Oracle Certified Professional: Java SE 8 Programmer II

Practice Tests

By: Udayan Khattry

DEDICATION

This book is dedicated to my wife Neha, with love.

26-Mar-2018:   v1.00 (1st Release)
11-Apr-2019:   v2.00 (2nd Release)
12-Sep-2019:   v2.01
10-Oct-2019:   v2.02
01-Nov-2021:   v2.03
15-Jun-2023:   v2.04

Author's Profile

Udayan Khattry

SCJP, SCWCD & Oracle Database SQL Certified Expert

Author has a master's degree in Computer Applications from Symbiosis International University, Pune, India and have completed following professional certifications:
- **SCJP** 1.6 (Sun Certified Programmer for J2SE 6.0)
- **SCWCD** 1.5 (Sun Certified Web Component Developer)
- **Oracle Database SQL Certified Expert**

After working as a software developer and consultant for over 9 years for various companies in India, Dubai & Singapore, he decided to follow his lifelong passion of teaching.

In the last 7 years, author has published multiple books and online courses on Java and Java certifications. He currently has 75000+ students from 140+ countries.

Audience

Anyone preparing for OCP (1Z0-809) certificate or interviews can take this book to assess his/her preparation.

Table of Content

Introduction

OCP - Java SE 8 Programmer II - Exam Information:

- **Exam Code: 1Z0-809**
- **Passing score: 65%**

OLD Pattern:

- Duration: 150 minutes
- Questions #: 85 (Multiple Choice / Multiple Select)

NEW Pattern (Strating Sep-2022):

- Duration: 120 minutes
- Questions #: 68 (Multiple Choice / Multiple Select)

Exam Curriculum:

- Java Class Design
- Advanced Java Class Design
- Generics and Collections
- Lambda Built-in Functional Interfaces
- Java Stream API
- Exceptions and Assertions
- Use Java SE 8 Date/Time API
- Java I/O Fundamentals
- Java File I/O (NIO.2)
- Java Concurrency
- Building Database Applications with JDBC
- Localization

All topics listed above are divided appropriately in **6 Practice Tests consisting 90 questions each i.e., 540 questions** in total. Questions are designed based on real examination questions in terms of pattern and complexity.

After each Practice Test, **correct answers** are provided with **explanation** for reference and understanding. **Relevant hints and how to approach a question in real examination setting is also provided in explanation.**

Completing all the tests successfully will boost your confidence to attempt Oracle Certified Professional (OCP) examination.

More information on detailed curriculum and assumptions, to be followed for examination is available on oracle certification page.
https://education.oracle.com/java-se-8-programmer-ii/pexam_1Z0-809

Disclaimer: These questions are not real examination questions / dumps. These questions are created to evaluate your preparation for certification exam.

For any questions / problems in above links send an email to: udayan.khattry@outlook.com.

Assumptions:

Questions mentioning line numbers: Because of wrapping one statement can be shown in multiple lines. If a question mentions line number, then consider the starting of line from the java statement / block perspective. In below code fragment, Line 14 represents 'catch(IllegalArgumentException | RuntimeException | Exception e) {' and not '| Exception e) {'.

There is no confusion for Line 15, it represents 'System.out.println(e.getMessage());' and Line 16 represents just the closing bracket, '}'

```
public static void main(String [] args) {
    try {
        convert("");
    }
    catch(IllegalArgumentException | RuntimeException
        | Exception e) { //Line 14
        System.out.println(e.getMessage()); //Line 15
    } //Line 16
    catch(Exception e) {
        e.printStackTrace();
    }
}
```

1   Practice Test-1

1.1   90 Questions covering all topics.

1.1.1   Consider the code of Test.java file:

```java
package com.udayan.ocp;

class Printer {
    private static int count = 0;
    private Printer() {
        count++;
    }

    static Printer getInstance() {
        return PrinterCreator.printer;
    }

    static class PrinterCreator {
        static Printer printer = new Printer();
    }

    static int getCount() {
        return count;
    }
}

public class Test {
    public static void main(String[] args) {
        Printer p1 = Printer.getInstance();
        Printer p2 = Printer.getInstance();
        Printer p3 = Printer.getInstance();
        System.out.println(Printer.getCount());
    }
}
```

What will be the result of compiling and executing Test class?

A. 0

B. 1

C. 2

D. 3

1.1.2   Consider the code of Test.java file:

```
package com.udayan.ocp;

class Player {
    String name;
    int age;

    Player() {
        this.name = "Yuvraj";
        this.age = 36;
    }

    public String toString() {
        return name + ", " + age;
    }

    public Class getClass() {
        return super.getClass();
    }
}

public class Test {
    public static void main(String[] args) {
        System.out.println(new Player());
    }
}
```

What will be the result of compiling and executing Test class?

A. Compilation error

B. null, 0

C. Yuvraj, 36

D. Text containing @ symbol

1.1.3 Given code of Test.java file:

```java
package com.udayan.ocp;

interface Printer1 {
  default void print() {
    System.out.println("Printer1");
  }
}

class Printer2 {
  public void print() {
    System.out.println("Printer2");
  }
}

class Printer extends Printer2 implements Printer1 {

}

public class Test {
  public static void main(String[] args) {
    Printer printer = new Printer();
    printer.print();
  }
}
```

What will be the result of compiling and executing Test class?

A. Compilation error for Printer1

B. Compilation error for Printer2

C. Compilation error for Printer

D. Printer1

E. Printer2

1.1.4   Consider the code of Test.java file:

```
package com.udayan.ocp;

enum Flags {
    TRUE, FALSE;

    Flags() {
        System.out.println("HELLO");
    }
}

public class Test {
    public static void main(String[] args) {
        Flags flags = new Flags();
    }
}
```

What will be the result of compiling and executing Test class?

A. HELLO is printed twice.

B. HELLO is printed once.

C. Exception is thrown at runtime.

D. None of the other options.

1.1.5   Which of the following statement is correct about java enums?

A. An enum can extend another class.

B. An enum can extend another enum.

C. An enum can implement interfaces.

D. All java enums implicitly extend from java.util.Enum class.

1.1.6   Given code:

```java
package com.udayan.ocp;

class Outer {
    private String name = "James Gosling";
    //Insert inner class definition here
}

public class Test {
    public static void main(String [] args) {
        new Outer().new Inner().printName();
    }
}
```

Which of the following Inner class definition inserted in the Outer class, will print 'James Gosling' in the output on executing Test class?

A.	```java
	class Inner {
	    public void printName() {
	        System.out.println(this.name);
	    }
	}
	``

B.	```java
	class Inner {
	    public void printName() {
	        System.out.println(name);
	    }
	}
	``

C.	```java
	inner class Inner {
	    public void printName() {
	        System.out.println(name);
	    }
	}
	``

D.	```java
	abstract class Inner {
	    public void printName() {
	        System.out.println(name);
	    }
	}
	``

1.1.7 What will be the result of compiling and executing class M?

```
package com.udayan.ocp;

class M {
    private int num1 = 100;
    class N {
        private int num2 = 200;
    }

    public static void main(String[] args) {
        M outer = new M();
        M.N inner = outer.new N();
        System.out.println(outer.num1 + inner.num2);
    }
}
```

A. Compilation error

B. 300

C. 100

D. 200

1.1.8 Given code:

```
package com.udayan.ocp;

class A {
    public void someMethod(final String name) {
        /*INSERT*/ {
            void print() {
                System.out.println("Hello " + name);
            }
        }
        new B().print();

    }
}

public class Test {
    public static void main(String[] args) {
        new A().someMethod("World!");
    }
}
```

Which of the following options can replace /*INSERT*/ such that on executing Test class, "Hello World!" is displayed in the output?

A.   **public class** B
B.   **protected class** B
C.   **class** B
D.   **private class** B
E.   **final class** B
F.   **abstract class** B

1.1.9   Below is the code of Test.java file:

```
package com.udayan.ocp;

interface Flyable {
    void fly();
}

public class Test {
    public static void main(String[] args) {
        /*INSERT*/
    }
}
```

Which of the following options can replace /*INSERT*/ such that there are no compilation errors?

A.	`Flyable flyable = new Flyable();`
B.	`Flyable flyable = new Flyable(){};`

C.	`Flyable flyable = new Flyable() {`
	`    public void fly() {`
	`        System.out.println("Flying high");`
	`    }`
	`}`

D.	`Flyable flyable = new Flyable() {`
	`    public void fly() {`
	`        System.out.println("Flying high");`
	`    }`
	`};`

1.1.10 Below is the code to Test.java file:

```java
package com.udayan.ocp;

enum ShapeType {
    CIRCLE, SQUARE, RECTANGLE;
}

abstract class Shape {
    private ShapeType type =
            ShapeType.SQUARE; //default ShapeType

    Shape(ShapeType type) {
        this.type = type;
    }

    public ShapeType getType() {
        return type;
    }

    abstract void draw();
}

public class Test {
    public static void main(String[] args) {
        Shape shape = new Shape() {
            @Override
            void draw() {
                System.out.println("Drawing a " + getType());
            }
        };
        shape.draw();
    }
}
```

What will be the result of compiling and executing Test class?

A. Drawing a CIRCLE

B. Drawing a SQUARE

C. Drawing a RECTANGLE

D. Compilation error

1.1.11 Below is the code of Test.java file:

```
package com.udayan.ocp;

class Outer {
    abstract static class Animal { //Line 2
        abstract void eat();
    }

    static class Dog extends Animal { //Line 6
        void eat() { //Line 7
            System.out.println("Dog eats biscuits");
        }
    }
}

public class Test {
    public static void main(String[] args) {
        Outer.Animal animal = new Outer.Dog(); //Line 15
        animal.eat();
    }
}
```

What will be the result of compiling and executing Test class?

A. Compilation error at Line 2

B. Compilation error at Line 6

C. Compilation error at Line 7

D. Compilation error at Line 15

E. Dog eats biscuits

1.1.12 What is the purpose of below lambda expression?

```
(x, y) -> x + y;
```

A. It accepts two int arguments, adds them and returns the int value

B. It accepts two String arguments, concatenates them and returns the String instance

C. It accepts a String and an int arguments, concatenates them and returns the String instance

D. Not possible to define the purpose

1.1.13 **What will be the result of compiling and executing Test class?**

```java
package com.udayan.ocp;

@FunctionalInterface
interface I5 {
    void print();
}

public class Test {
    int i = 100;

    I5 obj1 = new I5() {
        int i = 200;
        public void print() {
            System.out.println(this.i);
        }
    };

    I5 obj2 = () -> {
        int i = 300;
        System.out.println(this.i);
    };

    public static void main(String[] args) {
        Test ques = new Test();
        ques.obj1.print();
        ques.obj2.print();
    }
}
```

A.	100 100	B.	200 300
C.	200 100	D.	100 300

1.1.14 Given code of Test.java file:

```java
package com.udayan.ocp;

import java.util.Arrays;
import java.util.Comparator;
import java.util.List;

class Person {
    private String firstName;
    private String lastName;

    public Person(String firstName, String lastName) {
        this.firstName = firstName;
        this.lastName = lastName;
    }

    public String getFirstName() {
        return firstName;
    }

    public String getLastName() {
        return lastName;
    }

    public String toString() {
        return "{" + firstName + ", " + lastName + "}";
    }
}

public class Test {
    public static void main(String[] args) {
        List<Person> list = Arrays.asList(
            new Person("Tom", "Riddle"),
            new Person("Tom", "Hanks"),
            new Person("Yusuf", "Pathan"));

        list.stream().sorted(
            Comparator.comparing(Person::getFirstName)
            .reversed().thenComparing(Person::getLastName))
            .forEach(System.out::println);
    }
}
```

What will be the result of compiling and executing Test class?

A.	{Tom, Riddle} {Tom, Hanks} {Yusuf, Pathan}	B.	{Tom, Hanks} {Tom, Riddle} {Yusuf, Pathan}
C.	{Yusuf, Pathan} {Tom, Riddle} {Tom, Hanks}	D.	{Yusuf, Pathan} {Tom, Hanks} {Tom, Riddle}

1.1.15 Given code of Test.java file:

```
package com.udayan.ocp;

class T {
    @Override
    public String toString() {
        return "T";
    }
}

class Printer<T> {
    private T t;
    Printer(T t){
        this.t = t;
    }
    @Override
    public String toString(){
        return t.toString();
    }
}

public class Test {
    public static void main(String[] args) {
        Printer<T> obj = new Printer<>(new T());
        System.out.println(obj);

    }
}
```

What will be the result of compiling and executing Test class?

A. T

B. Compilation error in Printer<T> class

C. Compilation error in Test class

D. Compilation error in T class

1.1.16 Given code of Test.java file:

```java
package com.udayan.ocp;

class Printer<String> {
    private String t;
    Printer(String t){
        this.t = t;
    }
}

public class Test {
    public static void main(String[] args) {
        Printer<Integer> obj = new Printer<>(100);
        System.out.println(obj);
    }
}
```

What will be the result of compiling and executing Test class?

A. 100

B. Some text containing @ symbol

C. Compilation error in Printer class

D. Compilation error in Test class

1.1.17 Given code of Test.java file:

```
package com.udayan.ocp;

class Animal {}

class Dog extends Animal {}

class Cat extends Animal {}

class A<T> {
    T t;
    void set(T t) {
        this.t = t;
    }

    T get() {
        return t;
    }
}

public class Test {
    public static <T> void print1(A<? extends Animal> obj)
    {
        obj.set(new Dog()); //Line 22
        System.out.println(obj.get().getClass());
    }

    public static <T> void print2(A<? super Dog> obj) {
        obj.set(new Dog()); //Line 27
        System.out.println(obj.get().getClass());
    }

    public static void main(String[] args) {
        A<Dog> obj = new A<>();
        print1(obj); //Line 33
        print2(obj); //Line 34
    }
}
```

What will be the result of compiling and executing Test class?

A.	`class com.udayan.ocp.Dog` `class com.udayan.ocp.Dog`
B.	`null` `class com.udayan.ocp.Dog`
C.	`class com.udayan.ocp.Dog` `null`
D.	`Compilation error`
E.	`Runtime Exception`

1.1.18 Given code of Test.java file:

```java
package com.udayan.ocp;

import java.util.ArrayList;
import java.util.List;

public class Test {
    public static void main(String[] args) {
        List<? super String> list = new ArrayList<>();
        list.add("A");
        list.add("B");
        for(String str : list) {
            System.out.print(str);
        }
    }
}
```

What will be the result of compiling and executing Test class?

A. AB

B. Compilation error

C. Runtime exception

1.1.19 Consider below code:

```
package com.udayan.ocp;

public class Test {
    public static void main(String[] args) {
        Operation o1 = (x, y) -> x + y;
        System.out.println(o1.operate(5, 10));
    }
}
```

Which of the following functional interface definitions can be used here, so that the output of above code is: 15? Select ALL that apply.

A.	```interface Operation {` ` int operate(int x, int y);` `}```
B.	```interface Operation {` ` long operate(long x, long y);` `}```
C.	```interface Operation<T> {` ` T operate(T x, T y);` `}```
D.	```interface Operation<T extends Integer> {` ` T operate(T x, T y);` `}```

1.1.20 Given code of Test.java file:

```
package com.udayan.ocp;

import java.util.Arrays;
import java.util.List;
import java.util.ListIterator;

public class Test {
    public static void main(String[] args) {
        List<String> list = Arrays.asList("T", "S",
                                        "R", "I", "F");
        ListIterator<String> iter = list.listIterator(2);
        while(iter.hasNext()) {
            System.out.print(iter.next());
        }
    }
}
```

What will be the result of compiling and executing Test class?

A. IF

B. RIF

C. Runtime Exception

1.1.21 Given code of Test.java file:

```
package com.udayan.ocp;

import java.util.*;

class Student {
    private String name;
    private int age;

    Student(String name, int age) {
        this.name = name;
        this.age = age;
    }

    public int hashCode() {
        return name.hashCode() + age;
```

```java
        }

        public String toString() {
            return "Student[" + name + ", " + age + "]";
        }

        public boolean equals(Object obj) {
            if(obj instanceof Student) {
                Student stud = (Student)obj;
                return this.name.equals(stud.name)
                                && this.age == stud.age;
            }
            return false;
        }

        public String getName() {return name;}

        public int getAge() {return age;}

        public static int compareByName(Student s1, Student s2)
        {
            return s1.getName().compareTo(s2.getName());
        }
    }

public class Test {
    public static void main(String[] args) {
        Set<Student> students = new
                        TreeSet<>(Student::compareByName);
        students.add(new Student("James", 20));
        students.add(new Student("James", 20));
        students.add(new Student("James", 22));

        System.out.println(students.size());
    }
}
```

What will be the result of compiling and executing Test class?

A. 1

B. 2

C. 3

D. Runtime Exception

1.1.22 Given code of Test.java file:

```java
package com.udayan.ocp;

import java.util.*;

public class Test {
    public static void main(String[] args) {
        NavigableMap<Integer, String> map = new TreeMap<>();
        map.put(25, "Pune");
        map.put(32, "Mumbai");
        map.put(11, "Sri Nagar");
        map.put(39, "Chennai");

        System.out.println(map.headMap(25, true));
    }
}
```

What will be the result of compiling and executing Test class?

A. {11=Sri Nagar}

B. {11=Sri Nagar, 25=Pune}

C. {25=Pune, 32=Mumbai, 39=Chennai}

D. {32=Mumbai, 39=Chennai}

1.1.23 Given code of Test.java file:

```
package com.udayan.ocp;

import java.util.ArrayDeque;
import java.util.Deque;

public class Test {
    public static void main(String[] args) {
        Deque<Boolean> deque = new ArrayDeque<>();
        deque.push(new Boolean("abc"));
        deque.push(new Boolean("tRuE"));
        deque.push(new Boolean("FALSE"));
        deque.push(true);
        System.out.println(deque.pop() + ":"
                + deque.peek() + ":" + deque.size());
    }
}
```

What will be the result of compiling and executing Test class?

A. true:true:3

B. false:false:3

C. false:true:3

D. true:false:3

1.1.24 Given code of Test.java file:

```
package com.udayan.ocp;

import java.util.ArrayList;
import java.util.Arrays;
import java.util.List;

public class Test {
    public static void main(String[] args) {
        List<Integer> list = new ArrayList<>
                (Arrays.asList(1,2,3,4,5,6,7,8,9,10));
        list.removeIf(i -> i % 2 == 1);
        System.out.println(list);
    }
}
```

What will be the result of compiling and executing Test class?

A. Compilation Error

B. Runtime Exception

C. [2, 4, 6, 8, 10]

D. [1, 3, 5, 7, 9]

1.1.25 Given code of Test.java file:

```java
package com.udayan.ocp;

import java.util.Arrays;
import java.util.Comparator;

public class Test {
    public static void main(String[] args) {
        String [] arr = {"A5", "B4", "C3", "D2", "E1"};
        Arrays.sort(arr, Comparator.comparing(
                                s -> s.substring(1)));
        for(String str : arr) {
            System.out.print(str + " ");
        }
    }
}
```

What will be the result of compiling and executing Test class?

A. E1 D2 C3 B4 A5

B. A5 B4 C3 D2 E1

C. A1 B2 C3 D4 E5

D. E5 D4 C3 B2 A1

1.1.26 Given code of Test.java file:

```
package com.udayan.ocp;

import java.util.Arrays;

public class Test {
    public static void main(String[] args) {
        String [] cities = {"Seoul", "Tokyo", "Paris",
                    "London", "Hong Kong", "Singapore"};
        Arrays.stream(cities).sorted((s1,s2) ->
            s2.compareTo(s1)).forEach(System.out::println);
    }
}
```

What will be the result of compiling and executing Test class?

A.	Seoul Tokyo Paris London Hong Kong Singapore	B.	Hong Kong London Paris Seoul Singapore Tokyo
C.	Tokyo Singapore Seoul Paris London Hong Kong	D.	Compilation error

1.1.27 Given code of Test.java file:

```
package com.udayan.ocp;

import java.util.stream.IntStream;

public class Test {
    public static void main(String[] args) {
        IntStream stream = "OCP".chars();
        stream.forEach(c -> System.out.print((char)c));
        System.out.println(stream.count()); //Line 9
    }
}
```

What will be the result of compiling and executing Test class?

A. OCP3

B. Runtime exception

C. Compilation error

D. None of the other options

1.1.28 Given code of Test.java file:

```java
package com.udayan.ocp;

import java.util.Map;
import java.util.TreeMap;

public class Test {
    public static void main(String[] args) throws Exception {
        Map<Integer, String> map = new TreeMap<>();
        map.put(1, "one");
        map.put(2, "two");
        map.put(3, "three");
        map.put(null, "null");
        map.forEach((key, value) -> System.out.
                println("{" + key + ": " + value + "}"));
    }
}
```

What will be the result of compiling and executing Test class?

A.	{null: null} {1: one} {2: two} {3: three}	B.	{1: one} {2: two} {3: three} {null: null}
C.	{1: one} {2: two} {3: three}	D.	NullPointerException is thrown at runtime

1.1.29 Given code of Test.java file:

```java
package com.udayan.ocp;

import java.util.Arrays;
import java.util.List;
import java.util.function.Consumer;

interface StringConsumer extends Consumer<String> {
    @Override
    public default void accept(String s) {
        System.out.println(s.toUpperCase());
    }
}

public class Test {
    public static void main(String[] args) {
        StringConsumer consumer = s ->
                System.out.println(s.toLowerCase());
        List<String> list = Arrays.asList(
                        "Dr", "Mr", "Miss", "Mrs");
        list.forEach(consumer);
    }
}
```

What will be the result of compiling and executing Test class?

A.	dr mr miss mrs	B.	DR MR MISS MRS
C.	Compilation error	D.	Runtime exception

1.1.30 Given code of Test.java file:

```
package com.udayan.ocp;
import java.util.function.ToIntFunction;

public class Test {
    public static void main(String[] args) {
        String text = "Aa aA aB Ba aC Ca";
        ToIntFunction<String> func = text::indexOf;
        System.out.println(func.applyAsInt("a"));
    }
}
```

What will be the result of compiling and executing Test class?

A. 0

B. -1

C. 1

D. Compilation error

1.1.31 Given code of Test.java file:

```
package com.udayan.ocp;
import java.util.function.Consumer;

public class Test {
    public static void main(String[] args) {
        Consumer<Integer> consumer = System.out::print;
        Integer i = 5;
        consumer.andThen(consumer).accept(i++); //Line 7
    }
}
```

What will be the result of compiling and executing Test class?

A. 55

B. 56

C. 66

D. Compilation error

1.1.32 Given code of Test.java file:

```
package com.udayan.ocp;

import java.util.function.BiPredicate;

public class Test {
    public static void main(String[] args) {
        BiPredicate<String, String> predicate =
                                String::equalsIgnoreCase;
        System.out.println(predicate.test("JaVa", "Java"));
    }
}
```

What will be the result of compiling and executing Test class?

A. Compilation error

B. Runtime error

C. true

D. false

1.1.33 Given code of Test.java file:

```
package com.udayan.ocp;
import java.util.NavigableMap;
import java.util.TreeMap;
import java.util.function.BiConsumer;

public class Test {
    public static void main(String[] args) {
        NavigableMap<Integer, String> map = new TreeMap<>();
        BiConsumer<Integer, String> consumer
                                = map::putIfAbsent;
        consumer.accept(1, null);
        consumer.accept(2, "two");
        consumer.accept(1, "ONE");
        consumer.accept(2, "TWO");

        System.out.println(map);
    }
}
```

What will be the result of compiling and executing Test class?

A. {1=null, 2=two}

B. {1=ONE, 2=TWO}

C. {1=ONE, 2=two}

D. {1=null, 2=two}

E. {1=null, 2=TWO}

1.1.34 Given code of Test.java file:

```java
package com.udayan.ocp;

import java.util.function.BiPredicate;

public class Test {
    public static void main(String[] args) {
        String [] arr = {"A", "ab", "bab", "Aa", "bb",
            "baba", "aba", "Abab"};
        BiPredicate<String, String> predicate
                                = String::startsWith;

        for(String str : arr) {
            if(predicate.negate().test(str, "A"))
                System.out.println(str);
        }
    }
}
```

What will be the result of compiling and executing Test class?

A.	ab aba	B.	A Aa Abab
C.	ab bab bb baba aba	D.	bab bb baba

31

1.1.35 Given:

```
package com.udayan.ocp;

import java.util.function.Supplier;

class Document {
    void printAuthor() {
        System.out.println("Document-Author");
    }
}

class RFP extends Document {
    @Override
    void printAuthor() {
        System.out.println("RFP-Author");
    }
}

public class Test {
    public static void main(String[] args) {
        check(Document::new);
        check(RFP::new);
    }

    private static void check(_____ supplier) {
        supplier.get().printAuthor();
    }
}
```

Given options to fill the blanks:

```
Supplier<Document>
Supplier<? extends Document>
Supplier<? super Document>
Supplier<RFP>
Supplier<? extends RFP>
Supplier<? super RFP>
Supplier
```

How many of the above options can fill the blank space, such that output is:

```
Document-Author
RFP-Author
```

A. Only one option

B. Only two options

C. Only three options

D. More than three options

1.1.36 Given code of Test.java file:

```java
package com.udayan.ocp;

import java.util.Arrays;
import java.util.List;
import java.util.stream.Collectors;

class Book {
    String title;
    String author;
    double price;

    public Book(String title, String author, double price)
    {
        this.title = title;
        this.author = author;
        this.price = price;
    }

    public String getAuthor() {
        return this.author;
    }

    public String toString() {
      return "{" + title + "," + author + "," + price + "}";
    }
}

public class Test {
    public static void main(String[] args) {
        List<Book> books = Arrays.asList(
            new Book ("Head First Java","Kathy Sierra",24.5),
            new Book ("OCP", "Udayan Khattry", 20.99),
            new Book ("OCA", "Udayan Khattry", 14.99));
        books.stream().collect(
            Collectors.groupingBy(Book::getAuthor))
            .forEach((a,b) -> System.out.println(a));
```

```
        }
    }
```

What will be the result of compiling and executing Test class?

A.	[{Head First Java,Kathy Sierra,24.5}] [{OCP,Udayan Khattry,20.99}, {OCA,Udayan Khattry,14.99}]
B.	Kathy Sierra Udayan Khattry
C.	Runtime Exception

1.1.37 Given code of Test.java file:

```
package com.udayan.ocp;
import java.util.Arrays;
import java.util.List;
import java.util.function.Predicate;

public class Test {
    public static void main(String[] args) {
        List<Integer> list = Arrays.asList(-80, 100,
                                        -40, 25, 200);
        Predicate<Integer> predicate = num -> {
            int ctr = 1;
            boolean result = num > 0;
            System.out.print(ctr++ + ".");
            return result;
        };

        list.stream().filter(predicate).findFirst();
    }
}
```

What will be the result of compiling and executing Test class?

A. 1.

B. 1.1.

C. 1.2.

D. 1.2.3.4.5.

E. 1.1.1.1.1.

F. Nothing is printed on to the console.

1.1.38 Given code of Test.java file:

```java
package com.udayan.ocp;

import java.util.Arrays;
import java.util.List;

public class Test {
    public static void main(String[] args) {
        List<String> codes = Arrays.asList("1st",
                            "2nd", "3rd", "4th");
        System.out.println(codes.stream().filter(s ->
            s.endsWith("d")).reduce((s1, s2) -> s1 + s2));
    }
}
```

What will be the result of compiling and executing Test class?

A. 1st4th

B. 2nd3rd

C. Optional[1st4th]

D. Optional[2nd3rd]

1.1.39 Given code of Test.java file:

```
package com.udayan.ocp;

import java.util.ArrayList;
import java.util.List;

public class Test {
    public static void main(String[] args) {
        List<String> list = new ArrayList<>();
        System.out.println(list.stream().anyMatch(s ->
                                    s.length() > 0));
        System.out.println(list.stream().allMatch(s ->
                                    s.length() > 0));
        System.out.println(list.stream().noneMatch(s ->
                                    s.length() > 0));
    }
}
```

What will be the result of compiling and executing Test class?

A.	false false false	B.	true true true
C.	false true true	D.	true false false

1.1.40 Given code of Test.java file:

```
import java.util.Optional;

public class Test {
    public static void main(String[] args) {
        Optional<Integer> optional = Optional.
                                    ofNullable(null);
        System.out.println(optional);
    }
}
```

What will be the result of compiling and executing Test class?

A. Optional.empty

B. Optional[null]

C. Optional[0]

D. NullPointerException is thrown at runtime

1.1.41   **Given code of Test.java file:**

```
package com.udayan.ocp;

import java.util.OptionalDouble;

class MyException extends RuntimeException{}

public class Test {
    public static void main(String[] args) {
        OptionalDouble optional = OptionalDouble.empty();
        System.out.println(optional.
                            orElseThrow(MyException::new));
    }
}
```

What will be the result of compiling and executing Test class?

A. null

B. An instance of NoSuchElementException is thrown at runtime

C. An instance of RuntimeException is thrown at runtime

D. An instance of MyException is thrown at runtime

E. An instance of NullPointerException is thrown at runtime

F. Compilation error

1.1.42 Given code of Test.java file:

```
package com.udayan.ocp;

import java.util.stream.IntStream;

public class Test {
    public static void main(String[] args) {
        int sum = IntStream.rangeClosed(1,3).map(i -> i * i)
                .map(i -> i * i).sum();
        System.out.println(sum);
    }
}
```

What will be the result of compiling and executing Test class?

A. 6

B. 14

C. 98

D. None of the other options

1.1.43 Given code of Test.java file:

```
package com.udayan.ocp;

import java.util.stream.IntStream;

public class Test {
    public static void main(String[] args) {
        int res = 1;
        IntStream stream = IntStream.rangeClosed(1, 5);

        /*INSERT*/
    }
}
```

Which of the following options can replace /*INSERT*/ such that on executing Test class, 120 is printed in the output?
NOTE: 120 is the multiplication of numbers from 1 to 5. Select 2 options.

```
A.    System.out.println(stream.reduce(1, (i, j) -> i * j));
B.    System.out.println(stream.reduce(0, (i, j) -> i * j));
C.    System.out.println(stream.reduce(res, (i, j) -> i * j));
D.    System.out.println(stream.reduce(1, Integer::multiply));
E.    System.out.println(stream.reduce(0, Integer::multiply));
```

1.1.44 **Given code of Test.java file:**

```
package com.udayan.ocp;

import java.util.Set;
import java.util.stream.Collectors;
import java.util.stream.Stream;

public class Test {
    public static void main(String[] args) {
        Stream<String> stream = Stream.of("java",
            "python", "c", "c++", "java", "python");
        Set<String> set = stream.collect(Collectors.toSet());
        System.out.println(set.size());
    }
}
```

What will be the result of compiling and executing Test class?

A. 6

B. 5

C. 4

D. 0

1.1.45 Given code of Test.java file:

```
package com.udayan.ocp;

import java.util.stream.Stream;

public class Test {
    public static void main(String[] args) {
        Stream<Integer> stream = Stream.iterate(1,
                                        i -> i + 1);
        System.out.println(stream.anyMatch(i -> i > 1));
    }
}
```

What will be the result of compiling and executing Test class?

A. true

B. false

C. Nothing is printed on to the console as code runs infinitely

D. true is printed on to the console and code runs infinitely

1.1.46 Given code of Test.java file:

```
package com.udayan.ocp;

import java.util.HashMap;
import java.util.Map;

public class Test {
    public static void main(String[] args) {
        Map<Integer, String> map = new HashMap<>();
        map.put(1, "ONE");
        map.put(2, "TWO");
        map.put(3, "THREE");

        System.out.println(map.stream().count());
    }
}
```

What will be the result of compiling and executing Test class?

A. 3

B. 6

C. Runtime Exception

D. Compilation error

1.1.47 Given code of Test.java file:

```java
package com.udayan.ocp;

import java.util.ArrayList;
import java.util.List;

class Point {
    int x;
    int y;
    Point(int x, int y) {
        this.x = x;
        this.y = y;
    }

    public String toString() {
        return "Point(" + x + ", " + y + ")";
    }

    boolean filter() {
        return this.x == this.y;
    }

}
public class Test {
    public static void main(String[] args) {
        List<Point> list = new ArrayList<>();
        list.add(new Point(0, 0));
        list.add(new Point(1, 2));
        list.add(new Point(-1, -1));

        list.stream().filter(Point::filter)
            .forEach(System.out::println); //Line n1
    }
}
```

What will be the result of compiling and executing Test class?

A.	Line n1 causes compilation error	B.	Point(0, 0) Point(-1, -1)
C.	Point(0, 0) Point(1, 2) Point(-1, -1)	D.	Point(1, 2)

1.1.48 Given code of Test.java file:

```java
package com.udayan.ocp;
public class Test {
    public static void convert(String s)
        throws IllegalArgumentException,
        RuntimeException, Exception {
        if(s.length() == 0) {
            throw new RuntimeException("Length should " +
                "be greater than 0.");
        }
    }
    public static void main(String [] args) {
        try {
            convert("");
        }
        catch(IllegalArgumentException | RuntimeException
                                | Exception e) { //Line 14
            System.out.println(e.getMessage()); //Line 15
        } //Line 16
        catch(Exception e) {
            e.printStackTrace();
        }
    }
}
```

Line 14 is giving compilation error. Which of the following changes enables to code to print 'Length should be greater than 0.'?

A. Replace Line 14 with 'catch(RuntimeException | Exception e) {'

B. Replace Line 14 with 'catch(IllegalArgumentException | Exception e) {'

C. Replace Line 14 with 'catch(IllegalArgumentException | RuntimeException e) {'

D. Replace Line 14 with 'catch(RuntimeException e) {'

E. Comment out Line 14, Line 15 and Line 16

1.1.49 Given code of Test.java file:

```
package com.udayan.ocp;

public class Test {
    public static void main(String[] args) {
        try { //outer
            try { //inner
                System.out.println(1/0);
            } catch(ArithmeticException e) {
                System.out.println("Inner");
            } finally {
                System.out.println("Finally 1");
            }
        } catch(ArithmeticException e) {
            System.out.println("Outer");
        } finally {
            System.out.println("Finally 2");
        }
    }
}
```

What will be the result of compiling and executing Test class?

A.	Inner Finally 1	B.	Outer Finally 2
C.	Inner Finally 2	D.	Inner Finally 1 Finally 2

1.1.50 Consider the following interface declaration:

```
public interface I1 {
    void m1() throws java.io.IOException;
}
```

Which of the following incorrectly implements interface I1?

43

A.	`public class C1 implements I1 {`
	`    public void m1() {}`
	`}`

B.	`public class C2 implements I1 {`
	`    public void m1() throws`
	`            java.io.FileNotFoundException{}`
	`}`

C.	`public class C3 implements I1 {`
	`    public void m1() throws`
	`            java.io.IOException{}`
	`}`

D.	`public class C4 implements I1 {`
	`    public void m1() throws Exception{}`
	`}`

1.1.51 Given code of Test.java file:

```java
package com.udayan.ocp;

import java.sql.SQLException;

public class Test {
    private static void m() throws SQLException {
        try {
            throw new SQLException();
        } catch (Exception e) {
            throw e;
        }
    }

    public static void main(String[] args) {
        try {
            m();
        } catch(SQLException e) {
            System.out.println("Caught Successfully.");
        }
    }
}
```

What will be the result of compiling and executing Test class?

A. Method m() causes compilation error.

B. Method main(String []) causes compilation error.

C. Caught Successfully.

D. Program ends abruptly.

1.1.52 Given code of Test.java file:

```
package com.udayan.ocp;

import java.util.Scanner;

public class Test {
    public static void main(String[] args) {
        System.out.print("Enter some text: ");
        try(Scanner scan = new Scanner(System.in)) {
            String s = scan.nextLine();
            System.out.println(s);
            scan.close();
            scan.close();
        }
    }
}
```

What will be the result of compiling and executing Test class?

User input is: HELLO

A. Compilation error

B. Runtime Exception

C. On execution program terminates successfully after printing 'HELLO' on to the console

1.1.53 Given code of Test.java file:

```
//Test.java
package com.udayan.ocp;

class MyException extends RuntimeException {}

class YourException extends RuntimeException {}

public class Test {
    public static void main(String[] args) {
        try {
            throw new YourException();
        } catch(MyException e1 | YourException e2){
            System.out.println("Caught");
        }
    }
}
```

What will be the result of compiling and executing Test class?

A. Compilation error

B. Caught

C. Runtime Exception

1.1.54 Given code of Test.java file:

```
package com.udayan.ocp;

class MyResource implements AutoCloseable {
    @Override
    public void close() {
        System.out.println("Closing");
    }
}

public class Test {
    public static void main(String[] args) {
        try(AutoCloseable resource = new MyResource()) {

        }
    }
}
```

What will be the result of compiling and executing Test class?

A. Compilation error in MyResource class

B. Compilation error in Test class

C. Closing

1.1.55 Given code of Test.java file:

```
package com.udayan.ocp;

class Resource1 {
    public void close() {
        System.out.println("Resource1");
    }
}

class Resource2 {
    public void close() {
        System.out.println("Resource2");
    }
}
```

```
public class Test {
    public static void main(String[] args) {
        try(Resource1 r1 = new Resource1();
                    Resource2 r2 = new Resource2()) {
            System.out.println("Test");
        }
    }
}
```

What will be the result of compiling and executing Test class?

A.	Test Resource1 Resource2	B.	Test Resource2 Resource1
C.	Compilation Error		

1.1.56   Given code of Test.java file:

```
package com.udayan.ocp;

public class Test {
    private static void checkStatus() {
        assert 1 == 2 : 2 == 2;
    }

    public static void main(String[] args) {
        try {
            checkStatus();
        } catch (AssertionError ae) {
            System.out.println(ae.getCause());
        }
    }
}
```

What will be the result of executing Test class with below command?

java -ea com.udayan.ocp.Test

A. true

B. false

C. null

D. Compilation error

1.1.57 **Given code of Test.java file:**

```
package com.udayan.ocp;

import java.time.LocalDate;

public class Test {
    public static void main(String [] args) {
        LocalDate date = LocalDate.ofEpochDay(0);
        System.out.println(date);
    }
}
```

What will be the result of compiling and executing Test class?

A. 1970-01-01

B. Runtime Exception

C. 1970-00-01

D. 1970-1-1

1.1.58 **Given code of Test.java file:**

```
package com.udayan.ocp;

import java.time.*;

public class Test {
    public static void main(String [] args) {
        LocalTime t1 = LocalTime.now();
        LocalDateTime t2 = LocalDateTime.now();
        System.out.println(Duration.between(t2, t1));
    }
}
```

What will be the result of compiling and executing Test class?

A. Program terminates successfully after displaying the output

B. Compilation error

C. Runtime Exception

1.1.59 Given code of Test.java file:

```
package com.udayan.ocp;

import java.time.LocalTime;
import java.time.temporal.ChronoUnit;

public class Test {
    public static void main(String [] args) {
        LocalTime t1 = LocalTime.parse("11:03:15.987");
        System.out.println(t1.plus(22, ChronoUnit.HOURS)
                .equals(t1.plusHours(22)));
    }
}
```

What will be the result of compiling and executing Test class?

A. Runtime Exception

B. true

C. false

1.1.60 **Daylight saving time 2018 in United States (US) ends at 4-Nov-2018 2:00 AM. What will be the result of compiling and executing Test class?**

```
package com.udayan.ocp;

import java.time.*;

public class Test {
    public static void main(String [] args) {
        LocalDate date = LocalDate.of(2018, 11, 4);
        LocalTime time = LocalTime.of(13, 59, 59);
        ZonedDateTime dt = ZonedDateTime.of(date,
                time, ZoneId.of("America/New_York"));
        dt = dt.plusSeconds(1);
        System.out.println(dt.getHour() + ":" +
                dt.getMinute() + ":" + dt.getSecond());
    }
}
```

A. 12:0:0

B. 13:0:0

C. 14:0:0

1.1.61 **Given code of Test.java file:**

```
package com.udayan.ocp;

import java.time.LocalDateTime;
import java.time.format.DateTimeFormatter;
import java.time.format.FormatStyle;

public class Test {
    public static void main(String [] args) {
        LocalDateTime date = LocalDateTime.of(
                                2019, 1, 1, 10, 10);
        DateTimeFormatter formatter = DateTimeFormatter.
                ofLocalizedDate(FormatStyle.FULL);
        System.out.println(formatter.format(date));
    }
}
```

Will above code display time part on to the console?

A. Yes

B. No

1.1.62 Given code of Test.java file:

```
package com.udayan.ocp;

import java.time.*;

public class Test {
    public static void main(String[] args) {
        Instant instant = Instant.now();
        LocalDateTime obj = null; //Line n1
    }
}
```

Which of the following statements will replace null at Line n1 such that Instant object referred by 'instant' is converted to LocalDateTime object?

A. `instant.toLocalDateTime();`

B. `LocalDateTime.of(instant);`

C. `instant.atZone(ZoneId.systemDefault()).toLocalDateTime();`

D. `(LocalDateTime)instant;`

1.1.63 **Below is the directory structure of "F:/Test" directory:**

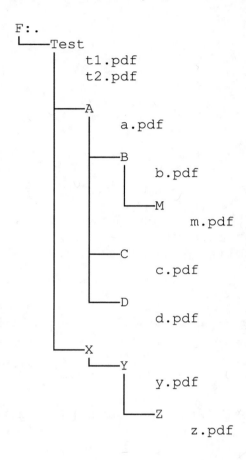

Given code of Test.java file:

```
package com.udayan.ocp;
import java.io.File;
import java.io.IOException;

public class Test {
    public static void main(String[] args)
                                throws IOException {
        deleteFiles(new File("F:\\Test"), ".pdf");
    }

    public static void deleteFiles(File dir,
            String extension) throws IOException {
        File[] list = dir.listFiles();
        if (list != null && list.length > 0) {
            for (File file : list) {
                if (file.isDirectory()) {
                    deleteFiles(file, extension);
                } else if (file.getName()
                            .endsWith(extension)) {
                    file.delete();
                }
            }
        }
    }
}
```

There is full permission to list/create/delete files and directories in F:.
What will be the result of compiling and executing Test class?

A.	All the pdf files in 'Test' directory and its sub-directories will be deleted successfully.
B.	Only t1.pdf and t2.pdf will get deleted.
C.	t1.pdf, t2.pdf and all the pdf files under 'A' and its sub-directories will be deleted successfully.
D.	t1.pdf, t2.pdf and all the pdf files under 'X' and its sub-directories will be deleted successfully.
E.	Only t1.pdf and t2.pdf will not get deleted, other pdf files will be successfully deleted.

54

1.1.64 Given code of Test.java file:

```
package com.udayan.ocp;
import java.io.Console;
import java.util.Optional;

public class Test {
    public static void main(String[] args) {
        Optional<Console> optional = Optional.
                        ofNullable(System.console());
        if(optional.isPresent()) {
            System.out.println(optional.get());
        }
    }
}
```

Which of the following statement are correct regarding above code?

A. Above code will never throw NullPointerException.

B. Above code may throw NullPointerException.

C. Above code will always print some output on to the console.

1.1.65 Given code of Test.java file:

```
package com.udayan.ocp;
import java.io.*;

public class Test {
    public static void main(String[] args)
                                throws IOException {
        File file = new File("F:\\temp.dat");
        try(
                DataOutputStream os = new DataOutputStream(
                        new FileOutputStream(file));
                DataInputStream is = new DataInputStream(
                        new FileInputStream(file))
        ) {
            os.writeChars("JAVA");
            System.out.println(is.readChar());
        }
    }
}
```

What will be the result of compiling and executing Test class?

A. J

B. A

C. V

D. None of the other options.

1.1.66 Imagine below path exists:

```
F:.
 └──A
     └──B
```

Given code of Test.java file:

```
package com.udayan.ocp;

import java.io.*;

public class Test {
    public static void main(String[] args) {
        File dir = new File("F:" + File.separator + "A"
                                + File.separator + "B");
        System.out.println(dir.getParentFile().getParent());
    }
}
```

What will be the result of compiling and executing Test class?

A. F:\

B. F:\A

C. Compilation error

D. NullPointerException is thrown at runtime

1.1.67 Given code of Test.java file:

```
package com.udayan.ocp;

import java.io.*;

public class Test {
    public static void main(String[] args)
                                throws IOException {
        try (FileInputStream fis = new FileInputStream(
                            "F:\\orig.png");
            FileOutputStream fos = new FileOutputStream(
                            "F:\\copy.png"))
        {
            int res;
            byte [] arr = new byte[500000]; //Line 10
            while((res = fis.read(arr)) != -1){ //Line 11
                fos.write(arr); //Line 12
            }
        }
    }
}
```

F: is accessible for reading/writing and contains 'orig.png' file.

Will above code create exact copy of 'orig.png' file?

A. Yes

B. No

1.1.68 Given code of Test.java file:

```java
package com.udayan.ocp;

import java.io.*;
import java.time.LocalDate;
import java.util.Optional;

public class Test {
    public static void main(String[] args)
            throws IOException, ClassNotFoundException {
        Optional<LocalDate> optional = Optional.of(
                            LocalDate.of(2018, 12, 1));
        try (ObjectOutputStream oos = new ObjectOutputStream(
                new FileOutputStream(("F:\\date.ser")));
            ObjectInputStream ois = new ObjectInputStream(
                new FileInputStream("F:\\date.ser")))
        {
            oos.writeObject(optional);

            Optional<?> object = (Optional<?>)ois.readObject();
            System.out.println(object.get());
        }
    }
}
```

F: is accessible for reading/writing and currently doesn't contain any files/directories.

What will be the result of compiling and executing Test class?

A. Compilation error

B. Runtime Exception

C. 2018-12-01

D. 01-12-2018

1.1.69 Given code of Test.java file:

```
package com.udayan.ocp;

import java.io.*;
import java.nio.file.Files;
import java.nio.file.Paths;

public class Test {
    public static void main(String[] args)
                                throws IOException {
        /*INSERT*/
    }
}
```

F: is accessible for reading and contains 'Book.java' file.

Which of the following statements, if used to replace /*INSERT*/, will successfully print contents of 'Book.java' on to the console?
Select 3 options.

A.	`Files.lines(Paths.get("F:\\Book.java")).forEach(System.out::println);`
B.	`Files.lines(Paths.get("F:\\Book.java")).stream().forEach(System.out::println);`
C.	`Files.readAllLines(Paths.get("F:\\Book.java")).forEach(System.out::println);`
D.	`Files.readAllLines(Paths.get("F:\\Book.java")).stream().forEach(System.out::println);`

1.1.70 Given code of Test.java file:

```
package com.udayan.ocp;

import java.io.IOException;
import java.nio.file.Files;
import java.nio.file.Path;
import java.nio.file.Paths;
import java.util.stream.Stream;

public class Test {
    public static void main(String[] args)
                                throws IOException {
        Stream<Path> files = Files.list(
                Paths.get(System.getProperty("user.home")));
        files.forEach(System.out::println);
    }
}
```

System.getProperty("user.home") returns the HOME directory of the User (Both in windows and Linux).

What will be the result of compiling and executing Test class?

A.	It will only print the paths of directories and files under HOME directory.
B.	It will print the paths of directories, sub-directories and files under HOME directory.
C.	It will only print the paths of files (not directories) under HOME directory.
D.	It will print the paths of files (not directories) under HOME directory and its sub-directories.

1.1.71 Given code of Test.java file:

```
package com.udayan.ocp;

import java.nio.file.Path;
import java.nio.file.Paths;

public class Test {
    public static void main(String[] args) {
        Path path = Paths.get("F:\\A\\B\\C\\Book.java");
        System.out.println(path.subpath(1,4));
    }
}
```

What will be the result of compiling and executing Test class?

A. Exception is thrown at runtime

B. A\B\C\Book.java

C. A\B\C

D. B\C\Book.java

1.1.72 Given code of Test.java file:

```
package com.udayan.ocp;

import java.nio.file.Path;
import java.nio.file.Paths;

public class Test {
    public static void main(String[] args) {
        Path path1 = Paths.get("F:\\A\\B\\C");
        Path path2 = Paths.get("F:\\A");
        System.out.println(path1.relativize(path2));
        System.out.println(path2.relativize(path1));
    }
}
```

What will be the result of compiling and executing Test class?

A.	Compilation error	B.	An exception is thrown at runtime
C.	B\C ..\..	D.	..\.. B\C

1.1.73 F: is accessible for reading/writing and below is the directory structure for F:

```
F:.
└───Parent
    │   a.txt
    │   b.txt
    │
    └───Child
            c.txt
            d.txt
```

Given code of Test.java file:

```java
package com.udayan.ocp;
import java.io.IOException;
import java.nio.file.Files;
import java.nio.file.Path;
import java.nio.file.Paths;
import java.nio.file.attribute.BasicFileAttributes;
import java.util.function.BiPredicate;
import java.util.stream.Stream;

public class Test {
    public static void main(String[] args)
                                    throws IOException {
        Path root = Paths.get("F:");
        BiPredicate<Path, BasicFileAttributes> predicate
                = (p,a) -> p.toString().endsWith("txt");
        try(Stream<Path> paths
                    = Files.find(root, 2, predicate))
        {
            paths.forEach(System.out::println);
        }
    }
}
```

What will be the result of compiling and executing Test class?

A.	Above program executes successfully and prints nothing on to the console.
B.	Above program executes successfully and prints below lines on to the console: F:Parent\a.txt F:Parent\b.txt
C.	Above program executes successfully and prints below lines on to the console: F:Parent\Child\c.txt F:Parent\Child\d.txt F:Parent\a.txt F:Parent\b.txt

1.1.74 **C:\ is accessible for reading/writing and below is the content of 'C:\TEMP' folder:**

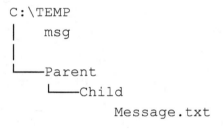

```
C:\TEMP
|    msg
|
L———Parent
       L———Child
              Message.txt
```

'msg' is a symbolic link file for 'C:\TEMP\Parent\Child\Message.txt'.

Message.txt contains following text:
Welcome!

Given code of Test.java file:

```java
package com.udayan.ocp;

import java.io.BufferedReader;
import java.io.IOException;
import java.nio.file.Files;
import java.nio.file.Path;
import java.nio.file.Paths;

public class Test {
    public static void main(String[] args)
                                    throws IOException {
        Path path = Paths.get("C:", "TEMP", "msg");

        try (BufferedReader reader =
                    Files.newBufferedReader(path)) {
            String str = null;
            while ((str = reader.readLine()) != null) {
                System.out.println(str);
            }
        }
    }
}
```

What will be the result of compiling and executing Test class?

A.	Compilation error.
B.	An exception is thrown at runtime.
C.	Program executes successfully and produces no output.
D.	Program executes successfully and prints 'Welcome!' on to the console.

1.1.75 Given structure of EMPLOYEE table:

```
EMPLOYEE (ID integer, FIRSTNAME varchar(100), LASTNAME
varchar(100), SALARY real, PRIMARY KEY (ID))
```

Given code of Test.java file:

```
package com.udayan.ocp;

import java.sql.Connection;
import java.sql.DriverManager;
import java.sql.SQLException;
import java.sql.Statement;

public class Test {
    public static void main(String[] args)
                                    throws SQLException {
        Connection connection = null;
        try (Connection con = DriverManager.getConnection(
                "jdbc:mysql://localhost:3306/ocp",
                "root", "password");)
        {
            connection = con;
        }
        Statement stmt = connection.createStatement();
        stmt.executeUpdate(
                "INSERT INTO EMPLOYEE VALUES(101, " +
                        "'John', 'Smith', 12000)");
        stmt.close();
        connection.close();
    }
}
```

Also assume:

URL, username and password are correct.

SQL query is correct and valid.

The JDBC 4.2 driver jar is configured in the classpath.

EMPLOYEE table doesn't have any records.

What will be the result of compiling and executing Test class?

A.	The program executes successfully and one record is inserted in the EMPLOYEE table.
B.	The program executes successfully but no record is inserted in the EMPLOYEE table.
C.	An exception is thrown at runtime.
D.	Compilation error.

1.1.76 **Given structure of EMPLOYEE table:**

```
EMPLOYEE (ID integer, FIRSTNAME varchar(100), LASTNAME
varchar(100), SALARY real, PRIMARY KEY (ID))
```

Given code of Test.java file:

```java
package com.udayan.ocp;

import java.sql.*;

public class Test {
    public static void main(String[] args) {
        try {
            Connection con = DriverManager.getConnection(
                    "jdbc:mysql://localhost:3306/ocp",
                    "root", "password");
            String query = "Select * FROM EMPLOYEE";
            Statement stmt = con.createStatement();
            ResultSet rs = stmt.executeQuery(query);
            while (rs.next()) { //Line 12
                System.out.println("ID: " + rs.getInt("ID"));
                System.out.println("First Name: "
                        + rs.getString("FIRSTNAME"));
                System.out.println("Last Name: "
                        + rs.getString("LASTNAME"));
                System.out.println("Salary: "
                        + rs.getDouble("SALARY"));
            }
            rs.close(); //Line 18
            stmt.close();
```

```
            con.close();
        } catch (SQLException ex) {
            ex.printStackTrace();
        }
    }
}
```

Also assume:

URL, username and password are correct.

SQL query is correct and valid.

The JDBC 4.2 driver jar is configured in the classpath.

EMPLOYEE table doesn't have any records.

What will be the result of compiling and executing Test class?

A.	Line 12 throws an exception at runtime.
B.	Line 18 throws an exception at runtime.
C.	Code executes fine and prints following on to the console: ID: 0 First Name: null Last Name: null Salary: 0.0
D.	Code executes fine and doesn't print anything on to the console.

1.1.77 **Given structure of EMPLOYEE table:**

```
EMPLOYEE (ID integer, FIRSTNAME varchar(100), LASTNAME
varchar(100), SALARY real, PRIMARY KEY (ID))
```

EMPLOYEE table contains below records:

```
101 John    Smith   12000
102 Sean    Smith   15000
103 Regina Williams   15500
104 Natasha   George 14600
```

Given code of Test.java file:

```java
package com.udayan.ocp;

import java.sql.*;

public class Test {
    public static void main(String[] args) {
        String url = "jdbc:mysql://localhost:3306/ocp";
        String user = "root";
        String password = "password";
        String query = "Select ID, FIRSTNAME, LASTNAME, " +
            "SALARY FROM EMPLOYEE " +
            "WHERE SALARY > 14900 ORDER BY ID";

        try (Connection con = DriverManager.getConnection(
                                    url, user, password);
            Statement stmt = con.createStatement(
                    ResultSet.TYPE_SCROLL_SENSITIVE,
                    ResultSet.CONCUR_UPDATABLE);
            ResultSet rs = stmt.executeQuery(query);) {
            rs.absolute(2);
            rs.updateDouble("SALARY", 20000);
        } catch (SQLException ex) {
            System.out.println("Error");
        }
    }
}
```

Also assume:

URL, username and password are correct.

SQL query is correct and valid.

The JDBC 4.2 driver jar is configured in the classpath.

What will be the result of compiling and executing Test class?

A.	'Error' is printed on to the console.
B.	Program executes successfully but no record is updated in the database.
C.	Program executes successfully and salary of Sean Smith is updated to 20000.
D.	Program executes successfully and salary of Regina Williams is updated to 20000.

1.1.78 **Given structure of MESSAGES table:**

```
MESSAGES (msg1 varchar(100), msg2 varchar(100))
```
MESSAGES table contains below records:
```
'Happy New Year!', 'Happy Holidays!'
```

Given code of Test.java file:
```java
package com.udayan.ocp;
import java.sql.*;
public class Test {
    public static void main(String[] args)
                                    throws SQLException {
        String url = "jdbc:mysql://localhost:3306/ocp";
        String user = "root";
        String password = "password";
        String query = "Select msg1 as msg, " +
                    "msg2 as msg FROM MESSAGES";
        try (Connection con = DriverManager
                    .getConnection(url, user, password);
            Statement stmt = con.createStatement(
                    ResultSet.TYPE_SCROLL_INSENSITIVE,
                    ResultSet.CONCUR_READ_ONLY);
            ResultSet rs = stmt.executeQuery(query);)
        {
            rs.absolute(1);
            System.out.println(rs.getString("msg"));
            System.out.println(rs.getString("msg"));
        }
```

```
        }
    }
```

Also assume:
URL is correct and db credentials are: root/password.
SQL query is correct and valid.
The JDBC 4.2 driver jar is configured in the classpath.

What will be the result of compiling and executing Test class?

A.	Happy New Year! Happy Holidays!	B.	Happy Holidays! Happy Holidays!
C.	Happy New Year! Happy New Year!	D.	An exception is thrown at runtime

1.1.79 **Given structure of MESSAGES table:**

```
MESSAGES (msg1 varchar(100), msg2 varchar(100))
```

MESSAGES table contains below records:

```
'Happy New Year!', 'Happy Holidays!'
```

Given code of Test.java file:

```java
package com.udayan.ocp;
import java.sql.*;

public class Test {
    public static void main(String[] args)
                                    throws SQLException {
        String url = "jdbc:mysql://localhost:3306/ocp";
        String user = "root";
        String password = "password";
        String query = "DELETE FROM MESSAGES";
        try (Connection con =
            DriverManager.getConnection(url, user, password);
            Statement stmt = con.createStatement())
        {
            System.out.println(stmt.execute(query));
        }
    }
}
```

Also assume:

URL is correct and db credentials are: root/password.

SQL query is correct and valid.

The JDBC 4.2 driver jar is configured in the classpath.

What will be the result of compiling and executing Test class?

A. 0

B. 1

C. true

D. false

1.1.80 **Given structure of EMPLOYEE table:**

```
EMPLOYEE (ID integer, FIRSTNAME varchar(100), LASTNAME
varchar(100), SALARY real, PRIMARY KEY (ID))
```

EMPLOYEE table contains below records:

```
101 John    Smith  12000
102 Sean    Smith  15000
103 Regina Williams  15500
104 Natasha    George 14600
```

Given code of Test.java file:

```java
package com.udayan.ocp;
import java.sql.*;

public class Test {
    public static void main(String[] args)
                                throws SQLException {
        String url = "jdbc:mysql://localhost:3306/ocp";
        String user = "root";
        String password = "password";
        String query = "Select ID, FIRSTNAME, LASTNAME, " +
            "SALARY FROM EMPLOYEE ORDER BY ID";
        try (Connection con = DriverManager
                    .getConnection(url, user, password);
            Statement stmt = con.createStatement(
                    ResultSet.TYPE_SCROLL_INSENSITIVE,
                    ResultSet.CONCUR_READ_ONLY);
        ) {
            ResultSet rs = stmt.executeQuery(query);
            rs.relative(-3);
            rs.relative(1);
            System.out.println(rs.getInt(1));
        }
    }
}
```

Also assume:

URL is correct and db credentials are: root/password.

SQL query is correct and valid.

The JDBC 4.2 driver jar is configured in the classpath.

What will be the result of compiling and executing Test class?

A. An exception is thrown at runtime.

B. 101

C. 102

D. 103

E. 104

1.1.81 Below is the content of 'F:\Message.properties' file:

```
key1=Good Morning!
key2=Good Evening!
```

Given code of Test.java file:

```
import java.io.FileInputStream;
import java.io.IOException;
import java.util.Properties;

public class Test {
    public static void main(String[] args)
                                throws IOException {
        Properties prop = new Properties ();
        FileInputStream fis = new FileInputStream (
                        F:\\Message.properties");
        prop.load(fis);
        System.out.println(prop.getProperty("key1"));
        System.out.println(prop.getProperty("key2",
                                "Good Day!"));
        System.out.println(prop.getProperty("key3",
                                "Good Day!"));
        System.out.println(prop.getProperty("key4"));
    }
}
```

There is full permission to list/create/delete files and directories in F:.
What will be the result of compiling and executing Test class?

A.	Good Morning! Good Day! Good Day! null	B.	Good Morning! Good Day! null null
C.	Good Morning! Good Evening! null null	D.	Good Morning! Good Evening! Good Day! null

1.1.82 Assume that proper import statements are available, and 'fr' is the language code for French language.

And you have the following code snippet:
```
Locale[] loc = Locale.getAvailableLocales();
```

Which of the following statements will print all the supported (by the JVM) French Language Locale on to the console?

Select ALL that apply.

A.	```Arrays.stream(loc).filter(x -> x.getLanguage().equals("fr")).forEach(System.out::println);```
B.	```Arrays.stream(loc).filter(x -> x.getLanguage().contains("FR")).forEach(System.out::println);```
C.	```Arrays.stream(loc).filter(x -> x.toString().contains("FR")).forEach(System.out::println);```
D.	```Arrays.stream(loc).filter(x -> x.startsWith("fr")).forEach(System.out::println);```
E.	```Arrays.stream(loc).filter(x -> x.toString().startsWith("fr")).forEach(System.out::println);```

1.1.83 **Below files are available for your project:**

```
//1.  ResourceBundle.properties
locale=French/Canada


//2.  ResourceBundle_CA.properties
locale=Canada


//3.  ResourceBundle_hi.properties
locale=Hindi


//4.  ResourceBundle_IN.properties
locale=India

//5.  Test.java
package com.udayan.ocp;

import java.util.Locale;
import java.util.ResourceBundle;

public class Test {
    public static void main(String[] args) {
        Locale.setDefault(new Locale("fr", "CA"));
        Locale loc = new Locale("en", "IN");
        ResourceBundle rb = ResourceBundle.getBundle(
                                "ResourceBundle", loc);
        System.out.println(rb.getObject("locale"));
    }
}
```

Assume that all the *.properties files are included in the CLASSPATH. What will be the output of compiling and executing Test class?

A. French/Canada

B. Canada

C. Hindi

D. India

E. Runtime Exception

1.1.84   **Below files are available for your project:**

```
//1. RB.properties
key1=one
key3=three

//2. RB_en.properties
key3=THREE

//3. RB_en_US.properties
key1=ONE
key2=TWO

//4. Test.java
package com.udayan.ocp;

import java.util.Enumeration;
import java.util.Locale;
import java.util.ResourceBundle;

public class Test {
    public static void main(String[] args) {
        Locale loc = new Locale("en", "US");
        ResourceBundle bundle = ResourceBundle
                                    .getBundle("RB", loc);
        Enumeration<String> enumeration = bundle.getKeys();
        while (enumeration.hasMoreElements()) {
            String key = enumeration.nextElement();
            String val = bundle.getString(key);
            System.out.println(key + "=" + val);
        }
    }
}
```

Assume that all the *.properties files are included in the CLASSPATH. What will be the output of compiling and executing Test class?

A.	key1=ONE key2=TWO	B.	key3=THREE
C.	key1=one key3=three	D.	key1=ONE key2=TWO key3=THREE
E.	key1=one key2=TWO key3=three		

1.1.85 Given code of Test.java file:

```
package com.udayan.ocp;

import java.util.concurrent.atomic.AtomicInteger;

class Counter implements Runnable {
    private static AtomicInteger ai = new AtomicInteger(3);

    public void run() {
        System.out.print(ai.getAndDecrement());
    }
}

public class Test {
    public static void main(String[] args) {
        Thread t1 = new Thread(new Counter());
        Thread t2 = new Thread(new Counter());
        Thread t3 = new Thread(new Counter());
        Thread[] threads = {t1, t2, t3};
        for(Thread thread : threads) {
            thread.start();
        }
    }
}
```

What will be the result of compiling and executing Test class?

A. It will always print 321

B. It will print three digits 321 but order can be different

C. It will always print 210

D. It will print three digits 210 but order can be different

E. None of the other options

1.1.86 Given code of Test.java file:

```
package com.udayan.ocp;

import java.util.concurrent.*;

class Player extends Thread {
    CyclicBarrier cb;

    public Player(){
        super();
    }

    public Player(CyclicBarrier cb) {
        this.cb = cb;
        this.start();
    }

    public void run() {
        try {
            cb.await();
        } catch (InterruptedException |
                BrokenBarrierException e) {}
    }
}

class Match implements Runnable {
    public void run() {
        System.out.println("Match is starting...");
    }
}

public class Test {
    public static void main(String[] args) {
        Match match = new Match();
        CyclicBarrier cb = new CyclicBarrier(2, match);
        Player p1 = new Player(cb);
        /*INSERT*/
    }
}
```

Which of the following statement, if used to replace /*INSERT*/, will print 'Match is starting...' on to the console and will successfully terminate the program?

A. p1.start();

B. new Player(cb);

C. new Player(cb).start();

D. cb.await();

E. new Player();

1.1.87 Given code of Test.java file:

```
package com.udayan.ocp;

import java.util.concurrent.*;

class MyThread implements Runnable {
    private String str;

    MyThread(String str) {
        this.str = str;
    }

    public void run() {
        System.out.println(str.toUpperCase());
    }
}

public class Test {
    public static void main(String[] args)
            throws ExecutionException, InterruptedException{
        ExecutorService es = Executors.
                newSingleThreadExecutor();
        MyThread thread = new MyThread("ocp");
        Future future = es.submit(thread);
        Integer tmp = (Integer) future.get(); //Line 22
        System.out.println(tmp);
        es.shutdown();
    }
}
```

What will be the result of compiling and executing Test class?

A.	Compilation error is caused by Line 22	B.	ClassCastException is thrown at runtime by Line 22
C.	ocp null	D.	OCP null
E.	OCP OCP		

1.1.88 Given code of Test.java file:

```
package com.udayan.ocp;

import java.util.concurrent.*;

class Printer implements Callable<String> {
    public String call() {
        System.out.println("DONE");
        return null;
    }
}

public class Test {
    public static void main(String[] args) {
        ExecutorService es = Executors.
                    newFixedThreadPool(1);
        es.submit(new Printer());
        System.out.println("HELLO");
        es.shutdown();
    }
}
```

What will be the result of compiling and executing Test class?

A. HELLO will always be printed before DONE.

B. DONE will always be printed before HELLO.

C. HELLO and DONE will be printed but printing order is not fixed.

D. HELLO will never be printed.

1.1.89 Given code of Test.java file:

```
package com.udayan.ocp;

import java.util.stream.IntStream;

public class Test {
    public static void main(String[] args) {
        IntStream.rangeClosed(1, 10).parallel()
                .forEachOrdered(System.out::println);
    }
}
```

What will be the result of compiling and executing Test class?

A. It will print numbers from 1 to 10 in ascending order.

B. It will print numbers form 1 to 10 in descending order.

C. It will print numbers form 1 to 10 but not in any specific order.

1.1.90 Given code of Test.java file:

```
package com.udayan.ocp;

import java.util.Arrays;
import java.util.List;
import java.util.concurrent.*;

public class Test {
    public static void main(String[] args) throws
            InterruptedException, ExecutionException {
        Callable<String> c = new Callable<String>() {
            @Override
            public String call() throws Exception {
                try {
                    Thread.sleep(3000);
                } catch (InterruptedException e) {}
                return "HELLO";
            }
        };

        ExecutorService es
                = Executors.newFixedThreadPool(10);
        List<Callable<String>> list
                = Arrays.asList(c,c,c,c,c);
        List<Future<String>> futures = es.invokeAll(list);
        System.out.println(futures.size());
        es.shutdown();
    }
}
```

Which of the following statement is correct about above code?

A. As each Thread sleeps for 3 secs, so program will take at least 15 secs. to print 5.

B. Program will always print 5 in exactly 3 secs.

C. Program will print 5 in any time greater than or equal to 3 secs.

D. Program will print 5 in less than 3 secs.

1.2 Answers of Practice Test - 1 with Explanation

1.1.1 Answer: B

Reason:
This is an example of Singleton class. static fields are initialize once, when class loads in the memory.
'printer' is static reference variable defined in PrinterCreator (static nested) class.
Printer p1 = Printer.getInstance(); => getInstance method loads the PrinterCreator class in the memory causing 'static Printer printer = new Printer();' to get executed. object of Printer class is created and variable count is incremented by 1.
Later invocation of Printer.getInstance(); method simply returns the reference of Printer object so Printer class's constructor is not invoked.
Variable count is incremented only once.

1.1.2 Answer: A

Reason:
getClass(), notify(), notifyAll() and overloaded wait methods are final in Object class and hence cannot be overridden.

1.1.3 Answer: E

Reason:
print() method is defined in interface Printer1 and class Printer2. class Printer inherits both the methods but there is no conflict in this case as print() method defined in Printer2 class is used.

'Printer2' is printed on to the console.

1.1.4 Answer: D

Reason:
new Flags() tries to invoke enum constructor but Enum constructor cannot be invoked.

1.1.5   Answer: C

Reason:
Java enums cannot extend from another class or enum but an enum can implement interfaces.
All java enums implicitly extend from java.lang.Enum class and not from java.util.Enum class.

1.1.6   Answer: B

Reason:
name can be referred either by name or Outer.this.name. There is no keyword with the name 'inner' in java.
As new Inner() is used in main method, hence cannot declare class Inner as abstract in this case. But note abstract or final can be used with regular inner classes.
Keyword 'this' inside Inner class refers to currently executing instance of Inner class and not the Outer class.
To access Outer class variable from within inner class you can use these 2 statements: System.out.println(name); OR System.out.println(Outer.this.name);

1.1.7   Answer: B

Reason:
Outer class (M) code has access to all the members of inner class (N) including private members, hence inner.num2 doesn't cause any compilation error.

1.1.8   Answer: C,E

Reason:
Method-local inner classes cannot be defined using explicit access modifiers (public, protected and private) but non-access modifiers: final and abstract can be used with method-local inner class. In this case, abstract is also not possible as new B() is used.

1.1.9   Answer: D

Reason:
new Flyable(); => Can't instantiate an interface.
new Flyable(){}; => fly() method is not implemented.

new Flyable() { public void fly() { System.out.println("Flying high"); } } => semicolon missing at the end
new Flyable() { public void fly() { System.out.println("Flying high"); } }; => correct syntax

1.1.10 Answer: D

Reason:
At the time of creating the instance of anonymous inner class, new Shape() is used, which means it is looking for a no-argument constructor in anonymous inner class code, which would invoke the no-argument constructor of super class, Shape. But as parameterized constructor is specified in Shape class, so no-argument constructor is not provided by the compiler and hence compilation error.

To correct the compilation error pass the enum constant while instantiating anonymous inner class.
Shape shape = new Shape(ShapeType.CIRCLE) {...}; or you can even pass null: Shape shape = new Shape(null) {...}; OR provide the no-argument constructor in the Shape class: Shape(){}

1.1.11 Answer: E

Reason:
A class can have multiple static nested classes. static nested class can use all 4 access modifiers (public, protected, default and private) and 2 non-access modifiers (final and abstract). No issues at Line 2.

static nested class can extend from a class and can implement multiple interfaces so Line 6 compiles fine. No overriding rules were broken while overriding eat() method, so no issues at Line 7.

Test class is outside the boundary of class Outer. So Animal can be referred by Outer.Animal and Dog can be referred by Outer.Dog. Polymorphism is working in this case, super class (Outer.Animal) reference variable is referring to the instance of sub class (Outer.Dog). So, no issues at Line 15 as well.

Test class compiles and executes successfully and prints "Dog eats biscuits" on to the console.

1.1.12 Answer: D

Reason:
Lambda expression doesn't work without target type and target type must be a functional interface.

In this case as the given lambda expression is not assigned to any target type, hence its purpose is not clear. In fact, given lambda expression causes compilation error without its target type.

1.1.13 Answer: C

Reason:
Keyword this within anonymous inner class code refers to the instance of anonymous inner class itself, so this.i in anonymous inner class code is 200.

Whereas, keyword this within lambda expression refers to the instance of enclosing class where lambda expression is written, so this.i in lambda expression is 100.

1.1.14 Answer: D

Reason:
In this case, sorted method accepts an instance of Comparator<Person> type.

Comparator.comparing(Person::getFirstName) => Returns a Comparator for sorting the records in ascending order of first name.
Comparator.comparing(Person::getFirstName).reversed() => Returns a Comparator for sorting the records in descending order of first name.
Comparator.comparing(Person::getFirstName).reversed().thenComparing(Person::getLastName) => Returns a Comparator for sorting the records in descending order of first name and in case first name matches, then ascending order of last name.

So correct answer is:
{Yusuf, Pathan}
{Tom, Hanks}
{Tom, Riddle}

1.1.15 Answer: A

Reason:
T is a valid identifier in Java, hence can be used as class name. toString() method has been correctly overridden by class T. No issues with class T.
Type parameter should not be a Java keyword and naming convention for Type parameter is to use uppercase single character. class Printer<T> correctly uses type parameter, T.
When using Generic types in the code, you need to specify the type argument. In Test class, 'Printer<T> obj' => T refers to class T and not type parameter, T.

System.out.println(obj); => Prints 'T' on to the console.

1.1.16 Answer: B

Reason:
Type parameter should not be a Java keyword & a valid Java identifier. Naming convention for Type parameter is to use uppercase single character.
In class Printer<String>, 'String' is a valid Java identifier and hence a valid type parameter even though it doesn't follow the naming convention of uppercase single character.
Printer<Integer> obj = new Printer<>(100); => Type argument is Integer and it correctly creates an instance of Printer class passing Integer object 100.
Printer class doesn't override toString() method and hence 'System.out.println(obj);' prints some text containing @ symbol.

1.1.17 Answer: D

Reason:
print1(A<? extends Animal> obj) => print1 method can accept arguments of A<Animal> or A<Dog> or A<Cat> types at runtime.
Suppose you have passed 'new A<Cat>()' as the argument of print1 method. Line 22 will not work in this case.
As compiler is not sure about the data that would come at runtime, hence it doesn't allow Line 22. Line 22 causes compilation failure.

print2(A<? super Dog> obj) => print2 method can accept arguments of A<Dog> or A<Animal> or A<Object> types at runtime.
All 3 arguments works with Line 27, hence no issues with Line 27.

1.1.18 Answer: B

Reason:

For 'List<? super String>' type of read objects is 'Object' and type of write objects is 'String' and its subclasses (no subclass of String as String is final).

'for(String str : list)' causes compilation failure. Correct syntax should be: 'for(Object str : list)'

1.1.19 Answer: A,B,D

Reason:

From the given syntax inside main method, it is clear that interface name is Operation and it has an abstract method operate which accepts 2 parameters of numeric type and returns the numeric result (as result of adding 5 and 10 is 15). So, int and long versions can be easily applied here.
Operation<T> will not work here as inside main method, raw type is used, which means x and y will be of Object type and x + y will cause compilation error as + operator is not defined when both the operands are of Object type.
For Operation<T extends Integer>, even though main method uses raw type, but x and y will be of Integer type and hence x + y will not cause any compilation error.

1.1.20 Answer: B

Reason:

listIterator(index); method allows to have the starting point at any index. Allowed values are between 0 and size of the list.
If next() method is called, then element at 'specified index' is returned and if previous() method is called, then element at 'specified index - 1' is returned.

1.1.21 Answer: A

Reason:

TreeSet requires you to provide either Comparable or Comparator. NOTE: To be used with TreeSet, it is not needed to override equals(Object) and hashCode() methods.
But in real world projects, it is a good practice to override hashCode() and equals(Object) methods for the classes to be used in Collection framework.

In this case 'new TreeSet<>(Student::compareByName);' provides the instance of Comparator<Student> type. Which compares the names only. All 3 Student objects have same name and hence only first Student object was added to this set.

1.1.22 Answer: B

Reason:
TreeMap is sorted map based on the natural ordering of keys. So, map has entries: {11=Sri Nagar, 25=Pune, 32=Mumbai, 39=Chennai}.

headMap(K toKey, boolean inclusive) => returns the map till toKey, if inclusive is true. Hence the output is: {11=Sri Nagar, 25=Pune}.

For the exam, you should know some of the methods from NavigableMap map. Below are the method calls and outputs for the map object used in this example:

//NavigableMap<K,V> tailMap(K fromKey, boolean inclusive); => Returns a view of the portion of this map whose keys are greater than (or equal to, if 'inclusive' is true) fromKey.
System.out.println(map.tailMap(25, true)); //{25=Pune, 32=Mumbai, 39=Chennai}

//Map.Entry<K,V> firstEntry(); => Returns a key-value mapping associated with the least key in this map.
System.out.println(map.firstEntry()); //11=Sri Nagar

//Map.Entry<K,V> lastEntry(); => Returns a key-value mapping associated with the greatest key in this map.
System.out.println(map.lastEntry()); //39=Chennai

//NavigableMap<K,V> descendingMap(); => Returns a reverse order view of the mappings contained in this map.
System.out.println(map.descendingMap()); //{39=Chennai, 32=Mumbai, 25=Pune, 11=Sri Nagar}

//K floorKey(K key); => Returns the greatest key less than or equal to the given key.
System.out.println(map.floorKey(30)); //25

//K ceilingKey(K key); => Returns the least key greater than or equal to the given key.
System.out.println(map.ceilingKey(30)); //32

1.1.23 Answer: D

Reason:

push, pop and peek are Stack's terminology.

push(E) calls addFirst(E), pop() calls removeFirst() and peek() invokes peekFirst(), it just retrieves the first element (HEAD) but doesn't remove it.

deque.push(new Boolean("abc")); => [*false]. * represents HEAD of the deque.
deque.push(new Boolean("tRuE")); => [*true, false].
deque.push(new Boolean("FALSE")); => [*false, true, false].
deque.push(true); => [*true, false, true, false].

deque.pop() => removes and returns the HEAD element, true in this case. deque => [*false, true, false].

deque.peek() => retrieves but doesn't remove the HEAD element, false in this case. deque => [*false, true, false].

deque.size() => 3. Hence output is 'true:false:3'.

1.1.24 Answer: C

Reason:

Arrays.asList(...) method returns a list backed with array, so items cannot be added to or removed from the list.

But if this list is passed to the constructor of ArrayList, then new ArrayList instance is created which copies the elements of passed list and elements can be added to or removed from this list.

List<Integer> list = new ArrayList<>(Arrays.asList(1,2,3,4,5,6,7,8,9,10)); => [1,2,3,4,5,6,7,8,9,10].

list.removeIf(i -> i % 2 == 1); => [2,4,6,8,10]. Remove the element for which passed Predicate is true.

1.1.25 Answer: A

Reason:

Sorting is working on 2nd letter of the array elements, which means 5, 4, 3, 2, 1. Sorting is in ascending order (1, 2, 3, 4, 5) hence the output is: E1 D2 C3 B4 A5

1.1.26 Answer: C

Reason:
Arrays class has overloaded stream(...) method to convert arrays to Stream.
sorted(...) method of Stream interface is also overloaded: sorted() => sorts on natural order and sorted(Comparator) => sorts on passed Comparator.

sorted((s1,s2) -> s2.compareTo(s1)) => sorts on descending order.

forEach(System.out::println); => Prints all the Stream data.

1.1.27 Answer: B

Reason:
forEach, count, toArray, reduce, collect, findFirst, findAny, anyMatch, allMatch, sum, min, max, average etc. are considered as terminal operations.
Once the terminal operation is complete, all the elements of the stream are considered as used. Any attempt to use the stream again causes IllegalStateException.
In this example, count() is used after using forEach() method and hence IllegalStateException is thrown.

1.1.28 Answer: D

Reason:
TreeMap cannot contain null keys. Hence, 'map.put(null, "null");' throws NullPointerException.

1.1.29 Answer: C

Reason:
Target type of lambda expression should be a functional interface. StringConsumer is not a Functional Interface as it just specifies one default method, abstract method is not available.

Statement 'StringConsumer consumer = s -> System.out.println(s.toLowerCase());' causes compilation error.

1.1.30 Answer: C

Reason:
'text::indexOf' is equivalent to lambda expression 'search -> text.indexOf(search)'.

ToIntFunction<T> has method: int applyAsInt(T value);.
In this case T is of String type.
func.applyAsInt("a") will invoke text.indexOf("a"), which returns the index of first occurrence of "a". In the given text, it is 1.

1.1.31 Answer: A

Reason:
andThen is the default method defined in Consumer interface, so it is invoked on consumer reference variable.

Value passed in the argument of accept method is passed to both the consumer objects. So, for understanding purpose Line 7 can be split into: consumer.accept(5); consumer.accept(5); So it prints '55' on to the console.

Check the code of andThen method defined in Consumer interface to understand it better.

1.1.32 Answer: C

Reason:
BiPredicate<T, U> : boolean test(T t, U u);
BiPredicate interface accepts 2 type parameters and these parameters (T,U) are passed to test method, which returns primitive boolean.
In this case, 'BiPredicate<String, String> predicate' means test method will have declaration: 'boolean test(String s1, String d2)'.

'String::equalsIgnoreCase' is equivalent to '(s1, s2) -> s1.equalsIgnoreCase(s2)'
This is an example of "Reference to an Instance Method of an Arbitrary Object of a Particular Type" and not "method reference to static method".
"JaVa".equalsIgnoreCase("Java") => returns true.

1.1.33 Answer: C

Reason:
Though reference variable of NavigableMap is used but putIfAbsent method is from Map interface. It is a default method added in JDK 8.0.
BiConsumer<T, U> : void accept(T t, U u);
Lambda expression corresponding to 'map::putIfAbsent;' is '(i, s) -> map.putIfAbsent(i, s)'
This is the case of "Reference to an Instance Method of a Particular Object".
TreeMap sorts the data on the basis of natural order of keys.

consumer.accept(1, null); => {1=null}.
consumer.accept(2, "two"); => {1=null, 2=two}.
consumer.accept(1, "ONE"); => {1=ONE, 2=two}. putIfAbsent method replaces null value with the new value.
consumer.accept(2, "TWO"); => {1=ONE, 2=two}. As value is available against '2', hence value is not replaced.

1.1.34 Answer: C

Reason:
startsWith is an instance method in String class. 'String::startsWith' corresponds to '(str1, str2) -> str1.startsWith(str2);'
Given predicate means return true for any text starting with uppercase 'A'.

But inside for loop predicate.negate() means, return true for any text not starting with uppercase 'A'.

1.1.35 Answer: B

Reason:
Blank space of check(_____ supplier) method needs to be filled such that check(...) method compiles, two statements invoking check(...) method compile and output is:
Document-Author
RFP-Author

'Document::new' is same as '() -> {return new Document();}' and 'RFP::new' is same as '() -> {return new RFP();}' and as these are the implementations of get method of Supplier interface, hence let's check all the options one by one:

94

1. Supplier<Document>:- Method parameter will be initialized as:
Supplier<Document> supplier = () -> {return new Document();};
or
Supplier<Document> supplier = () -> {return new RFP();};
No issues as get() method either returns Document or RFP instance.

2. Supplier<? extends Document>:- Method parameter will be initialize as:
Supplier<? extends Document> supplier = () -> {return new Document();};
or
Supplier<? extends Document> supplier = () -> {return new RFP();};

If target type is a wildcard-parameterized functional interface, then type inference of lambda expression is based on following from the JLS:
If T is a wildcard-parameterized functional interface type and the lambda expression is implicitly typed, then the ground target type is the non-wildcard parameterization of T. Based on above JLS statement, ground target type of above lambda expression will be:
Supplier<Document> and this means above expression is equivalent to:
Supplier<? extends Document> supplier = (Supplier<Document>)() -> {return new Document();};
or
Supplier<? extends Document> supplier = (Supplier<Document>)() -> {return new RFP();};
No issues as get() method either returns Document or RFP instance.

3. Supplier<? super Document>:- Method parameter will be initialize as:
Supplier<? super Document> supplier = () -> {return new Document();};
or
Supplier<? super Document> supplier = () -> {return new RFP();};
Based on above JLS statement, ground target type of above lambda expression will be:
Supplier<Document> and this means above expression is equivalent to:
Supplier<? super Document> supplier = (Supplier<Document>)() -> {return new Document();};
or
Supplier<? super Document> supplier = (Supplier<Document>)() -> {return new RFP();};
There is no issue with lambda expressions (method invocation) but get() method would return an Object type and invoking printAuthor() method on Object type is not possible. Hence compilation error.

4. Supplier<RFP>:- Method parameter will be initialized as:
Supplier<RFP> supplier = () -> {return new Document();};
or
Supplier<RFP> supplier = () -> {return new RFP();};
1st statement causes compilation failure.

5. Supplier<? extends RFP>:- Method parameter will be initialized as:
Supplier<? extends RFP> supplier = () -> {return new Document();};
or
Supplier<? extends RFP> supplier = () -> {return new RFP();};
Based on above JLS statement, ground target type of above lambda expression will be:
Supplier<RFP> and this means above expression is equivalent to:
Supplier<? extends RFP> supplier = (Supplier<RFP>)() -> {return new Document();};
or
Supplier<? extends RFP> supplier = (Supplier<RFP>)() -> {return new RFP();};
2nd statement compiles successfully but 1st statement fails to compile.

6. Supplier<? super RFP>:- Method parameter will be initialized as:
Supplier<? super RFP> supplier = () -> {return new Document();};
or
Supplier<? super RFP> supplier = () -> {return new RFP();};
Based on above JLS statement, ground target type of above lambda expression will be:
Supplier<RFP> and this means above expression is equivalent to:
Supplier<? super RFP> supplier = (Supplier<RFP>)() -> {return new Document();};
or
Supplier<? super RFP> supplier = (Supplier<RFP>)() -> {return new RFP();};
1st statement fails to compile. There is no issue with the lambda expression of 2nd
statement (method invocation) but get() method would return an Object type and
invoking printAuthor() method on Object type is not possible. Hence compilation error.

7. Supplier:- Doesn't compile as raw type's get() method returns Object type, so
printAuthor() method can't be invoked.

Hence out of given 7 options, only two options 'Supplier<Document>' and 'Supplier<?
extends Document>' will give the desired output.

1.1.36   Answer: B

Reason:
books --> [{Head First Java,Kathy Sierra,24.5}, {OCP,Udayan Khattry,20.99}, {OCA,Udayan Khattry,14.99}]. Ordered by insertion order.

books.stream() returns Stream<Book> type: [{Head First Java,Kathy Sierra,24.5}, {OCP,Udayan Khattry,20.99}, {OCA,Udayan Khattry,14.99}].

books.stream().collect(Collectors.groupingBy(Book::getAuthor)) returns a Map<String, List<Book>> type, key is the author name and value is the List of book objects.

map --> [{Kathy Sierra, {Head First Java,Kathy Sierra,24.5}}, {Udayan Khattry, {{OCP,Udayan Khattry,20.99}, {OCA,Udayan Khattry,14.99}}}].

forEach method accepts a BiConsumer<String, List<Book>> , so first parameter of accept method is key and 2nd parameter is value. So in the given lambda expression 'a' is key and 'b' is value.
System.out.println(a) prints keys(author names) to the console.

1.1.37   Answer: B

Reason:
findFirst() is terminal operation.

list.stream() => [-80, 100, -40, 25, 200].

filter(predicate) is executed for each element until just one element passes the test. Because findFirst() will terminate the operation on finding first matching element.

NOTE: a new instance of Predicate is used, hence every time ctr will be initialize to 1.

For -80, Output is '1.' but predicate returns false, hence findFirst() doesn't terminate the operation.

For 100, '1.' is appended to previous output, so on console you will see '1.1.' and predicate returns true, hence findFirst() finds an element and terminates the operation.

Final output is: '1.1.'

1.1.38 Answer: D

Reason:
filter method filters all the strings ending with "d".

'stream.reduce((s1, s2) -> s1 + s2)' returns 'Optional<String>' type whereas
'stream.reduce("", (s1, s2) -> s1 + s2)' returns 'String'.

1.1.39 Answer: C

Reason:
Method signatures:
boolean anyMatch(Predicate<? super T>) : Returns true if any of the stream element
matches the given Predicate. If stream is empty, it returns false and predicate is not
evaluated.

boolean allMatch(Predicate<? super T>) : Returns true if all the stream elements match
the given Predicate. If stream is empty, it returns true and predicate is not evaluated.

boolean noneMatch(Predicate<? super T>) : Returns true if none of the stream element
matches the given Predicate. If stream is empty, it returns true and predicate is not
evaluated.

In this case, as stream is empty anyMatch returns false whereas allMatch and
noneMatch both returns true.

1.1.40 Answer: A

Reason:
ofNullable method creates an empty Optional object if passed argument is null.

Optional.empty is printed on to the console for empty Optional.

1.1.41 Answer: D

Reason:
orElseThrow throws the instance of provided Exception if optional is empty.

In this case optional is an empty OptionalDouble, hence an instance of MyException is thrown at runtime.

1.1.42 Answer: C

Reason:
IntStream.rangeClosed(int start, int end) => Returns a sequential stream from start to end, both inclusive and with a step of 1.
IntStream.map(IntUnaryOperator) => Returns a stream consisting of the results of applying the given function to the elements of this stream.

IntStream.rangeClosed(1,3) => [1,2,3].
map(i -> i * i) => [1,4,9].
map(i -> i * i) => [1,16,81].
sum() => 1+16+81 = 98.

1.1.43 Answer: A,C

Reason:
Integer class doesn't have 'multiply' method, hence options containing 'Integer::multiply' will cause compilation failure.

To understand, 'stream.reduce(1, (i, j) -> i * j)' can be written as:

```
int result = 1;
for (int element : stream) {
   result = op.applyAsInt(result, element);
}
return result;
```

Above code is just for understanding purpose, you can't iterate a stream using given loop.

Note: 'op' in above code is of IntBinaryOperator and target type of given lambda expression.
Check IntPipeline class which implements IntStream for the details of reduce method.
If 1st argument of reduce is 0, then overall result will be zero.
'stream.reduce(1, (i, j) -> i * j)' and 'stream.reduce(res, (i, j) -> i * j)' are correct options.

1.1.44 Answer: C

Reason:
Set doesn't allow duplicates, which means generated set will have 4 elements ["java", "python", "c", "c++] and therefore set.size() will return 4.

1.1.45 Answer: A

Reason:
stream => {1, 2, 3, 4, 5, ... }. It is an infinite stream.
Predicate 'i -> i > 1' returns true for any Integer greater than 1.
As 2 > 1, so true is printed and operation is terminated. Code doesn't run infinitely.

NOTE: 'stream.allMatch(i -> i > 1)' returns false as 1st element of the stream (1) returns false for the predicate and 'stream.noneMatch(i -> i > 1)' returns false as 2nd element of the stream (2) returns true for the predicate.

1.1.46 Answer: D

Reason:
There is no stream() method available in Map interface and hence map.stream() causes compilation error.

Though you can first get either entrySet or keySet or values and then invoke stream() method.

For example, below code prints all the key value pairs available in the map:
map.entrySet().stream().forEach(x -> System.out.println(x.getKey() + ":" + x.getValue()));

1.1.47 Answer: B

Reason:
'Point::filter' is an example of "Reference to an Instance Method of an Arbitrary Object of a Particular Type". Equivalent lambda expression is: '(Point p) -> p.filter()'.
As filter(...) method accepts Predicate<? super Point> instance as an argument, hence given method reference syntax is the correct implementation of the Predicate. Line n1 compiles successfully.
Result of filtration is the Stream<Point> instance containing Point objects whose x == y. Therefore, this stream contains Point(0, 0) and Point(-1, -1).
forEach(System.out::println) prints Point(0, 0) and Point(-1, -1) on to the console.

1.1.48 Answer: D

Reason:
In multi-catch statement, classes with multi-level hierarchical relationship can't be used. RuntimeException is subclass of Exception, IllegalArgumentException is indirect subclass of Exception and IllegalArgumentException is subclass of RuntimeException, hence these pairs can't be used in multi-catch statement.

Only one option is left to replace Line 14 with 'catch(RuntimeException e) {'.

Commenting out Line 14, Line 15 and Line 16 will resolve the compilation error but it will print the whole stack trace rather than just printing the message.

1.1.49 Answer: D

Reason:
System.out.println(1/0); throws ArithmeticException, handler is available in inner catch block, it executes and prints "Inner" to the console.

Once we handled the exception, no other catch block will get executed unless we re-throw the exception.

Inner finally gets executed and prints "Finally 1" to the console.

Rule is finally block always gets executed, so outer finally gets executed and prints "Finally 2" to the console.

1.1.50 Answer: D

Reason:
NOTE: Question is asking for "incorrect" implementation and not "correct" implementation.

According to overriding rules, if super class / interface method declares to throw a checked exception, then overriding method of sub class / implementer class has following options:
1. May not declare to throw any checked exception,
2. May declare to throw the same checked exception thrown by super class / interface method,
3. May declare to throw the sub class of the exception thrown by super class / interface method,
4. Cannot declare to throw the super class of the exception thrown by super class / interface method.

1.1.51 Answer: C

Reason:
Even though it seems like method m() will not compile successfully, but starting with JDK 7, it is allowed to use super class reference variable in throw statement referring to sub class Exception object.

In this case, method m() throws SQLException and compiler knows that variable e (Exception type) refers to an instance of SQLException only and hence allows it.

Program executes successfully and prints 'Caught Successfully.' on to the console.

1.1.52 Answer: C

Reason:
Even though Scanner is created in try-with-resources block, calling close() method explicitly doesn't cause any problem.
Scanner class allows to invoke close() method multiple times. In this case, it will be called 3 times: twice because of scan.close() and once because of try-with-resources statement.

'HELLO' is printed on to the console and program terminates successfully.

1.1.53 Answer: A

Reason:
Wrong syntax for multi-catch block, only one reference variable is allowed.

Correct syntax of multi-catch statement is: 'catch(MyException | YourException e)'

1.1.54 Answer: B

Reason:
close() method in AutoCloseable interface has below declaration:
void close() throws Exception;

MyResource class correctly overrides close() method.

try-with-resources statement internally invokes resource.close() method.

resource is of AutoCloseable type, so compiler checks the close() method declaration of AutoCloseable interface.

close() method in AutoCloseable interface declares to throw Exception (checked exception) and hence handle or declare rule must be followed.

As main method neither declares to throw Exception nor provides catch block for Exception type, hence try-with-resources statement causes compilation error.

1.1.55 Answer: C

Reason:
Classes used in try-with-resources statement must implement java.lang.AutoCloseable or its sub interfaces such as java.io.Closeable.

As Resource1 and Resource2 don't implement AutoCloseable interface, hence try-with-resources statement causes compilation error.

1.1.56 Answer: C

Reason:
assert 1 == 2 : 2 == 2; => throws AssertionError and as 2 == 2 is true, hence message is set as true.

This doesn't make any changes to cause, which is still null.

If right side of the expression is an instance of Throwable type, then cause is set to that type.

main method catches AssertionError (though you are not supposed to handle Error and its subtype) and 'ae.getCause()' returns null.

1.1.57 Answer: A

Reason:
0th day in epoch is: 1970-01-01, 1st day in epoch is: 1970-01-02 and so on.

as toString() method of LocalDate class prints the LocalDate object in ISO-8601 format: "uuuu-MM-dd". Hence output is: '1970-01-01'.

1.1.58 Answer: C

Reason:
Signature of between method defined in Duration class is: 'Duration between(Temporal startInclusive, Temporal endExclusive)'.

As both LocalTime and LocalDateTime implement 'Temporal' interface, hence there is no compilation error.

If the Temporal objects are of different types as in this case, calculation is based on 1st argument and 2nd argument is converted to the type of 1st argument.
1st argument, 't2' is of LocalDateTime and 2nd argument, 't1' is of LocalTime. At runtime it is not possible to convert LocalTime to LocalDateTime and hence exception is thrown at runtime.

1.1.59 Answer: B

Reason:
Definition of plus method is: 'public LocalDate plus(long amountToAdd, TemporalUnit unit) {...}'.

TemporalUnit is mentioned in exam objectives and it is being used as method parameters in date time API. enum ChronoUnit implements this interface and it is used at various places in the API.

One such use as an argument in plus and minus methods of LocalDate, LocalDateTime and LocalTime classes.

t1.plus(22, ChronoUnit.HOURS) is same as t1.plusHours(22).

If you check the code of plus(long, TemporalUnit), you will find that it calls plusSeconds, plusMinutes, plusHours etc based on the passed enum value. 'ChronoUnit.HOURS' is passed in this case, hence t1.plus(22, ChronoUnit.HOURS) invokes t1.plusHours(22).

1.1.60 Answer: C

Reason:
You should be aware of Day light saving mechanism to answer this question.
Suppose daylight time starts at 2 AM on particular date.
Current time: 1:59:59 [Normal time].
Next second: 3:00:00 [Time is not 2:00:00 rather it is 3:00:00. It is Daylight saving time].
Clock just jumped from 1:59:59 to 3:00:00.

Now Suppose daylight time ends at 2 AM on particular date.
Current time: 1:59:59 [Daylight saving time].
Next second: 1:00:00 [Time is not 2:00:00 rather it is 1:00:00. Clock switched back to normal time].
Clock just went back from 1:59:59 to 1:00:00.

Now let's solve given code:
dt --> {2018-11-04T13:59:59}. Daylight saving time has already ended as it is PM and not AM. This is actually a normal time now.

dt.plusSeconds(1) => creates a new ZonedDateTime object {2018-11-04T14:00:00} and dt refers to it.

dt.getHour() = 14, dt.getMinute() = 0 and dt.getSecond() = 0.

1.1.61 Answer: B

Reason:
DateTimeFormatter.ofLocalizedDate(FormatStyle.FULL); statement returns formatter to format date part.

date is of LocalDateTime type hence it has both date part and time part.

'formatter.format(date)' simply formats the date part and ignores time part.

NOTE: You should aware of other formatter related methods for the OCP exam, such as: 'ofLocalizedTime' and 'ofLocalizedDateTime'

1.1.62 Answer: C

Reason:
Instant class doesn't have any method to convert to LocalDate, LocalDateTime or LocalTime and vice-versa. Hence, 'instant.toLocalDateTime();' and 'LocalDateTime.of(instant);' cause compilation error.
'(LocalDateTime)instant' also causes compilation failure as LocalDateTime and Instant are not related in multilevel inheritance.

Hence, the only option left is:
'instant.atZone(ZoneId.systemDefault()).toLocalDateTime();'.

Let us understand what is happening with above statement:
ZonedDateTime class has methods to convert to LocalDate, LocalDateTime and LocalTime instances. So, object of Instant is first converted to ZonedDateTime.
An Instant object doesn't store any information about the time zone, so to convert it to ZonedDateTime, the default zone (ZoneId.systemDefault()) is passed to atZone method.
'instant.atZone(ZoneId.systemDefault())' returns an instance of ZonedDateTime and toLocalDateTime() method returns the corresponding instance of LocalDateTime.

1.1.63 Answer: A

Reason:
File is used to represent both File and Directory.

deleteFiles(new File("F:\\Test"), ".pdf"); => A java file object referring to 'F:\Test' is created and on method call variable 'dir' refers to it.

dir.listFiles() method returns an File [], this contains the list of immediate files and directories.

NOTE: listFiles() method returns File[] and list() method returns String [].

In this case, array list will have 4 File objects:
[{F:\Test\t1.pdf},{F:\Test\t2.pdf},{F:\Test\A},{F:\Test\X}].

for loop iterates through each File object and if the File object is a Directory, then it recursively invokes deleteFiles method.

file.isDirectory() method checks if the file object is a File or Directory?

file.getName() returns the name (not the full path) of the file object (such as 't1.pdf', 't2.pdf', 'A' etc.).

file.delete() deletes the actual file from the disk.

1.1.64 Answer: A

Reason:
Two cases are possible:
1. If JVM is associated with the Console (such as running above code from command prompt/window):
System.console() will return the Console object, optional.isPresent() will return true and System.out.println(optional.get()); will print the Console reference (such as java.io.Console@48140564).

2. If JVM is not associated with the Console (such as running above code from an IDE or online):

System.console() will return null and Optional.ofNullable(System.console()); returns an EMPTY Optional.
For EMPTY optional, optional.isPresent() returns false and System.out.println(optional.get()); will not get executed. So you may not get any output in this case.

In both the cases, optional reference will always refer to some Optional object and will never be null. NullPointerException can't be thrown by calling methods on optional reference.

1.1.65   Answer: A

Reason:
writes 4 characters as 8 bytes of data.
readChar() method returns 2 bytes of data, interpreted as char. Return type is char and not int.

'J' is displayed in the output.

1.1.66   Answer: A

Reason:
File class has below 2 methods:
public File getParentFile() {...}
public String getParent() {...}

'dir' refers to File object for abstract path 'F:\A\B'.
dir.getParentFile() => returns a File object for abstract path 'F:\A'
dir.getParentFile().getParent() => returns a String object referring to 'F:\'

1.1.67   Answer: B

Reason:
It is very interesting question and frequently asked in interviews as well.

Initially length of arr is 500000 and all the elements are initialized with 0.
There are 2 options:
1. 'orig.png' file's size is way less than 500000, say 100000 bytes only. This means only 100000 array elements will be replaced and rest will remain 0.

fos.write(arr); => Writes whole array to the stream/file, which means along with 100000 data bytes 400000 extra bytes will also be written. In this case above code can't produce exact copy.

2. 'copy.png' file's size is not multiple of 500000, say 700000 bytes only.
1st invocation of 'fis.read(arr)' will populate all 500000 elements with data and 'fos.write(arr);' will correctly write first 500000 bytes to 'copy.png' file.
2nd invocation of 'fis.read(arr)' will replace 200000 elements with remaining data and leaving 300000 with the data read from previous read operation. This means 'fos.write(arr);' on 2nd invocation will write 300000 extra bytes. So for this case as well, above code cannot produce exact copy.

Solution is very simple. Use the overloaded version of write method.

res stores the number of bytes read into the arr. So to get exact copy replace line 12 with 'fos.write(arr, 0, res)'.

1.1.68 Answer: B

Reason:
There is no compilation error in this code.

Optional class doesn't implement Serializable interface, hence 'oos.writeObject(optional);' throws exception at runtime.

1.1.69 Answer: A,C,D

Reason:
Below are the declarations of lines and readAllLines methods from Files class:
public static Stream<String> lines(Path path) throws IOException {...}
public static List<String> readAllLines(Path path) throws IOException {...}

'Files.lines(Paths.get("F:\\Book.java"))' returns Stream<String> object. Hence forEach() can be invoked but stream() can't be invoked.

'Files.readAllLines(Paths.get("F:\\Book.java"))' returns List<String> object. Hence both forEach() and stream() methods can be invoked. List has both the methods. But converting list to stream() and then invoking forEach() method is not required but it is a legal syntax and prints the file contents.

1.1.70 Answer: A

Reason:
Files.list(Path) returns the object of Stream<Path> containing all the paths (files and directories) of current directory. It is not recursive.

For recursive access use overloaded Files.walk() methods.

1.1.71 Answer: D

Reason:
Root folder or drive is not considered in count and indexing. In the given path A is at 0th index, B is at 1st index, C is at 2nd index and Book.java is at 3rd index.

In 'subpath(int beginIndex, int endIndex)' method beginIndex in inclusive and endIndex is exclusive. So, in the given question, starting index is 1 and end index is 3.

So, 'path.subpath(1,4)' returns 'B\C\Book.java'.

1.1.72 Answer: D

Reason:
For 'path1.relativize(path2)' both path1 and path2 should be of same type. Both should either be relative or absolute.

In this case, path1 refers to 'F:\A\B\C' and path2 refers to 'F:\A'.

To easily tell the resultant path, there is a simple trick. Just remember this for the exam.

path1.relativize(path2) means how to reach path2 from path1. It is by doing 'cd ..\..' so, 1st output is '..\..'

path2.relativize(path1) means how to reach path1 from path2. It is by doing 'cd B\C' so, 2nd output is 'B\C'.

1.1.73 Answer: B

Reason:
String class has endsWith method, and the lambda expression '(p,a) -> p.toString().endsWith("txt")' will return all the paths ending with "txt".

Signature of find method is:
Stream<Path> find(Path start, int maxDepth, BiPredicate<Path, BasicFileAttributes> matcher, FileVisitOption... options)

and in the code, following syntax is used: Files.find(root, 2, predicate).

root refers to 'F:' and maxDepth is 2. This means look out for all the files under F: (depth 1) and all the files under the directories whose immediate parent is F: (depth 2).

So in this case, F: and Parent directory are searched for the matching files. 'F:Parent\a.txt' and 'F:Parent\b.txt' are printed on to the console.

1.1.74 Answer: D

Reason:
First of all I would like to tell you that Windows shortcut and symbolic links are different. Shortcut is just a regular file and symbolic link is a File System object.

To create symbolic link used in this question, I used below command:
C:\TEMP>mklink msg .\Parent\Child\Message.txt

And below message was displayed on to the console for the successful creation of symbolic link 'symbolic link created for msg <<===>> .\Parent\Child\Message.txt'.

Files class has methods such as newInputStream(...), newOutputStream(...), newBufferedReader(...) and newBufferedWriter(...) for files reading and writing. Given code doesn't cause any compilation error.

path refers to 'C\TEMP\msg', which is a symbolic link and hence Files.newBufferedReader(path) works with 'C:\TEMP\Parent\Child\Message.txt'.

Given code successfully reads the file and prints 'Welcome!' on to the console.

1.1.75 Answer: C

Reason:

Connection object is created inside try-with-resources statement. Both 'connection' and 'con' refer to the same Connection object.

con.close() method is invoked implicitly just before the closing bracket of try-with-resources statement.

connection.createStatement(); throws exception at runtime as no operations are allowed on closed Connection.

1.1.76 Answer: D

Reason:

Even if there are no records in EMPLOYEE table, ResultSet object returned by 'stmt.executeQuery(query);' will never be null.

rs.next() returns false and control doesn't enter while loop. Code executes fine and doesn't print anything on to the console.

1.1.77 Answer: B

Reason:

Given sql statement returns below records:

102 SeanSmith   15000
103 Regina   Williams 15500

'rs.absolute(2);' moves the cursor pointer to 2nd record.

'rs.updateDouble("SALARY", 20000);' updates the salary of 2nd record to 20000 but to update the records in the database, 'rs.updateRow();' statement must be invoked.

As 'rs.updateRow()' statement is missing hence no record is updated in the database.

Please note: there is no need to invoke con.commit(); method as by default Connection object is in auto-commit mode.

1.1.78 Answer: C

Reason:

In the given query, both the column aliases have same name 'msg'. 'rs.getString("msg")' always returns the first matching column.

In case of matching column names, column indexes can be used. rs.getString(1) would return 'Happy New Year!' and rs.getString(2) would return 'Happy Holidays!'.

1.1.79 Answer: D

Reason:

execute(String) method of Statement can accept all types of queries. It returns true if the first result is a ResultSet object; false if it is an update count or there are no results.

DELETE sql query returns the no. of deleted records, which is not a ResultSet hence record is deleted from the database and false is returned.

1.1.80 Answer: B

Reason:
Given query returns below records:
101   John Smith   12000
102   Sean Smith   15000
103   Regina   Williams 15500
104   Natasha George   14600

Initially cursor is just before the 1st record.

'rs.relative(-3);' doesn't throw any exception but keeps the cursor just before the 1st record. According to javadoc of relative method, "Attempting to move beyond the first/last row in the result set positions the cursor before/after the first/last row". Same is true for absolute method as well.

'rs.relative(1);' is identical to 'rs.next()' so it moves the cursor to the 1st record.

'rs.getInt(1)' returns 101.

1.1.81 Answer: D

Reason:
java.util.Properties extends Hashtable<Object, Object>, which is a map to store key value pairs.

load method accepts InputStream object and loads the key value pairs (present in InputStream object) to internal map of Properties class.

There are 2 overloaded versions of getProperty() method:
1. String getProperty(String key) => Returns value of the specified key and null if value is not found.

2. String getProperty(String key, String defaultValue) => Returns value of the specified key and defaultValue if value is not found.

'key1' and 'key2' are present in Properties file, so their corresponding values are returned.

As 'key3' is not present in the Properties file, hence 'prop.getProperty("key3", "Good Day!")' returns the defaultValue, "Good Day!" and as 'key4' is not present as well, hence 'prop.getProperty("key4")' returns null.

1.1.82 Answer: A,E

Reason:
'public static Locale[] getAvailableLocales() {...}' returns the Locale [] containing all the available locales supported by the JVM.

Language codes are stored in lower case, so syntax comparing upper case codes ('FR') is ruled out.

You are left with 3 options [working with lower case language code ('fr')]. 'x' in the lambda expression is of Locale type and Locale class doesn't have method startsWith, so 'x -> x.startsWith("fr")' causes compilation failure.

'x -> x.getLanguage().equals("fr")' and 'x -> x.toString().startsWith("fr")' correctly filters out expected Locale objects.

1.1.83 Answer: **A**

Reason:
ResourceBundle.getBundle("ResourceBundle", loc); => Base resource bundle file name should be 'ResourceBundle'.

Default Locale is: fr_CA and passed Locale to getBundle method is: en_IN

The search order for matching resource bundle is:
ResourceBundle_en_IN.properties [1st: Complete en_IN].
ResourceBundle_en.properties [2nd: Only language en].
ResourceBundle_fr_CA.properties [3rd: Complete default Locale fr_CA].
ResourceBundle_fr.properties [4th: Language of default Locale fr].
ResourceBundle.properties [5th: ResourceBundle's name without language or country].

Out of the given resource bundles, 'ResourceBundle.properties' matches.
This resource bundle has key 'locale' and value 'French/Canada'.
rb.getObject("locale") prints 'French/Canada' on to the console.

1.1.84 Answer: **D**

Reason:
If all the files have same keys and locale is en_US, then key-value pair of best match ('RB_en_US.properties') file will be considered.

If the files have different keys and locale is en_US, then key-value pair is searched in following order:
1. RB_en_US.properties [parent = 'RB_en.properties']
2. RB_en.properties [parent = 'RB.properties']
3. RB.properties [parent = null]

Hence bundle.getKeys(); returns an Enumeration<String> instance containing ("key1", "key2") from 'RB_en_US.properties' file and ("key3") from 'RB_en.properties' file.

I mentioned parent value above because there is relationship among above 3 files.
RB.properties is the ultimate parent, its child is 'RB_en.properties' and 'RB_en_US.properties is the child of 'RB_en.properties'.
So if I write below codes:

bundle.getString("key1"); value will be taken from 'RB_en_US.properties' file, so it returns ONE.
bundle.getString("key2"); value will be taken from 'RB_en_US.properties' file, so it returns ONE.
msgs.getString("key3"); this key is not available in 'RB_en_US.properties' file and hence it will be searched in its parent 'RB_en.properties'. And because "key3" key is available in 'RB_en.properties' file, hence it returns THREE.

You can iterate over Enumeration using hasMoreElements() and nextElement() methods.

Iteration logic prints key-value pair in the order of Enumeration elements ("key1", "key2", "key3"). Hence output will be:
key1=ONE
key2=TWO
key3=THREE

If you read the javadoc of getKeys(), getString(String) or getObject(String) methods, then you will find out that these methods work with current resource bundle and its parent.

1.1.85 Answer: B

Reason:
AtomicInteger's getAndDecrement() method will first retrieve the value and then decrement and it happens atomically.
So during the execution of getAndDecrement() method, another thread cannot execute getAndDecrement() method. This means output will have 3 digits 3, 2 and 1.

But execution of threads depend on OS/JVM implementation, hence order of output can be different.

1.1.86 Answer: B

Reason:
'new CyclicBarrier(2, match);' means 2 threads must call await() so that Cyclic Barrier is tripped and barrier action is executed, this means run() method of thread referred by match is invoked and this will print expected output on to the console.

'new Player(cb);' assigns passed CyclicBarrier instance to 'cb' property of the Player class and it also invokes start() method so that this Player thread becomes Runnable. run() method is invoked later which invokes cb.await() method.

One more 'cb.await();' call is needed to get the expected output.

'p1.start();' => Thread referred by p1 is already started in the constructor, calling start() again throws IllegalThreadStateException.
'new Player(cb);' => Just like previous statement, it will invoke the await() method on cb and CyclicBarrier will be tripped. This is correct option.
'new Player(cb).start();' => 'new Player(cb)' will invoke the await() method on cb and CyclicBarrier will be tripped. 'Match is starting...' will be printed on to the console. But calling start() method again throws IllegalThreadStateException and program is not terminated successfully.
'cb.await();' => await() method throws 2 checked exceptions: InterruptedException and BrokenBarrierException and these are not handled in the main method. Hence this will cause compilation error. If these 2 exceptions are handled inside main, then this could be one of the correct options.
'new Player();' => No-argument constructor of Player class doesn't assign value to 'cb' and doesn't invoke start() method as well. Hence, it will not have any affect.

1.1.87 Answer: D

Reason:
get() method throws 2 checked exceptions: InterruptedException and ExecutionException. And future.get() returns Object and it can be type-casted to Integer, so no compilation error.

run() method of MyThread prints 'OCP' on to the console and doesn't return anything, hence get() method of Future object returns null. null can be easily assigned to Integer. Hence 'System.out.println(tmp);' prints null on to the console.

1.1.88 Answer: C

Reason:
'es.submit(new Printer());' is asynchronous call, hence 2 threads(main and thread from pool) always run in asynchronous mode. Thread execution depends upon underlying OS/JVM's thread scheduling mechanism.

HELLO and DONE will be printed but their order cannot be predicted.

1.1.89   Answer: A

Reason:
IntStream.rangeClosed(1, 10) returns a sequential ordered IntStream but parallel() method converts it to a parallel stream.

forEachOrdered() will processes the elements of the stream in the order specified by its source (Encounter order), regardless of whether the stream is sequential or parallel, hence given code prints 1 to 10 in ascending order.

1.1.90   Answer: C

Reason:
There is a fixed thread pool of 10 threads, this means 10 threads can run in parallel. invokeAll() method causes the current thread (main) to wait, until all the Callable instances finish their execution. This means 'System.out.println(futures.size());' will execute once all the 5 tasks are complete.

Important point to note here is that all the Callable instances are executed in parallel. Even if all the tasks start at one instant, there will always be some overhead for sleeping thread to become running. In most of the cases it will be in nanoseconds/milliseconds. Hence overall time will be slightly greater than 3 secs.

2 Practice Test-2

2.1 90 Questions covering all topics.

2.1.1 Consider the code of Test.java file:

```java
//Test.java
package com.udayan.ocp;

class Player {
    String name;
    int age;

    Player() {
        this.name = "Virat";
        this.age = 29;
    }

    public int hashCode() {
        return 100;
    }
}

public class Test {
    public static void main(String[] args) {
        System.out.println(new Player());
    }
}
```

Hexadecimal representation of 100 is 64.

Which of the following option is correct?

A. Code doesn't compile successfully

B. Code compiles successfully and on execution always prints "com.udayan.ocp.Player@64" on to the console

C. Code compiles successfully but throws an exception on executing it

D. None of the other options

2.1.2   Given:

```
package com.udayan.ocp;

public class Initializer {
    static int a = 10000;

    static {
        --a;
    }

    {
        ++a;
    }

    public static void main(String[] args) {
        System.out.println(a);
    }
}
```

What is the result of compiling and executing Initializer class?

A. 10000

B. 9999

C. java.lang.ExceptionInInitailizerError

D. Compilation Error

2.1.3   Consider the code of Greet.java file:

```
package com.udayan.ocp;

public final class Greet {
    private String msg;
    public Greet(String msg) {
        this.msg = msg;
    }

    public String getMsg() {
        return msg;
    }

    public void setMsg(String msg) {
        this.msg = msg;
    }
}
```

Is Greet class an immutable class?

A. Yes

B. No

2.1.4 Given code of Test.java file:

```
package com.udayan.ocp;

interface Printer1 {
    default void print() {
        System.out.println("Printer1");
    }
}

interface Printer2 {
    default void print() {
        System.out.println("Printer2");
    }
}

class Printer implements Printer1, Printer2 {

}

public class Test {
    public static void main(String[] args) {
        Printer printer = new Printer();
        printer.print();
    }
}
```

What will be the result of compiling and executing Test class?

A. Compilation error for Printer1

B. Compilation error for Printer2

C. Compilation error for Printer

D. Printer1

E. Printer2

2.1.5   Consider the code of Test.java file:

```
package com.udayan.ocp;

enum Flags {
    TRUE, FALSE;

    Flags() {
        System.out.println("HELLO");
    }
}

public class Test {
    public static void main(String[] args) {
        Flags flags = Flags.TRUE;
    }
}
```

What will be the result of compiling and executing Test class?

A. HELLO is printed twice.

B. HELLO is printed once.

C. Exception is thrown at runtime.

D. None of the other options.

2.1.6 What will be the result of compiling and executing Test class?

```java
package com.udayan.ocp;

public class Test {
    enum TrafficLight {
        private String message;
        GREEN("go"), AMBER("slow"), RED("stop");

        TrafficLight(String message) {
            this.message = message;
        }

        public String getMessage() {
            return message;
        }
    }

    public static void main(String[] args) {
        System.out.println(
            TrafficLight.AMBER.getMessage().toUpperCase());
    }
}
```

A. slow

B. SLOW

C. NullPointerException is thrown at runtime

D. Compilation error

2.1.7   Given code:

```
package com.udayan.ocp;

public class Test {
    class A {
        void m() {
            System.out.println("INNER");
        }
    }

    public static void main(String [] args) {
        //Insert statement here
    }
}
```

Which statement when inserted in the main(String []) method will print "INNER" in the output?

A.	`A a1 = new Test().new A();` `a1.m();`
B.	`Test.A a2 = new Test().new A();` `a2.m();`
C.	`A a3 = this.new A();` `a3.m();`
D.	`Test.A a4 = this.new A();` `a4.m();`

2.1.8   What will be the result of compiling and executing class Test?

```java
package com.udayan.ocp;

class X {
    class Y {
        private void m() {
            System.out.println("INNER");
        }
    }

    public void invokeInner() {
        Y obj = new Y(); //Line 9
        obj.m(); //Line 10
    }
}

public class Test {
    public static void main(String[] args) {
        new X().invokeInner();
    }
}
```

A. INNER

B. Compilation error at Line 9 as instance of outer class (X) is needed to create the instance of inner class (Y).

C. Compilation error at Line 10 as private method m() cannot be invoked outside the body of inner class (Y).

D. Exception is thrown at runtime.

2.1.9 **What will be the result of compiling and executing Test class:**

```
package com.udayan.ocp;

class Outer {
    public void print(int x) {
        class Inner {
            public void getX() {
                System.out.println(++x);
            }
        }
        Inner inner = new Inner();
        inner.getX();
    }
}

public class Test {
    public static void main(String[] args) {
        new Outer().print(100);
    }
}
```

A. 100

B. 101

C. Compilation error

D. Runtime exception

2.1.10 Given code:

```
package com.udayan.ocp;

abstract class Greetings {
    abstract void greet();
}

public class Test {
    public static void main(String[] args) {
        Greetings obj = new Greetings() {
            @Override
            public void greet() {
                System.out.println("Hello");
            }
        };
        obj.greet();
    }
}
```

What will be the result of compiling and executing Test class?

A. Compilation error

B. NullPointerException

C. Hello

D. Nothing is printed on to the console

2.1.11 Below is the code of Test.java file:

```
package com.udayan.ocp;

public class Test {
    public static void main(String [] args) {
        System.out.println(new Object() {
            public String toString() {
                return "Anonymous";
            }
        });
    }
}
```

What will be the result of compiling and executing Test class?

A. Anonymous

B. Some text containing @ symbol

C. Compilation error

D. Runtime exception

2.1.12 Below is the code of Test.java file:

```
package com.udayan.ocp;

class Outer {
    static class Inner {
        static void greetings(String s) {
            System.out.println(s);
        }
    }
}

public class Test {
    public static void main(String[] args) {
        /*INSERT*/
    }
}
```

Which of the following 2 options can replace /*INSERT*/ such that there on executing class Test, output is: HELLO!?

A.	`Outer.Inner inner1 = new Outer().new Inner();` `inner1.greetings("HELLO!");`
B.	`Outer.Inner inner2 = new Outer.Inner();` `inner2.greetings("HELLO!");`
C.	`Outer.Inner.greetings("HELLO!");`
D.	`Inner.greetings("HELLO!");`

2.1.13 For the given code:

```
package com.udayan.ocp;

interface Operator {
    int operate(int i, int j);
}

public class Test {
    public static void main(String[] args) {
        Operator opr = new Operator() {
            public int operate(int i, int j) {
                return i + j;
            }
        };
        System.out.println(opr.operate(10, 20));
    }
}
```

Which of the following options successfully replace anonymous inner class code with lambda expression code?

```
A. Operator opr = (int x, int y) -> { return x + y; };
B. Operator opr = (x, y) -> { return x + y; };
C. Operator opr = (x, y) ->   return x + y;
D. Operator opr = (x, y) ->   x + y;
E. Operator opr = x, y ->   x + y;
```

2.1.14 **What will be the result of compiling and executing Test class?**

```
package com.udayan.ocp;

interface I9 {
    void print();
}

public class Test {
    public static void main(String[] args) {
        int i = 400;
        I9 obj = () -> System.out.println(i);
        obj.print();
        System.out.println(++i);
    }
}
```

A.	400 400	B.	400 401
C.	Compilation error	D.	Exception is thrown at runtime

2.1.15 Given code of Test.java file:

```
package com.udayan.ocp;

public class Test<T> {
    private T t;

    public T get() {
        return t;
    }

    public void set(T t) {
        this.t = t;
    }

    public static void main(String args[]) {
        Test obj = new Test();
        obj.set("OCP");
        obj.set(85);
        obj.set('%');

        System.out.println(obj.get());
    }
}
```

What will be the result of compiling and executing Test class?

A. Compilation error

B. Runtime exception

C. OCP85%

D. %

E. Output contains some text containing @ symbol

2.1.16 Given code of Test.java file:

```java
package com.udayan.ocp;

import java.util.Arrays;
import java.util.List;

public class Test {
    public static void main(String[] args) {
        List<String> list = Arrays.asList("7 Seven",
                        "Lucky 7", "77", "O7ne");
        list.stream().filter(str -> str.contains("7"))
            .forEach(System.out::println);
    }
}
```

What will be the result of compiling and executing Test class?

A.	7 Seven Lucky 7	B.	7 Seven Lucky 7 77
C.	7 Seven Lucky 7 O7ne	D.	7 Seven Lucky 7 77 O7ne
E.	7 Seven		

2.1.17 Given code of Test.java file:

```java
package com.udayan.ocp;

class Printer<String> {
    private String t;
    Printer(String t){
        this.t = t;
    }
    public String toString() {
        return null;
    }
}

public class Test {
    public static void main(String[] args) {
        Printer<Integer> obj = new Printer<>(100);
        System.out.println(obj);
    }
}
```

What will be the result of compiling and executing Test class?

A. 100

B. null

C. Compilation error in Printer class

D. Compilation error in Test class

2.1.18 Consider below codes:

```java
package com.udayan.ocp;

class A<T extends String> {

}

class B<T super String> {

}
```

Which of the following statement is correct?

A. Both class A and B compiles successfully

B. Only class A compiles successfully

C. Only class B compiles successfully

2.1.19 Given code of Test.java file:

```
package com.udayan.ocp;

import java.util.ArrayList;
import java.util.List;

public class Test {
    public static void main(String[] args) {
        List<String> list1 = new ArrayList<>();
        list1.add("A");
        list1.add("B");

        List<? extends Object> list2 = list1;
        list2.remove("A"); //Line 13
        list2.add("C"); //Line 14

        System.out.println(list2);
    }
}
```

What will be the result of compiling and executing Test class?

A. ABC

B. BC

C. Runtime exception

D. Compilation error

2.1.20 Given code of Test.java file:

```java
package com.udayan.ocp;

import java.util.Arrays;
import java.util.List;

public class Test {
    public static void main(String[] args) {
        List<String> list = Arrays.asList("A",
                                "E", "I", "O");
        list.add("U");
        list.forEach(System.out::print);
    }
}
```

What will be the result of compiling and executing Test class?

A. AEIO

B. AEIOU

C. UAEIO

D. Compilation error

E. Runtime exception

2.1.21 Given code of Test.java file:

```
package com.udayan.ocp;

import java.util.*;

enum TrafficLight {
    RED, YELLOW, GREEN
}

public class Test {
    public static void main(String[] args) {
        Map<TrafficLight, String> map = new TreeMap<>();
        map.put(TrafficLight.GREEN, "GO");
        map.put(TrafficLight.RED, "STOP");
        map.put(TrafficLight.YELLOW, "READY TO STOP");

        for(String msg : map.values()) {
            System.out.println(msg);
        }
    }
}
```

What will be the result of compiling and executing Test class?

A.	STOP READY TO STOP GO	B.	GO STOP READY TO STOP
C.	GO READY TO STOP STOP	D.	Printing order cannot be predicted.

2.1.22 Given code of Test.java file:

```
package com.udayan.ocp;

import java.util.*;

public class Test {
    public static void main(String[] args) {
        Set<String> set = new TreeSet<>(
                Arrays.asList(null,null,null));
        long count = set.stream().count();
        System.out.println(count);
    }
}
```

What will be the result of compiling and executing Test class?

A. 0

B. 1

C. 3

D. Runtime Exception

2.1.23 Given code of Test.java file:

```
package com.udayan.ocp;

import java.util.ArrayDeque;
import java.util.Deque;

public class Test {
    public static void main(String[] args) {
        Deque<Character> chars = new ArrayDeque<>();
        chars.add('A');
        chars.remove();
        chars.remove();

        System.out.println(chars);
    }
}
```

What will be the result of compiling and executing Test class?

A. []

B. [A]

C. Runtime Exception

2.1.24 **Given code of Test.java file:**

```
package com.udayan.ocp;

import java.util.Arrays;
import java.util.List;

public class Test {
    public static void main(String[] args) {
        List<Integer> list = Arrays.asList(0,2,4,6,8);
        list.replaceAll(i -> i + 1);
        System.out.println(list);
    }
}
```

What will be the result of compiling and executing Test class?

A. [0, 2, 4, 6, 8]

B. [1, 3, 5, 7, 9]

C. Runtime Exception

D. Compilation error

2.1.25 Given code of Test.java file:

```java
package com.udayan.ocp;

import java.util.Set;
import java.util.TreeSet;

class Employee implements Comparable<Employee> {
    private String name;
    private int age;

    Employee(String name, int age) {
        this.name = name;
        this.age = age;
    }

    @Override
    public String toString() {
        return "{" + name + ", " + age + "}";
    }

    @Override
    public int compareTo(Employee o) {
        return o.age - this.age;
    }
}
public class Test {
    public static void main(String[] args) {
        Set<Employee> employees = new TreeSet<>();
        employees.add(new Employee("Udayan", 31));
        employees.add(new Employee("Neha", 23));
        employees.add(new Employee("Hou Jian", 42));
        employees.add(new Employee("Smita", 29));

        System.out.println(employees);
    }
}
```

What will be the result of compiling and executing Test class?

A. [{Neha, 23}, {Smita, 29}, {Udayan, 31}, {Hou Jian, 42}]

B. [{Hou Jian, 42}, {Udayan, 31}, {Smita, 29}, {Neha, 23}]

C. [{Udayan, 31}, {Neha, 23}, {Hou Jian, 42}, {Smita, 29}]

D. Compilation error.

2.1.26 Given code of Test.java file:

```java
package com.udayan.ocp;

import java.util.Arrays;
import java.util.Collections;
import java.util.List;

class Name {
    String first;
    String last;

    public Name(String first, String last) {
        this.first = first;
        this.last = last;
    }

    public String getFirst() {
        return first;
    }

    public String getLast() {
        return last;
    }

    public String toString() {
        return first + " " + last;
    }

}

public class Test {
    public static void main(String[] args) {
        List<Name> names = Arrays.asList(
            new Name("Peter", "Lee"),
            new Name("John", "Smith"),
            new Name("bonita", "smith"));

        /*INSERT*/

        System.out.println(names);
    }
}
```

Currently on executing Test class, [Peter Lee, John Smith, bonita smith] is displayed in the output.

Which of the following options can replace /*INSERT*/ such that on executing Test class, [bonita smith, John Smith, Peter Lee] is displayed in the output?
The names list must be sorted in ascending order of first name in case-insensitive manner. Select 3 options.

A.	`Collections.sort(names, (o1, o2) -> o1.getFirst().compareTo(o2.getFirst()));`
B.	`Collections.sort(names, (o1, o2) -> o1.getFirst().toLowerCase().compareTo(o2.getFirst().toLowerCase()));`
C.	`Collections.sort(names, (o1, o2) -> o1.getFirst().toUpperCase().compareTo(o2.getFirst().toUpperCase()));`
D.	`Collections.sort(names, (o1, o2) -> o1.getFirst().compareToIgnoreCase(o2.getFirst()));`

2.1.27 Given code of Test.java file:

```java
package com.udayan.ocp;

import java.util.stream.IntStream;

public class Test {
    public static void main(String[] args) {
        System.out.println(IntStream.range(10,1).count());
    }
}
```

What will be the result of compiling and executing Test class?

A. 10

B. 9

C. 0

D. Runtime Exception

2.1.28 **Given code of Test.java file:**

```
package com.udayan.ocp;

import java.util.Date;
import java.util.function.*;

public class Test {
    public static void main(String[] args) {
        /*INSERT*/ obj = Date::new; //Constructor reference
                                    // for Date() constructor
        Date date = obj.get(); //Creates an instance
                                    // of Date class.
        System.out.println(date);
    }
}
```

Which of the following options can replace /*INSERT*/ such that on executing Test class, current date and time is displayed in the output?

A. Supplier

B. Supplier<Object>

C. Supplier<Date>

D. Function

E. Function<Date>

F. Function<Object>

2.1.29 Given code of Test.java file:

```java
package com.udayan.ocp;

import java.util.Arrays;
import java.util.List;
import java.util.function.Consumer;

interface StringConsumer extends Consumer<String> {
    @Override
    public default void accept(String s) {
        System.out.println(s.toUpperCase());
    }
}

public class Test {
    public static void main(String[] args) {
        StringConsumer consumer = new StringConsumer() {
            @Override
            public void accept(String s) {
                System.out.println(s.toLowerCase());
            }
        };
        List<String> list = Arrays.asList("Dr",
                            "Mr", "Miss", "Mrs");
        list.forEach(consumer);
    }
}
```

What will be the result of compiling and executing Test class?

A.	dr mr miss mrs	B.	DR MR MISS MRS
C.	Compilation error	D.	Runtime exception

2.1.30 Given code of Test.java file:

```
package com.udayan.ocp;

import java.util.function.BiFunction;

public class Test {
    public static void main(String[] args) {
        BiFunction<Integer, Integer, Character>
                        compFunc = (i, j) -> i + j;
        System.out.println(compFunc.apply(0, 65));
    }
}
```

NOTE: ASCII value of A is 65.

What will be the result of compiling and executing Test class?

A. Compilation error
B. 65
C. A

2.1.31 Given code of Test.java file:

```
package com.udayan.ocp;

import java.util.*;
import java.util.function.DoublePredicate;

class Employee {
    private String name;
    private double salary;

    public Employee(String name, double salary) {
        this.name = name;
        this.salary = salary;
    }

    public String getName() {
        return name;
    }
```

```java
    public double getSalary() {
        return salary;
    }

    public void setSalary(double salary) {
        this.salary = salary;
    }

    public String toString() {
        return "{" + name + ", " + salary + "}";
    }
}

public class Test {
    public static void main(String[] args) {
        List<Employee> employees = Arrays.asList(
            new Employee("Jack", 8000),
            new Employee("Lucy", 12000));
        updateSalary(employees, d -> d < 10000);
        employees.forEach(System.out::println);
    }

    private static void updateSalary(List<Employee> list,
                            DoublePredicate predicate) {
        for(Employee e : list) {
            if(predicate.negate().test(e.getSalary())) {
                e.setSalary(e.getSalary() + 2000);
            }
        }
    }
}
```

What will be the result of compiling and executing Test class?

A.	{Jack, 8000.0} {Lucy, 12000.0}	B.	{Jack, 10000.0} {Lucy, 12000.0}
C.	{Jack, 8000.0} {Lucy, 14000.0}	D.	{Jack, 10000.0} {Lucy, 14000.0}

2.1.32 Given code of Test.java file:

```
package com.udayan.ocp;

import java.util.function.BiFunction;

public class Test {
    public static void main(String[] args) {
        BiFunction<String, String, String>
                          func = String::concat;
        System.out.println(func.apply("James",
                                "Gosling"));
    }
}
```

What will be the result of compiling and executing Test class?

A. JamesGosling

B. James Gosling

C. GoslingJames

D. Gosling James

E. Gosling

F. James

2.1.33 Given code of Test.java file:

```
package com.udayan.ocp;

import java.util.Arrays;
import java.util.List;

public class Test {
    public static void main(String[] args) {
        List<String> list = Arrays.asList(
                "north", "east", "west", "south");
        list.replaceAll(s -> s.substring(0,1)
            .toUpperCase().concat(s.substring(1)));

        System.out.println(list);
```

```
        }
    }
```

What will be the result of compiling and executing Test class?

A. [north, east, west, south]

B. [North, East, West, South]

C. [NORTH, EAST, WEST, SOUTH]

D. [N, E, W, S]

E. [n, e, w, s]

2.1.34 **Given code of Test.java file:**

```
package com.udayan.ocp;

import java.util.LinkedHashMap;
import java.util.Map;
import java.util.function.BiConsumer;
import java.util.function.BiFunction;

public class Test {
    public static void main(String[] args) {
        Map<Integer, Integer> map = new LinkedHashMap<>();
        map.put(1, 10);
        map.put(2, 20);
        BiConsumer<Integer, Integer> consumer = (k, v) -> {
            System.out.println(k + ":" + v);
        };

        BiFunction<Integer, Integer, Integer> function
                = (k, v) -> {
                    System.out.println(k + ":" + v);
                    return null;
        };
        //Line n1

    }
}
```

Which of the following options will replace //Line n1 such that below output is printed to the console?
```
1:10
2:20
```

A. `map.forEach(consumer);`

B. `map.forEach(function);`

C. `map.forEachOrdered(consumer);`

D. `map.forEachOrdered(function);`

2.1.35 Given code of Test.java file:

```java
package com.udayan.ocp;

import java.util.Arrays;
import java.util.List;
import java.util.Map;
import java.util.stream.Collectors;

enum Color {
    RED, YELLOW, GREEN
}

class TrafficLight {
    String msg;
    Color color;

    TrafficLight(String msg, Color color) {
        this.msg = msg;
        this.color = color;
    }

    public String getMsg() {
        return msg;
    }

    public Color getColor() {
        return color;
    }

    public String toString() {
        return "{" + color + ", " + msg + "}";
    }
}

public class Test {
```

```
public static void main(String[] args) {
    TrafficLight tl1 = new TrafficLight("Go", Color.GREEN);
    TrafficLight tl2 = new TrafficLight("Go Now!",
                                        Color.GREEN);
    TrafficLight tl3 = new TrafficLight("Ready to stop",
                                        Color.YELLOW);
    TrafficLight tl4 = new TrafficLight("Slow Down",
                                        Color.YELLOW);
    TrafficLight tl5 = new TrafficLight("Stop", Color.RED);

    List<TrafficLight> list = Arrays.asList(tl1,
                                    tl2, tl3, tl4, tl5);

    Map<Color, List<String>> map = list.stream()
        .collect(Collectors.groupingBy(TrafficLight::getColor,
                Collectors.mapping(TrafficLight::getMsg,
                                    Collectors.toList()))));

    System.out.println(map.get(Color.YELLOW));
    }
}
```

What will be the result of compiling and executing Test class?

A. [Ready to stop, Slow Down]

B. [Ready to stop]

C. [Slow Down]

D. Some text containing @ symbol

2.1.36 **Given code of Test.java file:**

```java
package com.udayan.ocp;

import java.util.Arrays;
import java.util.List;
import java.util.function.Predicate;

public class Test {
    public static void main(String[] args) {
        List<Integer> list = Arrays.asList(-80,
                            100, -40, 25, 200);
        Predicate<Integer> predicate = num -> {
            int ctr = 1;
            boolean result = num > 0;
            System.out.print(ctr++ + ".");
            return result;
        };

        list.stream().filter(predicate).sorted();
    }
}
```

What will be the result of compiling and executing Test class?

A. 1.

B. 1.1.

C. 1.2.

D. 1.2.3.4.5.

E. 1.1.1.1.1.

F. Nothing is printed on to the console

2.1.37 Given code of Test.java file:

```
package com.udayan.ocp;

import java.util.Arrays;
import java.util.Comparator;
import java.util.List;

public class Test {
    public static void main(String[] args) {
        List<Integer> list = Arrays.asList(10, 20, 8);

        System.out.println(list.stream().max(
            Comparator.comparing(a -> a)).get()); //Line 1

        System.out.println(list.stream().max(
            Integer::compareTo).get()); //Line 2

        System.out.println(list.stream().max(
            Integer::max).get()); //Line 3
    }
}
```

Which of the following statement is true?

A. Line 1, Line 2 and Line 3 print same output.

B. Line 1 and Line 2 print same output.

C. Line 1 and Line 3 print same output.

D. Line 2 and Line 3 print same output.

2.1.38 Given code of Test.java file:

```
package com.udayan.ocp;

import java.util.ArrayList;
import java.util.List;

public class Test {
    public static void main(String[] args) {
        int ref = 10;
        List<Integer> list = new ArrayList<>();
        list.stream().anyMatch(i -> {
            System.out.println("HELLO");
            return i > ref;
        });
    }
}
```

What will be the result of compiling and executing Test class?

A. HELLO

B. Compilation error

C. Program executes successfully but nothing is printed on to the console.

2.1.39 Given code of Test.java file:

```
package com.udayan.ocp;

import java.util.Optional;
import java.util.stream.Stream;

public class Test {
    public static void main(String[] args) {
        Stream<Number> stream = Stream.of();
        Optional<Number> optional = stream.findFirst();
        System.out.println(optional.orElse(-1));
    }
}
```

What will be the result of compiling and executing Test class?

A. null

B. 0

C. -1

D. Optional.empty

2.1.40 Given code of Test.java file:

```
package com.udayan.ocp;

import java.util.OptionalInt;

class MyException extends Exception{}

public class Test {
    public static void main(String[] args) {
        OptionalInt optional = OptionalInt.empty();
        System.out.println(
            optional.orElseThrow(MyException::new));
    }
}
```

What will be the result of compiling and executing Test class?

A. null

B. An instance of NoSuchElementException is thrown at runtime

C. An instance of RuntimeException is thrown at runtime

D. An instance of MyException is thrown at runtime

E. An instance of NullPointerException is thrown at runtime

F. Compilation error

2.1.41 Given code of Test.java file:

```java
package com.udayan.ocp;

import java.util.Arrays;
import java.util.stream.Stream;

public class Test {
    public static void main(String[] args) {
        Stream<Integer> stream = Arrays.asList(
                        1,2,3,4,5).stream();
        System.out.println(stream.sum());
    }
}
```

What will be the result of compiling and executing Test class?

A. 15

B. Runtime Exception

C. Compilation error

2.1.42 Given code of Test.java file:

```java
package com.udayan.ocp;

import java.util.stream.IntStream;

public class Test {
    public static void main(String[] args) {
        int res = 1;
        IntStream stream = IntStream.rangeClosed(1, 4);

        System.out.println(stream.reduce(res++,
                                (i, j) -> i * j));
    }
}
```

What will be the result of compiling and executing Test class?

A. 24

B. 48

C. 12

D. 6

E. Compilation error as res should be effectively final

2.1.43 Given code of Test.java file:

```java
package com.udayan.ocp;

import java.util.List;
import java.util.Map;
import java.util.stream.Collectors;
import java.util.stream.Stream;

class Certification {
    String studId;
    String test;
    int marks;

    Certification(String studId, String test, int marks) {
        this.studId = studId;
        this.test = test;
        this.marks = marks;
    }

    public String toString() {
        return "{" + studId + ", " + test + ", "
                                + marks + "}";
    }

    public String getStudId() {
        return studId;
    }

    public String getTest() {
        return test;
    }

    public int getMarks() {
        return marks;
```

```java
        }
}

public class Test {
    public static void main(String[] args) {
        Certification c1 =
                new Certification("S001", "OCA", 87);
        Certification c2 =
                new Certification("S002", "OCA", 82);
        Certification c3 =
                new Certification("S001", "OCP", 79);
        Certification c4 =
                new Certification("S002", "OCP", 89);
        Certification c5 =
                new Certification("S003", "OCA", 60);
        Certification c6 =
                new Certification("S004", "OCA", 88);

        Stream<Certification> stream
            = Stream.of(c1, c2, c3, c4, c5, c6);
        Map<Boolean, List<Certification>> map =
            stream.collect(Collectors
                .partitioningBy(s -> s.equals("OCA")));
        System.out.println(map.get(true));
    }
}
```

What will be the result of compiling and executing Test class?

A. [{S001, OCA, 87}, {S002, OCA, 82}, {S003, OCA, 60}, {S004, OCA, 88}]

B. []

C. [{S001, OCA, 87}, {S002, OCA, 82}, {S001, OCP, 79}, {S002, OCP, 89}, {S003, OCA, 60}, {S004, OCA, 88}]

D. [{S001, OCP, 79}, {S002, OCP, 89}]

2.1.44 Given code of Test.java file:

```
package com.udayan.ocp;

import java.util.stream.Stream;

public class Test {
    public static void main(String[] args) {
        System.out.println(Stream.of(10, 0, -10)
                    .sorted().findAny().orElse(-1));
    }
}
```

Which of the following statements are true about the execution of Test class?

A. It can print any number from the stream.

B. It will always print 10 on to the console.

C. It will always print -10 on to the console.

D. It will always print 0 on to the console.

E. It will never print -1 on to the console.

2.1.45 Given code of Test.java file:

```
package com.udayan.ocp;

import java.util.ArrayList;
import java.util.List;

class Rope {
    int length;
    String color;

    Rope(int length, String color) {
        this.length = length;
        this.color = color;
    }

    public String toString() {
        return "Rope [" + color + ", " + length + "]";
    }
```

```
        static class RedRopeFilter {
            boolean filter(Rope rope) {
                return rope.color.equalsIgnoreCase("Red");
            }
        }
    }

public class Test {
    public static void main(String[] args) {
        List<Rope> list = new ArrayList<>();
        list.add(new Rope(5, "red"));
        list.add(new Rope(10, "Red"));
        list.add(new Rope(7, "RED"));
        list.add(new Rope(10, "green"));
        list.add(new Rope(7, "Blue"));

        list.stream().filter(
            new Rope.RedRopeFilter()::filter)
                .forEach(System.out::println); //Line n1
    }
}
```

What will be the result of compiling and executing Test class?

A.	Line n1 causes compilation error	B.	Rope [Red, 10]
C.	Rope [red, 5] Rope [Red, 10] Rope [RED, 7]	D.	Rope [green, 10] Rope [Blue, 7]
E.	Rope [red, 5] Rope [Red, 10] Rope [RED, 7] Rope [green, 10] Rope [Blue, 7]		

2.1.46 Given code of Test.java file:

```java
package com.udayan.ocp;

import java.util.ArrayList;
import java.util.List;

class MyString {
    String str;
    MyString(String str) {
        this.str = str;
    }
}

public class Test {
    public static void main(String[] args) {
        List<MyString> list = new ArrayList<>();
        list.add(new MyString("Y"));
        list.add(new MyString("E"));
        list.add(new MyString("S"));

        list.stream().map(s -> s).forEach(System.out::print);
    }
}
```

Which of the following statements are correct?

A. On execution, above code prints "YES" on to the console

B. Above code terminates successfully without printing anything on to the console

C. Above code terminates successfully after printing text other than "YES" on to the console

D. Above code causes compilation error

2.1.47 **Given code of Test.java file:**

```
package com.udayan.ocp;

class Resource1 implements AutoCloseable {
    public void m1() throws Exception {
        System.out.print("A");
        throw new Exception("B");
    }
    public void close() {
        System.out.print("C");
    }
}

class Resource2 implements AutoCloseable {
    public void m2() {
        System.out.print("D");
    }
    public void close() throws Exception {
        System.out.print("E");
    }
}

public class Test {
    public static void main(String[] args) {
        try (Resource1 r1 = new Resource1();
             Resource2 r2 = new Resource2()) {
            r1.m1();
            r2.m2();
        } catch (Exception e) {
            System.out.print(e.getMessage());
        }
    }
}
```

What will be the result of compiling and executing Test class?

A. Compilation error

B. ABEC

C. ABCE

D. ACEB

E. AECB

2.1.48 Given code of Test.java file:

```java
package com.udayan.ocp;

import java.io.*;

class ReadTheFile {
    static void print() { //Line 4
        throw new IOException(); //Line 5
    }
}

public class Test {
    public static void main(String[] args) { //Line 10
        ReadTheFile.print(); //Line 11
        //Line 12
    }
}
```

Which 2 changes are necessary so that code compiles successfully?

A.	Replace Line 4 with **static void** print() **throws** Exception {
B.	Replace Line 4 with **static void** print() **throws** Throwable {
C.	Replace Line 10 with **public static void** main(String[] args) **throws** IOException {

D.	Surround Line 11 with below try-catch block:
	``
	try {
	    ReadTheFile.print();
	} catch(IOException e) {
	    e.printStackTrace();
	}
	``

E.	Surround Line 11 with below try-catch block:
	``
	try {
	    ReadTheFile.print();
	} catch(IOException | Exception e) {
	    e.printStackTrace();
	}
	``

F.	Surround Line 11 with below try-catch block:
	``
	try {
	    ReadTheFile.print();
	} catch(Exception e) {
	    e.printStackTrace();
	}
	``

2.1.49 Given code of Test.java file:

```java
package com.udayan.ocp;

import java.sql.SQLException;

public class Test {
    private static void m() throws SQLException {
        try {
            throw new SQLException();
        } catch (Exception e) {
            e = new SQLException();
            throw e;
        }
    }

    public static void main(String[] args) {
        try {
            m();
        } catch(SQLException e) {
            System.out.println("Caught Successfully.");
        }
    }
}
```

What will be the result of compiling and executing Test class?

A. Method m() causes compilation error.

B. Method main(String []) causes compilation error.

C. Caught Successfully.

D. Program ends abruptly.

2.1.50 Given code of Test.java file:

```java
package com.udayan.ocp;

import java.io.FileNotFoundException;
import java.io.FileReader;

public class Test {
    public static void main(String[] args) {
        try(FileReader fr = new FileReader(
                                "C:/temp.txt")) {

        } catch (FileNotFoundException e) {
            e.printStackTrace();
        }
    }
}
```

Does above code compile successfully?

A. YES

B. NO

2.1.51 Given code of Test.java file:

```java
package com.udayan.ocp;

import java.io.PrintWriter;

public class Test {
    public static void main(String[] args) {
        try(PrintWriter writer
                    = new PrintWriter(System.out)) {
            writer.println("Hello");
        } catch(Exception ex) {
            writer.close();
        }
    }
}
```

What will be the result of compiling and executing Test class?

A. Hello

B. Compilation error

C. Program ends abruptly

2.1.52 Given code of Test.java file:

```java
package com.udayan.ocp;

import java.io.IOException;
import java.sql.SQLException;

class MyResource implements AutoCloseable {
    @Override
    public void close() throws IOException{
        throw new IOException("IOException");
    }

    public void execute() throws SQLException {
        throw new SQLException("SQLException");
    }
}

public class Test {
    public static void main(String[] args) {
        try(MyResource resource = new MyResource()) {
            resource.execute();
        } catch(Exception e) {
            System.out.println(e.getMessage());
        }
    }
}
```

What will be the result of compiling and executing Test class?

A. IOException

B. SQLException

C. Compilation error

2.1.53 Given code of Test.java file:

```
package com.udayan.ocp;

class Resource1 implements AutoCloseable {
    @Override
    public void close() {
        System.out.println("Resource1");
    }
}

class Resource2 implements AutoCloseable {
    @Override
    public void close() {
        System.out.println("Resource2");
    }
}

public class Test {
    public static void main(String[] args) {
        try(Resource1 r1 = new Resource1();
            Resource2 r2 = new Resource2()) {
            System.out.println("Test");
        }
    }
}
```

What will be the result of compiling and executing Test class?

A.	Test Resource1 Resource2	B.	Test Resource2 Resource1
C.	Compilation Error		

2.1.54 Given code of Test.java file:

```
package com.udayan.ocp;

import java.util.Scanner;

public class Test {
    public static void main(String[] args) {
        try(Scanner scanner = new Scanner(System.in)) {
            int i = scanner.nextInt();
            if(i % 2 != 0) {
                assert false;
            }
        } catch(Exception ex) {
            System.out.println("ONE");
        } catch(Error ex) {
            System.out.println("TWO");
        }
    }
}
```

What will be the result of compiling and executing Test class?

User input: 1

A. ONE

B. TWO

C. Program ends abruptly

D. No output and program terminates successfully

2.1.55 Given code of Test.java file:

```
package com.udayan.ocp;

public class Test {
    enum STATUS {
        PASS, FAIL;
    }

    private static boolean checkStatus(STATUS status) {
        switch(status) {
            case PASS:
                return true;
            case FAIL:
                return false;
            default: {
                assert false : "<<<DANGER ZONE>>>";
                return false;
            }
        }
    }

    public static void main(String[] args) {
        checkStatus(null);
    }
}
```

What will be the result of executing Test class with below command?

java -ea com.udayan.ocp.Test

A. AssertionError is thrown and program ends abruptly

B. NullPointerException is thrown and program ends abruptly

C. No output and program terminates successfully

2.1.56 Given code of Test.java file:

```
package com.udayan.ocp;

import java.time.LocalDate;

public class Test {
    public static void main(String [] args) {
        LocalDate date = LocalDate.ofEpochDay(1);
        System.out.println(date);
    }
}
```

What will be the result of compiling and executing Test class?

A. 1970-01-01

B. 1970-01-02

C. 1970-1-1

D. 1970-1-2

2.1.57 Given code of Test.java file:

```
package com.udayan.ocp;

import java.time.*;

public class Test {
    public static void main(String [] args) {
        Period period = null;
        System.out.println(period);
    }
}
```

2022 FIFA world cup in Qatar is scheduled to start on 21st Nov 2022. Which of the following statement, if used to replace null, will tell you the period left for 2022 world cup?

A. `Period.between(LocalDateTime.now(),
   LocalDateTime.parse("2022-11-21"))`
B. `Period.between(LocalDateTime.now(), LocalDate.parse("2022-11-21"))`
C. `Period.between(LocalDate.now(), LocalDateTime.parse("2022-11-21"))`
D. `Period.between(LocalDate.now(), LocalDate.parse("2022-11-21"))`

2.1.58 Given code of Test.java file:

```
package com.udayan.ocp;

import java.time.*;

public class Test {
    public static void main(String [] args) {
        LocalDate d1 = LocalDate.now();
        LocalDateTime d2 = LocalDateTime.now();
        System.out.println(Duration.between(d1, d2));
    }
}
```

What will be the result of compiling and executing Test class?

A. Program terminates successfully after displaying the output

B. Compilation error

C. Runtime Exception

2.1.59 Given code of Test.java file:

```
package com.udayan.ocp;

import java.time.*;

public class Test {
    public static void main(String [] args) {
        LocalDate date1 = LocalDate.of(2019, 1, 2);
        date1.minus(Period.ofDays(1));
        LocalDate date2 = LocalDate.of(2018, 12, 31);
        date2.plus(Period.ofDays(1));
        System.out.println(date1.equals(date2) + ":"
                            + date1.isEqual(date2));
    }
}
```

What will be the result of compiling and executing Test class?

A. true:true

B. false:false

C. false:true

D. true:false

2.1.60   Daylight saving time 2018 in United States (US) ends at 4-Nov-2018 2:00 AM. What will be the result of compiling and executing Test class?

```java
package com.udayan.ocp;

import java.time.*;

public class Test {
    public static void main(String [] args) {
        LocalDate date = LocalDate.of(2018, 11, 4);
        LocalTime time = LocalTime.of(1, 59, 59);
        ZonedDateTime dt = ZonedDateTime.of(date, time,
                        ZoneId.of("America/New_York"));
        dt = dt.plusSeconds(1);
        System.out.println(dt.getHour() + ":"
                + dt.getMinute() + ":" + dt.getSecond());
    }
}
```

A.   2:0:0

B.   1:0:0

C.   3:0:0

2.1.61   Given code of Test.java file:

```java
package com.udayan.ocp;

import java.time.*;
import java.util.Date;

public class Test {
    public static void main(String[] args) {
        Date date = new Date();
        LocalDate localDate = null; //Line n1
    }
}
```

Which of the following two statements will replace null at Line n1 such that Date object referred by 'date' is converted to LocalDate object?

A. `(LocalDate)date;`

B. `date.toLocalDate();`

C. `LocalDate.of(date);`

D. `date.toInstant().atZone(ZoneId.systemDefault())`
`.toLocalDate();`

E. `Instant.ofEpochMilli(date.getTime())`
`.atZone(ZoneId.systemDefault()).toLocalDate();`

2.1.62 Given code of Test.java file:

```
package com.udayan.ocp;

import java.io.*;

public class Test {
    public static void main(String[] args)
                                throws IOException {
        BufferedReader br = new BufferedReader(
            new InputStreamReader(System.in));
        System.out.print(
            "Enter any number between 1 and 10: ");
        int num = br.read();
        System.out.println(num);
    }
}
```

On execution above code prompts user with following message:

Enter any number between 1 and 10:

Which of the following statement is true if user types 2 and press Enter?

A. 2 will be printed on to the console.

B. 2 will not be printed on to the console.

C. Runtime Exception

2.1.63 **Which of the following will correctly accept and print the entered password on to the console?**

A.	```Console console = System.console();String pwd = console.readPassword("Enter Password: ");System.out.println(pwd);```
B.	```Console console = new Console(System.in);String pwd = console.readPassword("Enter Password: ");System.out.println(pwd);```
C.	```Console console = new Console(System.in);char [] pwd = console.readPassword("Enter Password: ");System.out.println(new String(pwd));```
D.	```Console console = System.console();char [] pwd = console.readPassword("Enter Password: ");System.out.println(new String(pwd));```

2.1.64 Given code of Test.java file:

```java
package com.udayan.ocp;

import java.io.*;

class Counter implements Serializable {
    private static int count = 0;
    public Counter() {
        count++;
    }

    public static int getCount() {
        return count;
    }
}

public class Test {
    public static void main(String[] args)
                throws IOException, ClassNotFoundException {
        Counter ctr = new Counter();
        try( ObjectOutputStream oos = new ObjectOutputStream(
            new FileOutputStream("C:\\Counter.dat")) ){
                oos.writeObject(ctr);
        }

        new Counter(); new Counter();

        try( ObjectInputStream ois = new ObjectInputStream(
            new FileInputStream("C:\\Counter.dat")) ){
                ctr = (Counter)ois.readObject();
                System.out.println(Counter.getCount());
        }
    }
}
```

There is full permission to list/create/delete files and directories in C:.
What will be the result of compiling and executing Test class?

A. Runtime Exception
B. 1
C. 2
D. 3

2.1.65 Given code of Test.java file:

```
package com.udayan.ocp;

import java.io.IOException;
import java.io.PrintWriter;

public class Test {
    public static void main(String[] args) {
        try(PrintWriter bw = new PrintWriter("F:\\test.txt"))
        {
            bw.close();
            bw.write(1);
        } catch(IOException e) {
            System.out.println("IOException");
        }
    }
}
```

F: is accessible for reading/writing purposes.

Which of the following statement is true about above code?

A. Class Test compiles and executes fine and no output is displayed on to the console

B. On execution, IOException is printed on to the console

C. Compilation error

D. test.txt file will be successfully created and 1 will be written to it

2.1.66 Imagine below path exists:

```
F:.
  └──A
      └──B
```

Given code of Test.java file:

```java
package com.udayan.ocp;

import java.io.*;

public class Test {
    public static void main(String[] args) {
        File dir = new File("F:" + File.separator
                        + "A" + File.separator + "B");
        System.out.println(/*INSERT*/);
    }
}
```

Which of the following replaces /*INSERT*/, such that on execution 'F:\' is displayed on to the console? Select 2 options.

A. dir.getParentFile().getParentFile()

B. dir.getParentFile().getParent()

C. dir.getParent().getParentFile()

D. dir.getParent().getParent()

2.1.67 Given code of Test.java file:

```
package com.udayan.ocp;

import java.io.*;

public class Test {
    public static void main(String[] args)
                            throws IOException {
        BufferedWriter bw = new BufferedWriter(
                    new FileWriter("F:\\temp.tmp"));
        try(BufferedWriter writer = bw) { //Line 8

        } finally {
            bw.flush(); //Line 11
        }
    }
}
```

What will be the result of compiling and executing Test class?

A. Line 8 causes Compilation error

B. Line 11 causes Compilation error

C. Line 8 causes Runtime exception

D. Line 11 causes Runtime exception

2.1.68 Given code of Test.java file:

```
package com.udayan.ocp;

import java.io.*;
import java.nio.file.Path;
import java.nio.file.Paths;

public class Test {
    public static void main(String[] args)
                                throws IOException {
        Path path = Paths.get("F:\\A\\B\\C\\");
        System.out.printf("%d, %s, %s",
                    path.getNameCount(),
                    path.getFileName(),
                    path.getName(2));
    }
}
```

F: is accessible for reading/writing but is currently blank.

What will be the result of compiling and executing Test class?

A. 4, C, B

B. 4, null, B

C. 3, C, B

D. 3, C, C

E. Runtime Exception

2.1.69 **F: is accessible for reading and below is the directory structure for F:**

```
F:.
  └──A
      └──B
          └──C
                  Book.java
```

'Book.java' file is available under 'C' directory.

Given code of Test.java file:

```java
package com.udayan.ocp;

import java.nio.file.Path;
import java.nio.file.Paths;

public class Test {
    public static void main(String[] args) {
        Path file = Paths.get("F:\\A\\B\\Book.java");
        System.out.println(file.toAbsolutePath());
    }
}
```

What will be the result of compiling and executing Test class?

A. NoSuchFileException is thrown at runtime.

B. FileNotFoundException is thrown at runtime.

C. F:\A\B\Book.java

D. Book.java

2.1.70 **F: is accessible for reading and below is the directory structure for F:**

```
F:.
└──A
    └──B
        └──C
                Book.java
```

Given code of Test.java file:

```java
package com.udayan.ocp;

import java.io.IOException;
import java.nio.file.Files;
import java.nio.file.Path;
import java.nio.file.Paths;
import java.io.File;

public class Test {
    public static void main(String[] args)
                                    throws IOException{
        Path path = Paths.get("F:\\A\\B");
        /*INSERT*/
    }
}
```

Which of the following statements, if used to replace /*INSERT*/, will successfully print 'true' on to the console?
Select 3 options.

A. System.out.println(Files.isDirectory(path));

B. System.out.println(path.toFile().isDirectory());

C. System.out.println(Files.getAttribute(path, "isDirectory"));

D. System.out.println(File.isDirectory(path));

E. System.out.println(new File(path).isDirectory());

2.1.71 **F: is accessible for reading/writing and below is the directory structure for F:**

```
F:.
└──X
```

Directory X exists under F:.

Given code of Test.java file:

```
package com.udayan.ocp;

import java.io.IOException;
import java.nio.file.Files;
import java.nio.file.Path;
import java.nio.file.Paths;

public class Test {
    public static void main(String[] args)
                                throws IOException{
        Path path = Paths.get("F:\\X\\Y\\Z");
        Files.createDirectory(path);
    }
}
```

What will be the result of compiling and executing Test class?

A. Directory Y will be created under X and directory Z will be created under Y.

B. Only directory Y will be created under X.

C. An exception is thrown at runtime.

2.1.72 Given code of Test.java file:

```
package com.udayan.ocp;

import java.nio.file.Path;
import java.nio.file.Paths;

public class Test {
    public static void main(String[] args) {
        Path path1 = Paths.get("C:\\A\\B\\C");
        Path path2 = Paths.get("D:\\A");
        System.out.println(path1.relativize(path2));
        System.out.println(path2.relativize(path1));
    }
}
```

What will be the result of compiling and executing Test class?

A.	Compilation error	B.	An exception is thrown at runtime
C.	B\C ..\..	D.	..\.. B\C

2.1.73 C:\ is accessible for reading/writing and below is the content of 'C:\TEMP' folder:

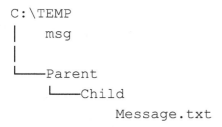

```
C:\TEMP
|    msg
|
└──Parent
     └──Child
           Message.txt
```

'msg' is a symbolic link file for 'C:\TEMP\Parent\Child\Message.txt'.

Given code of Test.java file:

```
package com.udayan.ocp;

import java.io.IOException;
import java.nio.file.Files;
import java.nio.file.Path;
import java.nio.file.Paths;

public class Test {
    public static void main(String[] args)
                                    throws IOException {
        Path src = Paths.get("C:", "TEMP", "msg");

        Path tgt = Paths.get(
                    "C:", "TEMP", "Parent", "copy");
        Files.copy(src, tgt);

        System.out.println(Files.isSymbolicLink(src)
                    + ":" + Files.isSymbolicLink(tgt));
    }
}
```

What will be the result of compiling and executing Test class?

A. true:true

B. true:false

C. false:false

D. false:true

2.1.74 Which of the 4 interfaces must be implemented by a JDBC driver?

A. java.sql.DriverManager

B. java.sql.Driver

C. java.sql.Statement

D. java.sql.ResultSet

E. java.sql.Connection

F. java.sql.Date

2.1.75 Given structure of EMPLOYEE table:

```
EMPLOYEE (ID integer, FIRSTNAME varchar(100), LASTNAME
varchar(100), SALARY real, PRIMARY KEY (ID))
```

EMPLOYEE table contains below records:

```
101 John    Smith   12000
102 Sean    Smith   15000
103 Regina Williams  15500
104 Natasha    George 14600
```

Given code of Test.java file:

```java
package com.udayan.ocp;

import java.sql.*;
import java.util.Properties;

public class Test {
    public static void main(String[] args)
                                    throws SQLException {
        String url = "jdbc:mysql://localhost:3306/ocp";
        Properties prop = new Properties();
        prop.put("username", "root");
        prop.put("password", "password");
        String query = "Select ID, FIRSTNAME, LASTNAME, " +
            "SALARY FROM EMPLOYEE ORDER BY ID";

        try (Connection con = DriverManager
                        .getConnection(url, prop);
            Statement stmt = con.createStatement(
                ResultSet.TYPE_SCROLL_INSENSITIVE,
                ResultSet.CONCUR_READ_ONLY);
            ResultSet rs = stmt.executeQuery(query);) {
            rs.relative(1);
            System.out.println(rs.getString(2));
        }
    }
}
```

Also assume:

URL is correct and db credentials are: root/password.

SQL query is correct and valid.

The JDBC 4.2 driver jar is configured in the classpath.

What will be the result of compiling and executing Test class?

A. John

B. Sean

C. Smith

D. An exception is thrown at runtime.

2.1.76   Consider 'con' refers to a valid Connection instance.

Which of the following successfully creates Statement instance? Select All that apply.

A.	`con.createStatement(ResultSet.`*`TYPE_SCROLL_INSENSITIVE`*`);`
B.	`con.createStatement(ResultSet.`*`CONCUR_READ_ONLY`*`);`
C.	`con.createStatement(ResultSet.`*`TYPE_SCROLL_INSENSITIVE`*`,` `ResultSet.`*`CONCUR_READ_ONLY`*`);`
D.	`con.createStatement();`

2.1.77   Given structure of EMPLOYEE table:

```
EMPLOYEE (ID integer, FIRSTNAME varchar(100), LASTNAME
varchar(100), SALARY real, PRIMARY KEY (ID))
```

EMPLOYEE table contains below records:

```
101 John    Smith  12000
102 Sean    Smith  15000
103 Regina Williams  15500
104 Natasha    George 14600
```

Given code of Test.java file:

```java
package com.udayan.ocp;

import java.sql.*;

public class Test {
    public static void main(String[] args)
                                    throws SQLException {
        String url = "jdbc:mysql://localhost:3306/ocp";
        String user = "root";
        String password = "password";
        String query = "Select * from EMPLOYEE";
        Connection con = DriverManager
                    .getConnection(url, user, password);
        try (Statement stmt = con.createStatement())
        {
            ResultSet rs = stmt.executeQuery(query);
        }
    }
}
```

Also assume:

URL is correct and db credentials are: root/password.

SQL query is correct and valid.

The JDBC 4.2 driver jar is configured in the classpath.

Which of the following objects will get closed? Select ALL that apply.

A. Connection object

B. Statement object

C. ResultSet object

D. None of the objects will get closed as close() method is not invoked.

2.1.78 Given structure of EMPLOYEE table:

```
EMPLOYEE (ID integer, FIRSTNAME varchar(100), LASTNAME
varchar(100), SALARY real, PRIMARY KEY (ID))
```

EMPLOYEE table contains below records:

```
101 John    Smith  12000
102 Sean    Smith  15000
103 Regina Williams  15500
104 Natasha    George 14600
```

Given code of Test.java file:

```java
package com.udayan.ocp;
import java.sql.*;

public class Test {
    public static void main(String[] args)
                                    throws Exception {
        String url = "jdbc:mysql://localhost:3306/ocp";
        String user = "root";
        String password = "password";
        String query = "Select ID, FIRSTNAME, LASTNAME, " +
            "SALARY FROM EMPLOYEE";
        try (Connection con = DriverManager
                    .getConnection(url, user, password);
            Statement stmt = con.createStatement(
                ResultSet.TYPE_SCROLL_SENSITIVE,
                ResultSet.CONCUR_UPDATABLE);
        ) {
            ResultSet rs = stmt.executeQuery(query);
            rs.afterLast();
            while (rs.previous()) {
              rs.updateDouble(4, rs.getDouble(4) + 1000);
            }
            rs.updateRow();

            rs = stmt.executeQuery(query);
            while(rs.next()) {
                System.out.println(rs.getDouble(4));
            }
        }
    }
```

```
        }
}
```

Also assume:

URL, username and password are correct.

SQL query is correct and valid.

The JDBC 4.2 driver jar is configured in the classpath.

What will be the result of compiling and executing Test class?

A.	12000.0 15000.0 15500.0 14600.0	B.	13000.0 16000.0 16500.0 15600.0
C.	13000.0 15000.0 15500.0 14600.0	D.	12000.0 15000.0 15500.0 15600.0
E.	An exception is thrown at runtime		

2.1.79 Given structure of LOG table:

```
LOG (ID integer, MESSAGE varchar(1000), PRIMARY KEY (ID))
```

Given code of Test.java file:

```java
package com.udayan.ocp;
import java.sql.*;

public class Test {
    public static void main(String[] args)
                                    throws SQLException {
        String url = "jdbc:mysql://localhost:3306/ocp";
        String user = "root";
        String password = "password";
        String query = "Select ID, MESSAGE FROM LOG";
        try (Connection con = DriverManager
                    .getConnection(url, user, password);
            Statement stmt = con.createStatement(
                        ResultSet.TYPE_SCROLL_SENSITIVE,
                        ResultSet.CONCUR_UPDATABLE);
        )
        {
          stmt.executeUpdate(
          "INSERT INTO LOG VALUES(1001,'Login Successful')");
          stmt.executeUpdate(
          "INSERT INTO LOG VALUES(1002,'Login Failure')");

          con.setAutoCommit(false);

          stmt.executeUpdate(
          "INSERT INTO LOG VALUES(1003,'Not Authorized')");
        }
    }
}
```

Also assume:

URL, username and password are correct.

SQL query is correct and valid.

The JDBC 4.2 driver jar is configured in the classpath.

LOG table doesn't have any records.

What will be the result of compiling and executing Test class?

A. Records for IDs 1001, 1002 and 1003 will be successfully inserted in the database table.

B. Records for IDs 1001 and 1002 will be successfully inserted in the database table.

C. Records for ID 1003 will be successfully inserted in the database table.

D. No records will be inserted in the database table.

2.1.80 Given structure of EMPLOYEE table:

```
EMPLOYEE (ID integer, FIRSTNAME varchar(100), LASTNAME
varchar(100), SALARY real, PRIMARY KEY (ID))
```

EMPLOYEE table contains below records:

```
101 John    Smith  12000
102 Sean    Smith  15000
103 Regina Williams  15500
104 Natasha    George 14600
```

Given code of Test.java file:

```java
package com.udayan.ocp;

import java.sql.*;

public class Test {
    public static void main(String[] args) throws Exception
{
        String url = "jdbc:mysql://localhost:3306/ocp";
        String user = "root";
        String password = "password";
        String query = "Select ID, FIRSTNAME, LASTNAME,
                        SALARY FROM EMPLOYEE ORDER BY ID";
        try (Connection con = DriverManager.getConnection(
                                    url, user, password);
            Statement stmt = con.createStatement(
                    ResultSet.TYPE_SCROLL_SENSITIVE,
                    ResultSet.CONCUR_UPDATABLE);
        ) {
            ResultSet rs = stmt.executeQuery(query);

            rs.absolute(3);
            rs.updateString(3, "Gales");
            rs.updateRow();
            rs.refreshRow();
            System.out.println(rs.getString(2) + " "
                                + rs.getString(3));
        }
    }
}
```

Also assume:

URL is correct and db credentials are: root/password.

SQL query is correct and valid.

The JDBC 4.2 driver jar is configured in the classpath.

Updates on EMPLOYEE table are being done by Test.java code only.

What will be the result of compiling and executing Test class?

A. Regina Gales

B. Regina Williams

C. John Smith

D. Natasha George

2.1.81 Given code of Test.java file:

```java
package com.udayan.ocp;

import java.util.Locale;

public class Test {
    public static void main(String[] args) {
        Locale locale = new Locale("temp", "UNKNOWN"); //Line 7
        System.out.println(locale.getLanguage()
            + ":" + locale.getCountry()); //Line 8
        System.out.println(locale); //Line 9
    }
}
```

What will be the result of compiling and executing Test class?

A.	Compilation error
B.	Line 7 throws exception at runtime
C.	Line 8 throws exception at runtime
D.	Line 9 throws exception at runtime
E.	temp:UNKNOWN temp_UNKNOWN

2.1.82 Given code of Test.java file:

```
package com.udayan.ocp;

import java.util.Locale;

public class Test {
    public static void main(String[] args) {
        Locale loc = new Locale("it", "IT"); //Line 7
        loc.setDefault(loc); //Line 8
        System.out.println(Locale.getDefault());
    }
}
```

Which of the following statement is correct about above code?

A. Code compiles and executes successfully and prints it_IT on to the console.

B. Line 8 causes compilation failure.

C. Code compiles and execute successfully but may print text other than it_IT.

2.1.83 Below files are available for your project:

```
//1. ResourceBundle.properties
```
locale=French/Canada

```
//2. ResourceBundle_CA.properties
```
locale=Canada

```
//3. ResourceBundle_hi.properties
```
locale=Hindi

```
//4. ResourceBundle_IN.properties
```
locale=India

```
//5. Test.java
package com.udayan.ocp;

import java.util.Locale;
import java.util.ResourceBundle;

public class Test {
    public static void main(String[] args) {
        Locale.setDefault(new Locale("fr", "CA"));
        Locale loc = new Locale("en", "IN");
        ResourceBundle rb = ResourceBundle.getBundle(
                              "MyResourceBundle", loc);
        System.out.println(rb.getObject("locale"));
    }
}
```

Assume that all the *.properties files are included in the CLASSPATH. What will be the output of compiling and executing Test class?

A. French/Canada

B. Canada

C. Hindi

D. India

E. Runtime Exception

2.1.84 **Given code of Test.java file:**

```
package com.udayan.ocp;

import java.util.concurrent.*;

class MyCallable implements Callable<Integer> {
    private Integer i;

    public MyCallable(Integer i) {
        this.i = i;
    }

    public Integer call() throws Exception {
        return --i;
    }
}

public class Test {
    public static void main(String[] args)
        throws InterruptedException, ExecutionException {
        ExecutorService es
                = Executors.newSingleThreadExecutor();
        MyCallable callable = new MyCallable(100);
        System.out.println(es.submit(callable).get());
        System.out.println(es.submit(callable).get());
        es.shutdown();
    }
}
```

What will be the result of compiling and executing Test class?

A.	98 98	B.	99 99
C.	99 98	D.	100 100
E.	100 99		

2.1.85 Given code of Test.java file:

```
package com.udayan.ocp;

import java.util.concurrent.*;

class Printer implements Runnable {
    public void run() {
        System.out.println("Printing");
    }
}

public class Test {
    public static void main(String[] args) {
        ExecutorService es = Executors
                        .newFixedThreadPool(1);
        /*INSERT*/
        es.shutdown();
    }
}
```

Which of the following statements, if used to replace /*INSERT*/, will print 'Printing' on to the console? Select 2 options.

A. es.submit(new Printer());

B. es.execute(new Printer());

C. es.run(new Printer());

D. es.start(new Printer());

2.1.86 Given code of Test.java file:

```java
package com.udayan.ocp;

import java.util.ArrayList;
import java.util.List;
import java.util.concurrent.CopyOnWriteArrayList;

public class Test {
    public static void main(String[] args) {
        List<String> list1 = new ArrayList<>();
        list1.add("Melon");
        list1.add("Apple");
        list1.add("Banana");
        list1.add("Mango");
        List<String> list2
                    = new CopyOnWriteArrayList<>(list1);
        for(String s : list2) {
            if(s.startsWith("M")){
                list2.remove(s);
            }
        }
        System.out.println(list1);
        System.out.println(list2);
    }
}
```

What will be the result of compiling and executing Test class?

A.	[Melon, Apple, Banana, Mango] [Melon, Apple, Banana, Mango]
B.	[Apple, Banana] [Apple, Banana]
C.	[Melon, Apple, Banana, Mango] [Apple, Banana]
D.	An exception is thrown at runtime

2.1.87   Fill in the blanks:

The states of the threads involved in _____ constantly change with regard to one another, with no overall progress made.

A. deadlock

B. livelock

C. synchronization

D. CyclicBarrier

2.1.88   Given code of Test.java file:

```java
package com.udayan.ocp;
import java.util.concurrent.*;

class Player extends Thread {
    CyclicBarrier cb;

    public Player(CyclicBarrier cb) {
        this.cb = cb;
    }

    public void run() {
        try {
            cb.await();
        } catch (InterruptedException
                    | BrokenBarrierException e) {}
    }
}

class Match implements Runnable {
    public void run() {
        System.out.println("Match is starting...");
    }
}

public class Test {
    public static void main(String[] args) {
        Match match = new Match();
        CyclicBarrier cb = new CyclicBarrier(2, match);
        ExecutorService es
                    = Executors.newFixedThreadPool(1);
        es.execute(new Player(cb));
        es.execute(new Player(cb));
        es.shutdown();
    }
}
```

What will be the result of compiling and executing Test class?

A.   'Match is starting...' is printed on to the console and program doesn't terminate.

B.   'Match is starting...' is printed on to the console and program terminates successfully.

C.   'Match is starting...' is never printed on to the console and program waits indefinitely.

2.1.89 Given code of Test.java file:

```
package com.udayan.ocp;

import java.util.ArrayList;
import java.util.List;
import java.util.concurrent.*;

class Accumulator {
    private List<Integer> list = new ArrayList<>();

    public synchronized void accumulate(int i) {
        list.add(i);
    }

    public List<Integer> getList() {
        return list;
    }
}

public class Test {
    public static void main(String [] args) {
        ExecutorService s =
                Executors.newFixedThreadPool(1000);
        Accumulator a = new Accumulator();
        for(int i=1; i<=1000; i++) {
            int x = i;
            s.execute(() -> a.accumulate(x));
        }
        s.shutdown();
        System.out.println(a.getList().size());
    }
}
```

What will be the result of compiling and executing Test class?

A. It will always print 1000 on to the console.

B. It can print any number between 0 and 1000.

C. The program will wait indefinitely.

2.1.90 Fill in the blanks:

```
package com.udayan.ocp;

import java.util.concurrent.*;

public class Task extends _____ {
    @Override
    protected Long compute() {
        return null;
    }
}
```

Select All that apply.

A. RecursiveTask<Long>
B. RecursiveTask
C. RecursiveAction
D. RecursiveAction<Long>
E. RecursiveTask<Object>
F. RecursiveAction<Object>

2.2 Answers of Practice Test - 2 with Explanation

2.1.1 Answer: B

Reason:
If toString() method is not overridden, then Object class's version is invoked.
The toString() method in Object class has below definition:
```
public String toString() {
 return getClass().getName() + "@" + Integer.toHexString(hashCode());
}
```

So, in the output you get: fully-qualified-name-of-the-class@hexadecimal-representation-of-hash-code. NOTE: hashCode() method is called for that.
Player class overrides the hashCode() method so, toString() method calls this overriding hashCode() method. Output string will always contain 64.

2.1.2 Answer: B

Reason:
You can write statements inside initialization blocks, variable a is of static type so both static and instance initialization blocks can access it.

Instance of Initializer block is not created in this case, so instance initialization block is not executed.
Execution of static initialization block decrements the value of a by 1. Hence the output is 9999.

2.1.3   Answer: B

Reason:
Immutable class should have private fields and no setters.
In this case it is possible to change the msg after an instance of Greet class is created.
Check below code:

```
public class Test {
    public static void main(String[] args) {
        Greet greet = new Greet("Hello"); //msg refers to "Hello"
        greet.setMsg("Welcome"); //msg refers to "Welcome"
        System.out.println(greet.getMsg()); //Prints "Welcome" on to the console.
    }
}
```

To make Greet class immutable, delete the setter and add modifier 'final' for variable msg.
```
final class Greet {
    private final String msg;
    public Greet(String msg) {
        this.msg = msg;
    }

    public String getMsg() {
        return msg;
    }
}
```

Once value is assigned to msg variable in the constructor, it cannot be changed later.

2.1.4   Answer: C

Reason:
Starting with JDK 8, a Java interface can have default and static methods. So, no issues in Printer1 and Printer2 interfaces.

Printer class inherits both the default methods and hence compilation error.

To resolve this error, override the print() method in Printer class:

```
public void print() {
   System.out.println("Printer");
}
```

To invoke print() method of Parent interfaces from within the overriding method, you can use below syntax:

```
public void print() {
   System.out.println("Printer");
   Printer1.super.print();
   Printer2.super.print();
}
```

2.1.5   Answer: A

Reason:
Enum constructor is invoked once for every constant.
For 'Flags.TRUE', enum constructor is invoked for TRUE as well as FALSE.

2.1.6   Answer: D

Reason:
Enum constant list must be the first item in an enum.
GREEN("go"), AMBER("slow"), RED("stop"); should be the first line inside TrafficLight enum.

2.1.7   Answer: A, B

Reason:
There are 2 parts: 1st one is referring the name of inner class, A and 2nd one is creating the instance of inner class, A.
main method is inside Test class only, so inner class can be referred by 2 ways: A or Test.A.

As, A is Regular inner class, so instance of outer class is needed for creating the instance of inner class. As keyword 'this' is not allowed inside main method, so instance of outer class, Test can only be obtained by new Test(). Instance of inner class can be created by: new Test().new A();

Also note, keyword 'this' is not allowed static main method.

2.1.8   Answer: A

Reason:
invokeInner() is instance method of outer class, X. So, implicit 'this' reference is available for this method. this reference refers to the currently executing instance of outer class, X. So Java compiler converts Y obj = new Y(); to Y obj = this.new Y(); and hence this syntax has no issues. So Line 9 is fine.

Because of the special relationship between Outer and inner class, Outer and Inner class can very easily access each other's private members. Hence, no issues with Line 10 as well.
Given code compiles and executes fine and prints INNER to the console.

2.1.9   Answer: C

Reason:
class Inner is method local inner class and it is accessing parameter variable x.
Starting with JDK 8, a method local inner class can access local variables and parameters of the enclosing block that are final or effectively final.
But the statement System.out.println(++x); tries to increment the value of variable x and hence compilation error.

2.1.10 Answer: C

Reason:
obj refers to an anonymous inner class instance extending from Greetings class and the anonymous inner class code correctly overrides greet() method.
Code executes and prints Hello on to the console.

2.1.11 Answer: A

Reason:
System.out.println(new Object()); invokes the toString() method defined in Object class, which prints fully qualified class name, @ symbol and hexadecimal value of hash code [Similar to java.lang.Object@15db9742].

In the given code, an instance of anonymous class extending Object class is passed to System.out.println() method and the anonymous class overrides the toString() method. Thus, at runtime overriding method is invoked, which prints "Anonymous" to the console.

2.1.12 Answer: B, C

Reason:
Outside of top-level class, Outer, static nested class can be referred by using TOP-LEVEL-CLASS.STATIC-NESTED-CLASS. So, in this case correct way to refer static nested class is Outer.Inner. greetings(String) is a static method, so it can be invoked by using the class name, which is by the statement: Outer.Inner.greetings("...");

Even though it is not preferred to invoke static method in non-static manner, but you can use the instance of class to invoke its static method.
To Create the instance of static nested class, syntax is: new TOP-LEVEL-CLASS.STATIC-NESTED-CLASS(...);
in this case, new Outer.Inner();

2.1.13 Answer: A,B,D

Reason:
Operator opr = (int x, int y) -> { return x + y; }; => Correct, operate(int, int) method accepts two int type parameters and returns the addition of passed parameters.

Operator opr = (x, y) -> { return x + y; }; => Correct, type is removed from left part, type inference handles it.

Operator opr = (x, y) -> return x + y; => Compilation error, if there is only one statement in the right side then semicolon inside the body, curly brackets and return statement(if available) can be removed. But all should be removed. You can't just remove one and leave others.

Operator opr = (x, y) -> x + y; => Correct, semicolon inside the body, curly brackets and return statement, all 3 are removed from right side.

Operator opr = x, y -> x + y; => Compilation error, if there are no parameters or more than one parameter available, then round brackets cannot be removed from left side.

2.1.14   Answer: C

Reason:
variable i a is local variable and it is used in the lambda expression. So, it should either be final or effectively final.
The last statement inside main(String []) method, increments value of i, which means it is not effectively final and hence compilation error.

2.1.15   Answer: D

Reason:
Test<T> is generic type and Test is raw type. When raw type is used then T is Object, which means set method will have signature: set(Object t).

Test obj = new Test(); => Test object is created and obj refers to it.

obj.set("OCP"); => Instance variable t refers to "OCP".
obj.set(85); => Instance variable t refers to Integer object, 85. Auto-boxing converts int literal to Integer object.
obj.set('%'); => Instance variable t refers to Character object, %. Auto-boxing converts char literal to Character object.

obj.get() => this returns Character object as as Character class overrides toString() method, % is printed on to the console.

2.1.16   Answer: D

Reason:
contains("7") method checks if '7' is available anywhere in the String object. All 4 String objects contain 7 and hence all 4 String objects are printed on to the console.

2.1.17 Answer: C

Reason:
Type parameter should not be a Java keyword & a valid Java identifier. Naming convention for Type parameter is to use uppercase single character.

In class Printer<String>, 'String' is a valid Java identifier and hence a valid type parameter even though it doesn't follow the naming convention of uppercase single character.

But within Printer<String> class, 'String' is considered as type parameter and not java.lang.String class. Return value of toString() method is java.lang.String class and not type parameter 'String'. So toString() method caused compilation error in Printer class.

To resolve the compilation error, you can use below code:

```
public java.lang.String toString() {
   return null;
}
```

2.1.18 Answer: B

Reason:
super is used with wildcard (?) only.

2.1.19 Answer: D

Reason:
list1 is of List<String> type and contains 2 elements "A" and "B".

list2 is of List<? extends Object> type, which means any List whose type extends from Object. As String extends Object, hence 'List<? extends Object> list2 = list1;' works.

list2.remove("A"); => remove is non-generic method. remove(Object) will be invoked and it will successfully remove "A" from list2.

list2.add("C"); => add is a generic method. add(? extends Object) would be invoked. This means it can take an instance of any UnknownType (extending from Object class).

Compiler can never be sure whether passed argument is a subtype of UnknownType (extending from Object class). Line 14 causes compilation failure.

NOTE: Compiler works with reference types and not instances.

Simple way to remember is that as upper-bounded wildcard is used, hence add operation is not supported. Line 14 causes compilation failure.

2.1.20 Answer: E

Reason:
You cannot add or remove elements form the list returned by Arrays.asList(T...) method but elements can be re-positioned.

list.add("U"); throws UnsupportedOperationException at runtime.

2.1.21 Answer: A

Reason:
TreeMap is the sorted map on the basis on natural ordering of keys (if comparator is not provided).

enum TrafficLight is used as a key for TreeMap. The natural order for enum elements is the sequence in which they are defined. Value corresponding to 'RED' is printed first, followed by value corresponding to 'YELLOW' and finally value for 'GREEN' is printed.

2.1.22 Answer: D

Reason:
TreeSet cannot contain null values. Hence, 'new TreeSet<>(Arrays.asList(null,null,null));' throws NullPointerException.

2.1.23 Answer: C

Reason:
Deque's add() method invokes addLast(E) method and remove() method invokes removeFirst() method.

chars.add('A'); => [A],

chars.remove(); => [],
chars.remove(); => No elements left to remove() and hence
java.util.NoSuchElementException is thrown at runtime.

2.1.24 Answer: B

Reason:
replaceAll(UnaryOperator<E> operator) is a default method available in List interface, it replaces each element of this list with the result of applying the operator to that element.

list.replaceAll(i -> i + 1); => Adds 1 to each element of the list. Result is [1, 3, 5, 7, 9].

2.1.25 Answer: B

Reason:
Comparable interface has compareTo(...) method and Comparator interface has compare(...) method.
In this case, class Employee correctly implements Comparable interface.

return o.age - this.age; => This will help to sort the Employee objects in descending order of age and not in ascending order.

As no Comparator is passed in TreeSet, hence it sorts on the basis of implementation of Comparable interface, which means Employee objects will be sorted in descending order of their age.

2.1.26 Answer: B,C,D

Reason:
Collections.sort(names, (o1, o2) -> o1.getFirst().compareTo(o2.getFirst())); => It sorts in the ascending order of first name in case-sensitive manner and displays [John Smith, Peter Lee, bonita smith] in the output.
Collections.sort(names, (o1, o2) ->
o1.getFirst().toLowerCase().compareTo(o2.getFirst().toLowerCase())); => At the time of comparison, first names in lower case are considered, this doesn't change the case of displayed output. Output is: [bonita smith, John Smith, Peter Lee].
Collections.sort(names, (o1, o2) ->
o1.getFirst().toUpperCase().compareTo(o2.getFirst().toUpperCase())); => At the time of

comparison, first names in upper case are considered, this doesn't change the case of displayed output. Output is: [bonita smith, John Smith, Peter Lee].
Collections.sort(names, (o1, o2) -> o1.getFirst().compareToIgnoreCase(o2.getFirst())); => compareToIgnoreCase method compares the first names in case-insensitive manner and displays [bonita smith, John Smith, Peter Lee] in the output.

2.1.27   Answer: C

Reason:
IntStream.range(int start, int end) => start is inclusive and end is exclusive and incremental step is 1.

count() => Returns the count of elements in this stream.

IntStream.range(10,1) => Returns an empty stream as start > end, this means stream doesn't have any elements. That is why count() returns 0.

2.1.28   Answer: C

Reason:
Date date = obj.get(); means get() method of the interface is invoked. get() method is declared in Supplier interface. All options of Function interface are incorrect.
Supplier interface's declaration is: public interface Supplier<T> { T get(); }.

Note: No parameters are specified in get() method, this means no-argument constructor of Date class is invoked by Date::new.
Supplier<Date> can replace /*INSERT*/.

If you use raw type, Supplier or parameterized type Supplier<Object>, then obj.get() method would return Object type. So Date date = obj.get(); will have to be converted to Date date = (Date)obj.get(); but you are allowed to replace /*INSERT*/ only, hence Supplier and Supplier<Object> are incorrect options.

2.1.29   Answer: A

Reason:
list is of List<String> type, so list.forEach(...) method can accept argument of Consumer<String> type.

interface StringConsumer extends Consumer<String>, which means instances of StringConsumer will also be instances of Consumer<String>.

Note: StringConsumer is not a Functional Interface as it just specifies one default method.

Reference variable 'consumer' refers to an instance of anonymous subclass of StringConsumer and overrides accept(String) method.

list.forEach(consumer); => Prints list elements in lower case as overriding version of anonymous inner class is used.

2.1.30 Answer: A

Reason:
BiFunction<T, U, R> : R apply(T t, U u);

BiFunction interface accepts 3 type parameters, first 2 parameters (T,U) are passed to apply method and 3rd type parameter is the return type of apply method.

In this case, 'BiFunction<Integer, Integer, Character>' means apply method will have declaration: 'Character apply(Integer d1, Integer d2)'.

Lambda expression should accept 2 Integer type parameters and must return Character object. Lambda expression is:

'(i, j) -> i + j', i + j returns an int type and int cannot be implicitly casted to Character and this causes compilation error.

2.1.31 Answer: C

Reason:
There are 3 primitive interfaces corresponding to Predicate interface:
DoublePredicate : boolean test(double value);
IntPredicate : boolean test(int value);
LongPredicate : boolean test(long value);

Lambda expression 'd -> d < 10000' in this case can be easily assigned to DoublePredicate target type. 'd -> d < 10000' returns true if value is less than 10000.

But note: negate() method is used, which means a new DoublePredicate is returned which is just opposite of the given DoublePredicate. After negation, the resultant predicate is 'd -> d >= 10000'.
Salary is incremented only for Lucy and not Jack.

2.1.32 Answer: A

Reason:
BiFunction<String, String, String> interface's apply method signature will be: String apply(String str1, String str2).

'String::concat' is equivalent to LAMBDA expression '(str1, str2) -> str1.concat(str2)'. concat method returns new String object after concatenation.

Hence, func.apply("James", "Gosling") returns 'JamesGosling'.

2.1.33 Answer: B

Reason:
replaceAll(UnaryOperator<E> operator) is the default method added in List interface.

interface UnaryOperator<T> extends Function<T, T>.

As List is of String type, this means operator must be of UnaryOperator<String> type only. Its accept method should have signature: String apply(String s);

Lambda expression 's -> s.substring(0,1).toUpperCase().concat(s.substring(1))' is correctly defined for apply method.

The lambda expression is applied for all the elements of the list. Let's check it for first element "north".

"north".substring(0,1) => "n",
"n".toUpperCase() => "N",
"N".concat("north".substring(1)) => "N".concat("orth") => "North".

Hence, the output is: [North, East, West, South]

2.1.34 Answer: A

Reason:
In JDK 1.8, Map interface had added the default method: "default void forEach(BiConsumer)". This method performs the BiConsumer action (passed as an argument) for each entry in the Map. From the given options, 'map.forEach(consumer);' is the only valid option.
There is no method with the name 'forEachOrdered' in Map interface.

2.1.35 Answer: A

Reason:
Though it looks like very complex code, but it is simple.
TrafficLight class stores the enum Color and text message to be displayed with the color.
tl1 --> {GREEN, "Go"}.
tl2 --> {GREEN, "Go Now!"}.
tl3 --> {YELLOW, "Ready to stop"}.
tl4 --> {YELLOW, "Slow Down"}.
tl5 --> {RED, "Stop"}.

list.stream() --> [{GREEN, "Go"}, {GREEN, "Go Now!"}, {YELLOW, "Ready to stop"}, {YELLOW, "Slow Down"}, {RED, "Stop"}].

Collectors.groupingBy(TrafficLight::getColor, Collectors.mapping(TrafficLight::getMsg, Collectors.toList())); => Group above stream on the basis of Color (key is enum constant Color: RED, GREEN, YELLOW).

So, intermediate object returned by 'Collectors.groupingBy(TrafficLight::getColor)' is of Map<Color, List<TrafficLight>> type. But the 2nd argument, 'Collectors.mapping(TrafficLight::getMsg, Collectors.toList())' passed to groupingBy(...) method converts List<TrafficLight> to List<String> and returns 'Map<Color, List<String>>'

map --> {GREEN=[Go, Go Now!], YELLOW=[Ready to stop, Slow Down], RED=[Stop]}.

System.out.println(map.get(Color.YELLOW)); prints [Ready to stop, Slow Down] on to the console.

2.1.36 Answer: F

Reason:
Streams are lazily evaluated and as sorted() is an intermediate operation, hence stream is not evaluated and you don't get any output on to the console.

2.1.37 Answer: B

Reason:
In Comparator.comparing(a -> a), keyExtractor is not doing anything special, it just implements Comparator to sort integers in ascending order.

Integer::compareTo is a method reference syntax for the Comparator to sort integers in ascending order.

NOTE: Comparator implementations must return following:
-1 (if 1st argument is less than 2nd argument),
0 (if both arguments are equal) and
1 (if 1st argument is greater than 2nd argument).

Integer::max accepts 2 arguments and returns int value but in this case as all the 3 elements are positive, so value will always be positive.

Line 3 will print different output as it will not sort the list properly.

2.1.38 Answer: C

Reason:
Method signature for anyMatch method:
boolean anyMatch(Predicate<? super T>) : Returns true if any of the stream element matches the given Predicate. If stream is empty, it returns false and predicate is not evaluated.

As given stream is empty, hence predicate is not evaluated and nothing is printed on to the console.

2.1.39 Answer: C

Reason:
Stream.of() creates an empty stream.
stream.findFirst(); => returns an empty Optional. Hence, orElse method is executed and prints -1 on to the console.

2.1.40 Answer: F

Reason:
MyException is a checked exception, so 'handle or declare' rule must be followed.

'orElseThrow(MyException::new)' can throw checked exception at runtime, so it must be surrounded by a try-catch block or main method should declare proper throws clause.

2.1.41 Answer: C

Reason:
Generic Stream<T> interface has following methods:
Optional<T> min(Comparator<? super T> comparator);
Optional<T> max(Comparator<? super T> comparator);

Primitive Stream interfaces (IntStream, LongStream & DoubleStream) has methods min(), max(), sum(), average() and summaryStatistics().

In this case, as stream is a generic interface, hence stream.sum() causes compilation error.

2.1.42 Answer: A

Reason:
IntStream.rangeClosed(1, 4); => [1, 2, 3, 4]

To understand, 'stream.reduce(res++, (i, j) -> i * j)' can be somewhat written as:

```
int result = res++;
for (int element : stream) {
   result = accumulator.applyAsInt(result, element);
}
```

return result;

Above code is just for understanding purpose, you can't iterate a stream using given loop.

result will be initialized to 1 and after that res will be incremented to 2. But value of 'result' is used and not 'res'.
Hence output will be result of '1 * 1 * 2 * 3 * 4', which is 24.

2.1.43 Answer: B

Reason:
Rest of the code is very simple, let us concentrate on partitioning code.

Collectors.partitioningBy(s -> s.equals("OCA")) => s in this lambda expression is of Certification type and not String type.
This means predicate 's -> s.equals("OCA")' will return false for "OCA". None of the certification object will return true and hence no element will be stored against 'true'.

[] will be printed in the output.

Correct predicate will be: 's -> s.getTest().equals("OCA")'.

For above predicate, output for 'System.out.println(map.get(true));' will be:
[{S001, OCA, 87}, {S002, OCA, 82}, {S003, OCA, 60}, {S004, OCA, 88}]

2.1.44 Answer: A,E

Reason:
findAny() may return any element from the stream and as stream is not parallel, it will most likely return first element from the sorted stream, which is -10. But this is not the guaranteed result.
As this stream has 3 elements, hence -1 will never get printed on to the console.

2.1.45 Answer: C

Reason:
'new Rope.RedRopeFilter()::filter' is an example of "Reference to an Instance Method of a Particular Object". Equivalent lambda expression is: '(Rope r) -> new Rope.RedRopeFilter().filter(r)'.
As filter(...) method accepts Predicate<? super Point> instance as an argument, hence given method reference syntax is the correct implementation of the Predicate. Line n1 compiles successfully.
Result of filtration is the Stream<Rope> instance containing Rope objects of 'red' color. Please note string 'red' can be in any case(upper, lower or mixed) Therefore, this stream contains Rope [red, 5], Rope [Red, 10] and Rope [RED, 7].
forEach(System.out::println) prints Rope [red, 5], Rope [Red, 10] and Rope [RED, 7]) on to the console.

If 'filter(Rope)' is declared as static, then to achieve same output, you will have to change the method reference syntax to: 'filter(Rope.RedRopeFilter::filter)'.

2.1.46 Answer: C

Reason:
MyString class doesn't override toString() method, hence when instance of MyString class passed to System.out.print(...) method, it prints <fully-qualified-class-name>@<hex-value-of-hashcode>.
list.stream() returns an object of Stream<MyString> and this stream object has 3 instances of MyString class.
map(s -> s) returns the Stream<MyString> object containing exactly same 3 instances of MyString class.
forEach(System.out::print) prints text in the format <fully-qualified-class-name>@<hex-value-of-hashcode> for all the 3 instances.
Text in above format is printed for the 3 elements of the stream and program terminates successfully.
Hence correct option is: 'Above code terminates successfully after printing text other than "YES" on to the console'

To print "YES" on to the console, change the last statement to: list.stream().map(s -> s.str).forEach(System.out::print);
's' represents the instance of MyString class and as MyString class is defined within the same package, hence instance variable 'str' can be accessed using dot operator.

2.1.47 Answer: E

Reason:
AutoCloseable interface has abstract method: void close() throws Exception;

Both Resource1 and Resource2 implement the close() method correctly and main method specified handler for Exception type, hence no compilation error.

Resources are always closes, even in case of exceptions. And in case of multiple resources, these are closed in the reverse order of their declaration. So r2 is closed first and then r1. Output will have 'EC' together.

r1.m1(); prints 'A' on to the console. An exception (with message 'B') is thrown so close methods are invoked.

After close() methods of r2 and r1 are invoked successfully, output will be: 'AEC'.
Exception is caught in main method and e.getMessage() returns 'B'.
So the overall output will be; 'AECB'.

2.1.48 Answer: A,F

Reason:
This question is tricky as 2 changes are related and not independent. Let's first check the reason for compilation error. Line 5 throws a checked exception, IOException but it is not declared in the throws clause. So, print method should have throws clause for IOException or the classes in top hierarchy such as Exception or Throwable.

Based on this deduction, Line 4 can be replaced with either "static void print() throws Exception {" or "static void print() throws Throwable" but we will have to select one out of these as after replacing Line 4, Line 11 will start giving error as we are not handling the checked exception at Line 11.

This part is easy, do we have other options, which mention "Throwable"? NO. Then mark the first option as "Replace Line 4 with static void print() throws Exception {".
As, print() method throws Exception, so main method should handle Exception or its super type and not it's subtype. Two options working only with IOException can be ruled out.

Multi-catch statement "catch(IOException | Exception e)" causes compilation error as IOException and Exception are related to each other in multilevel inheritance. So you are left with only one option to pair with our 1st choice:

Surround Line 11 with below try-catch block:

```
try {
    ReadTheFile.print();
} catch(Exception e) {
    e.printStackTrace();
}
```

2.1.49 Answer: A

Reason:

If you don't initialize variable e inside catch block using 'e = new SQLException();' and simply throw e, then code would compile successfully as compiler is certain that e would refer to an instance of SQLException only.

But the moment compiler finds 'e = new SQLException();', 'throw e;' causes compilation error as at runtime e may refer to any Exception type.

2.1.50 Answer: B

Reason:

close() method of FileReader class throws IOException, which is a checked exception and hence handle or declare rule applies in this case.

As main method neither declares to throw IOException nor a catch block is available for IOException, hence code doesn't compile.

2.1.51 Answer: B

Reason:

Scope of writer variable is with-in the boundary of try-with-resources block. It is not accessible inside catch block and hence 'writer.close()' causes compilation failure.

NOTE: PrintWriter constructor and println method don't throw any exception but it is OK to catch Exception type. Compiler allows to catch Exception type even if code within try block doesn't throw any exception.

2.1.52 Answer: B

Reason:
execute() method throws an instance of SQLException.

Just before finding the matching handler, Java runtime executes close() method. This method throws an instance of IOException but it gets suppressed and an instance of SQLException is thrown.

e.getMessage() prints SQLException on to the console.

NOTE: e.getSuppressed() returns Throwable [] and this helps to get all the suppressed exceptions.

2.1.53 Answer: B

Reason:
Resources are closed in the reverse order of their declaration. So r2 is closed first and then r1.

2.1.54 Answer: D

Reason:
Assertions are disabled by default, so assert false; statement is not executed.

No output is shown and program terminates successfully.

If above program is run with -ea option, the 'TWO' will be printed on to the console as AssertionError extends Error.

NOTE: It is not a good programming practice to validate user input using assertion.

2.1.55 Answer: B

Reason:
switch(status) tries to extract the enum constant and as status is null, NullPointerException is thrown and program ends abruptly.

2.1.56   Answer: B

Reason:
0th day in epoch is: 1970-01-01, 1st day in epoch is: 1970-01-02 and so on.

as toString() method of LocalDate class prints the LocalDate object in ISO-8601 format: "uuuu-MM-dd". Hence output is: '1970-01-02'.

2.1.57   Answer: D

Reason:
Signature of Period.between method is: Period between(LocalDate startDateInclusive, LocalDate endDateExclusive) {...}
Both the parameters are of 'LocalDate' type.

2.1.58   Answer: C

Reason:
Signature of between method defined in Duration class is: 'Duration between(Temporal startInclusive, Temporal endExclusive)'.

As both LocalDate and LocalTime implement 'Temporal' interface, hence there is no compilation error.

Time part must be available to calculate duration but as LocalDate object referred by d1 doesn't have time part, hence an exception is thrown at runtime.

2.1.59   Answer: B

Reason:
Both the methods public "boolean isEqual(ChronoLocalDate)" and "public boolean equals(Object)" return true if date objects are equal otherwise false.
NOTE: LocalDate implements ChronoLocalDate.

date1 --> {2019-01-02}
date1.minus(Period.ofDays(1)); As LocalDate is immutable, this statement creates another instance of LocalDate class. and date1 still refers to previous object.

Similarly date2 refers to {2018-12-31}

and 'date2.plus(Period.ofDays(1));' creates another instance of LocalDate class.

As date1 and date2 are not logically same, equals and isEqual methods return false.

2.1.60 Answer: B

Reason:
You should be aware of Day light saving mechanism to answer this question.
Suppose daylight time starts at 2 AM on particular date.
Current time: 1:59:59 [Normal time].
Next second: 3:00:00 [Time is not 2:00:00 rather it is 3:00:00. It is Daylight saving time].
Clock just jumped from 1:59:59 to 3:00:00.

Now Suppose daylight time ends at 2 AM on particular date.
Current time: 1:59:59 [Daylight saving time].
Next second: 1:00:00 [Time is not 2:00:00 rather it is 1:00:00. Clock switched back to normal time].
Clock just went back from 1:59:59 to 1:00:00.

Now let's solve given code:
dt --> {2018-11-04T01:59:59}. Daylight saving time will end at next second.

dt.plusSeconds(1) => creates a new ZonedDateTime object {2018-11-04T01:00:00} and dt refers to it.

dt.getHour() = 1, dt.getMinute() = 0 and dt.getSecond() = 0.

2.1.61 Answer: D, E

Reason:
java.util.Date class doesn't have any method to convert to LocalDate, LocalDateTime or LocalTime and vice-versa. Hence, 'date.toLocalDate();' and 'LocalDate.of(date);' cause compilation error.
'(LocalDate)date' also causes compilation failure as LocalDate and Date are not related in multilevel inheritance.

Hence, two correct options left are:
'date.toInstant().atZone(ZoneId.systemDefault()).toLocalDate();' and
'Instant.ofEpochMilli(date.getTime()).atZone(ZoneId.systemDefault()).toLocalDate();'.

Let us understand what is happening with above statements:
java.util.Date class has toInstant() method which converts java.util.Date object to java.time.Instant object. If you check the code of toInstant() method, you will find below one statement inside it:
'return Instant.ofEpochMilli(getTime());'
This means 'date.toInstant()' is same as 'Instant.ofEpochMilli(date.getTime())'. Both statements return the object of Instant class.
ZonedDateTime class has methods to convert to LocalDate, LocalDateTime and LocalTime instances. So, object of Instant is first converted to ZonedDateTime.
An Instant object doesn't store any information about the time zone, so to convert it to ZonedDateTime, the default zone (ZoneId.systemDefault()) is passed to atZone method. 'instant.atZone(ZoneId.systemDefault())' returns an instance of ZonedDateTime and toLocalDate() method returns the corresponding instance of LocalDate.

2.1.62 Answer: B

Reason:
InputStreamReader class has a constructor 'public InputStreamReader(InputStream in)', hence System.in, which is an instance of InputStream can be passed to it.

br.read() reads a single character, so it reads user input as '2' and not 2. ASCII code for character '2' is not 2. In fact, it is 50.

So, 50 will be shown in the output.

OCP exam doesn't expect you to know exact corresponding ASCII codes but you should know that read() method returns single character (16-bit: 0 to 65535) but as return type is int hence it returns the ASCII value in this case.

If you want to retrieve the user input then use below code:
String s = br.readLine();
int i = Integer.parseInt(s); //In case you want to convert to int.
System.out.println(i);

2.1.63 Answer: D

Reason:
new Console(...) causes compilation error as it doesn't have matching constructor. It's no-argument constructor is private.
Correct way to get Console instance is by System.console();

readPassword method is overloaded:
char [] readPassword() {...}
char [] readPassword(String fmtString, Object... args) {...}

console.readPassword("Enter Password: "); => compiles and executes successfully as there are no format specifier in 1st argument, so it is OK to provide just one argument to this method.

Return type of readPassword(...) method is char [] and not String.

2.1.64 Answer: D

Reason:
Counter class implements Serializable, hence objects of Counter class can be serialized using ObjectOutputStream.

State of transient and static fields are not persisted.

While de-serializing, transient fields are initialized to default values (null for reference type and respective Zeros for primitive types) and static fields refer to current value.

In this case, count is static, so it is not persisted. On de-serializing, current value of count is used.

new Counter(); simply increments the variable count by 1.

System.out.println(Counter.getCount()); => Prints 3 on to the console.

2.1.65 Answer: A

Reason:
new PrintWriter("F:\\test.txt") creates a blank file 'F:\test.txt'.

new PrintWriter("F:\\test.txt") can throw FileNotFoundException at runtime and given catch handler can access FileNotFoundException as it extends IOException.

public methods of PrintWriter don't throw IOException. In case of IOException, internal flag variable, 'trouble' is set to true.

bw.write(1); is invoked after bw.close() and hence nothing is written to the file.

2.1.66 Answer: A,B

Reason:
File class has below 2 methods:
public File getParentFile() {...}
public String getParent() {...}

toString() method of File class prints the abstract path of file object on to the console.

dir.getParentFile() => returns a File object for abstract path 'F:\A'.

dir.getParentFile().getParentFile() => returns a File object for abstract path 'F:\', when this file object is passed to println method, its toString() method is invoked and 'F:\' gets printed on to the console.

dir.getParentFile().getParent() => Returns a String object containing "F:\".

dir.getParent() returns String and String class doesn't contain getParentFile() and getParent() methods.

2.1.67 Answer: D

Reason:
As variable 'bw' is created outside of try-with-resources block, hence it can easily be accessed in finally block.

There is no issue with 'try(BufferedWriter writer = bw)' as well.

NOTE: writer and bw are referring to the same object.

Just before finishing the try-with-resources block, Java runtime invokes writer.close() method, which closes the stream referred by writer object.

But as writer and bw are referring to the same object, hence when bw.flush(); is invoked in finally block, it throws IOException.

2.1.68 Answer: D

Reason:
Root folder or drive is not considered in count and indexing. In the given path A is at 0th index, B is at 1st index and C is at 2nd index.
path.getName(2) returns 'C'.

path.getNameCount() returns 3 (A,B,C) and path.getFileName() returns the last name of the path, which is 'C'.

Given methods doesn't need actual path to physically exist and hence no exception is thrown at Runtime.

2.1.69 Answer: C

Reason:
toAbsolutePath() method doesn't care if given path elements are physically available or not. It just returns the absolute path.

As file already refers to absolute path, hence the same path is printed on to the console.

2.1.70 Answer: A,B,C

Reason:
'B' is a directory.

java.nio.file.Files (not java.io.File) class has static method isDirectory(Path) to check if the farthest element of given path is directory or not. 'Files.isDirectory(path)' returns true.

Interface Path has toFile() method to return the java.io.File object representing this path. And java.io.File class has isDirectory() method to check if given File object is directory or not. 'path.toFile().isDirectory()' returns true.

Files.getAttribute(Path path, String attribute, LinkOption... options) returns the value corresponding to passed attribute. IllegalArgumentException is thrown if attribute is not spelled correctly.

Files.getAttribute(path, "isDirectory") returns true.

There is no static method, isDirectory(Path) in java.io.File class, hence 'File.isDirectory(path)' causes compilation error.

There is no constructor of File class accepting Path, hence new File(path) causes compilation error.

2.1.71 Answer: C

Reason:
'Files.createDirectory(path);' creates the farthest directory element but all parents must exist.

In this case, createDirectory method tries to create 'Z' directory under F:\X\Y.

F:\X exists but F:\X\Y doesn't exist and hence NoSuchFileException is thrown at runtime.

2.1.72 Answer: B

Reason:
For 'path1.relativize(path2)' both path1 and path2 should be of same type. Both should either be relative or absolute.

In this case, path1 refers to 'C:\A\B\C' and path2 refers to 'D:\A'.

Even though both paths are absolute but their roots are different, hence IllegalArgumentException is thrown at runtime.

2.1.73 Answer: B

Reason:
First of all I would like to tell you that Windows shortcut and symbolic links are different. Shortcut is just a regular file and symbolic link is a File System object.

To create symbolic link used in this question, I used below command:
C:\TEMP>mklink msg .\Parent\Child\Message.txt

And below message was displayed on to the console for the successful creation of symbolic link 'symbolic link created for msg <<===>> .\Parent\Child\Message.txt'.

When copy() method is used for symbolic link, then by default target file is copied and not the symbolic link.

So, 'src' is a symbolic link an 'tgt' is a regular file. 'true:false' is printed on to the console.

NOTE: For the job, if you want to copy symbolic link, then use 'Files.copy(src, tgt, LinkOption.NOFOLLOW_LINKS);' but make sure that user should have 'symbolic' LinkPermission.

2.1.74 Answer: B,C,D,E

Reason:
DriverManager and Date are classes and hence not correct options.

A JDBC drive must provide implementation for Driver, Statement, PreparedStatement, CallableStatement, ResultSet and Connection interfaces.

2.1.75 Answer: D

Reason:
As credentials are passed as java.util.Properties so user name should be passed as "user" property and password should be passed as "password" property.

In the given code, 'prop.put("username", "root");' name of property is 'username' and not 'user' and that is why SQLException is thrown at runtime.

2.1.76 Answer: C, D

Reason:
Method createStatement is overloaded: createStatement(), createStatement(int, int) and createStatement(int, int, int).

2.1.77 Answer: B,C

Reason:
Statement object is created inside try-with-resources statement. So, close() method is invoked on Statement object implicitly.

According to the javadoc of close() method, "When a Statement object is closed, its current ResultSet object, if one exists, is also closed". Hence, ResultSet object is also closed.

Connection object is created outside of try-with-resources statement, hence close() method of Connection object is not invoked implicitly.

2.1.78   Answer: E

Reason:
Method updateRow() must be called after every updated ResultSet row. In this case updateRow() method was called after updating salary in all 4 rows and hence it throws an exception at runtime.

NOTE: To update the salary of all the records successfully, move rs.updateRow() statement inside while loop after rs.updateDouble(...) method call.

2.1.79   Answer: B

Reason:
According to javadoc of java.sql.Connection, "By default a Connection object is in auto-commit mode, which means that it automatically commits changes after executing each statement. If auto-commit mode has been disabled, the method commit must be called explicitly in order to commit changes; otherwise, database changes will not be saved".

First 2 executeUpdate(...) method invocation inserts the records in the database table. So records for IDs 1001 and 1002 are available in the database table.

After that 'con.setAutoCommit(false);' is invoked which disables the auto-commit mode. The next stmt.executeUpdate(...) statement doesn't commit the row in the database unless 'con.commit();' OR 'con.setAutoCommit(true);' is invoked.

Record for ID 1003 is not committed to the database table.

2.1.80   Answer: A

Reason:
Given query returns below records:
101 John   Smith   12000
102 Sean   Smith   15000
103 Regina Williams   15500
104 Natasha George 14600

'rs.absolute(3);' moves the cursor to the 3rd row.
'rs.updateString(3, "Gales");' updates LASTNAME field of 3rd row from 'Williams' to 'Gales'.

'rs.updateRow();' commits the changes to the database.

'rs.refreshRow();' It refreshes the current row (which is 3rd now) with its most recent value in the database. There is no change to the cursor position.

System.out.println(rs.getString(2) + " " + rs.getString(3)); prints the 2nd and 3rd column values of 3rd row, which are 'Regina' and 'Gales'.

2.1.81 Answer: E

Reason:
Locale class has overloaded constructors:
Locale(String language)
Locale(String language, String country)
Locale(String language, String country, String variant)

For the exam, you should know that Locale instance can be created by passing incorrect country and language and in fact getLanguage(), getCountry() and toString() method prints the passed strings.
NOTE: It may cause problem later on, when you try to retrieve resource bundle.

2.1.82 Answer: A

Reason:
setDefault(Locale) is a static method defined inside Locale class but static method can be invoked using instance reference as well.

Compiler changes 'loc.setDefault(loc);' to 'Locale.setDefault(loc);'.

Line 8 doesn't cause any compilation error and on execution it sets the default locale to it_IT.

Hence, Locale.getDefault() will always return it_IT.

2.1.83 Answer: E

Reason:
ResourceBundle.getBundle("MyResourceBundle", loc); => Base resource bundle file name should be 'MyResourceBundle'.

Default Locale is: fr_CA and passed Locale to getBundle method is: en_IN

The search order for matching resource bundle is:
MyResourceBundle_en_IN.properties [1st: Complete en_IN].
MyResourceBundle_en.properties [2nd: Only language en].
MyResourceBundle_fr_CA.properties [3rd: Complete default Locale fr_CA].
MyResourceBundle_fr.properties [4th: Language of default Locale fr].
MyResourceBundle.properties [5th: ResourceBundle's name without language or country].

None of the properties files match with above search list, hence
MissingResourceException is thrown at runtime.

2.1.84   Answer: C

Reason:
'Executors.newSingleThreadExecutor();' creates an Executor that uses a single worker thread.

'new MyCallable(100);' creates MyCallable object and initializes its property i to 100.

'es.submit(callable)' invokes the call method and returns a Future object containing Integer value 99. get() method prints this value on to the console.

'es.submit(callable)' is invoked again for the same MyCallable instance, call method returns a Future object containing Integer value 98. get() method prints this value on to the console.

2.1.85   Answer: A, B

Reason:
ExecutorService interface has following methods:
Future<?> submit(Runnable task);
<T> Future<T> submit(Runnable task, T result);
<T> Future<T> submit(Callable<T> task);

Hence, 'es.submit(new Printer());' is one of the correct options.

ExecutorService interface extends Executor interface and it has 'void execute(Runnable command);' method. Hence, 'es.execute(new Printer());' is the 2nd correct option.

2.1.86 Answer: C

Reason:
'new CopyOnWriteArrayList<>(list1);' creates a thread-safe list containing the elements of list1. list1 and list2 are not linked, hence changes made to one list doesn't affect other list.

CopyOnWriteArrayList allows add/set/remove while iterating through the list. On every modification, a fresh copy of underlying array is created, leaving the iterator object unchanged.
'Melon' and 'Mango' are deleted from list2.

list1 refers to [Melon, Apple, Banana, Mango] and list2 refers to [Apple, Banana].

2.1.87 Answer: B

Reason:
In deadlock, threads' state do not change but in livelock threads' state change constantly. In both cases, process hangs.

2.1.88 Answer: C

Reason:
ExecutorService can handle 1 thread, but 2 threads are submitted. The first thread calls await() and wait endlessly.

CyclicBarrier needs 2 threads to call await() method but as this is not going to happen, hence the program waits endlessly. 'Match is starting...' is never printed on to the console and program waits indefinitely.

NOTE: To trip the CyclicBarrier, replace 'Executors.newFixedThreadPool(1);' with 'Executors.newFixedThreadPool(2);'.

2.1.89 Answer: B

Reason:
As 'list.add(i);' is invoked inside synchronized method, hence adding to list is thread-safe.

shutdown() doesn't wait for previously submitted tasks to complete execution and as all submitted tasks execute in parallel hence list can contain any number of elements between 1 and 1000. It will be a rare case when none of the tasks were completed and shutdown() invoked before that, but still that's a chance and if it happens then list will have no elements.

2.1.90   Answer: A,B,E

Reason:
RecursiveTask is a generic class which extends from ForkJoinTask<V> class.
RecursiveTask<V> declares compute() method as: 'protected abstract V compute();'
In the given code overriding method returns Long, so classes from which class Task can extend are: RecursiveTask<Long>, RecursiveTask<Object> [co-variant return type in overriding method] and RecursiveTask [co-variant return type in overriding method].

RecursiveAction is a non-generic class which extends from ForkJoinTask<Void> class.
RecursiveAction declared compute() method as: 'protected abstract void compute();'
In the given code overriding method returns Long, hence RecursiveAction can't be used as super class of Task.

3   Practice Test-3

3.1   90 Questions covering all topics.

3.1.1   Consider below code:

```
//Child.java
package com.udayan.ocp;

class Parent {
    public void m() {
        System.out.println("Parent");
    }
}

public abstract class Child extends Parent { //Line 9
    public static void main(String [] args) { //Line 10
        new Parent().m(); //Line 11
    }
}
```

What will be the result of compiling and executing Child class?

A.   Compilation error at Line 9

B.   Compilation error at Line 10

C.   Compilation error at Line 11

D.   Parent

3.1.2 Consider the code of Test.java file:

```
package com.udayan.ocp;

class Player {
    String name;
    int age;

    Player(String name, int age) {
        this.name = name;
        this.age = age;
    }

    public String toString() {
        return name + ", " + age;
    }

    public boolean equals(Player player) {
        if(player != null
                && this.name.equals(player.name)
                && this.age == player.age) {
            return true;
        }
        return false;
    }
}

public class Test {
    public static void main(String[] args) {
        Object p1 = new Player("Sachin", 44);
        Object p2 = new Player("Sachin", 44);
        System.out.println(p1.equals(p2));
    }
}
```

What will be the result of compiling and executing Test class?

A. true

B. false

C. Compilation error in Player class

D. Compilation error in Test class

3.1.3   Consider the code of Test.java file:

```
package com.udayan.ocp;

class Point {
    private int x;
    private int y;

    Point(){
        Point(10, 20);
    }

    Point(int x, int y) {
        this.x = x;
        this.y = y;
    }

    @Override
    public String toString() {
        return "Point{" + x + ", " + y + "}";
    }
}

public class Test {
    public static void main(String[] args) {
        Point p = new Point();
        System.out.println(p);
    }
}
```

What will be the result of compiling and executing Test class?

A. Point{10, 20}

B. Point{0, 0}

C. Compilation error in Point class

D. Compilation error in Test class

3.1.4 Given code of Test.java file:

```
package com.udayan.ocp;

interface Printer1 {
    default void print() {
        System.out.println("Printer1");
    }
}

interface Printer2 {
    public static void print() {
        System.out.println("Printer2");
    }
}

class Printer implements Printer1, Printer2 {

}

public class Test {
    public static void main(String[] args) {
        Printer printer = new Printer();
        printer.print();
    }
}
```

What will be the result of compiling and executing Test class?

A. Compilation error for Printer1

B. Compilation error for Printer2

C. Compilation error for Printer

D. Printer1

E. Printer2

3.1.5 Consider the code of Test.java file:

```java
public class Test {
    enum TrafficLight {
        RED, YELLOW, GREEN;
    }

    public static void main(String[] args) {
        TrafficLight tl = TrafficLight.valueOf(args[1]);
        switch(tl) {
            case TrafficLight.RED:
                System.out.println("STOP");
                break;
            case TrafficLight.YELLOW:
                System.out.println("SLOW");
                break;
            case TrafficLight.GREEN:
                System.out.println("GO");
                break;
        }
    }
}
```

What will be the result of compiling and executing Test class by using the commands:
```
javac Test.java
java Test RED AMBER
```

A. STOP

B. No output

C. IllegalArgumentException is thrown

D. None of the other options

3.1.6 **What will be the result of compiling and executing Test class?**

```java
package com.udayan.ocp;

public class Test {
    enum JobStatus {
        SUCCESS, FAIL; //Line 3
    }

    enum TestResult {
        PASS, FAIL; //Line 7
    }

    public static void main(String[] args) {
        JobStatus js = JobStatus.FAIL;
        TestResult tr = TestResult.FAIL;

        System.out.println(js.equals(tr)); //Line 14
        System.out.println(js == tr); //Line 15
    }
}
```

A.	Compilation error at Line 14	B.	Compilation error at Line 15
C.	true true	D.	false false

3.1.7 Given code:

```
package com.udayan.ocp;

class Outer {
    class Inner {
        public void m() {
            System.out.println("WELCOME!");
        }
    }
}

public class Test {
    public static void main(String[] args) {
        //Insert statement here
    }
}
```

Which statement when inserted in the main(String []) method will print "WELCOME!" in the output?

A.	`Outer.Inner obj1 = new Outer().new Inner();` `obj1.m();`
B.	`Inner obj2 = new Outer().new Inner();` `obj2.m();`
C.	`Outer.Inner obj3 = this.new Inner();` `obj3.m();`
D.	`Inner obj4 = this.new Inner();` `obj4.m();`

3.1.8 What will be the result of compiling and executing class Test?

```java
package com.udayan.ocp;

class P {
    private int var = 100;
    class Q {
        String var = "Java";
        void print() {
            System.out.println(var);
        }
    }
}

public class Test {
    public static void main(String[] args) {
        new P().new Q().print();
    }
}
```

A. Java

B. 100

C. Compilation error

D. Exception is thrown at runtime

3.1.9 Given Code:

```java
class Outer {
    public static void sayHello() {}
    static {
        class Inner {
            /*INSERT*/
        }
        new Inner();
    }
}

public class TestOuter {
    public static void main(String[] args) {
        Outer.sayHello();
    }
}
```

Which of the following options can replace /*INSERT*/ such that on executing TestOuter class, "HELLO" is printed in the output?

A.	```\n{\n System.out.println("HELLO");\n}\n```
B.	```\nstatic {\n System.out.println("HELLO");\n}\n```
C.	```\nInner() {\n System.out.println("HELLO");\n}\n```
D.	```\nInner(String s) {\n System.out.println(s);\n}\n```

3.1.10 Given code:

```
package com.udayan.ocp;

class Message {
    public void printMessage() {
        System.out.println("Hello!");
    }
}

public class Test {
    public static void main(String[] args) {
        Message msg = new Message() {
            @Override
            public void PrintMessage() {
                System.out.println("HELLO!");
            }
        };
        msg.printMessage();
    }
}
```

What will be the result of compiling and executing Test class?

A. Compilation error

B. Runtime error

C. Hello!

D. HELLO!

3.1.11 Below is the code of TestSellable.java file:

```
package com.udayan.ocp;

interface Sellable {
    double getPrice();
}

public class TestSellable {
    private static void printPrice(Sellable sellable) {
        System.out.println(sellable.getPrice());
    }

    public static void main(String[] args) {
        /*INSERT*/
    }
}
```

Which of the following options can replace /*INSERT*/ such that there are no compilation errors?

A.	`printPrice(null);`
B.	`printPrice(new Sellable());`

C.	`printPrice(new Sellable() {`
	
	`});`

D.	`printPrice(new Sellable() {`
	`    @Override`
	`    public double getPrice() {`
	`        return 45.34;`
	`    }`
	`});`

3.1.12 Will below code compile successfully?

```java
package com.udayan.ocp;

interface I1 {
    void m1();

    interface I2 {
        void m2();
    }

    abstract class A1 {
        public abstract void m3();
    }

    class A2 {
        public void m4() {
            System.out.println(4);
        }
    }
}
```

A. Yes

B. No

3.1.13 Which of the annotation is used for Functional Interface?

A. @Functional

B. @FI

C. @FunctionalInterface

D. @Functional Interface

3.1.14 Given code of Test.java file:

```
package com.udayan.ocp;

interface I10 {
    void m(String s);
}

public class Test {
    public static void main(String[] args) {
        method(new I10() {
            @Override
            public void m(String s) {
                System.out.println(s.toUpperCase());
            }

        }, "good morning!");
    }

    private static void method(I10 obj, String text) {
        obj.m(text);
    }
}
```

Which of the following code replaces the anonymous inner class code with lambda expression?

A.	`method(s -> {`
	`System.out.println(s.toUpperCase()) }, "good`
	`morning!");`

B.	`method(s -> System.out.println(s.toUpperCase()),` `"good morning!");`
C.	`method(s -> s.toUpperCase(), "good morning!");`
D.	`method(s ->` `System.out.println(s.toUpperCase()));`

3.1.15 Given code of Test.java file:

```java
package com.udayan.ocp;

import java.util.Arrays;
import java.util.Comparator;
import java.util.List;

class Student implements Comparator<Student> {
    private String name;
    private String exam;

    public Student() {
        super();
    }

    public Student(String name, String exam) {
        this.name = name;
        this.exam = exam;
    }

    public int compare(Student s1, Student s2) {
        return s2.name.compareToIgnoreCase(s1.name);
    }

    public String toString() {
        return '{' + name + ", " + exam + '}';
    }
}

public class Test {
    public static void main(String[] args) {
        Student stud1 = new Student("John", "OCA");
        Student stud2 = new Student("Jack", "OCP");
        Student stud3 = new Student("Rob", "OCP");
        List<Student> list = Arrays.asList(stud1,
                                    stud2, stud3);
        list.sort(new Student());
        list.forEach(System.out::println);
    }
}
```

What will be the result of compiling and executing Test class?

A.	Runtime exception	B.	Compilation error
C.	{Rob, OCP} {John, OCA} {Jack, OCP}	D.	{Jack, OCP} {John, OCA} {Rob, OCP}

3.1.16 Does below code compile successfully?

```
class GenericPrinter<T> {}

abstract class AbstractGenericPrinter<X,Y,T>
                        extends GenericPrinter<T>{}
```

A. Yes

B. No

3.1.17 Given code of Test.java file:

```
package com.udayan.ocp;

import java.util.*;

public class Test {
    public static void main(String[] args) {
        List<? extends String> list = new ArrayList<>
            (Arrays.asList("A", "E", "I", "O")); //Line 8
        list.add("U"); //Line 9
        list.forEach(System.out::print);
    }
}
```

What will be the result of compiling and executing Test class?

A. AEIO

B. AEIOU

C. Line 8 causes compilation error

D. Line 9 causes compilation error

E. Runtime exception

3.1.18 Given code of Test.java file:

```
package com.udayan.ocp;

public class Test<T> {
    static T obj;
}
```

Does above code compile successfully?

A. Yes

B. No

3.1.19 For the given code:

```
package com.udayan.ocp;

interface Operator<T> {
    public abstract T operation(T t1, T t2);
}

public class Test {
    public static void main(String[] args) {
        System.out.println(new Operator<String>() {
            public String operation(String s1, String s2) {
                return s1 + s2;
            }
        });
    }
}
```

Which of the following options successfully replace anonymous inner class code with lambda expression code?

A.	`System.out.println((String s1, String s2) -> s1 + s2);`
B.	`System.out.println((s1, s2) -> s1 + s2);`
C.	`System.out.println((s1, s2) -> { return s1 + s2; });`
D.	None of the other options

3.1.20 Given code of Test.java file:

```java
package com.udayan.ocp;

import java.util.Arrays;
import java.util.List;
import java.util.ListIterator;

public class Test {
    public static void main(String[] args) {
        List<String> list = Arrays.asList("T",
                                "S", "R", "I", "F");
        ListIterator<String> iter = list.listIterator(5);
        while(iter.hasPrevious()) {
            System.out.print(iter.previous());
        }
    }
}
```

What will be the result of compiling and executing Test class?

A. IRST

B. FIRST

C. TSRIF

D. Runtime Exception

3.1.21 **Given code of Test.java file:**

```
package com.udayan.ocp;

import java.util.*;

enum TrafficLight {
    RED, YELLOW, GREEN
}

public class Test {
    public static void main(String[] args) {
        Map<TrafficLight, String> map = new TreeMap<>();
        map.put(TrafficLight.GREEN, "GO");
        map.put(TrafficLight.RED, "STOP");
        map.put(TrafficLight.YELLOW, "STOP IN 3 Seconds");
        map.put(TrafficLight.YELLOW, "READY TO STOP");

        for(String msg : map.values()) {
            System.out.println(msg);
        }
    }
}
```

What will be the result of compiling and executing Test class?

A.	STOP READY TO STOP STOP IN 3 Seconds GO	B.	STOP STOP IN 3 Seconds READY TO STOP GO
C.	STOP READY TO STOP GO	D.	STOP STOP IN 3 Seconds GO
E.	Printing order cannot be predicted.		

3.1.22 Given code of Test.java file:

```
package com.udayan.ocp;

import java.util.LinkedList;
import java.util.List;
import java.util.Queue;

public class Test {
    public static void main(String[] args) {
        List<String> list = new LinkedList<>();
        list.add("ONE");
        list.add("TWO");
        list.remove(1);
        System.out.println(list);

        Queue<String> queue = new LinkedList<>();
        queue.add("ONE");
        queue.add("TWO");
        queue.remove();
        System.out.println(queue);
    }
}
```

What will be the result of compiling and executing Test class?

A.	[ONE] [TWO]	B.	[TWO] [ONE]
C.	[TWO] [TWO]	D.	[ONE] [ONE]

3.1.23 For the code below:

```
package com.udayan.ocp;

import java.util.Arrays;

public class Test {
    public static void main(String[] args) {
        String [] arr
            = {"**", "***", "*", "*****", "****"};
        Arrays.sort(
            arr, (s1, s2) -> s1.length()-s2.length());
        for(String str : arr) {
            System.out.println(str);
        }
    }
}
```

What do you need to do so that above code gives following output?
```
*
**
***
****
*****
```

A. Add the import statement for the Comparator interface: import java.util.Comparator;

B. Existing code without any changes displays above output.

C. Change the lambda expression to (s1, s2) -> s2.length()-s1.length()

D. Change the lambda expression to (s2, s1) -> s1.length()-s2.length()

3.1.24 Given code of Test.java file:

```java
package com.udayan.ocp;

import java.util.Arrays;
import java.util.Collections;
import java.util.Comparator;
import java.util.List;

public class Test {
    public static void main(String[] args) {
        List<String> emails = Arrays.asList(
            "udayan@outlook.com", "sachin@outlook.com",
            "sachin@gmail.com", "udayan@gmail.com");
        Collections.sort(emails, Comparator.comparing(str ->
                    str.substring(str.indexOf("@") + 1)));
        for(String email : emails) {
            System.out.println(email);
        }
    }
}
```

What will be the result of compiling and executing Test class?

A.	sachin@gmail.com udayan@gmail.com sachin@outlook.com udayan@outlook.com	B.	sachin@gmail.com udayan@gmail.com udayan@outlook.com sachin@outlook.com
C.	sachin@outlook.com udayan@outlook.com sachin@gmail.com udayan@gmail.com	D.	sachin@outlook.com udayan@outlook.com udayan@gmail.com sachin@gmail.com

3.1.25 Given code of Test.java file:

```
package com.udayan.ocp;

import java.util.Arrays;
import java.util.Collections;
import java.util.List;

public class Test {
    public static void main(String[] args) {
        List<String> list
                    = Arrays.asList("M", "R", "A", "P");
        Collections.sort(list, null);
        System.out.println(list);
    }
}
```

What will be the result of compiling and executing Test class?

A. [M, R, A, P]

B. [A, M, P, R]

C. [R, P, M, A]

D. Runtime Exception

3.1.26 Given code of Test.java file:

```
package com.udayan.ocp;

import java.util.Arrays;
import java.util.Collections;
import java.util.List;

public class Test {
    public static void main(String[] args) {
        List<String> list
                    = Arrays.asList("M", "R", "A", "P");
        Collections.sort(list, null);
        list.stream().peek(System.out::print);
    }
}
```

What will be the result of compiling and executing Test class?

A. MRAP

B. AMPR

C. RPMA

D. Runtime Exception

E. None of the other options

3.1.27 Given code of Test.java file:

```java
package com.udayan.ocp;

public class Test {
    private static boolean isDirection(int ch) {
        switch(ch) {
            case 'N':
            case 'E':
            case 'W':
            case 'S':
                return true;
        }
        return false;
    }

    public static void main(String[] args) {
        String str = "North East West South";
        str.chars().filter(Test::isDirection)
            .forEach(c -> System.out.print((char)c));
    }
}
```

What will be the result of compiling and executing Test class?

A. orth ast est outh

B. N E W S

C. NEWS

D. None of the other options

3.1.28 Given code of Test.java file:

```
package com.udayan.ocp;

import java.util.ArrayDeque;
import java.util.Arrays;
import java.util.Deque;
import java.util.List;

public class Test {
  public static void main(String[] args) throws Exception {
      List<String> list = Arrays.asList("oca",
                  null, "ocp", "java", "null"); //Line n1
      Deque<String> deque
                  = new ArrayDeque<String>(list); //Line n2
      System.out.println(deque.size()); //Line n3
    }
}
```

What will be the result of compiling and executing Test class?

A. 3

B. 4

C. 5

D. NullPointerException is thrown at runtime

3.1.29 Given code of Test.java file:

```
package com.udayan.ocp;

import java.util.function.Supplier;

public class Test {
    public static void main(String[] args) {
        Supplier<StringBuilder> supplier = () ->
                    new StringBuilder(" olleH")
                .reverse().append("!dlroW").reverse();
        System.out.println(supplier.get());
    }
}
```

What will be the result of compiling and executing Test class?

A. >World! olleH<

B. >Hello World!<

C. > olleHWorld!<

D. > olleH!dlroW<

E. >World!Hello <

3.1.30 Given code of Test.java file:

```
package com.udayan.ocp;

import java.util.Arrays;
import java.util.List;
import java.util.function.UnaryOperator;

public class Test {
    public static void main(String[] args) {
        List<Integer> list = Arrays.asList (2, 3, 4);
        UnaryOperator<Long> operator = s -> s*s*s;
        list.replaceAll(operator);
        list.forEach(System.out::println);
    }
}
```

What will be the result of compiling and executing Test class?

A.	8 27 64	B.	2 3 4
C.	Compilation error	D.	Runtime exception

3.1.31 Consider below code:

```java
package com.udayan.ocp;

import java.util.function.Function;

public class Test {
    public static void main(String[] args) {
        Function<Integer, Integer> f = x -> x + 10;
        Function<Integer, Integer> g = y -> y * y;

        Function<Integer, Integer> fog
                        = g.compose(f); //Line 8
        System.out.println(fog.apply(10));
    }
}
```

On execution, Test class prints 400 on to the console. Which of the statements can replace Line 8 such that there is no change in the output?

A.	Function<Integer, Integer> fog = f.compose(g);
B.	Function<Integer, Integer> fog = f.andThen(g);
C.	Function<Integer, Integer> fog = g.andThen(f);

3.1.32 Given code of Test.java file:

```
package com.udayan.ocp;

import java.util.function.Consumer;

class Counter {
    static int count = 1;
}
public class Test {
    public static void main(String[] args) {
        Consumer<Integer> add = i -> Counter.count += i;
        Consumer<Integer> print = System.out::println;
        add.andThen(print).accept(10); //Line 10
    }
}
```

What will be the result of compiling and executing Test class?

A. 11

B. 10

C. 1

D. Compilation error

3.1.33 Which of the following is the only Functional interface available for boolean primitive type?

A. BooleanConsumer

B. BooleanSupplier

C. BooleanPredicate

D. BooleanFunction

3.1.34 Given code of Test.java file:

```
package com.udayan.ocp;

import java.util.Arrays;
import java.util.List;

public class Test {
    public static void main(String[] args) {
        List<Integer> list = Arrays.asList(10, 100, 1000);
        list.replaceAll(i -> -i++);

        System.out.println(list);
    }
}
```

What will be the result of compiling and executing Test class?

A. Compilation error

B. [10, 100, 1000]

C. [-10, -100, -1000]

D. [-11, -101, -1001]

E. [-9, -99, -999]

3.1.35 Given code of Test.java file:

```
package com.udayan.ocp;

import java.util.function.BiFunction;
import java.util.function.BiPredicate;

public class Test {
  public static void main(String[] args) {
      BiPredicate<String, String> predicate
                              = String::contains;
      BiFunction<String, String, Boolean> func
                              = (str1, str2) -> {
          return predicate.test(str1, str2) ? true : false;
      };

      System.out.println(func.apply("Tomato", "at"));
    }
}
```

What will be the result of compiling and executing Test class?

A. true

B. false

C. null

D. Compilation error

3.1.36 Given code of Test.java file:

```java
package com.udayan.ocp;

import java.util.Optional;

class Message {
    private String msg = "Good Morning!";
    public Message(String msg) {
        this.msg = msg;
    }

    public Message() {super();}

    public String getMsg() {
        return msg;
    }

    public String toString() {
        return msg;
    }
}

public class Test {
    public static void main(String[] args) {
        Message message = null;
        Optional<Message> optional =
                Optional.ofNullable(message);
        System.out.println(optional.isPresent() ?
                optional.get().getMsg() : new Message());
    }
}
```

What will be the result of compiling and executing Test class?

A. null

B. Text containing @ symbol

C. Good Morning!

D. NullPointerException is thrown at runtime

3.1.37 Given code of Test.java file:

```
package com.udayan.ocp;

import java.util.Arrays;
import java.util.List;
import java.util.function.Predicate;

public class Test {
    public static void main(String[] args) {
        List<Integer> list = Arrays.asList(-80, 100,
                                           -40, 25, 200);
        Predicate<Integer> predicate = num -> {
            int ctr = 1;
            boolean result = num > 0;
            System.out.print(ctr++ + ".");
            return result;
        };

        list.stream().filter(predicate).count();
    }
}
```

What will be the result of compiling and executing Test class?

A. 2.4.5.

B. 1.1.1.

C. 1.2.3.

D. 1.2.3.4.5.

E. 1.1.1.1.1.

3.1.38 Given code of Test.java file:

```
package com.udayan.ocp;

import java.util.ArrayList;
import java.util.List;

public class Test {
    public static void main(String[] args) {
        int ref = 10;
        List<Integer> list = new ArrayList<>();
        list.stream().anyMatch(i -> {
            System.out.println("HELLO");
            return i > ++ref;
        });
    }
}
```

What will be the result of compiling and executing Test class?

A. HELLO

B. Compilation error

C. Program executes successfully but nothing is printed on to the console.

3.1.39 Given code of Test.java file:

```
package com.udayan.ocp;

import java.util.Optional;

public class Test {
    public static void main(String[] args) {
        Optional<Integer> optional
                         = Optional.of(null); //Line 8
        System.out.println(optional.orElse(-1)); //Line 9
    }
}
```

What will be the result of compiling and executing Test class?

A. null

B. -1

C. Line 8 throws NullPointerException

D. Line 9 throws NullPointerException

3.1.40 Which of the following are Primitive variant of Optional class?

A. ByteOptional

B. IntOptional

C. OptionalBoolean

D. OptionalFloat

E. OptionalDouble

3.1.41 Given code of Test.java file:

```
package com.udayan.ocp;

import java.util.Arrays;
import java.util.stream.Stream;

public class Test {
    public static void main(String[] args) {
        Stream<Integer> stream =
                Arrays.asList(1,2,3,4,5).stream();
        System.out.println(stream.mapToInt(i -> i)
                .average().getAsInt());
    }
}
```

What will be the result of compiling and executing Test class?

A. 3

B. Runtime Exception

C. Compilation error

3.1.42 Given code of Test.java file:

```
package com.udayan.ocp;

import java.util.Arrays;
import java.util.stream.Stream;

public class Test {
    public static void main(String[] args) {
        Stream<String> stream =
            Arrays.asList("One", "Two", "Three").stream();
        System.out.println(stream.reduce(null,
                                (s1, s2) -> s1 + s2));
    }
}
```

What will be the result of compiling and executing Test class?

A. OneTwoThree

B. nullOneTwoThree

C. NullPointerException is thrown at runtime

D. OneTwoThreenull

3.1.43 Given code of Test.java file:

```
package com.udayan.ocp;

import java.util.stream.Stream;

public class Test {
    public static void main(String[] args) {
        Stream<String> stream = Stream.of("d",
                                "cc", "bbb", "aaaa");
        stream.sorted().forEach(System.out::println);
    }
}
```

Which of the following needs to be done, so that output is:

```
d
cc
bbb
aaaa
```

A. No need to make any changes, on execution given code prints expected result.

B. Replace 'stream.sorted()' with 'stream.sorted((s1,s2) -> s1.length() - s2.length())'

C. Replace 'stream.sorted()' with 'stream.sorted((s1,s2) -> s2.length() - s1.length())'

3.1.44 Given code of Test.java file:

```
package com.udayan.ocp;

import java.util.Set;
import java.util.TreeSet;
import java.util.stream.Collectors;
import java.util.stream.Stream;

public class Test {
    public static void main(String[] args) {
        Stream<String> stream = Stream.of("java",
                "python", "c", "c++", "java", "python");
        Set<String> set = stream.collect(
                Collectors.toCollection(TreeSet::new));
        System.out.println(set);
    }
}
```

What will be the result of compiling and executing Test class?

A. [c, c++, java, python]

B. [c++, c, java, python]

C. [java, python, c, c++]

D. Order of elements can't be predicted in the output.

3.1.45 Given code of Test.java file:

```
package com.udayan.ocp;

import java.util.stream.Stream;

public class Test {
    public static void main(String[] args) {
        Stream<String> stream = Stream.of("ocp");
        stream._____(s -> s.chars())
                .forEach(i -> System.out.print((char)i));
    }
}
```

Which code snippet, when filled into the blank, allows the class to compile?

A. flatMap

B. flatMapToInt

C. flatMapToDouble

D. flatMapToLong

3.1.46 Given code of Test.java file:

```java
package com.udayan.ocp;

import java.util.ArrayList;
import java.util.Comparator;
import java.util.List;

class Fruit implements Comparable<Fruit>, Comparator<Fruit>
{
    String name;
    String countryOfOrigin;

    Fruit() {}

    Fruit(String name, String countryOfOrigin) {
        this.name = name;
        this.countryOfOrigin = countryOfOrigin;
    }

    public String toString() {
        return name + ":" + countryOfOrigin;
    }

    @Override
    public int compareTo(Fruit o) {
        return this.name.compareToIgnoreCase(o.name);
    }

    @Override
    public int compare(Fruit o1, Fruit o2) {
        return o1.countryOfOrigin
            .compareToIgnoreCase(o2.countryOfOrigin);
    }
```

```
    public static int comp(String s1, String s2) {
        return s2.compareToIgnoreCase(s1);
    }
}

public class Test {
    public static void main(String[] args) {
        List<Fruit> list = new ArrayList<>();
        list.add(new Fruit("Olive", "Middle East"));
        list.add(new Fruit("Mango", "India"));
        list.add(new Fruit("Cranberry", "North America"));
        list.add(new Fruit("Watermelon", "Africa"));
        list.add(new Fruit("Peach", "China"));
        list.add(new Fruit("Fig", "Middle East"));
        list.add(new Fruit("Blueberry", "North America"));

        /* INSERT */
    }
}
```

Which of the following two options can replace /* INSERT */ such that output is:

Cranberry:North America

Blueberry:North America

Olive:Middle East

Fig:Middle East

Mango:India

Peach:China

Watermelon:Africa

A. `list.stream().sorted().forEach(System.out::println);`

B. `list.stream().sorted(new Fruit())`
   `                    .forEach(System.out::println);`

C. `list.stream().sorted(new Fruit().reversed())`
   `                    .forEach(System.out::println);`

D. `list.stream().sorted(Comparator`
   `    .comparing(f -> f.countryOfOrigin, Fruit::comp))`
   `                    .forEach(System.out::println);`

3.1.47 Given code of Test.java file:

```java
package com.udayan.ocp;

public class Test {
    private static void m1() throws Exception {
        throw new Exception();
    }

    public static void main(String[] args) {
        try {
            m1();
        } finally {
            System.out.println("A");
        }
    }
}
```

What will be the result of compiling and executing Test class?

A. A is printed to the console and program ends normally.

B. A is printed to the console, stack trace is printed and then program ends normally.

C. A is printed to the console, stack trace is printed and then program ends abruptly.

D. Compilation error.

3.1.48 Given code of Test.java file:

```
package com.udayan.ocp;

public class Test {
    public static void main(String[] args) {
        try {
            try {
                System.out.println(1/0);
            } catch(ArithmeticException e) {
                System.out.println("Inner");
                throw e;
            } finally {
                System.out.println("Finally 1");
            }
        } catch(ArithmeticException e) {
            System.out.println("Outer");
        }
    }
}
```

What will be the result of compiling and executing Test class?

A.	Inner Finally 1	B.	Inner Finally 1 Outer
C.	Inner Outer Finally 1	D.	Compilation Error.

3.1.49 Given code of Test.java file:

```
package com.udayan.ocp;

public class Test {
    public static void main(String[] args) {
        try {
            main(args);
        } catch (Exception ex) {
            System.out.println("CATCH-");
        }
        System.out.println("OUT");
    }
}
```

What will be the result of compiling and executing Test class?

A. CATCH-OUT

B. OUT

C. None of the System.out.println statements are executed

D. Compilation error

3.1.50   Given code of Test.java file:

```java
package com.udayan.ocp;

public class Test {
    private static void div(int i, int j) {
        try {
            System.out.println(i / j);
        } catch (ArithmeticException e) {
            throw (RuntimeException)e;
        }
    }

    public static void main(String[] args) {
        try {
            div(5, 0);
        } catch (ArithmeticException e) {
            System.out.println("AE");
        } catch (RuntimeException e) {
            System.out.println("RE");
        }
    }
}
```

What will be the result of compiling and executing Test class?

A. Compilation error

B. Program ends abruptly

C. AE

D. RE

3.1.51 Given code of Test.java file:

```java
package com.udayan.ocp;

import java.sql.SQLException;

public class Test {
    private static void m() throws SQLException {
        try {
            throw new SQLException();
        } catch (Exception e) {
            throw null; //Line 10
        }
    }

    public static void main(String[] args) {
        try {
            m(); //Line 16
        } catch (SQLException e) {
            System.out.println("Caught Successfully.");
        }
    }
}
```

What will be the result of compiling and executing Test class?

A. Caught Successfully.

B. Program ends abruptly.

C. Line 10 causes compilation failure.

D. Line 16 causes compilation failure.

3.1.52 Given code of Test.java file:

```
package com.udayan.ocp;

import java.io.PrintWriter;

public class Test {
    public static void main(String[] args) {
        try(PrintWriter writer = null) {
            System.out.println("HELLO");
        }
    }
}
```

What will be the result of compiling and executing Test class?

A. HELLO

B. Compilation error

C. NullPointerException is thrown at runtime

3.1.53 Given code of Test.java file:

```java
package com.udayan.ocp;

class MyException extends RuntimeException {
    public void log() {
        System.out.println("Logging MyException");
    }
}

class YourException extends RuntimeException {
    public void log() {
        System.out.println("Logging YourException");
    }
}

public class Test {
    public static void main(String[] args) {
        try {
            throw new MyException();
        } catch(MyException | YourException ex){
            ex.log();
        }
    }
}
```

What will be the result of compiling and executing Test class?

A. Logging MyException

B. Logging YourException

C. Compilation error

D. Runtime Exception

3.1.54 Given code of Test.java file:

```java
package com.udayan.ocp;

import java.io.IOException;
import java.sql.SQLException;

class MyResource implements AutoCloseable {
    @Override
    public void close() throws IOException{
        throw new IOException("IOException");
    }

    public void execute() throws SQLException {
        throw new SQLException("SQLException");
    }
}

public class Test {
    public static void main(String[] args) {
        try(MyResource resource = new MyResource()) {
            resource.execute();
        } catch(Exception e) {
            System.out.println(
                    e.getSuppressed()[0].getMessage());
        }
    }
}
```

What will be the result of compiling and executing Test class?

A. IOException

B. SQLException

C. Compilation error

3.1.55 Given code of Test.java file:

```java
package com.udayan.ocp;

public class Test {
    private static String msg = "Hello";

    private static String changeMsg(String m) {
        msg = m;
        return null;
    }

    public static void main(String[] args) {
        if(args.length == 0) {
            assert false : changeMsg("Bye");
        }
        System.out.println(msg);
    }
}
```

What will be the result of executing Test class with below command?

java -ea com.udayan.ocp.Test

A. Hello

B. Bye

C. AssertionError is thrown at runtime and program terminates abruptly

3.1.56 Given code of Test.java file:

```java
package com.udayan.ocp;

import java.time.LocalDate;

public class Test {
    public static void main(String [] args) {
        LocalDate date = LocalDate.ofEpochDay(-1);
        System.out.println(date);
    }
}
```

What will be the result of compiling and executing Test class?

A. 1970-01-01

B. 1969-12-31

C. Runtime Exception

3.1.57 Given code of Test.java file:

```java
package com.udayan.ocp;

import java.time.Instant;

public class Test {
    public static void main(String [] args) {
        System.out.println(Instant.EPOCH);
    }
}
```

What will be the result of compiling and executing Test class?

A. 1970-01-01T00:00:00

B. 1970-01-01T00:00:00Z

C. 1970-01-01T00:00:00.000

D. 1970-01-01T00:00:00.000Z

3.1.58 Given code of Test.java file:

```
package com.udayan.ocp;

import java.time.*;

public class Test {
    public static void main(String [] args) {
        System.out.println(Duration.ofDays(-2));
    }
}
```

What will be the result of compiling and executing Test class?

A. P-2D

B. P2D

C. PT-48H

D. PT48H

3.1.59 Given code of Test.java file:

```
package com.udayan.ocp;

import java.time.*;

public class Test {
    public static void main(String [] args) {
        LocalDate date = LocalDate.of(2019, 1, 1);
        LocalTime time = LocalTime.of(0, 0);
        ZoneId india = ZoneId.of("Asia/Kolkata");
        ZonedDateTime zIndia = ZonedDateTime.of(date,
                                            time, india);

        ZoneId us = ZoneId.of("America/Los_Angeles");
        ZonedDateTime zUS = /*INSERT*/;

        System.out.println(Duration.between(
                                zIndia, zUS)); //Line 15
    }
}
```

Current time in India is: 2019-01-01T00:00. Indians have started celebrating New Year. Line 15 prints the duration for which Los Angeles citizen has to wait to celebrate the new year.

Which of the following statement replace /*INSERT*/ such that Line 15 prints the correct duration?

A. zIndia.withZoneSameLocal(us)

B. zIndia.withZoneSameInstant(us)

C. Cannot be achieved by just replacing /*INSERT*/

3.1.60   Given code of Test.java file:

```
package com.udayan.ocp;

import java.time.*;
import java.time.format.DateTimeFormatter;

public class Test {
    public static void main(String [] args) {
        LocalDate date = LocalDate.of(2018, 11, 4);
        DateTimeFormatter formatter =
                DateTimeFormatter.ofPattern("dd-MM-uuuu");
        System.out.println(formatter.format(date)
                        .equals(date.format(formatter)));
    }
}
```

What will be the result of compiling and executing Test class?

A. Compilation Error

B. true

C. false

3.1.61   Given statement:

_____ represents date-based amount of time whereas _____ represents time-based amount of time.

Which of the following two options correctly fill the blanks in order?

A. Period, Duration

B. Duration, Period

C. Duration, Instant

D. Instant, Duration

3.1.62 Below is the content of 'F:\message.txt':

```
sdaleteftdeagncedk
```

message.txt file contains secret message received.

Below code is for decoding the secret message.

```java
package com.udayan.ocp;

import java.io.*;

public class Test {
    public static void main(String[] args)
                                throws IOException {
        try (InputStreamReader reader =
                new InputStreamReader(
                  new FileInputStream("F:\\message.txt"))) {
            while (reader.ready()) {
                reader.skip(1);
                reader.skip(1);
                System.out.print((char) reader.read());
            }
        }
    }
}
```

What will be the result of compiling and executing Test class?

A. sledge

B. defend

C. attack

D. None of the other options

3.1.63 Given code of Test.java file:

```java
package com.udayan.ocp;

public class Test {
    public static void main(String[] args) {
        System.out.format("A%nB%nC");
    }
}
```

What will be the result of compiling and executing Test class?

A.	Runtime Exception	B.	ABC
C.	A B C	D.	A

3.1.64 Given code of Test.java file:

```java
package com.udayan.ocp;

import java.io.*;

class Student {
    private String name;
    private int age;

    Student(String name, int age) {
        this.name = name;
        this.age = age;
    }

    public String getName() {
        return name;
    }

    public int getAge() {
        return age;
    }
}
```

```java
    public void setName(String name) {
        this.name = name;
    }

    public void setAge(int age) {
        this.age = age;
    }
}

public class Test {
    public static void main(String[] args)
            throws IOException, ClassNotFoundException {
        Student stud = new Student("John", 20);

        try( ObjectOutputStream oos = new ObjectOutputStream(
            new FileOutputStream("C:\\Student.dat")) )

        {
            oos.writeObject(stud);
        }

        try( ObjectInputStream ois = new ObjectInputStream(
            new FileInputStream("C:\\Student.dat")) ){
            stud = (Student)ois.readObject();
            System.out.printf("%s : %d",
                        stud.getName(), stud.getAge());
        }
    }
}
```

There is full permission to list/create/delete files and directories in C:.
What will be the result of compiling and executing Test class?

A. Compilation error

B. Runtime Exception

C. John : 20

D. null : 0

3.1.65 Given code of Test.java file:

```java
package com.udayan.ocp;

import java.io.*;

public class Test {
    public static void main(String[] args) {
        try(BufferedWriter bw = new BufferedWriter(
                        new FileWriter("F:\\test.txt")))
        {
            bw.close();
            bw.newLine();
        } catch(IOException e) {
            System.out.println("IOException");
        }
    }
}
```

F: is accessible for reading/writing purposes.

Which of the following statement is true about above code?

A. Class Test compiles and executes fine and no output is displayed on to the console

B. On execution, IOException is printed on to the console

C. Compilation error

3.1.66   Given code of Test.java file:

```
package com.udayan.ocp;

import java.io.*;

public class Test {
    public static void main(String[] args)
                                throws IOException {
        BufferedOutputStream bos
                    = new BufferedOutputStream(
            new FileOutputStream("F:\\file.tmp"));
        bos.write(2);
        bos.close();
    }
}
```

Which of the following statement regarding above code is true?

A. Above code causes compilation error.

B. There is no chance of resource leak.

C. There is a chance of resource leak.

3.1.67 Given code of Test.java file:

```
package com.udayan.ocp;

import java.io.*;

public class Test {
    public static void main(String[] args)
                                    throws IOException {
        File f1 = new File("F:\\f1.txt");
        FileWriter fw = new FileWriter("F:\\dir\\f2.txt");
        PrintWriter pw = new PrintWriter("F:\\f3.txt");
    }
}
```

F: is accessible for reading/writing and currently doesn't contain any files/directories.

On executing Test class, how many physical files will be created on the disc?

A. 0

B. 1

C. 2

D. 3

3.1.68 **Below is the directory structure for F:**

```
F:.
 └──A
     └──B
         └──C
                    Book.java
```

Given code of Test.java file:

```java
import java.io.IOException;
import java.nio.file.Files;
import java.nio.file.Path;
import java.nio.file.Paths;

public class Test {
    public static void main(String[] args)
                                    throws IOException {
        Path src = Paths.get("F:\\A\\B\\C\\Book.java");
        Path tgt = Paths.get("F:\\A\\B");
        Files.copy(src, tgt);
    }
}
```

What will be the result of compiling and executing Test class?

A. java.io.FileNotFoundException is thrown at runtime.

B. java.nio.file.FileAlreadyExistsException is thrown at runtime.

C. Program terminates successfully without copying 'Book.java' file.

D. 'Book.java' will be copied successfully to 'F:\A\B\' directory.

3.1.69 F: is accessible for reading and below is the directory structure for F:

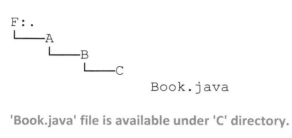

```
F:.
 └──A
     └──B
         └──C
                    Book.java
```

'Book.java' file is available under 'C' directory.

Given code of Test.java file:

```
package com.udayan.ocp;

import java.nio.file.Path;
import java.nio.file.Paths;

public class Test {
    public static void main(String[] args) {
        Path file = Paths.get("Book.java");
        System.out.println(file.toAbsolutePath());
    }
}
```

Actual path of generated class file is: "C:\classes\Test.class".

What will be the result of compiling and executing Test class?

A. NoSuchFileException is thrown at runtime.

B. FileNotFoundException is thrown at runtime.

C. F:\A\B\Book.java

D. C:\classes\Book.java

3.1.70 **F: is accessible for reading and below is the directory structure for F:**

```
F:.
└───process
        file.txt
        file.docx
        file.pdf
```

Above 3 files contain HELLO as the only word in the files. "file.txt" is a text file, "file.docx" is a Microsoft Word document and "file.pdf" is a PDF file.

Given code of Test.java file:

```java
package com.udayan.ocp;

import java.io.IOException;
import java.nio.file.Files;
import java.nio.file.Path;
import java.nio.file.Paths;
import java.util.stream.Stream;

public class Test {
    public static void main(String[] args)
                                throws IOException {
        Stream<Path> paths = Files.walk(
                    Paths.get("F:\\process"));
        paths.filter(
            path -> !Files.isDirectory(path)).forEach(
            path -> {
                try {
                    Files.readAllLines(path).stream()
                        .forEach(System.out::println);
                } catch (IOException e) {
                    System.out.println("FAILED");
                }
            }
        );
    }
}
```

What will be the result of compiling and executing Test class?

A. HELLO will be printed thrice on to the console.

B. HELLO will be printed twice and FAILED will be printed once.

C. HELLO will be printed once and FAILED will be printed twice.

D. FAILED will be printed thrice.

3.1.71   F: is accessible for reading/writing and below is the directory structure for F:

```
F:.
└──X
```

Directory X exists under F:.

Given code of Test.java file:

```java
package com.udayan.ocp;

import java.io.IOException;
import java.nio.file.Files;
import java.nio.file.Path;
import java.nio.file.Paths;

public class Test {
    public static void main(String[] args) throws IOException{
        Path path = Paths.get("F:\\X\\Y\\Z");
        Files.createDirectories(path);
    }
}
```

What will be the result of compiling and executing Test class?

A. Directory Y will be created under X and directory Z will be created under Y.

B. Only directory Y will be created under X.

C. An exception is thrown at runtime.

3.1.72 Given code of Test.java file:

```
package com.udayan.ocp;

import java.nio.file.Path;
import java.nio.file.Paths;

public class Test {
    public static void main(String[] args)  {
        Path path
            = Paths.get("F:", "user", "..", "udayan..");
        System.out.println(path.normalize());
    }
}
```

What will be the result of compiling and executing Test class?

A. F:\

B. F:\user

C. F:\user\udayan

D. F:\udayan..

3.1.73 C:\ is accessible for reading/writing and below is the content of 'C:\TEMP' folder:

```
C:\TEMP
|   msg
|
|
└──Parent
    └──Child
            Message.txt
```

'msg' is a symbolic link file for 'C:\TEMP\Parent\Child\Message.txt'.

Given code of Test.java file:

```java
package com.udayan.ocp;

import java.io.IOException;
import java.nio.file.Files;
import java.nio.file.Path;
import java.nio.file.Paths;

public class Test {
    public static void main(String[] args)
                                    throws IOException {
        Path src = Paths.get("C:", "TEMP", "msg");
        Files.delete(src);
    }
}
```

What will be the result of compiling and executing Test class?

A. The code executes successfully but doesn't delete anything.

B. The code executes successfully and deletes symbolic link file 'msg'.

C. The code executes successfully and deletes the file referred by symbolic link 'Message.txt'.

D. The code executes successfully and deletes all the directories and files in the path 'C:\TEMP\Parent\Child\Message.txt'.

3.1.74 Given structure of EMPLOYEE table:

```
EMPLOYEE (ID integer, FIRSTNAME varchar(100), LASTNAME
varchar(100), SALARY real, PRIMARY KEY (ID))
```

Given code of Test.java file:

```
package com.udayan.ocp;

import java.sql.*;

public class Test {
    public static void main(String[] args)
                                throws SQLException {
      String query = "Select * FROM EMPLOYEE";
      try (Connection con = DriverManager.getConnection(
      "jdbc:mysql://localhost:3306/ocp", "root", "password");
          Statement stmt = con.createStatement();
          ResultSet rs = stmt.executeQuery(query);) {
          System.out.println(rs.getMetaData()
                    .getColumnCount());  //Line 11
        }
    }
}
```

Also assume:

URL, username and password are correct.

SQL query is correct and valid.

The JDBC 4.2 driver jar is configured in the classpath.

EMPLOYEE table doesn't have any records.

What will be the result of compiling and executing Test class?

A. Compilation error

B. NullPointerException is thrown at Line 11

C. SQLException is thrown at Line 11

D. Code executes successfully and prints 4 on to the console.

3.1.75 Given structure of EMPLOYEE table:

```
EMPLOYEE (ID integer, FIRSTNAME varchar(100), LASTNAME
varchar(100), SALARY real, PRIMARY KEY (ID))
```

EMPLOYEE table contains below records:

```
101 John    Smith   12000
102 Sean    Smith   15000
103 Regina Williams  15500
104 Natasha    George 14600
```

Given code of Test.java file:

```java
package com.udayan.ocp;

import java.sql.*;
import java.util.Properties;

public class Test {
    public static void main(String[] args)
                             throws SQLException {
        String url = "jdbc:mysql://localhost:3306/ocp";
        Properties prop = new Properties();
        prop.put("user", "root");
        prop.put("password", "password");
        String query = "Select ID, FIRSTNAME, LASTNAME, " +
            "SALARY FROM EMPLOYEE ORDER BY ID";

        try (Connection con =
                DriverManager.getConnection(url, prop);
            Statement stmt = con.createStatement(
                ResultSet.TYPE_SCROLL_INSENSITIVE,
                ResultSet.CONCUR_READ_ONLY);
            ResultSet rs = stmt.executeQuery(query);) {
            rs.relative(1);
            System.out.println(rs.getString(2));
        }
    }
}
```

Also assume:

URL is correct and db credentials are: root/password.

SQL query is correct and valid.

The JDBC 4.2 driver jar is configured in the classpath.

What will be the result of compiling and executing Test class?

A. John

B. Sean

C. Smith

D. An exception is thrown at runtime.

3.1.76 Given structure of MESSAGES table:

```
MESSAGES (msg1 varchar(100), msg2 varchar(100))
```

MESSAGES table contains below records:

```
'Happy New Year!', 'Happy Holidays!'
```

Given code of Test.java file:

```java
package com.udayan.ocp;
import java.sql.*;

public class Test {
    public static void main(String[] args)
                            throws SQLException {
        String url = "jdbc:mysql://localhost:3306/ocp";
        String user = "root";
        String password = "password";
        String query = "DELETE FROM MESSAGES";
        try (Connection con =
                DriverManager.getConnection(url, user, password);
             Statement stmt = con.createStatement();
             ResultSet rs = stmt.executeQuery(query);)
        {
            rs.next();
            System.out.println(rs.getInt(1));
        }
    }
}
```

Also assume:
URL is correct and db credentials are: root/password.
SQL query is correct and valid.
The JDBC 4.2 driver jar is configured in the classpath.

What will be the result of compiling and executing Test class?

A. 0

B. 1

C. Compilation error

D. An exception is thrown at runtime

3.1.77 Given structure of EMPLOYEE table:

```
EMPLOYEE (ID integer, FIRSTNAME varchar(100), LASTNAME
varchar(100), SALARY real, PRIMARY KEY (ID))
```

EMPLOYEE table contains below records:
101 John   Smith 12000
102 Sean   Smith 15000
103 Regina Williams 15500
104 Natasha   George 14600

Given code of Test.java file:

```java
package com.udayan.ocp;

import java.sql.*;
import java.util.Properties;

public class Test {
    public static void main(String[] args)
                                    throws Exception {
        String url = "jdbc:mysql://localhost:3306/ocp";
        Properties prop = new Properties();
        prop.put("user", "root");
        prop.put("password", "password");
        String query = "Select ID, FIRSTNAME, LASTNAME, " +
            "SALARY FROM EMPLOYEE ORDER BY ID";
        try (Connection con =
                DriverManager.getConnection(url, prop);
            Statement stmt = con.createStatement(
                ResultSet.TYPE_SCROLL_INSENSITIVE,
                ResultSet.CONCUR_READ_ONLY);
            ResultSet rs = stmt.executeQuery(query);)
        {
            rs.afterLast();
            rs.relative(-1);
            rs.previous();
            System.out.println(rs.getInt(1));
        }
    }
}
```

Also assume:

URL, username and password are correct.

SQL query is correct and valid.

The JDBC 4.2 driver jar is configured in the classpath.

What will be the result of compiling and executing Test class?

A. 101

B. 102

C. 103

D. 104

3.1.78 **Given structure of EMPLOYEE table:**

```
EMPLOYEE (ID integer, FIRSTNAME varchar(100), LASTNAME
varchar(100), SALARY real, PRIMARY KEY (ID))
```

EMPLOYEE table contains below records:

```
101 John    Smith   12000
102 Sean    Smith   15000
103 Regina Williams  15500
104 Natasha    George 14600
```

Given code of Test.java file:

```java
package com.udayan.ocp;
import java.sql.*;

public class Test {
    public static void main(String[] args)
                                    throws Exception {
        String url = "jdbc:mysql://localhost:3306/ocp";
        String user = "root";
        String password = "password";
        String query = "Select ID, FIRSTNAME, LASTNAME, " +
            "SALARY FROM EMPLOYEE ORDER BY ID";
        try (Connection con = DriverManager
                        .getConnection(url, user, password);
            Statement stmt = con.createStatement(
                ResultSet.TYPE_SCROLL_SENSITIVE,
                ResultSet.CONCUR_UPDATABLE);
        ) {
            ResultSet rs = stmt.executeQuery(query);
            rs.afterLast();
            while (rs.previous()) {
                rs.updateDouble(4, rs.getDouble(4) + 1000);
                rs.updateRow();
            }

            rs = stmt.executeQuery(query);
            while(rs.next()) {
                System.out.println(rs.getDouble(4));
            }
        }
    }
}
```

Also assume:

URL, username and password are correct.

SQL query is correct and valid.

The JDBC 4.2 driver jar is configured in the classpath.

What will be the result of compiling and executing Test class?

A.	12000.0	B.	13000.0
	15000.0		16000.0
	15500.0		16500.0
	14600.0		15600.0
C.	13000.0	D.	12000.0
	15000.0		15000.0
	15500.0		15500.0
	14600.0		15600.0
E.	15600.0		
	16500.0		
	16000.0		
	13000.0		

3.1.79 Given structure of EMPLOYEE table:

```
EMPLOYEE (ID integer, FIRSTNAME varchar(100), LASTNAME
varchar(100), SALARY real, PRIMARY KEY (ID))
```

EMPLOYEE table contains below records:

```
101 John    Smith  12000
102 Sean    Smith  15000
103 Regina Williams  15500
104 Natasha   George 14600
```

Given code of Test.java file:

```java
package com.udayan.ocp;

import java.sql.*;

public class Test {
    public static void main(String[] args)
                                    throws SQLException {
        String url = "jdbc:mysql://localhost:3306/ocp";
        String user = "root";
        String password = "password";
        try (Connection con = DriverManager
                    .getConnection(url, user, password);
            Statement stmt = con.createStatement(
                ResultSet.TYPE_SCROLL_INSENSITIVE,
                ResultSet.CONCUR_READ_ONLY);
        ) {
            ResultSet res1 = stmt.executeQuery(
              "SELECT * FROM EMPLOYEE ORDER BY ID");
            ResultSet res2 = stmt.executeQuery(
              "SELECT * FROM EMPLOYEE ORDER BY ID DESC");
            res1.next();
            System.out.println(res1.getInt(1));
            res2.next();
            System.out.println(res2.getInt(1));
        }
    }
}
```

Also assume:

URL is correct and db credentials are: root/password.

SQL query is correct and valid.

The JDBC 4.2 driver jar is configured in the classpath.

What will be the result of compiling and executing Test class?

A.	101 104	B.	104 101
C.	An exception is thrown at runtime	D.	None of the other options

3.1.80 Which of the following code will create/return a Locale object for the JVM, on which your code is running?

A. Locale.getDefaultLocale();

B. Locale.getLocale();

C. System.getDefault();

D. Locale.getDefault();

3.1.81 Given code of Test.java file:

```java
package com.udayan.ocp;

import java.util.Locale;

public class Test {
    public static void main(String[] args) {
        Locale loc = new Locale("it", "IT");
        System.out.println(loc
            .getDisplayCountry()); //Line 8
        System.out.println(loc
            .getDisplayCountry(Locale.CHINA)); //Line 9
        System.out.println(loc
            .getDisplayLanguage()); //Line 10
        System.out.println(loc
            .getDisplayLanguage(Locale.CHINA)); //Line 11
    }
}
```

Which of the following statement is correct about above code?

A. Line 8 and Line 10 cause compilation error.

B. Line 9 and Line 11 cause compilation error.

C. Given code compiles successfully.

3.1.82 Which of the following statements successfully create a Locale instance?
Select ALL that apply.

A. `Locale loc1 = new Locale();`

B. `Locale loc2 = new Locale(loc1);`

C. `Locale loc3 = new Locale("");`

D. `Locale loc4 = new Locale("", "");`

E. `Locale loc5 = new Locale("", "", "");`

3.1.83 Given code of Test.java file:

```
package com.udayan.ocp;

import java.text.*;
import java.time.format.DateTimeFormatter;
import java.util.Locale;

public class Test {
    public static void main(String[] args) {
        DateTimeFormatter dateFormatter = DateTimeFormatter
                    .ofPattern("dd-MM-uuuu"); //Line n1

        System.out.println(dateFormatter
                        .parse("10-5-2019")); //Line n2

        NumberFormat currFormatter = NumberFormat
                .getCurrencyInstance(Locale.US); //Line n3
        System.out.println(currFormatter
                        .parse("$7.00")); //Line n4
    }
}
```

What will be the result of compiling and executing Test class?

A. Code compiles successfully and on execution no exception is thrown at runtime

B. Code compiles successfully and on execution an exception is raised by Line n2

C. Code compiles successfully and on execution an exception is thrown by Line n4

D. Line n2 causes compilation failure

E. Line n4 causes compilation failure

3.1.84 Given code of Test.java file:

```java
package com.udayan.ocp;

class Counter implements Runnable {
    private static int i = 3;

    public void run() {
        System.out.print(i--);
    }
}

public class Test {
    public static void main(String[] args) {
        Thread t1 = new Thread(new Counter());
        Thread t2 = new Thread(new Counter());
        Thread t3 = new Thread(new Counter());
        Thread[] threads = {t1, t2, t3};
        for(Thread thread : threads) {
            thread.start();
        }
    }
}
```

What will be the result of compiling and executing Test class?

A. It will always print 321

B. It will print three digits 321 but order can be different

C. It will always print 210

D. It will print three digits 210 but order can be different

E. None of the other options

3.1.85 Given code of Test.java file:

```java
package com.udayan.ocp;

import java.util.concurrent.*;

class MyCallable implements Callable<Integer> {
    private Integer i;

    public MyCallable(Integer i) {
        this.i = i;
    }

    public Integer call() throws Exception {
        return --i;
    }
}

public class Test {
    public static void main(String[] args) {
        ExecutorService es =
            Executors.newSingleThreadExecutor();
        MyCallable callable = new MyCallable(1);
        System.out.println(es.submit(callable).get());
        es.shutdown();
    }
}
```

What will be the result of compiling and executing Test class?

A. 1

B. 0

C. Compilation error

D. An exception is thrown at runtime

3.1.86 Given code of Test.java file:

```java
package com.udayan.ocp;

import java.util.List;
import java.util.concurrent.CopyOnWriteArrayList;

public class Test {
    public static void main(String[] args) {
        List<String> list = new CopyOnWriteArrayList<>();
        list.add("Melon");
        list.add("Apple");
        list.add("Banana");
        list.add("Mango");
        for(String s : list) {
            list.removeIf(str -> str.startsWith("M"));
            System.out.println(s);
        }
    }
}
```

What will be the result of compiling and executing Test class?

A.	Melon Apple Banana Mango	B.	Apple Banana
C.	An exception is thrown at runtime	D.	Compilation error

3.1.87 Given code of Test.java file:

```
package com.udayan.ocp;

import java.util.concurrent.*;

public class Test {
    public static void main(String[] args)
            throws InterruptedException, ExecutionException {
        ExecutorService es =
                Executors.newSingleThreadExecutor();
        Future<String> f = es.submit(() -> "HELLO");
        System.out.println(f.get());
        es.shutdown();
    }
}
```

What will be the result of compiling and executing Test class?

A. Compilation error

B. null

C. HELLO

D. An exception is thrown at runtime

3.1.88 Given code of Test.java file:

```
package com.udayan.ocp;

import java.util.stream.IntStream;

public class Test {
    public static void main(String[] args) {
        IntStream.rangeClosed(1, 10).parallel()
            .forEach(System.out::println);
    }
}
```

What will be the result of compiling and executing Test class?

A. It will print numbers from 1 to 10 in ascending order.

B. It will print numbers form 1 to 10 in descending order.

C. It will print numbers form 1 to 10 but not in any specific order.

3.1.89 Given code of Test.java file:

```
package com.udayan.ocp;

import java.util.stream.IntStream;

public class Test {
    public static void main(String[] args) {
        int res = IntStream.rangeClosed(1, 1000).parallel()
            .filter( i -> i > 50).findFirst().getAsInt();
        System.out.println(res);
    }
}
```

What will be the result of compiling and executing Test class?

A. It will always print 51.

B. It will print any number between 51 and 1000.

C. It will always print 50.

D. It will print any number between 1 and 50.

3.1.90   Given code of Test.java file:

```java
package com.udayan.ocp;

import java.util.concurrent.*;

class Adder extends RecursiveAction {
    private int from;
    private int to;
    int total = 0;

    Adder(int from, int to) {
        this.from = from;
        this.to = to;
    }

    @Override
    protected void compute() {
        if ((to - from) <= 4) {
            int sum = 0;
            for(int i = from; i <= to; i++) {
                sum += i;
            }
            total+=sum;
        } else {
            int mid = (from + to) / 2;
            Adder first = new Adder(from, mid);
            Adder second = new Adder(mid + 1, to);
            invokeAll(first, second);
        }
    }
}

public class Test {
    public static void main(String[] args) {
        Adder adder = new Adder(1, 5); //Line 34
        ForkJoinPool pool = new ForkJoinPool(4);
        pool.invoke(adder);
        System.out.println(adder.total);
    }
}
```

What will be the result of compiling and executing Test class?

A. It will print 0 on to the console.

B. It will print 15 on to the console.

C. It can print any number between 0 and 15.

D. None of the other options.

3.2   Answers of Practice Test - 3 with Explanation

3.1.1   Answer: D

Reason:
Parent is a concrete class.
In java it is possible for abstract class to not have any abstract methods. class Child is abstract, it extends Parent and doesn't contain any abstract method. It contains special main method, so JVM can invoke this method.

Rest of the code is normal java code. new Parent().m(); creates an instance of Parent class and invokes method m() on that instance. "Parent" is printed on to the console.

3.1.2   Answer: B

Reason:
Object class contains:
```
public boolean equals(Object obj) {
    return (this == obj);
}
```

class Player doesn't override equals(Object) method rather it overloads the equals method: equals(Player).
As p2 is of Object type, p1.equals(p2) invokes the equals(Object) method defined in Object class and as this method compares the reference (memory address), hence it returns false in this case.

Below code will correctly override equals(Object) method in the Player class:
```
public boolean equals(Object player) {
    if(player instanceof Player) {
        Player p = (Player)player;
        if(this.name.equals(p.name) && this.age == p.age)
            return true;
    }
    return false;
}
```

3.1.3   Answer: C

Reason:
To call another constructor of the class use this(10, 20);
No-argument constructor of Point class causes compilation error.

3.1.4   Answer: D

Reason:
Starting with JDK 8, a Java interface can have default and static methods. So, no issues in Printer1 and Printer2 interfaces.

Printer class implements both the interfaces: Printer1 and Printer 2. static method cannot be overridden, hence doesn't conflict with default method.

No compilation error anywhere. On execution default method is invoked and 'Printer1' is printed on to the console.

If you want to invoke static method defined in Printer2 interface, then use:
Printer2.print();

3.1.5   Answer: D

Reason:
case labels accept constant names only.
case TrafficLight.RED:, case TrafficLight.YELLOW: and case TrafficLight.GREEN: cause compilation error.

Correct case labels should be:
case RED:, case YELLOW: and case GREEN:

3.1.6   Answer: B

Reason:
enums JobStatus and TestResult are siblings as both implicitly extend from java.lang.Enum class.

Siblings cannot be compared using double equals operator (==).

equals(Object) method accepts any instance which Object can refer to, which means all the instances.

3.1.7   Answer: A

Reason:
There are 2 parts: 1st one is referring the name of inner class, Inner and 2nd one is creating an instance of inner class, Inner.
Now main method is outside Outer class only, so inner class can be referred by one way only and that is by using outer class name: Outer.Inner.

As, Inner is Regular inner class, so instance of outer class is needed for creating the instance of inner class. Instance of outer class, Outer can only be obtained by new Outer(). So, instance of inner class can be created by: new Outer().new Inner();
Also note, keyword 'this' is not allowed static main method.

3.1.8   Answer: A

Reason:
In this example, inner class's variable var shadows the outer class's variable var. So output is Java.
Few points to note here:
1. If inner class shadows the variable of outer class, then Java compiler prepends 'this.' to the variable. System.out.println(var); is replaced by System.out.println(this.var);
 2. If inner class does not shadow the variable of outer class, then Java compiler prepends "outer_class.this." to the variable. So, if class Q doesn't override the variable of class P, then System.out.println(var); would be replaced by System.out.println(P.this.var);

In the given example, if you provide System.out.println(P.this.var); inside print() method, then output would be 100.

3.1.9   Answer: A, C

Reason:
static initialization block defined inside Outer class is invoked when static method sayHello is invoked.

Method-local inner class can be defined inside methods(static and non-static) and initialization blocks(static and non-static).
But like Regular inner class, method-local inner class cannot define anything static, except static final variables.

new Inner(); invokes the no-argument constructor of Inner class. So, System.out.println("HELLO") can either be provided inside no-argument constructor or instance initialization block.

3.1.10   Answer: A

Reason:
@Override annotation is used for overriding method. But PrintMessage (P in upper case) method of anonymous inner class doesn't override printMessage (p in lower case) method of its super class, Message. Hence, @Override annotation causes compilation error.

3.1.11   Answer: A, D

Reason:
Instance of anonymous inner class can be assigned to static variable, instance variable, local variable, method parameter and return value.
In this question, anonymous inner class instance is assigned to method parameter.

printPrice(null); => No compilation error as asked in the question but it would throw NullPointerException at runtime,
printPrice(new Sellable()); => Cannot create an instance of Sellable type,
printPrice(new Sellable() {}); => getPrice() method is not implemented.

3.1.12 Answer: A

Reason:
interface I2 is implicitly public and static (Nested interface). class A1 is implicitly public and static (Nested class). class A2 is implicitly public and static (Nested class).

You cannot explicitly specify protected, default and private for nested classes and nested interfaces inside an interface.

3.1.13 Answer: C

Reason:
@FunctionalInterface annotation is used to tag a functional interface.

3.1.14 Answer: B

Reason:
Lambda expression can be assigned to static variable, instance variable, local variable, method parameter or return type. method(I10, String) accepts two arguments, hence method(s -> System.out.println(s.toUpperCase())); would cause compilation error.

When curly brackets are used then semicolon is necessary, hence method(s -> { System.out.println(s.toUpperCase()) }, "good morning!"); would cause compilation error.

method(s -> s.toUpperCase(), "good morning!"); is a legal syntax but, nothing is printed to the console.

3.1.15 Answer: C

Reason:
In real world programming you will hardly find a bean class implementing Comparator but it is a legal code. A bean class generally implements Comparable interface to define natural ordering.

Student class in this case correctly implements Comparator<Student> interface by overriding compare(Student, Student) method. Note, this compare method will sort in descending order of Student's name.

list.sort(...) accepts an argument of Comparator<Student> type. new Student() provides the instance of Comparator<Student> type. It sorts list in descending order of Students' name.

Output is:
{Rob, OCP}
{John, OCA}
{Jack, OCP}

3.1.16 Answer: A

Reason:
'GenericPrinter<T>' is generic type and is defined correctly.

'AbstractGenericPrinter<X,Y,T>' is also a generic type and extends another generic type 'GenericPrinter<T>'.

NOTE: If a class extends from generic type, then it must pass type arguments to its super class. Third type parameter, 'T' in 'AbstractGenericPrinter<X,Y,T>' correctly passed type argument to super class, 'GenericPrinter<T>'.

Below codes will not compile:
abstract class AbstractGenericPrinter<X,Y> extends GenericPrinter<T>{} => No way to pass type argument to the type parameter, T of super class.
abstract class AbstractGenericPrinter extends GenericPrinter<T>{} => No way to pass type argument to the type parameter, T of super class.

But below codes will compile successfully:
abstract class AbstractGenericPrinter<X,Y> extends GenericPrinter<String>{} => Type argument, 'String' is passed to the type parameter, T of super class.
abstract class AbstractGenericPrinter extends GenericPrinter<String>{} => Type argument, 'String' is passed to the type parameter, T of super class.

3.1.17 Answer: D

Reason:
Line 8 is a valid syntax but as upper-bounded wildcard is used, hence add operation is not supported. Line 9 causes compilation failure.

3.1.18 Answer: B

Reason:
static declaration of type parameter is not allowed, only instance declaration is possible.

'static T obj;' causes compilation failure.

3.1.19 Answer: D

Reason:
Reference variable to which lambda expression is assigned is known as target type. Target type can be a static variable, instance variable, local variable, method parameter or return type. Lambda expression doesn't work without target type and target type must be a functional interface.
In this case, println(Object) method is invoked but Object is a class and not a functional interface, hence no lambda expression can be passed directly to println method.

But you can first assign lambda expression to target type and then pass the target type reference variable to println(Object) method:
Operator<String> operator = (s1, s2) -> s1 + s2;
System.out.println(operator);

Or you can typecast lambda expression to target type. e.g. following works:
System.out.println((Operator<String>)(String s1, String s2) -> s1 + s2);
System.out.println((Operator<String>)(s1, s2) -> s1 + s2);
System.out.println((Operator<String>)(s1, s2) -> { return s1 + s2; });

3.1.20 Answer: B

Reason:
listIterator(index); method allows to have the starting point at any index. Allowed values are between 0 and size of the list.

ListIterator extends Iterator and can be used to iterate in both the directions. If you want to iterate backward then pass the no. of elements in the list to listIterator(index) method. In this case, 'list.listIterator(5);'.

To iterate backward, use hasPrevious() and previous() methods.

3.1.21 Answer: C

Reason:
TreeMap is the sorted map on the basis on natural ordering of keys (if comparator is not provided).
enum TrafficLight is used as a key for TreeMap. The natural order for enum elements is the sequence in which they are defined.

A map doesn't allow duplicate keys. 'map.put(TrafficLight.YELLOW, "READY TO STOP");' replaces the previous value corresponding to 'TrafficLight.YELLOW' with the new value 'READY TO STOP'.

Value corresponding to 'RED' is printed first, followed by value corresponding to 'YELLOW' and finally value for 'GREEN' is printed.

3.1.22 Answer: A

Reason:
LinkedList implements both List and Queue. In this example reference type controls the LinkedList behavior.

```
list.add("ONE"); => [ONE].
list.add("TWO"); => [ONE,TWO]. Adds to the last.
list.remove(1); => [ONE]. Removes from the specified index.
System.out.println(list); => [ONE].

queue.add("ONE"); => [*ONE].  * represents HEAD of the queue.
queue.add("TWO"); => [*ONE,TWO]. Adds to the end of the queue.
queue.remove(); => [*TWO]. Removes from the HEAD of the queue.
System.out.println(queue); => [TWO].
```

3.1.23 Answer: B

Reason:
Even though lambda expression is for the compare method of Comparator interface, but in the code name "Comparator" is not used hence import statement is not needed here.
Expressions
(s1, s2) -> s2.length()-s1.length() and (s2, s1) -> s1.length()-s2.length() displays the output in reversed order.

3.1.24   Answer: B

Reason:
Comparator is comparing on the basis of email domain: gmail.com and outlook.com.
Insertion order is:
udayan@outlook.com
sachin@outlook.com
sachin@gmail.com
udayan@gmail.com

gmail records should appear before outlook records. So sorting order is:
sachin@gmail.com
udayan@gmail.com
udayan@outlook.com
sachin@outlook.com

NOTE: It is not specified, what to do in case email domain is matching. So, for matching email domain, records are left at insertion order.

3.1.25   Answer: B

Reason:
If null Comparator is passed to sort method, then elements are sorted in natural order (based on Comparable interface implementation).

As list is of String type and String implements Comparable, hence list elements are sorted in ascending order.

3.1.26   Answer: E

Reason:
Streams are lazily evaluated, which means if terminal operations such as: forEach, count, toArray, reduce, collect, findFirst, findAny, anyMatch, allMatch, sum, min, max, average etc. are not present, the given stream pipeline is not evaluated and hence peek() method doesn't print anything on to the console.

3.1.27 Answer: C

Reason:
chars() method in String class returns IntStream, all the elements in this stream are stored as int value of corresponding char.

filter(Test::isDirection) => Returns the stream consisting of int (char) for which isDirection method returns true. isDirection method returns true for 'N', 'E', 'W' and 'S' only for other characters (including whitespace character) it returns false.

forEach(c -> System.out.print((char)c)); => forEach method typecast int value to char and hence NEWS is printed on to the console.

3.1.28 Answer: D

Reason:
ArrayDeque cannot store null, hence Line n2 throws NullPointerException exception. ArrayDeque doesn't store null because its poll() method returns null in case ArrayDeque is empty. If null element was allowed, then it would be not possible to find out whether poll() method is returning null element or ArrayDeque is empty.

3.1.29 Answer: A

Reason:
Syntax is correct and without any errors. Methods are chained from left to right.
new StringBuilder(" olleH") => " olleH"
" olleH".reverse() => "Hello "
"Hello ".append("!dlroW") => "Hello !dlroW"
"Hello !dlroW".reverse() => "World! olleH"

3.1.30 Answer: C

Reason:
replaceAll(UnaryOperator<E> operator) is the default method added in List interface.

interface UnaryOperator<T> extends Function<T, T>.

326

As List is of Integer type, this means operator must be of UnaryOperator<Integer> type only.

'list.replaceAll(operator);' causes compilation error as operator is of UnaryOperator<Long> type.

3.1.31 Answer: B

Reason:
compose & andThen are default methods defined in Function interface. Starting with JDK 8, interfaces can define default and static methods.

g.compose(f); means first apply f and then g. Same result is achieved by f.andThen(g); => first apply f and then g.
f.apply(10) = 10 + 10 = 20 and g.apply(20) = 20 * 20 = 400.

3.1.32 Answer: B

Reason:
andThen is the default method defined in Consumer interface, so it is invoked on consumer reference variable.

Value passed in the argument of accept method is passed to both the consumer objects. So, for understanding purpose Line 10 can be split into: add.accept(10); print.accept(10);

add.accept(10) is executed first and it increments the count variable by 10, so count becomes 11.

Then print.accept(10); method prints 10 on to the console.

Check the code of andThen method defined in Consumer interface to understand it better.

3.1.33 Answer: B

Reason:
There is only BooleanSupplier available in JDK 8.0.

3.1.34 Answer: C

Reason:
replaceAll(UnaryOperator<E> operator) is the default method added in List interface.

interface UnaryOperator<T> extends Function<T, T>.

As List is of Integer type, this means operator must be of UnaryOperator<Integer> type only. Its accept method should have signature: Integer apply(Integer s);

Lambda expression 'i -> -i++' is correctly defined for apply method.

Unary post increment(++) operator has higher precedence than unary minus(-) operator.

i -> -i++ = i -> -(i++). NO COMPILATION ERROR here.

Post increment operator is applied after the value is used, which means in this case list elements are replaced with -10, -100 and -1000.

3.1.35 Answer: A

Reason:
BiPredicate<T, U> : boolean test(T t, U u);
BiPredicate interface accepts 2 type parameters and these parameters (T,U) are passed to test method, which returns primitive boolean.
In this case, 'BiPredicate<String, String>' means test method will have declaration: 'boolean test(String s1, String s2)'.
'String::contains' is equivalent to '(str1, str2) -> str1.contains(str2)'
This is an example of "Reference to an Instance Method of an Arbitrary Object of a Particular Type" and not "method reference to static method", predicate declaration is correct.

BiFunction<T, U, R> : R apply(T t, U u);
BiFunction interface accepts 3 type parameters, first 2 parameters (T,U) are passed to apply method and 3rd type parameter is the return type of apply method.
In this case, 'BiFunction<String, String, Boolean>' means apply method will have declaration: 'Boolean apply(String str1, String str2)'. Given lambda expression '(str1, str2)

-> { return predicate.test(str1, str2) ? true : false; };' is the correct implementation of BiFunction<String, String, Boolean> interface.

Please note, the lambda expressions makes use of predicate declared above.

func.apply("Tomato", "at") returns true as "Tomato" contains "at", hence true is printed on to the console.

Also note that usage of ternary operator (?:) is not needed here, you can simply write 'return predicate.test(str1, str2);' as well.

3.1.36 Answer: C

Reason:
optional --> [null]
optional.isPresent() returns false, hence Message object is returned. 'msg' filed of this object refers to "Good Morning!", which is returned by toString() method.

3.1.37 Answer: E

Reason:
count() is terminal operation and it needs all the elements of the stream to return the result. So, all the stream elements will be processed.

list.stream() => [-80, 100, -40, 25, 200].

NOTE: a new instance of Predicate is used, hence every time ctr will be initialize to 1.

For -80, Output is '1.' but predicate returns false, hence element is not included.

For 100, '1.' is appended to previous output, so on console you will see '1.1.' and predicate returns true, hence element is included.

You don't have to count the filtered elements as result of count() is not printed.

As 5 elements in the stream so final output will be: '1.1.1.1.1.'

3.1.38 Answer: B

Reason:
Method signature for anyMatch method:
boolean anyMatch(Predicate<? super T>) : Returns true if any of the stream element matches the given Predicate. If stream is empty, it returns false and predicate is not evaluated.

ref is a local variable and it is used within lambda expression. ++ref causes compilation failure as variable ref should be effectively final.

3.1.39 Answer: C

Reason:
Optional.of(null); throws NullPointerException as null argument is passed.

You can use 'Optional.ofNullable(null);' to create an empty optional.

3.1.40 Answer: E

Reason:
Only 3 primitive variants available: OptionalDouble, OptionalInt and OptionalLong.

3.1.41 Answer: C

Reason:
stream.mapToInt(i -> i) => returns an instance of IntStream.

average() method of all the 3 primitive streams (IntStream, LongStream & DoubleStream) return an instance of OptionalDouble. OptionalDouble has getAsDouble() method and not getAsInt() method.

3.1.42 Answer: B

Reason:
Given reduce method concatenates null + "One" + "Two" + "Three" and hence the output is: 'nullOneTwoThree'.

To concatenate just the stream contents, use below code:

stream.reduce("", (s1, s2) -> s1 + s2)
OR
stream.reduce((s1, s2) -> s1 + s2).get()

3.1.43 Answer: B

Reason:
Given code sorts the stream in natural order (a appears before b, b appears before c and so on).

To get the expected output, stream should be sorted in ascending order of length of the string. Replacing 'stream.sorted()' with 'stream.sorted((s1,s2) -> s1.length() - s2.length())' will do the trick.

3.1.44 Answer: A

Reason:
'TreeSet::new' is same as '() -> new TreeSet()'

TreeSet contains unique elements and in sorted order, in this case natural order.

Output will always be: [c, c++, java, python]

3.1.45 Answer: B

Reason:
s -> s.chars() is of IntStream type as chars() method returns instance of IntStream type.

All 4 are valid method names but each specify different parameters. Only faltMapToInt can accept argument of IntStream type.

3.1.46   Answer: C, D

Reason:
As Comparable and Comparator are interfaces, so Fruit class can implement both the interfaces.
Given code compiles successfully.
compareTo(Fruit) method of Comparable interface will help to sort in ascending order of Fruit's name and compare(Fruit, Fruit) method of Comparator interface will help to sort in ascending order of Fruit's country of origin.
By looking at the expected output it is clear that output is arranged in descending order of Fruit's country of origin. This means Comparator needs to be used in reversed order.
Out of the given options 'list.stream().sorted(new Fruit().reversed()).forEach(System.out::println);' will display the expected output.

'list.stream().sorted()' sorts Fruit instances on the basis of ascending order of their names, not the correct option.
'list.stream().sorted(new Fruit())' sorts Fruit instances on the basis of ascending order of their country of origin, not the correct option.
'list.stream().sorted(Comparator.comparing(f -> f.countryOfOrigin, Fruit::comp))':
keyExtractor is accepting Fruit object and returning countryOfOrigin, which is of String type. The 2nd argument passed is Fruit::comp, which is keyComparator and it sorts the Fruit objects in descending order of the key (courntryOfOrigin) in this case. Hence this is also a correct option.

3.1.47   Answer: D

Reason:
Method m1() throws Exception (checked) and it declares to throw it, so no issues with method m1().

But main() method neither provides catch handler nor throws clause and hence main method causes compilation error.

Handle or Declare rule should be followed for checked exception if you are not re-throwing it.

3.1.48 Answer: B

Reason:
System.out.println(1/0); throws ArithmeticException, handler is available in inner catch block, it executes and prints "Inner" to the console.
throw e; re-throws the exception.

But before exception instance is forwarded to outer catch block, inner finally gets executed and prints "Finally 1" to the console.
In outer try-catch block, handler for ArithmeticException is available, so outer catch block gets executed and prints "Outer" to the console.

3.1.49 Answer: C

Reason:
main(args) method is invoked recursively without specifying any exit condition, so this code ultimately throws java.lang.StackOverflowError. StackOverflowError is a subclass of Error type and not Exception type, hence it is not handled. Stack trace is printed to the console and program ends abruptly.

Java doesn't allow to catch specific checked exceptions if these are not thrown by the statements inside try block.
catch(java.io.FileNotFoundException ex) {} will cause compilation error in this case as main(args); will never throw FileNotFoundException. But Java allows to catch Exception type, hence catch (Exception ex) {} doesn't cause any compilation error.

3.1.50 Answer: C

Reason:
Any RuntimeException can be thrown without any need it to be declared in throws clause of surrounding method.

'throw (RuntimeException)e;' doesn't cause any compilation error.

Even though variable 'e' is type casted to RuntimeException but exception object is still of ArithmeticException, which is caught in main method and 'AE' is printed to the console.

3.1.51 Answer: B

Reason:
Classes in Exception framework are normal java classes, hence null can be used wherever instances of Exception classes are used, so Line 10 compiles successfully.
No issues with Line 16 as method m() declares to throw SQLException and main method code correctly handles it.

Program compiles successfully but on execution, NullPointerException is thrown, stack trace is printed on to the console and program ends abruptly.

If you debug the code, you would find that internal routine for throwing null exception causes NullPointerException.

3.1.52 Answer: A

Reason:
For null resources, close() method is not called and hence NullPointerException is not thrown at runtime.

HELLO is printed on to the console.

3.1.53 Answer: C

Reason:
In a multi-catch block, type of reference variable (ex in this case) is the common base class of all the Exception types mentioned, 'MyException' and 'YourException'.
This means ex is of RuntimeException. Method log() is not available in RuntimeException or its super classes.

ex.log(); causes compilation failure.

3.1.54   Answer: A

Reason:
execute() method throws an instance of SQLException.

Just before finding the matching handler, Java runtime executes close() method. This method throws an instance of IOException but it gets suppressed and an instance of SQLException is thrown.

e.getSuppressed() returns Throwable [] whose 1st element is the instance of suppressed exception, IOException.

'e.getSuppressed()[0].getMessage()' prints IOException on to the console.

3.1.55   Answer: C

Reason:
On execution, 'args.length == 0' returns true and 'assert false : changeMsg("Bye");' is executed.
'changeMsg("Bye")' method makes msg to refer to "Bye" and null is returned.
An instance of AssertionError is thrown with message null.
Remaining statements are ignored and program terminates abruptly.

NOTE: Though this class compiles successfully but Assertion mechanism is not implemented appropriately. There are 2 issues:
1. Assertion mechanism is used to validate the arguments of public method and
2. changeMsg("Bye") method causes side effect as it changes the class variable, 'msg'.

3.1.56   Answer: B

Reason:
0th day in epoch is: 1970-01-01, 1st day in epoch is: 1970-01-02 and so on.

And if you pass a negative number, then it represents earlier days.

LocalDate.ofEpochDay(-1); --> {1969-12-31}.

3.1.57 Answer: B

Reason:
DateTimeFormatter.ISO_INSTANT is used by the toString() method of Instant class and it formats or parses an instant in UTC, such as '2018-10-01T15:02:01.231Z'.

EPOCH instant is: 1970-01-01T00:00:00Z and it is printed to the console.

NOTE: nano portion is 0 in EPOCH instant, hence it is ignored by toString() method.

3.1.58 Answer: C

Reason:
As Period is expressed in terms of Years, Months and Days, Duration is expressed in terms of Hours, Minutes and Seconds.
String representation of Period starts with "P" whereas String representation of Duration starts with "PT".

You should be aware of following 'of' methods for the exam:
Duration.ofDays(long days) => Returns a Duration instance with specified number of days converted to hours. -2 days equals to -48 hours.
Duration.ofHours(long hours) => Returns a Duration instance with specified number of hours.
Duration.ofMinutes(long minutes) => Returns a Duration instance with specified number of minutes.
Duration.ofSeconds(long seconds) => Returns a Duration instance with specified number of seconds, nanos field is set to 0. NOTE: if nanos field is 0, toString ignores it.
Duration.ofMillis(long millis) => Returns a Duration instance with passed value converted to seconds and nano seconds.
Duration.ofNanos(long nanos) => Returns a Duration instance with passed value converted to seconds and nono seconds.

3.1.59 Answer: A

Reason:
zIndia --> {2019-01-01T00:00+05:30[Asia/Kolkata]}.
zIndia.withZoneSameLocal(us) => {2019-01-01T00:00-08:00[America/Los_Angeles]}. It just changes the Zone but keeps the date and time same and this is what zUS supposed to refer to.

Duration.between(zIndia, zUS) returns 'PT13H30M' in this case. So, people of Los Angeles have to wait for 13 hours 30 minutes to celebrate the new year.

zIndia.withZoneSameInstant(us) => {2018-12-31T10:30-08:00[America/Los_Angeles]}. It just converts India time to Los Angeles time.
As both zIndia and zUS will refer to same instance of time, hence 'Duration.between(zIndia, zUS)' would return 'PT0S'. And this is not expected.

NOTE: If you intend to use 'zIndia.withZoneSameInstant(us);', then Line 15 should be changed as below:

System.out.println(Duration.between(zUS.toLocalDateTime(), zIndia.toLocalDateTime())); // would print 'PT13H30M'.

To get positive duration value, first parameter should be earlier date/time.

3.1.60 Answer: B

Reason:
DateTimeFormatter.ofPattern(String) accepts String argument. Format string is also correct.
d represents day-of-month, M represents month-of-year and u represents year.

New Date/Time API has format method in DateTimeFormatter as well as LocalDate, LocalTime, LocalDateTime, ZonedDateTime classes.

formatter.format(date) returns "04-11-2018" and date.format(formatter) returns "04-11-2018" and hence 'true' is printed on to the console.

3.1.61 Answer: A

Reason:
Correct statement is:
Period represents date-based amount of time whereas Duration represents time-based amount of time.

Period is date-based, such as '10 years, 5 months and 3 days'.
Duration is time-based, such as '5 hours, 10 minutes and 44 seconds'.

Oracle Certified Professional: Java SE 8 Programmer II

Instant is to just represent an instantaneous point on the time-line.

Check the Javadoc of above classes.

3.1.62   Answer: C

Reason:
reader.ready() => Returns true if input buffer is not empty or if bytes are available to be read from the underlying byte stream, otherwise false.

reader.skip(long n) => This method is inherited from Reader class and skips the passed n characters.

Let's check how the file contents are processed. Initially available stream: "sdaleteftdeagncedk".

reader.ready() => returns true.
reader.skip(1); => skips 's'. Available Stream: "daleteftdeagncedk".
reader.skip(1); => skips 'd'. Available Stream: "aleteftdeagncedk".
reader.read(); => Reads 'a' and prints it. Available Stream: "leteftdeagncedk".

reader.ready() => returns true.
reader.skip(1); => skips 'l'. Available Stream: "eteftdeagncedk".
reader.skip(1); => skips 'e'. Available Stream: "teftdeagncedk".
reader.read(); => Reads 't' and prints it. Available Stream: "eftdeagncedk".

And so on, until whole stream is exhausted.

'attack' will be printed on to the console.

3.1.63   Answer: C

Reason:
Format specifier, 'n' is for newline.

NOTE: System.out.printf(...) is same as System.out.format(...).

3.1.64 Answer: B

Reason:
As Student class doesn't implement Serializable or Externalizable, hence 'oos.writeObject(stud);' throws java.io.NotSerializableException.

To persist Student objects using ObjectInputStream, Student class should implement Serializable.

3.1.65 Answer: B

Reason:
Once the close() method is called on BufferedWriter, same stream cannot be used for writing.

bw.newLine(); tries to append a newline character to the closed stream and hence IOException is thrown. catch handler is provided for IOException. Control goes inside and prints 'IOException' on to the console.

3.1.66 Answer: C

Reason:
main method declares to throw IOException, hence given code compiles successfully.

Even though, bos.close(); method is invoked but it is not invoked in finally block. If statements before bos.close(); throw any exception, then bos.close() will not execute and this will result in resource leak.

To avoid resource leak, either use try-with-resources statement or provide try-finally block.

3.1.67 Answer: A

Reason:
Initially F:\ is blank.

new File("F:\\f1.txt"); => It just creates a Java object containing abstract path 'F:\f1.txt'. NO physical file is created on the disc.

Constructors of FileWriter and PrintWriter can create a new file but not directory.

new FileWriter("F:\\dir\\f2.txt"); => Throws IOException as 'dir' is a folder, which doesn't exist. This constructor can't create folders/directories.

new PrintWriter("F:\\f3.txt"); would have created 'f3.txt' on the disk but as previous statement threw IOException, hence program ends abruptly after printing the stack trace.

3.1.68 Answer: B

Reason:
Path is an abstract path and farthest element can be a file or directory.

src refers to Path object, F:\\A\\B\\C\\Book.java and its farthest element, 'Book.java' is a file (and it exists).

tgt refers to Path object, F:\\A\\B and its farthest element, 'B' is a directory (and it exists).

Files.copy(src, tgt) copies the farthest element. 'Book.java' can't be copied to 'B' as it is a directory and it is not allowed to have file and directory of same name to be present at same location. Hence, java.nio.file.FileAlreadyExistsException is thrown at runtime.

If you change tgt to Paths.get("F:\\A\\C\\"); then 'Files.copy(src, tgt);' will successfully copy 'Book.java' to 'C' ('C' will be a file in that case, containing the contents from 'Book.java' file).

3.1.69   Answer: D

Reason:
Paths.get("Book.java"); represents a relative path. This means relative to current directory.

'Test.class' file is available under "C:\classes" directory, hence path of 'Book.java' is calculated relative to C:\classes.
file.toAbsolutePath() returns 'C:\classes\Book.java'.

NOTE: toAbsolutePath() method doesn't care if given path elements are physically available or not. It just returns the absolute path.

3.1.70   Answer: C

Reason:
Files.walk(Paths.get("F:\\process")) returns the object of Stream<Path> containing "F:\\process", "F:\\process\file.txt", "F:\\process\file.docx" and "F:\\process\file.pdf".

paths.filter(path -> !Files.isDirectory(path)) filters out the directory "F:\\process" and process the 3 files.

Files.readAllLines method reads all the lines from the files using StandardCharsets.UTF_8 but as pdf and docx files use different Charset, hence exception is thrown for reading these files.

FAILED will be printed twice for pdf and docx files. And HELLO (content of file.txt) will be printed once.

Files.readAllLines(path, StandardCharsets.ISO_8859_1) may allow you to read all the 3 files without Exception but these files store lots of other information font, formatting etc. so output may not make any sense.

Oracle Certified Professional: Java SE 8 Programmer II

3.1.71 Answer: A

Reason:
'Files.createDirectories(path);' creates a directory by creating all nonexistent parent directories first. So this method first creates directory Y under X and then directory Z under Y.

3.1.72 Answer: D

Reason:
path --> {F:\user\..\udayan..}. path.normalize() will return {F:\udayan..}.

NOTE: double dot with 'udayan' is not removed as these are not path symbol.

3.1.73 Answer: B

Reason:
According to the javadoc comment of delete method, if the file is a symbolic link then the symbolic link itself, not the final target of the link, is deleted.

3.1.74 Answer: D

Reason:
Even if there are no records in EMPLOYEE table, ResultSet object returned by 'stmt.executeQuery(query);' will never be null.

rs.getMetaData().getColumnCount() returns number of columns of EMPLOYEE table, hence 4 is printed on to the console.

3.1.75 Answer: A

Reason:
As credentials are passed as java.util.Properties so user name should be passed as "user" property and password should be passed as "password" property.

In the given code, correct property names 'user' and 'password' are used. As URL and DB credentials are correct, hence no issues in connecting the database.

Given sql query returns below records:

101 John Smith   12000
102 SeanSmith   15000
103 Regina   Williams 15500
104 Natasha George   14600

Initially the cursor stays just before the first record.

'rs.relative(1);' moves the cursor to the first record.

Column index starts with 1 and not 0, so 'rs.getString(2)' returns 'John'.

3.1.76 Answer: D

Reason:
stmt.executeQurey(String) method can accept any String and it returns ResultSet
instance, hence no compilation error.

But stmt.executeQuery(String) method cannot issue INSERT, UPDATE and DELETE
statements. Hence, 'stmt.executeQuery(query)' throws SQLException at runtime.

To issue INSERT, UPDATE or DELETE statements either use stmt.execute(String) method
OR stmt.executeUpdate(String) method.

```
try (Connection con = DriverManager.getConnection(url, user, password);
    Statement stmt = con.createStatement();)
{
   boolean res = stmt.execute(query);
   System.out.println(stmt.getUpdateCount());
}
```

OR

```
try (Connection con = DriverManager.getConnection(url, user, password);
    Statement stmt = con.createStatement();)
{
   System.out.println(stmt.executeUpdate(query));
}
```

3.1.77 Answer: C

Reason:

As credentials are passed as java.util.Properties so user name should be passed as "user" property and password should be passed as "password" property.

In the given code, correct property names 'user' and 'password' are used. As URL and DB credentials are correct, hence no issues in connecting the database.

Given query returns below records:

```
101  John Smith      12000
102  SeanSmith       15000
103  Regina    Williams 15500
104  Natasha  George   14600
```

'rs.afterLast();' moves the cursor after 4th record.
'rs.relative(-1);' moves the cursor to the 4th record.
'rs.previous()' moves the cursor to the 3rd record.
'rs.getInt(1)' returns 103.

3.1.78 Answer: B

Reason:
Given query returns below records:
```
101  John Smith      12000
102  SeanSmith       15000
103  Regina    Williams 15500
104  Natasha  George   14600
```

'rs.afterLast();' moves the cursor just after the last record.

'rs.previous()' inside while loop moves the cursor from last to first and the codes inside while loop increment the salary of each record by 1000.

'rs.updateRow();' makes sure that salary is updated in the database.

Next while loop simply prints the updated salaries on to the console.

3.1.79   Answer: C

Reason:

executeQuery method closes the previously opened ResultSet object on the same Statement object.

ResultSet object referred by res1 gets closed when 2nd executeQuery method is executed. So 'res1.next()' throws SQLException at runtime.

3.1.80   Answer: D

Reason:

Locale.getDefault(); returns the default Locale for the currently running instance of JVM and getDefault() method is from Locale class and not from System class.

3.1.81   Answer: C

Reason:

getDisplayCountry() and getDisplayLanguage() methods are overloaded to accept Locale type.

Given Test class compiles successfully.

3.1.82   Answer: C,D,E

Reason:

Question only talks about successful creation of Locale instance.
Locale class has 3 public overloaded constructors:
Locale(String language)
Locale(String language, String country)
Locale(String language, String country, String variant)

But constructor with no-argument and constructor that accepts another Locale instance are not available. Hence 'new Locale();' and 'new Locale(loc1);' causes compilation error.

Passing blank string is OK and Locale objects are successfully created.

NOTE: If you pass null as argument to any of the overloaded constructors, then NullPointerException will be thrown and Locale objects will not be successfully created in that case.

3.1.83 Answer: E

Reason:
parse(...) method defined in new Date/Time API such as LocalDate, LocalTime, LocalDateTime and DateTimeFormatter can throw java.time.DateTimeException (which is a RuntimeException) but parse(...) method defined in NumberFormat class declares to throw java.text.ParseException (which is a checked exception) and hence needs to follow declare or handle rule.
As main(...) method doesn't provide try-catch block around Lind n4 and also it doesn't declares to throw ParseException, so Line n4 causes compilation failure.

3.1.84 Answer: E

Reason:
Given program will print 3 digits but all 3 digits can be different or same as variable i is not accessed in synchronized manner.

3.1.85 Answer: C

Reason:
get() method throws 2 checked exceptions: InterruptedException and ExecutionException.

As the given code neither handles these exceptions using catch block nor declares these exceptions in throws clause, hence call to get() method causes compilation failure.

3.1.86 Answer: A

Reason:
removeIf method accepts Predicate, hence no compilation error.
Enhanced for loop uses an internal iterator and as CopyOnWriteArrayList is used, add/set/remove operations while iterating doesn't cause any exception.

In first iteration, removeIf method removes 'Melon' and 'Mango' from the list. On every modification, a fresh copy of underlying array is created, leaving the iterator object unchanged. 'Melon' is printed on to he console.

In 2nd iteration, removeIf method doesn't remove anything as list doesn't contain any element starting with 'M'. But iterator still has 4 elements. 2nd iteration prints 'Apple' on to the console. And so on.

3.1.87 Answer: C

Reason:
submit method of ExecutorService interface is overloaded: submit(Runnable) and submit(Callable). Both Runnable and Callable are Functional interfaces.

Given lambda expression '() -> "HELLO"', it accepts no parameter and returns a String, hence it matches with the call() method implementation of Callable interface.
f.get() would return 'HELLO'.

Notice, get() method throws 2 checked exceptions InterruptedException and ExecutionException and main method declares to throw these exceptions, hence no compilation error.

3.1.88 Answer: C

Reason:
IntStream.rangeClosed(1, 10) returns a sequential ordered IntStream but parallel() method converts it to a parallel stream. Hence, forEach method doesn't guarantee the order for printing numbers.

3.1.89 Answer: A

Reason:
First element that matches the filter is 51.
In this case, base stream is sequential ordered IntStream (it has specific Encounter Order), hence findFirst() method will always return 51 regardless of whether the stream is sequential or parallel.

3.1.90 Answer: B

Reason:
RecursiveAction class has an abstract method 'void compute()' and Adder class correctly overrides it.

new Adder(1, 5); instantiate an Adder object with from = 1, to = 5 and total = 0.

5 - 1 = 4, which is less than or equal to 4 hence else block will not get executed. compute() method will simply add the numbers from 1 to 5 and will update the total field of Adder object created at Line 34.

So when 'System.out.println(adder.total);' is executed, it prints 15 on to the console.

If Line 34 is replaced with 'Adder adder = new Adder(1, 6);', then else block of compute() method will create more Adder objects and total filed of those Adder objects will be updated and not the Adder object created at Line 34. So, in this case output will be 0.

Best solution would be to add below code as the last statement in the else block so that total field of Adder object created at Line 34 is updated successfully:
total = first.total + second.total;

It will give the expected result in all the cases.

4 Practice Test-4

4.1 90 Questions covering all topics.

4.1.1 Consider the code of Test.java file:

```
package com.udayan.ocp;

class Player {
    String name;
    int age;

    Player() {
        this.name = "Virat";
        this.age = 29;
    }

    public int hashcode() {
        return 100;
    }
}

public class Test {
    public static void main(String[] args) {
        System.out.println(new Player());
    }
}
```

Hexadecimal representation of 100 is 64.

Which of the following option is correct?

A. Code doesn't compile successfully

B. Code compiles successfully and on execution always prints "com.udayan.ocp.Player@64" on to the console

C. Code compiles successfully but throws an exception on executing it

D. None of the other options

4.1.2   Consider the code of Test.java file:

```
package com.udayan.ocp;

class Player {
    String name;
    int age;

    Player() {
        this.name = "Sachin";
        this.age = 44;
    }

    public Object toString() {
        return name + ", " + age;
    }
}

public class Test {
    public static void main(String[] args) {
        System.out.println(new Player());
    }
}
```

What will be the result of compiling and executing Test class?

A. Compilation error

B. null, 0

C. Sachin, 44

D. Text containing @ symbol

4.1.3   Consider the code of Test.java file:

```
package com.udayan.ocp;

abstract class Animal {
    public static void vaccinate() {
        System.out.println("Vaccinating...");
    }

    abstract void treating();
}

public class Test {
    public static void main(String[] args) {
        Animal.vaccinate();
    }
}
```

What will be the result of compiling and executing Test class?

A.   Compilation error in Test class

B.   Compilation error in Animal class

C.   Vaccinating...

4.1.4   Given code of Test.java file:

```
package com.udayan.ocp;

interface Printer {
    default void print() {
        System.out.println("Printer");
    }
}

@FunctionalInterface
interface ThreeDPrinter extends Printer {
    @Override
    void print();
}

public class Test {
    public static void main(String[] args) {
        ThreeDPrinter p = () ->
                    System.out.println("3DPrinter");
        p.print();
    }
}
```

What will be the result of compiling and executing Test class?

A. Printer

B. 3DPrinter

C. Compilation error in ThreeDPrinter class

D. Compilation error in Test class

4.1.5 Consider the code of Test.java file:

```
package com.udayan.ocp;

enum Flags {
    TRUE, FALSE;

    public Flags() {
        System.out.println("HELLO");
    }
}

public class Test {
    public static void main(String[] args) {
        Flags flags = Flags.TRUE;
    }
}
```

What will be the result of compiling and executing Test class?

A. HELLO is printed twice.

B. HELLO is printed once.

C. Exception is thrown at runtime.

D. Compilation error.

4.1.6   Given:

```
package com.udayan.ocp;

enum TrafficLight {
    RED, YELLOW, GREEN;
}

public class Test {
    public static void main(String[] args) {
        TrafficLight tl1 = TrafficLight.GREEN;
        TrafficLight tl2 = tl1.clone(); //Line 10
        System.out.println(tl2); //Line 11
    }
}
```

What will be the result of compiling and executing Test class?

A. GREEN

B. Compilation error at Line 10

C. Line 11 throws CloneNotSupportedException at runtime

4.1.7   Given:

```java
package com.udayan.ocp;

class A {
    private String str = "Hello";
    public class B {
        public B(String s) {
            if(s != null)
                str = s;
        }
        public void m1() {
            System.out.println(str);
        }
    }
}

public class Test {
    public static void main(String[] args) {
        //Insert statement here
    }
}
```

Which statement when inserted in the main(String []) method will print "Hello" in the output?

A.	`new A().new B().m1();`
B.	`new A.B().m1();`
C.	`new A().new B("hello").m1();`
D.	`new A().new B(null).m1();`

4.1.8   What will be the result of compiling and executing Test class?

```
package com.udayan.ocp;

class Foo {
    static { //static initialization block
        System.out.print(1);
    }
    class Bar {
        static { //static initialization block
            System.out.print(2);
        }
    }
}

public class Test {
    public static void main(String [] args) {
        new Foo().new Bar();
    }
}
```

A. 12

B. 21

C. Compilation error

D. Exception is thrown at runtime

4.1.9   **Given Code:**

```java
package com.udayan.ocp;

class A {
    public void print(String name) {
        class B {
            B() {
                System.out.println(name);  //Line 5
            }
        }
    }
    B obj = new B();  //Line 9
}

public class Test {
    public static void main(String[] args) {
        new A().print("OCP");  //Line 14
    }
}
```

What will be the result of compiling and executing Test class?

A. OCP

B. Compilation error at Line 5

C. Compilation error at Line 9

D. Compilation error at Line 14

4.1.10 Given code:

```
package com.udayan.ocp;

class Message {
    public void printMessage() {
        System.out.println("Hello!");
    }
}

public class Test {
    public static void main(String[] args) {
        Message msg = new Message() {
            public void PrintMessage() {
                System.out.println("HELLO!");
            }
        };
        msg.PrintMessage();
    }
}
```

What will be the result of compiling and executing Test class?

A. Compilation error

B. Runtime error

C. Hello!

D. HELLO!

4.1.11 Can an anonymous inner class implement multiple interfaces?

A. Yes

B. No

4.1.12 Below is the code of Test.java file:

```
package com.udayan.ocp;

class Outer {
    private static int i = 10;
    private int j = 20;

    static class Inner {
        void add() {
            System.out.println(i + j);
        }
    }
}

public class Test {
    public static void main(String[] args) {
        Outer.Inner inner = new Outer.Inner();
        inner.add();
    }
}
```

What will be the result of compiling and executing Test class?

A. Compilation error in Test class code

B. Compilation error in Inner class code

C. 30

D. Exception is thrown at runtime

4.1.13 For the given code:

```
package com.udayan.ocp;

abstract class Greetings {
    abstract void greet(String s);
}

public class Test {
    public static void main(String[] args) {
        Greetings obj = new Greetings() {
            public void greet(String s) {
                System.out.println(s);
            }
        };
        obj.greet("Happy New Year!");
    }
}
```

Which of the following options successfully replace anonymous inner class code with lambda expression code?

A.	`Greetings obj = (String s) -> {System.out.println(s.toUpperCase());};`
B.	`Greetings obj = (String s) -> {System.out.println(s.toUpperCase());};`
C.	`Greetings obj = s -> System.out.println(s.toUpperCase());`
D.	Lambda expression cannot be used in this case

4.1.14 Consider below interface:

```
interface I2 {
    int calc(int x);
}
```

Which of the following is the correct lambda expression for I2?

A.	`I2 obj1 = x -> return x*x;`
B.	`I2 obj2 = (x) -> return x*x;`
C.	`I2 obj3 = x - > x*x;`
D.	`I2 obj4 = x -> x*x;`

4.1.15 Is below functional interface correctly defined?

```
@FunctionalInterface
interface I8 {
    boolean equals(Object obj);
}
```

A. Yes

B. No

4.1.16 Given code of Test.java file:

```
package com.udayan.ocp;

class A{}
interface M{}
interface N{}

class B extends A {}
class C extends A implements M {}
class D extends A implements M, N {}

class Generic<T extends A & M & N> {}

public class Test {
    public static void main(String[] args) {
        /*INSERT*/
    }
}
```

Which of the following statements, if used to replace /*INSERT*/, will not cause any compilation error?

A. Generic<A> obj = new Generic<>();

B. Generic<M> obj = new Generic<>();

C. Generic<N> obj = new Generic<>();

D. Generic<D> obj = new Generic<>();

E. All options will work

4.1.17 Given code of Test.java file:

```
package com.udayan.ocp;

class Printer<T implements Cloneable> {}

public class Test {
    public static void main(String[] args) {
        Printer<String> printer = new Printer<>();
        System.out.println(printer);
    }
}
```

What will be the result of compiling and executing Test class?

A. Some text containing @ symbol

B. Compilation error for Printer class

C. Compilation error for Test class

4.1.18 Given code of Test.java file:

```
package com.udayan.ocp;

public class Test {
    private <T extends Number> static void print(T t) {
        System.out.println(t.intValue());
    }

    public static void main(String[] args) {
        print(new Double(5.5));
    }
}
```

What will be the result of compiling and executing Test class?

A. 5

B. 6

C. Compilation error

D. Runtime Exception

4.1.19 Given code of Test.java file:

```java
package com.udayan.ocp;
import java.util.ArrayList;
import java.util.List;

public class Test {
    public static void main(String[] args) {
        List list = new ArrayList<String>();
        list.add(1);
        list.add("2");
        list.forEach(System.out::print);
    }
}
```

Which of the following is correct? Select 2 options.

A. Code compiles without any errors and warnings.

B. Code compiles with some warnings.

C. Exception is thrown at runtime.

D. 12 is displayed on to the console.

4.1.20 Given code of Test.java file:

```java
package com.udayan.ocp;
import java.util.*;

public class Test {
    public static void main(String[] args) {
        List<String> colors = new ArrayList<>();
        colors.add("RED");
        colors.add("GREEN");
        colors.add("BLUE");
        Iterator<String> iter = colors.iterator();
        while(iter.hasNext()) {
            iter.remove();
            iter.next();
        }
        System.out.println(colors.size());
    }
}
```

What will be the result of compiling and executing Test class?

A. 0

B. 2

C. Runtime exception

4.1.21   Given code of Test.java file:

```java
package com.udayan.ocp;

import java.util.*;

public class Test {
    public static void main(String[] args) {
        Map<Integer, String> map = new LinkedHashMap<>();
        map.put(null, "zero");
        map.put(1, "one");

        System.out.println(map);
    }
}
```

What will be the result of compiling and executing Test class?

A. {null=zero, 1=one}

B. {1=one, null=zero}

C. Order cannot be predicted

D. Runtime Exception

4.1.22 Given code of Test.java file:

```
package com.udayan.ocp;

import java.util.*;

public class Test {
    public static void main(String[] args) {
        Set<Character> set = new TreeSet<>(
            Arrays.asList('a','b','c','A','a','c'));
        set.stream().forEach(System.out::print);
    }
}
```

What will be the result of compiling and executing Test class?

A. abcAac

B. Aaabcc

C. Aabc

D. abc

4.1.23 Given code of Test.java file:

```
package com.udayan.ocp;

import java.util.*;

public class Test {
    public static void main(String[] args) {
        NavigableSet<String> set = new TreeSet<>(
            Arrays.asList("red", "green", "blue", "gray"));
        System.out.println(set.ceiling("gray"));
        System.out.println(set.floor("gray"));
        System.out.println(set.higher("gray"));
        System.out.println(set.lower("gray"));
    }
}
```

What will be the result of compiling and executing Test class?

A.	gray gray green blue	B.	green blue gray gray
C.	green blue green blue	D.	gray gray gray gray

4.1.24 Consider below code:

```
package com.udayan.ocp;

import java.util.Arrays;
import java.util.Collections;
import java.util.Comparator;
import java.util.List;

public class Test {
    public static void main(String [] args) {
        List<String> names = Arrays.asList(
                        "James", "diana", "Anna");

        /*INSERT*/

        System.out.println(names);
    }
}
```

Currently on executing Test class, [James, diana, Anna] is printed in the output.

Which of the following options can replace /*INSERT*/ such that on executing Test
class, [Anna, diana, James] is printed in the output?

A.	`Collections.sort(names, new`
	`Comparator<String>() {`
	`    public int compare(String o1, String`
	`o2) {`
	`        return o1.compareTo(o2);`
	`    }`
	`});`

B.	`Collections.sort(names, new`
	`Comparator<String>() {`
	`    public int compare(String o1, String`
	`o2) {`
	`        return o1.compareToIgnoreCase(o2);`
	`    }`
	`});`

C.	`Collections.sort(names, new`
	`Comparator<String>() {`
	`    public int compare(String o1, String`
	`o2) {`
	`        return o2.compareTo(o1);`
	`    }`
	`});`

D.	`Collections.sort(names);`

4.1.25 **What will be the result of compiling and executing Test class?**

```java
package com.udayan.ocp;

import java.util.ArrayList;
import java.util.Collections;
import java.util.Comparator;
import java.util.List;

class Point {
    private int x;
    private int y;

    public Point(int x, int y) {
        this.x = x;
        this.y = y;
    }
    public int getX() {
        return x;
    }
    public int getY() {
        return y;
    }
    @Override
    public String toString() {
        return "Point(" + x + ", " + y + ")";
    }
}

public class Test {
    public static void main(String [] args) {
        List<Point> points = new ArrayList<>();
        points.add(new Point(4, 5));
        points.add(new Point(6, 7));
        points.add(new Point(2, 2));

        Collections.sort(points, new Comparator<Point>() {
            public int compare(Point o1, Point o2) {
                return o2.getX() - o1.getX();
            }
        });

        System.out.println(points);
    }
}
```

A. [Point(2, 2), Point(4, 5), Point(6, 7)]

B. [Point(6, 7), Point(4, 5), Point(2, 2)]

C. [Point(4, 5), Point(6, 7), Point(2, 2)]

D. Compilation error

4.1.26 Given code of Test.java file:

```
package com.udayan.ocp;

import java.util.*;

public class Test {
    public static void main(String[] args) {
        int i = 2000;
        Deque<Integer> deque = new ArrayDeque<>();
        deque.add(1000);
        deque.add(i);
        deque.add(3000);

        /*INSERT*/
    }
}
```

Which of the following statements, if used to replace /*INSERT*/, will print following on to the console:
1000
2000
3000

A.	`deque.forEach(System.out::print);`
B.	`deque.forEach(System.out::println);`
C.	`deque.forEach(i -> System.out.println(i));`
D.	`deque.forEach(s -> System.out.println(s));`

4.1.27 Given code of Test.java file:

```java
package com.udayan.ocp;

import java.util.*;

class Employee {
    private String name;
    private double salary;

    public Employee(String name, double salary) {
        this.name = name;
        this.salary = salary;
    }

    public String getName() {
        return name;
    }

    public double getSalary() {
        return salary;
    }

    public void setSalary(double salary) {
        this.salary = salary;
    }

    public String toString() {
        return "{" + name + ", " + salary + "}";
    }
}

public class Test {
    public static void main(String[] args) {
        List<Employee> employees = Arrays.asList(
            new Employee("Jack", 10000),
            new Employee("Lucy", 12000));
        employees.stream().peek(
            e -> e.setSalary(e.getSalary() + 1000))
            .forEach(System.out::println);
    }
}
```

What will be the result of compiling and executing Test class?

A.	{Jack, 10000.0} {Lucy, 12000.0}	B.	{Jack, 11000.0} {Lucy, 13000.0}
C.	{Lucy, 12000.0} {Jack, 10000.0}	D.	{Lucy, 13000.0} {Jack, 11000.0}

4.1.28 Built-in functional interfaces are part of which java package?

A. java.lang

B. java.util

C. java.util.function

D. java.function

4.1.29 You have to create below functional interface:

```
interface Generator<T, U> {
    U generate(T t);
}
```

Which of the following built-in interface you can use instead of above interface?

A. Supplier

B. Function

C. Predicate

D. Consumer

4.1.30 Given code of Test.java file:

```java
package com.udayan.ocp;

import java.util.function.Consumer;

public class Test {

    public static void main(String[] args) {
        Consumer<String> c1 = str -> {
            System.out.println(new StringBuilder(str)
                    .reverse().toString().substring(2));
        };
        c1.accept("!yppahnu");
    }
}
```

What will be the result of compiling and executing Test class?

A. ppahnu

B. unhapp

C. !yppah

D. happy!

4.1.31 Given code of Test.java file:

```java
package com.udayan.ocp;

import java.util.function.Predicate;

public class Test {
    public static void main(String[] args) {
        String [] arr = {"A", "ab", "bab", "Aa", "bb",
                             "baba", "aba", "Abab"};

        Predicate<String> p1 = s -> s.startsWith("A");
        Predicate<String> p2 = s -> s.startsWith("a");
        Predicate<String> p3 = s -> s.length() >= 3;

        processStringArray(arr, p1.or(p2).and(p3));
    }

    private static void processStringArray(String [] arr,
                            Predicate<String> predicate) {
        for(String str : arr) {
            if(predicate.test(str)) {
                System.out.println(str);
            }
        }
    }
}
```

What will be the result of compiling and executing Test class?

A.	Abab	B.	aba Abab
C.	bab baba aba Abab	D.	A ab Aa aba Abab

4.1.32 Given code of Test.java file:

```
package com.udayan.ocp;

import java.util.stream.LongStream;

public class Test {
    public static void main(String[] args) {
        LongStream.rangeClosed(51,75)
            .filter(l -> l % 5 == 0)
            .forEach(l -> System.out.print(l + " "));
    }
}
```

What will be the result of compiling and executing Test class?

A. 55 60 65 70 75

B. 55 60 65 70

C. 75 70 65 60 55

D. 75 70 65 60

4.1.33 Given code of Test.java file:

```
package com.udayan.ocp;

import java.util.function.BiFunction;
import java.util.function.BiPredicate;

public class Test {
    public static void main(String[] args) {
        BiFunction<String, String, String> func =
            (str1, str2) -> {
                return (str1 + str2);
        };

        BiPredicate<String, String> predicate =
            (str1, str2) -> {
                return func.apply(str1, str2).length() > 10;
        };

        String [] arr = {"vention", "historic",
                        "sident", "sentation", "vious"};

        for(String str : arr) {
            if(predicate.test("pre", str)) {
                System.out.println(func.apply("pre", str));
            }
        }
    }
}
```

What will be the result of compiling and executing Test class?

A.	prevention prehistoric president presentation previous	B.	prevention prehistoric president presentation
C.	prevention prehistoric presentation	D.	prehistoric presentation
E.	presentation	F.	Program terminates successfully without printing anything on to the console

4.1.34 Given code of Test.java file:

```java
package com.udayan.ocp;

import java.util.stream.Stream;

public class Test {
    public static void main(String[] args) {
        Stream<StringBuilder> stream = Stream.of();
        stream.map(s -> s.reverse())
                    .forEach(System.out::println);
    }
}
```

What will be the result of compiling and executing Test class?

A. Compilation error

B. NullPointerException is thrown at runtime

C. ClassCastException is thrown at runtime

D. Program executes successfully but nothing is printed on to the console

4.1.35 Given code of Test.java file:

```java
package com.udayan.ocp;

import java.util.Optional;
import java.util.stream.Stream;

public class Test {
    public static void main(String[] args) {
        Optional<String> optional =
            Stream.of("red", "green", "blue", "yellow")
            .sorted().findFirst();
        System.out.println(optional.get());
    }
}
```

What will be the result of compiling and executing Test class?

A. red

B. blue

C. green

D. yellow

4.1.36 Given code of Test.java file:

```java
package com.udayan.ocp;

import java.util.Optional;
import java.util.function.Predicate;
import java.util.stream.Stream;

public class Test {
    public static void main(String[] args) {
        Stream<String> stream = Stream.of("and", "Or",
                    "not", "Equals", "unary", "binary");
        Optional<String> optional = stream
          .filter(((Predicate<String>)Test::isFirstCharVowel)
          .negate()).findFirst();
        System.out.println(optional.get());
    }

    private static boolean isFirstCharVowel(String str) {
        str = str.substring(0, 1).toUpperCase();
        switch(str) {
            case "A":
            case "E":
            case "I":
            case "O":
            case "U":
                return true;
        }
        return false;
    }
}
```

What will be the result of compiling and executing Test class?

A. and

B. not

C. binary

D. Or

4.1.37 Given code of Test.java file:

```
package com.udayan.ocp;

import java.util.Random;
import java.util.stream.IntStream;

public class Test {
    public static void main(String[] args) {
        IntStream stream = IntStream.generate(() ->
                    new Random().nextInt(100)).limit(5);
        stream.filter(i -> i > 0 && i < 10)
                        .findFirst()._____;
    }
}
```

Which code snippet, when filled into the blank, allows the class to compile?

A.   get()
B.   map(i -> i * i)
C.   forEach(System.out::println)
D.   ifPresent(System.out::println)

4.1.38 Given code of Test.java file:

```
package com.udayan.ocp;

import java.util.stream.IntStream;

public class Test {
    public static void main(String[] args) {
        IntStream stream = IntStream
            .rangeClosed(1, 20).filter(i -> i % 2 == 0);
        System.out.println(stream.summaryStatistics());
    }
}
```

Which of the following statements is true for above code?

A. On execution only sum and average data will be printed on to the console.

B. On execution only max, min and count data will be printed on to the console.

C. On execution sum, average, max, min and count data will be printed on to the console.

D. On execution a text containing @ symbol will be printed on to the console.

4.1.39 Given code of Test.java file:

```java
package com.udayan.ocp;

import java.util.Arrays;
import java.util.stream.Stream;

public class Test {
    public static void main(String[] args) {
        Stream<Double> stream =
            Arrays.asList(1.8, 2.2, 3.5).stream();

        /*INSERT*/
    }
}
```

Which of the following options can replace /*INSERT*/ such that on executing Test class, all the stream elements are added and result is printed on to the console? Select all that apply.

A.	`System.out.println(stream.reduce(0.0, (d1, d2) -> d1 + d2));`
B.	`System.out.println(stream.reduce(0.0, Double::sum));`
C.	`System.out.println(stream.reduce(0, (d1, d2) -> d1 + d2));`
D.	`System.out.println(stream.reduce(0, Double::sum));`
E.	`System.out.println(stream.sum());`

4.1.40 Given code of Test.java file:

```
package com.udayan.ocp;

import java.util.Comparator;
import java.util.stream.Stream;

public class Test {
    public static void main(String[] args) {
        Stream<String> stream = Stream.of("d", "a",
                                "mm", "bb", "zzz", "www");
        Comparator<String> lengthComp = (s1, s2) ->
                                s1.length() - s2.length();
        stream.sorted(lengthComp)
                        .forEach(System.out::println);
    }
}
```

Which of the following needs to be done, so that output is:

a

d

bb

mm

www

zzz

A. No need to make any changes, on execution given code prints expected result.

B. Replace 'stream.sorted(lengthComp)' with
   'stream.sorted(lengthComp.thenComparing(String::compareTo))'

C. Replace 'stream.sorted(lengthComp)' with 'stream.sorted(lengthComp.reversed())'

4.1.41 Given code of Test.java file:

```java
package com.udayan.ocp;

import java.util.List;
import java.util.stream.Collectors;
import java.util.stream.Stream;

public class Test {
    public static void main(String[] args) {
        Stream<String> stream =
            Stream.of("java", "python", "c", "c++");
        List<String> list = stream.sorted()
                        .collect(Collectors.toList());
        System.out.println(list);
    }
}
```

What will be the result of compiling and executing Test class?

A. [c++, c, java, python]

B. [python, java, c++, c]

C. [c, c++, java, python]

D. [java, python, c, c++]

4.1.42   Given code of Test.java file:

```
package com.udayan.ocp;

import java.util.Map;
import java.util.TreeMap;
import java.util.function.Function;
import java.util.stream.Collectors;
import java.util.stream.Stream;

class Person {
    int id;
    String name;
    Person(int id, String name) {
        this.id = id;
        this.name = name;
    }
    public String toString() {
        return "{" + id + ", " + name + "}";
    }

    public boolean equals(Object obj) {
        if(obj instanceof Person) {
            Person p = (Person) obj;
            return this.id == p.id;
        }
        return false;
    }

    public int hashCode() {
        return new Integer(this.id).hashCode();
    }
}

public class Test {
    public static void main(String[] args) {
        Person p1 = new Person(1010, "Sean");
        Person p2 = new Person(2843, "Rob");
        Person p3 = new Person(1111, "Lucy");

        Stream<Person> stream = Stream.of(p1, p2, p3);
        Map<Integer, Person> map =
                            stream.collect(/*INSERT*/);
        System.out.println(map.size());
    }
}
```

Which of the following statements can replace /*INSERT*/ such that output is 3?

```
1. Collectors.toMap(p -> p.id, Function.identity())
2. Collectors.toMap(p -> p.id, p -> p)
3. Collectors.toCollection(TreeMap::new)
```

A. Only 1

B. Only 2

C. Only 3

D. Both 1 & 2

E. Both 2 & 3

F. All 1, 2 & 3

4.1.43 Given code of Test.java file:

```java
package com.udayan.ocp;

import java.util.ArrayList;
import java.util.Arrays;
import java.util.List;

public class Test {
    public static void main(String[] args) {
        List<String> list =
            new ArrayList<>(Arrays.asList("Z", "Y", "X"));
        list.stream().sorted().findFirst().get();
        System.out.println(list.get(2));
    }
}
```

What will be the result of compiling and executing Test class?

A. X

B. Z

C. Y

D. Runtime Exception

4.1.44 Given code of Test.java file:

```
package com.udayan.ocp;

import java.util.Arrays;
import java.util.List;
import java.util.function.BinaryOperator;

public class Test {
    public static void main(String[] args) {
        List<Boolean> list =
            Arrays.asList(false, new Boolean(null),
                    new Boolean("1"), new Boolean("0"));
        BinaryOperator<Boolean> operator =
                                    (b1, b2) -> b1 || b2;
        System.out.println(list.stream()
                            .reduce(false, operator));
    }
}
```

What will be the result of compiling and executing Test class?

A. Compilation error

B. true

C. false

D. NullPointerException is thrown at runtime

4.1.45 Given code of Test.java file:

```
package com.udayan.ocp;

import java.io.FileNotFoundException;
import java.io.IOException;

abstract class Super {
    public abstract void m1() throws IOException;
}

class Sub extends Super {
    @Override
    public void m1() throws IOException {
        throw new FileNotFoundException();
    }
}

public class Test {
    public static void main(String[] args) {
        Super s = new Sub();
        try {
            s.m1();
        } catch (FileNotFoundException e) {
            System.out.print("X");
        } catch (IOException e) {
            System.out.print("Y");
        } finally {
            System.out.print("Z");
        }
    }
}
```

What will be the result of compiling and executing Test class?

A. XZ

B. YZ

C. XYZ

D. Compilation Error

4.1.46 Given code of Test.java file:

```java
package com.udayan.ocp;

import java.io.FileNotFoundException;
import java.io.IOException;

abstract class Super {
    public abstract void m1() throws IOException;
}

class Sub extends Super {
    @Override
    public void m1() throws IOException {
        throw new FileNotFoundException();
    }
}

public class Test {
    public static void main(String[] args) {
        Super s = new Sub();
        try {
            s.m1();
        } catch (FileNotFoundException e) {
            System.out.print("M");
        } finally {
            System.out.print("N");
        }
    }
}
```

What will be the result of compiling and executing Test class?

A. MN

B. N

C. Compilation error.

D. Program ends abruptly.

4.1.47 What will be the result of compiling and executing the following program?

```
package com.udayan.ocp;

public class Test {
    private static String s;
    public static void main(String[] args) {
      try {
          System.out.println(s.length());
      } catch(NullPointerException | RuntimeException ex) {
          System.out.println("DONE");
      }
    }
}
```

A. DONE

B. Executes successfully but no output

C. Compilation error

4.1.48 Given code of Test.java file:

```
package com.udayan.ocp;

class Base {
    public void m1() throws NullPointerException {
        System.out.println("Base: m1()");
    }
}

class Derived extends Base {
    public void m1() throws RuntimeException {
        System.out.println("Derived: m1()");
    }
}

public class Test {
    public static void main(String[] args) {
        Base obj = new Derived();
        obj.m1();
    }
}
```

What will be the result of compiling and executing Test class?

A. Base: m1()

B. Derived: m1()

C. Compilation error in Derived class

D. Compilation error in Test class

4.1.49 Given code of Test.java file:

```
package com.udayan.ocp;

import java.util.Scanner;

public class Test {
    public static void main(String[] args) {
        try(Scanner scan = new Scanner(System.in)) {
            String s = scan.nextLine();
            System.out.println(s);
            scan = null;
        }
    }
}
```

What will be the result of compiling and executing Test class?

A. Normal Termination

B. Exception is thrown at runtime

C. Compilation error

4.1.50   Given code of Test.java file:

```
package com.udayan.ocp;

class MyException extends RuntimeException {}

class YourException extends RuntimeException {}

public class Test {
    public static void main(String[] args) {
        try {
            throw new YourException();
        } catch(MyException | YourException e){
            e = null;
        }
    }
}
```

What will be the result of compiling and executing Test class?

A. Compilation error

B. Runtime Exception

C. Nothing is printed on to the console and program terminates successfully

4.1.51 Given code of Test.java file:

```java
package com.udayan.ocp;

class MyResource implements AutoCloseable {
    public void execute() {
        System.out.println("Executing");
    }

    @Override
    public void close() {
        System.out.println("Closing");
    }
}

public class Test {
    public static void main(String[] args) {
        try(MyResource resource = new MyResource()) {
            resource.execute();
        }
    }
}
```

What will be the result of compiling and executing Test class?

A.	Compilation Error	B.	Executing
C.	Executing Closing	D.	Runtime Exception

4.1.52 Given code of Test.java file:

```
package com.udayan.ocp;

class Resource implements AutoCloseable {
    public void close() {
        System.out.println("CLOSE");
    }
}

public class Test {
    public static void main(String[] args) {
        try(Resource r = null) {
            r = new Resource();
            System.out.println("HELLO");
        }
    }
}
```

What will be the result of compiling and executing Test class?

A.	HELLO	B.	HELLO
			CLOSE
C.	Compilation error	D.	NullPointerException is thrown at runtime

4.1.53 Given code of Test.java file:

```
package com.udayan.ocp;
public class Test {
    private static void checkStatus(boolean flag) {
        assert flag = true : flag = false;
    }

    public static void main(String[] args) {
        checkStatus(false);
    }
}
```

What will be the result of executing Test class with below command?

```
java -ea:com.udayan... com.udayan.ocp.Test
```

A. No output and program terminates successfully

B. AssertionError is thrown and program terminates abruptly

C. Compilation error

4.1.54 Given code of Test.java file:

```java
package com.udayan.ocp;

public class Test {
  public static void main(String[] args) {
    try {
        check();
    } catch(RuntimeException e) {
      System.out.println(e.getClass().getName()); //Line n1
    }
  }

  private static void check() {
    try {
        RuntimeException re
                        = new RuntimeException(); //Line n2
        throw re; //Line n3
    } catch(RuntimeException e) {
        System.out.println(1);
        ArithmeticException ex
                        = (ArithmeticException)e; //Line n4
        System.out.println(2);
        throw ex;
    }
  }
}
```

What will be the result of compiling and executing Test class?

A.	1 2 java.lang.RuntimeException	B.	1 2 java.lang.ArithmeticException
C.	1 java.lang.ArithmeticException	D.	1 java.lang.RuntimeException
E.	1 java.lang.ClassCastException		

4.1.55 Given code of Test.java file:

```
package com.udayan.ocp;
import java.time.LocalDate;

public class Test {
    public static void main(String [] args) {
        LocalDate date = LocalDate.ofYearDay(2018, 0);
        System.out.println(date);
    }
}
```

What will be the result of compiling and executing Test class?

A. 2018-01-01

B. 2018-1-1

C. 2017-12-31

D. Runtime Exception

4.1.56 Given code of Test.java file:

```
package com.udayan.ocp;

import java.time.LocalTime;

public class Test {
    public static void main(String [] args) {
        LocalTime time = LocalTime.parse("14:14:59.1111");
        System.out.println(time);
    }
}
```

What will be the result of compiling and executing Test class?

A. Runtime Exception

B. 14:14:59.1111

C. 14:14:59.111100

D. 14:14:59.111100000

4.1.57 Given code of Test.java file:

```
package com.udayan.ocp;

import java.time.LocalDateTime;

public class Test {
    public static void main(String [] args) {
        LocalDateTime dt = LocalDateTime.parse(
                "2018-03-16t10:15:30.22");
        System.out.println(
            dt.toLocalDate() + dt.toLocalTime());
    }
}
```

What will be the result of compiling and executing Test class?

A. 2018-03-1610:15:30.22

B. 2018-03-1610:15:30.220

C. Compilation error

D. Runtime exception

4.1.58 Given code of Test.java file:

```
package com.udayan.ocp;

import java.time.*;

public class Test {
    public static void main(String [] args) {
        Period period = Period.ofWeeks(100);
        System.out.println(period);
    }
}
```

What will be the result of compiling and executing Test class?

A. P100W

B. p100w

C. p700d

D. P700D

4.1.59 Given code of Test.java file:

```
package com.udayan.ocp;

import java.time.*;

public class Test {
    public static void main(String [] args) {
        LocalTime t1 = LocalTime.now();
        LocalDateTime t2 = LocalDateTime.now();
        System.out.println(Duration.between(t1, t2));
    }
}
```

What will be the result of compiling and executing Test class?

A. Program terminates successfully after displaying the output

B. Compilation error

C. Runtime Exception

4.1.60 Given code of Test.java file:

```
package com.udayan.ocp;

import java.time.LocalDate;
import java.time.format.DateTimeFormatter;
import java.util.Locale;

public class Test {
    public static void main(String [] args) {
        Locale.setDefault(new Locale("en", "US"));
        LocalDate date = LocalDate.parse("2018-09-10");
        System.out.println(date.format(DateTimeFormatter
                            .ofPattern("dd-MMM-yyyy")));
    }
}
```

What will be the result of compiling and executing Test class?

A. 10-SEP-2018

B. 10-Sep-2018

C. 10-SEPTEMBER-2018

D. 10-September-2018

4.1.61   F: is accessible for reading/writing. Currently there is no 'err.log' file under F:.

Given code of Test.java file:

```java
package com.udayan.ocp;

import java.io.*;

public class Test {
    public static void main(String[] args)
                                    throws IOException {
        System.setOut(new PrintStream("F:\\err.log"));
        try {
            System.out.println("ONE");
            System.out.println(1 / 0);
        } catch (ArithmeticException e) {
            System.err.println("TWO");
        }
    }
}
```

What will be the result of compiling and executing Test class?

A.	No err.log file will be created.
B.	err.log file will be created and it will contain following texts: ONE
C.	err.log file will be created and it will contain following texts: TWO
D.	err.log file will be created and it will contain following texts: ONE TWO
E.	err.log will be created but it will not have any texts inside.

4.1.62 Given code of Test.java file:

```
package com.udayan.ocp;

public class Test {
    public static void main(String[] args) {
        System.out.printf("%2$d + %1$d", 10, 20);
    }
}
```

What will be the result of compiling and executing Test class?

A. 30

B. 10 + 20

C. 20 + 10

D. None of the other options

4.1.63 Given code of Test.java file:

```java
package com.udayan.ocp;
import java.io.*;
class Student implements Serializable {
    private transient String name;
    private int age;

    Student(String name, int age) {
        this.name = name;
        this.age = age;
    }

    public String getName() {
        return name;
    }

    public int getAge() {
        return age;
    }

    public void setName(String name) {
        this.name = name;
    }

    public void setAge(int age) {
        this.age = age;
    }
}
public class Test {
    public static void main(String[] args)
            throws IOException, ClassNotFoundException {
        Student stud = new Student("John", 20);

        try(ObjectOutputStream oos = new ObjectOutputStream(
            new FileOutputStream("C:\\Student.dat")) ){
            oos.writeObject(stud);
        }

        try( ObjectInputStream ois = new ObjectInputStream(
            new FileInputStream("C:\\Student.dat")) ){
            stud = (Student)ois.readObject();
            System.out.printf("%s : %d",
                    stud.getName(), stud.getAge());
        }
    }
}
```

There is full permission to list/create/delete files and directories in C:.
What will be the result of compiling and executing Test class?

A. Compilation error

B. Runtime Exception

C. John : 20

D. null : 20

E. null : 0

4.1.64 Given code of Test.java file:

```
package com.udayan.ocp;
import java.io.*;
public class Test {
    public static void main(String[] args) {
        File dirs = new File("F:\\A\\B\\C");
        System.out.println(dirs.mkdirs());
        File dir = new File("F:\\A");
        System.out.println(dir.mkdir());
        System.out.println(dir.delete());
    }
}
```

F: is accessible for reading/writing and currently doesn't contain any files/directories.

What will be the result of compiling and executing Test class?

A.	true false true	B.	false false false
C.	true true true	D.	false true true
E.	true false false		

4.1.65 Given code of Test.java file:

```
package com.udayan.ocp;

import java.io.*;

public class Test {
    public static void main(String[] args)
                                throws IOException {
        Console console = System.console();
        String name
            = console.readLine("What's your name? ");
        System.out.printf("You entered: %s", name);
    }
}
```

Which of the following statement is correct regarding above program, if it is executed from the command line?

A. It causes compilation failure.

B. It compiles fine but can cause NullPointerException at runtime.

C. It compiles fine and will never cause NullPointerException at runtime.

D. It waits indefinitely for the user input after displaying the text: What's your name?

E. It waits for 1 min for the user input and then terminates.

4.1.66 F: is accessible for reading and below is the directory structure for F:

```
F:.
└──A
    └──B
        └──C
                Book.java
```

'Book.java' file is available under 'C' directory.

Given code of Test.java file:

```
package com.udayan.ocp;

import java.io.IOException;
import java.nio.file.Path;
import java.nio.file.Paths;

public class Test {
    public static void main(String[] args)
                            throws IOException {
        Path file = Paths.get(
            "F:\\A\\.\\B\\C\\D\\..\\Book.java");
        System.out.println(file.toRealPath());
    }
}
```

What will be the result of compiling and executing Test class?

A. NoSuchFileException is thrown at runtime.

B. FileNotFoundException is thrown at runtime.

C. F:\A\B\C\Book.java

D. F:\A\.\B\C\D\..\Book.java

E. Book.java

4.1.67 Given code of Test.java file:

```
package com.udayan.ocp;

import java.nio.file.Path;
import java.nio.file.Paths;

public class Test {
    public static void main(String[] args) {
        Path file1 = Paths.get("F:\\A\\B\\C");
        Path file2 = Paths.get("Book.java");
        System.out.println(file1.resolve(file2));
        System.out.println(file1.resolveSibling(file2));
    }
}
```

What will be the result of compiling and executing Test class?

A.	Book.java Book.java	B.	F:\A\B\Book.java F:\A\B\C\Book.java
C.	F:\A\B\C\Book.java F:\A\B\Book.java	D.	F:\A\B\C\Book.java Book.java
E.	Book.java F:\A\B\Book.java		

4.1.68 F: is accessible for reading/writing and below is the directory structure for F:

```
F:.
└──A
    └──B
        └──C
                Book.java
```

Given code of Test.java file:

```java
package com.udayan.ocp;

import java.io.IOException;
import java.nio.file.Files;
import java.nio.file.Path;
import java.nio.file.Paths;

public class Test {
    public static void main(String[] args)
                                    throws IOException{
        Path src = Paths.get("F:\\A\\B\\C\\Book.java");
        Path tgt = Paths.get("F:\\A\\B\\Book.java");
        Path copy = Files.copy(src, tgt);
        System.out.println(Files.isSameFile(src, copy));
        System.out.println(Files.isSameFile(tgt, copy));
    }
}
```

What will be the result of compiling and executing Test class?

A.	true true	B.	true false
C.	false false	D.	false true

4.1.69 Given code of Test.java file:

```
package com.udayan.ocp;

import java.nio.file.Path;
import java.nio.file.Paths;

public class Test {
    public static void main(String[] args) {
        Path path = Paths.get("F:\\A\\B\\C\\Book.java");
        System.out.println(path.subpath(1,5));
    }
}
```

What will be the result of compiling and executing Test class?

A. Exception is thrown at runtime

B. A\B\C\Book.java

C. A\B\C

D. F:\A\B\C\Book.java

4.1.70 Given code of Test.java file:

```
package com.udayan.ocp;
import java.nio.file.*;

public class Test {
    public static void main(String[] args) {
        Path path = Paths.get("F:\\A");
        System.out.println(
            path.getRoot().equals(path.getParent()));
    }
}
```

What will be the result of compiling and executing Test class?

A. true

B. false

C. NullPointerException is thrown at runtime

4.1.71 F: is accessible for reading/writing and below is the directory structure for F:

```
F:.
├───Parent
│       └───Child
│               Message.txt
│
├───Shortcut
│       Child.lnk
│
└───Other
        └───Logs
```

Given code of Test.java file:

```java
package com.udayan.ocp;
import java.nio.file.Path;
import java.nio.file.Paths;

public class Test {
    public static void main(String[] args) {
        Path path1 = Paths.get("F:", "Other", "Logs");
        Path path2 = Paths.get("..", "..", "Shortcut",
                            "Child.lnk", "Message.txt");

        Path path3 = path1.resolve(path2).normalize();
        Path path4 = path1.resolveSibling(path2)
                                        .normalize();

        System.out.println(path3.equals(path4));

    }
}
```

What will be the result of compiling and executing Test class?

A. An exception is thrown at runtime.

B. true

C. false

4.1.72 Given structure of EMPLOYEE table:

EMPLOYEE (ID integer, FIRSTNAME varchar(100), LASTNAME varchar(100), SALARY real, PRIMARY KEY (ID))

EMPLOYEE table contains below record:
101, John, Smith, 12000

Given code of Test.java file:

```java
package com.udayan.ocp;

import java.sql.*;

public class Test {
    public static void main(String[] args) {
        try {
            Connection con =
                DriverManager.getConnection(
                        "jdbc:mysql://localhost:3306/ocp",
                        "root", "password");
            String query = "Select * FROM EMPLOYEE";
            Statement stmt = con.createStatement();
            ResultSet rs = stmt.executeQuery(query);
            while (rs.next()) {
              System.out.println("ID: " + rs.getInt("IDD"));
              System.out.println("First Name: "
                              + rs.getString("FIRSTNAME"));
              System.out.println("Last Name: "
                              + rs.getString("LASTNAME"));
              System.out.println("Salary: "
                              + rs.getDouble("SALARY"));
            }
            rs.close();
            stmt.close();
            con.close();
        } catch (SQLException ex) {
            System.out.println("An Error Occurred!");
        }
    }
}
```

Also assume:

URL, username and password are correct.

SQL query is correct and valid.

The JDBC 4.2 driver jar is configured in the classpath.

What will be the result of compiling and executing Test class?

A.	Compilation Error
B.	'An Error Occurred!' is printed on to the console.
C.	Code executes fine and prints following on to the console: ID: 101 First Name: John Last Name: Smith Salary: 12000
D.	Code executes fine and prints following on to the console: ID: 0 First Name: John Last Name: Smith Salary: 12000
E.	Code executes fine and doesn't print anything on to the console.

4.1.73 Given structure of EMPLOYEE table:

```
EMPLOYEE (ID integer, FIRSTNAME varchar(100), LASTNAME
varchar(100), SALARY real, PRIMARY KEY (ID))
```

EMPLOYEE table contains below record:

```
101 John    Smith  12000
102 Sean    Smith  15000
103 Regina Williams  15500
104 Natasha    George 14600
```

Given code of Test.java file:

```java
package com.udayan.ocp;

import java.sql.*;

public class Test {
    public static void main(String[] args)
                                throws SQLException {
        String url = "jdbc:mysql://localhost:3306/ocp";
        String user = "root";
        String password = "password";
        String query = "Select ID, FIRSTNAME, LASTNAME, " +
            "SALARY FROM EMPLOYEE ORDER BY ID";

        try (Connection con = DriverManager
                        .getConnection(url, user, password);
            Statement stmt = con.createStatement(
                ResultSet.TYPE_SCROLL_INSENSITIVE,
                ResultSet.CONCUR_READ_ONLY);
            ResultSet rs = stmt.executeQuery(query);) {
            rs.absolute(-2);
            rs.relative(-1);
            System.out.println(rs.getInt(1));
        }
    }
}
```

Also assume:

URL, username and password are correct.

SQL query is correct and valid.

The JDBC 4.2 driver jar is configured in the classpath.

What will be the result of compiling and executing Test class?

A. 101
B. 102
C. 103
D. 104

4.1.74 Database URL starts with _____.

A. db:

B. jdbc:

C. database:

D. url:

4.1.75 Given structure of MESSAGES table:

```
MESSAGES  (msg1 varchar(100), msg2 varchar(100))
```

MESSAGES table contains below records:

```
'Happy New Year!', 'Happy Holidays!'
```

Given code of Test.java file:

```
package com.udayan.ocp;

import java.sql.*;

public class Test {
    public static void main(String[] args)
                            throws SQLException {
        String url = "jdbc:mysql://localhost:3306/ocp";
        String user = "root";
        String password = "password";
        String query = "Select msg1 as msg, " +
                        "msg2 as msg FROM MESSAGES";
        try (Connection con = DriverManager
                    .getConnection(url, user, password);
            Statement stmt = con.createStatement(
                ResultSet.TYPE_SCROLL_INSENSITIVE,
                ResultSet.CONCUR_READ_ONLY);
            ResultSet rs = stmt.executeQuery(query);)
        {
            int colCount = rs.getMetaData().getColumnCount();
            for(int i = 1; i <= colCount; i++) {
                System.out.println(rs.getString(i));
            }
        }
    }
}
```

Also assume:
URL is correct and db credentials are: root/password.
SQL query is correct and valid.
The JDBC 4.2 driver jar is configured in the classpath.

What will be the result of compiling and executing Test class?

A.	Happy New Year! Happy Holidays!	B.	Happy Holidays! Happy Holidays!
C.	Happy New Year! Happy New Year!	D.	An exception is thrown at runtime

4.1.76 Which of the following is a valid ResultSet type?

A. TYPE_BACKWARD_ONLY

B. TYPE_FORWARD_ONLY

C. TYPE_BOTH

D. TYPE_SCROLL

4.1.77 Given structure of EMPLOYEE table:

```
EMPLOYEE (ID integer, FIRSTNAME varchar(100), LASTNAME
varchar(100), SALARY real, PRIMARY KEY (ID))
```

EMPLOYEE table contains below record:

```
101 John    Smith  12000
102 Sean    Smith  15000
103 Regina Williams  15500
104 Natasha    George 14600
```

Given code of Test.java file:

```
package com.udayan.ocp;

import java.sql.*;

public class Test {
    public static void main(String[] args) throws Exception
    {
        String url = "jdbc:mysql://localhost:3306/ocp";
        String user = "root";
        String password = "password";
        String query = "Select ID, FIRSTNAME, LASTNAME,
                        SALARY FROM EMPLOYEE ORDER BY ID";
        try (Connection con =
           DriverManager.getConnection(url, user, password);
           Statement stmt = con.createStatement(
                      ResultSet.TYPE_FORWARD_ONLY,
                      ResultSet.CONCUR_UPDATABLE);
        ) {
           ResultSet rs = stmt.executeQuery(query);
```

```
            rs.moveToInsertRow();
            rs.updateInt(1, 105);
            rs.updateString(2, "Chris");
            rs.updateString(3, "Lee");
            rs.updateDouble(4, 16000);
            rs.refreshRow(); //Line n1
            rs.insertRow(); //Line n2
            rs.last();
            System.out.println(rs.getInt(1)); //Line n3
        }
    }
}
```

Also assume:

URL, username and password are correct.

SQL query is correct and valid.

The JDBC 4.2 driver jar is configured in the classpath.

What will be the result of compiling and executing Test class?

A. 105

B. 104

C. An exception is raised by Line n1

D. An exception is raised by Line n2

E. An exception is raised by Line n3

4.1.78 Which of the following will always represent Locale object for English in US? Select ALL that apply.

A. Locale l1 = Locale.US;

B. Locale l2 = new Locale(Locale.US);

C. Locale l3 = Locale.getInstance("us");

D. Locale l4 = Locale.getDefault();

E. Locale l5 = new Locale("en", "US");

4.1.79 **Given codes of 4 Java files:**

```java
//1. MyResourceBundle.java
package com.udayan.ocp;

import java.util.ListResourceBundle;

public class MyResourceBundle extends ListResourceBundle {
    @Override
    protected Object[][] getContents() {
        Object [][] arr = {{"surprise", "SURPRISE!"}};
        return arr;
    }
}


//2. MyResourceBundle_en_CA.java
package com.udayan.ocp;

import java.util.ListResourceBundle;

public class MyResourceBundle_en_CA extends
                            ListResourceBundle {
    @Override
    protected Object[][] getContents() {
        Object [][] arr = {{"surprise", 12.64}};
        return arr;
    }
}

//3. MyResourceBundle_fr.java
package com.udayan.ocp;

import java.util.ListResourceBundle;

public class MyResourceBundle_fr extends ListResourceBundle {
    @Override
    protected Object[][] getContents() {
        Object [][] arr = {{"surprise", 1001}};
        return arr;
    }
}

//4. Test.java
package com.udayan.ocp;
```

```
import java.util.Locale;
import java.util.ResourceBundle;

public class Test {
    public static void main(String[] args) {
        Locale.setDefault(new Locale("fr", "IT"));
        Locale loc = new Locale("en", "US");
        ResourceBundle rb = ResourceBundle.getBundle(
                "com.udayan.ocp.MyResourceBundle", loc);
        System.out.println(rb.getObject("surprise"));
    }
}
```

What will be the result of compiling and executing Test class?

A. SURPRISE!

B. 12.64

C. 1001

D. MissingResourceException is thrown at runtime

4.1.80 Given code of Test.java file:

```
package com.udayan.ocp;

import java.util.Locale;

public class Test {
    public static void main(String[] args) {
        Locale loc = Locale.ENGLISH;
        loc.setCountry("en");
        loc.setCountry("CA");

        System.out.println(loc.getDisplayCountry());
    }
}
```

'CA' is the country code for 'Canada'.

What will be the result of compiling and executing Test class?

A. Canada

B. United States

C. English

D. Compilation error

E. No text is displayed in the output

4.1.81 Below files are available for your project:
```
//1. ResourceBundle.properties
k1=1
k2=2

//2. ResourceBundle_EN.properties
k3=EN3
k4=EN4

//3. ResourceBundle_US.properties
k2=US2
k3=US3

//4. Test.java
package com.udayan.ocp;

import java.util.Enumeration;
import java.util.Locale;
import java.util.ResourceBundle;

public class Test {
    public static void main(String[] args) {
        Locale loc = Locale.US;
        ResourceBundle bundle =
            ResourceBundle.getBundle("ResourceBundle", loc);
        Enumeration<String> enumeration = bundle.getKeys();
        while (enumeration.hasMoreElements()) {
            String key = enumeration.nextElement();
            String val = bundle.getString(key);
            System.out.println(key + "=" + val);
        }
    }
}
```

Assume that all the *.properties files are included in the CLASSPATH. What will be the output of compiling and executing Test class?

A.	k2=US2 k3=US3 k3=EN3 k4=EN4 k1=1 k2=2	B.	k1=1 k2=2 k3=EN3 k4=EN4 k2=US2 k3=US3
C.	k3=EN3 k4=EN4 k1=1 k2=2	D.	k1=1 k2=2 k3=EN3 k4=EN4
E.	k2=US2 k3=US3 k4=EN4 k1=1		

4.1.82 Given code of Test.java file:

```java
package com.udayan.ocp;
import java.util.concurrent.*;

class Caller implements Callable<Void> {
    String str;

    public Caller(String s) {
        this.str = s;
    }

    public Void call() throws Exception {
        System.out.println(str.toUpperCase());
        return null;
    }
}

public class Test {
    public static void main(String[] args)
            throws InterruptedException, ExecutionException {
        ExecutorService es =
                        Executors.newSingleThreadExecutor();
        Future<Void> future = es.submit(new Caller("Call"));
        System.out.println(future.get());
    }
}
```

What will be the result of compiling and executing Test class?

A.	The program doesn't terminate but prints following: CALL CALL
B.	The program doesn't terminate but prints following: null null
C.	The program doesn't terminate but prints following: CALL Null
D.	The program terminates after printing: CALL Null

4.1.83 Given code of Test.java file:

```
package com.udayan.ocp;

import java.util.concurrent.*;

public class Test {
    public static void main(String[] args)
            throws InterruptedException, ExecutionException {
        ExecutorService es =
                        Executors.newSingleThreadExecutor();
        Future<String> f = es.execute(() -> "HELLO");
        System.out.println(f.get());
        es.shutdown();
    }
}
```

What will be the result of compiling and executing Test class?

A. Compilation error

B. null

C. HELLO

D. An exception is thrown at runtime

4.1.84 Can all streams be converted to parallel stream?

A. Yes

B. No

4.1.85 Given code of Test.java file:

```java
package com.udayan.ocp;

import java.util.concurrent.ExecutionException;
import java.util.concurrent.ExecutorService;
import java.util.concurrent.Executors;
import java.util.concurrent.Future;

public class Test {
    private static void print() {
        System.out.println("PRINT");
    }

    private static Integer get() {
        return 10;
    }

    public static void main(String [] args)
            throws InterruptedException, ExecutionException {
        ExecutorService es =
                        Executors.newFixedThreadPool(10);
        Future<?> future1 = es.submit(Test::print);
        Future<?> future2 = es.submit(Test::get);
        System.out.println(future1.get());
        System.out.println(future2.get());
        es.shutdown();
    }
}
```

What will be the result of compiling and executing Test class?

A.	Compilation error	B.	PRINT null 10
C.	null 10 PRINT	D.	PRINT 10 null
E.	null PRINT 10		

4.1.86   *Given code of Test.java file:*

```java
package com.udayan.ocp;

import java.util.concurrent.*;

class Adder extends RecursiveAction {
    private int from;
    private int to;
    int total = 0;

    Adder(int from, int to) {
        this.from = from;
        this.to = to;
    }

    @Override
    protected void compute() {
        if ((to - from) <= 4) {
            int sum = 0;
            for(int i = from; i <= to; i++) {
                sum += i;
            }
            total+=sum;
        } else {
            int mid = (from + to) / 2;
            Adder first = new Adder(from, mid);
            Adder second = new Adder(mid + 1, to);
            invokeAll(first, second);
        }
    }
}

public class Test {
    public static void main(String[] args) {
        Adder adder = new Adder(1, 20); //Line 34
        ForkJoinPool pool = new ForkJoinPool(4);
        pool.invoke(adder);
        System.out.println(adder.total);
    }
}
```

What will be the result of compiling and executing Test class?

A. It will print 0 on to the console.

B. It will print 210 on to the console.

C. It can print any number between 0 and 210.

D. None of the other options.

4.1.87 Which of the following instances can be passed to invoke() method of ForkJoinPool class?

Select ALL that apply.

A. ForkJoinTask

B. RecursiveAction

C. RecursiveTask

D. Runnable

E. Callable

4.1.88 Performance with parallel stream is always better than sequential streams.

A. true

B. false

4.1.89   Given code of Test.java file:

```
package com.udayan.ocp;

import java.util.Arrays;
import java.util.List;

public class Test {
    private static StringBuilder RES = new StringBuilder();

    public static void main(String[] args) {
        List<String> list = Arrays.asList("A", "B", "C",
                        "D", "E", "F", "G", "H", "I", "J");
        list.parallelStream().forEach(RES::append);
        System.out.println(RES);
    }
}
```

What will be the result of compiling and executing Test class?

A.   It will always print ABCDEFGHIJ.

B.   Output cannot be predicted.

C.   Compilation error.

4.1.90 Given code of Test.java file:

```
package com.udayan.ocp;

import java.util.stream.IntStream;

public class Test {
    public static void main(String[] args) {
        IntStream stream = IntStream.rangeClosed(1, 5);
        System.out.println(stream.parallel()
                .reduce((x, y) -> x + y).getAsInt());
    }
}
```

What will be the result of compiling and executing Test class?

A. It will print 15 on to the console.

B. It can print any number between 1 and 15.

C. It will print 0 on to the console.

D. None of the other options.

4.2   Answers of Practice Test - 4 with Explanation

4.1.1   Answer: D

Reason:

If toString() method is not overridden, then Object class's version is invoked.
The toString() method in Object class has below definition:
public String toString() {
        return getClass().getName() + "@" + Integer.toHexString(hashCode());
}

So, in the output you get: fully-qualified-name-of-the-class@hexadecimal-representation-of-hash-code. NOTE: hashCode() method is called for that.
Player class doesn't override the hashCode() method, rather it defines a new method hashcode() [NOTE: c in lower case in the method name].

Hence, hashcode() is never invoked and no guarantee of getting 64 always.

4.1.2   Answer: A

Reason:
The toString() method in Object class has below definition:
public String toString() {
 return getClass().getName() + "@" + Integer.toHexString(hashCode());
}

class Player doesn't override it correctly, return type should be String and not Object.

4.1.3   Answer: C

Reason:
Abstract class can have static methods and those can be called by using
Class_Name.method_name.

class Animal is declared with package(default) scope, which means it can be extended by other classes in the same package(com.udayan.ocp).

Above code executes fine and prints 'Vaccinating...' on to the console.

4.1.4   Answer: B

Reason:
An interface can override the default method of parent interface and declare it as abstract as well.

ThreeDPrinter is a functional interface as it has one non-overriding abstract method. No issues with ThreeDPrinter interface.

Lambda syntax is correct and p.print() method invokes 'System.out.println("3DPrinter");' of lambda expression, hence '3DPrinter' is printed in the output.

4.1.5   Answer: D

Reason:
Enum constructors are implicitly private, even though you can provide private access modifier but it will be redundant.
Using 'public' or 'protected' for enum constructors is not allowed.

4.1.6   Answer: B

Reason:
Every enum extends from java.lang.Enum class and it contains following definition of clone method:

```
protected final Object clone() throws CloneNotSupportedException {
    throw new CloneNotSupportedException();
}
```

Every enum constant (RED, YELLOW, GREEN) is an instance of TrafficLight enum and as clone method is protected in Enum class so it cannot be accessed in com.udayan.ocp package using reference variable.

4.1.7   Answer: D

Reason:
new B() will cause compilation error as no-argument constructor is not defined in inner class B.

new A.B() is invalid syntax for creating the instance of Regular inner classes.

new A().new B("hello").m1(); is a valid syntax but it will print "hello" in the output and not "Hello".

4.1.8 Answer: C

Reason:
Regular inner class cannot define anything static, except static final variables. In this case, static initialization block inside inner class Bar is not allowed.

4.1.9 Answer: C

Reason:
Instance of method-local inner class can only be created within the boundary of enclosing initialization block or enclosing method.

B obj = new B(); is written outside the closing curly bracket of print(String) method and hence Line 9 causes compilation error.

Starting with JDK 8, a method local inner class can access local variables and parameters of the enclosing block that are final or effectively final so no issues with Line 5.

4.1.10 Answer: A

Reason:
Even though anonymous inner class allows to define methods not available in its super class but these methods cannot be invoked from outside the anonymous inner class code.

Reason is very simple, methods are invoked on super class reference variable (msg) which is of Message type.

And class Message is aware of the methods declared or defined within its boundary, printMessage() method in this case.

So using Message class reference variable, methods defined in sub class cannot be invoked. So, msg.PrintMessage(); statement causes compilation error.

4.1.11 Answer: B

Reason:
Unlike other inner classes, an anonymous inner class can either extend from one class or can implement one interface. It cannot extend and implement at the same time and it cannot implement multiple interfaces.

4.1.12 Answer: B

Reason:
static nested class cannot access non-static member of the Outer class using static reference. Hence usage of variable j in Inner class causes compilation error.

4.1.13 Answer: D

Reason:
Reference variable to which lambda expression is assigned is known as target type. Target type can be a static variable, instance variable, local variable, method parameter or return type.

Lambda expression doesn't work without target type and target type must be a functional interface. Functional interface was added in JDK 8 and it contains one non-overriding abstract method.

As Greetings is abstract class, so lambda expression cannot be used in this case.

4.1.14 Answer: D

Reason:
If curly brackets are removed from lambda expression body, then return keyword should also be removed. There should not be space between - and >.
For one parameter, parentheses or round brackets () can be removed.

4.1.15 Answer: B

Reason:
Functional interface must have one and only one non-overriding abstract method.

boolean equals(Object) is declared and defined in Object class, hence it is not non-overriding abstract method.

@FunctionalInterface annotation causes compilation error.

4.1.16 Answer: D

Reason:
T is with multiple bounds, so the type argument must be a subtype of all bounds.

Oracle Certified Professional: Java SE 8 Programmer II

4.1.17   Answer: B

Reason:
For bounds, extends keyword is used for both class and interface.

Correct declaration of Printer class should be:
class Printer<T extends Cloneable> {}

4.1.18   Answer: C

Reason:
A generic method is defined in non-generic class.
Type parameter for the method should be defined just before the return type of the method. In this case, '<T extends Number>' is not appearing just before void and hence compilation error.

4.1.19   Answer: B, D

Reason:
Compiler warning for unchecked call to add and forEach.

list can store all objects and when each element is passed to System.out.print() method, toString() method for passed element is invoked.

Both Integer and String class overrides toString() method and hence 12 is printed on to the console.

4.1.20   Answer: C

Reason:
Iterator and ListIterator allow to remove elements while iterating. But next() should be called before remove().

In this case, remove() is called before next() and hence IllegalStateException is thrown at runtime.

4.1.21   Answer: A

Reason:
HashMap and LinkedHashMap can accept 1 null key but TreeMap cannot accept null keys.

433

LinkedHashMap by default keeps an insertion order so every time you iterate the map, you get same result.

Output will always be: {null=zero, 1=one}

4.1.22 Answer: C

Reason:
TreeSet requires you to provide either Comparable or Comparator. If you don't provide Comparator explicitly, then for natural ordering your class should implement Comparable interface.

Character and all wrapper classes implement Comparable interface, hence Characters are sorted in ascending order. Uppercase characters appears before lowercase characters.

Set doesn't allow duplicate, hence output will always be: 'Aabc'.

4.1.23 Answer: A

Reason:
new TreeSet<>(Arrays.asList("red", "green", "blue", "gray")); => [blue, gray, green, red].
set.ceiling("gray") => Returns the least value greater than or equal to the given value, 'gray'.
set.floor("gray") => Returns the greatest value less than or equal to the given value, 'gray'.
set.higher("gray") => Returns the least value strictly greater than the given value, 'green'.
set.lower("gray") => Returns the greatest value strictly less than the given value, 'blue'.

4.1.24 Answer: B

Reason:
If you sort String in ascending order, then upper case letters appear before the lower case letters.
So in this case if I sort the list in ascending order then the output will be [Anna, James, diana] and this is what Collections.sort(names); and o1.compareTo(o2); method calls do.

o2.compareTo(o1); sorts the same list in descending order: [diana, James, Anna] but you have to sort the list such that [Anna, diana, James] is printed in the output,
which means sort the names in ascending order but in case-insensitive manner. String class has compareToIgnoreCase() method for such purpose.

4.1.25 Answer: B

Reason:

return o2.getX() - o1.getX(); means the Comparator is sorting the Point objects on descending value of x of Point objects.
To sort the Point objects in ascending order of x, use: return o1.getX() - o2.getX();
To sort the Point objects in ascending order of y, use: return o1.getY() - o2.getY();
To sort the Point objects in descending order of y, use: return o2.getY() - o1.getY();

4.1.26 Answer: B,D

Reason:

Iterator<T> interface has forEach(Consumer) method. As Consumer is a Functional Interface, hence a lambda expression or method reference syntax can be passed as argument to forEach() method.

deque.forEach(System.out::print); => This will print 100020003000 without any newline character in between.
deque.forEach(System.out::println); => This prints desired output
deque.forEach(i -> System.out.println(i)); => Causes compilation failure as lambda expression variable 'i' conflicts with local variable.
deque.forEach(s -> System.out.println(s)); => Prints desired output.

NOTE: 'System.out::print' is a method reference syntax corresponding to lambda expression 's -> System.out.println(s)'.

4.1.27 Answer: B

Reason:
employees.stream() => [{"Jack",10000.0},{"Lucy",12000.0}].

peek(e -> e.setSalary(e.getSalary() + 1000)) => [{"Jack",11000.0},{"Lucy",13000.0}].
peek(Consumer) method applies the passed lambda expression to all the elements of the stream and returns the same elements in the stream.

forEach(System.out::println); => Prints both the elements of the stream.

Arrays.asList(...) method returns sequential List object, so order of elements remain same.

Output is:
{Jack, 11000.0}
{Lucy, 13000.0}

NOTE: peek() method is for debugging the streams and should not be used in production ready code.

4.1.28 Answer: C

Reason:
All the built-in functional interfaces are defined inside java.util.function package.

4.1.29 Answer: B

Reason:
It is always handy to remember the names and methods of four important built-in functional interfaces:
Supplier<T> : T get();
Function<T, R> : R apply(T t);
Consumer<T> : void accept(T t);
Predicate<T> : boolean test(T t);
Rest of the built-in functional interfaces are either similar to or dependent upon these four interfaces.

Clearly, interface Function can be used instead or defining Generator interface.

4.1.30 Answer: D

Reason:
Consumer<T> interface has void accept(T) method, which means in this case, Consumer<String> interface has void accept(String) method.

Given lambda expression accepts String argument and does some operation.

First String is converted to StringBuilder object to use the reverse method. new StringBuilder("!yppahnu").reverse().toString() returns "unhappy!" and "unhappy!".substring(2) returns "happy!", which is printed by System.out.println method.

4.1.31 Answer: B

Reason:
"or" and "and" method of Predicate interface works just like short-circuit || and && operators.

p1.or(p2) will return {"A", "ab", "Aa", "aba", "Abab"} and after that and method will retrieve strings of length greater than or equal to 3, this means you would get {"aba", "Abab"} as the final result.

4.1.32 Answer: A

Reason:
There are 3 primitive streams especially to handle primitive data: DoubleStream, IntStream and LongStream.

There are some important methods available in Stream class:
Stream<T> filter(Predicate<? super T> predicate);
<R> Stream<R> map(Function<? super T, ? extends R> mapper);
void forEach(Consumer<? super T> action);
public static<T> Stream<T> generate(Supplier<T> s){...}

Corresponding primitive streams have similar methods working with primitive version of Functional interfaces:
Double Stream:
DoubleStream filter(DoublePredicate predicate);
DoubleStream map(DoubleUnaryOperator mapper); [Operator is similar to Function]
void forEach(DoubleConsumer action);
public static DoubleStream generate(DoubleSupplier s){...}

IntStream:
IntStream filter(IntPredicate predicate);
IntStream map(IntUnaryOperator mapper); [Operator is similar to Function]
void forEach(IntConsumer action);
public static IntStream generate(IntSupplier s) {...}

LongStream:
LongStream filter(LongPredicate predicate);
LongStream map(LongUnaryOperator mapper); [Operator is similar to Function]
void forEach(LongConsumer action);
public static LongStream generate(LongSupplier s) {...}

For exams, you will have to remember some of the important methods and their signature.

LongStream.rangeClosed(51,75) => [51,52,53,...,75]. Both start and end are inclusive.
filter(l -> l % 5 == 0) => [55,60,65,70,75]. filter method accepts LongPredicate and filters the data divisible by 5.
forEach(l -> System.out.print(l + " ")) => Prints the stream data on to the console.

4.1.33 Answer: D

Reason:

BiFunction<T, U, R> : R apply(T t, U u);
BiFunction interface accepts 3 type parameters, first 2 parameters (T,U) are passed to apply method and 3rd type parameter is the return type of apply method.
In this case, 'BiFunction<String, String, String>' means apply method will have declaration: 'String apply(String str1, String str2)'. Given lambda expression '(str1, str2) -> { return (str1 + str2); };' is the correct implementation of BiFunction<String, String, String> interface. It simply concatenates the passed strings.

BiPredicate<T, U> : boolean test(T t, U u);
BiPredicate interface accepts 2 type parameters and these parameters (T,U) are passed to test method, which returns primitive boolean.
In this case, 'BiPredicate<String, String>' means test method will have declaration: 'boolean test(String s1, String s2)'. Given lambada expression '(str1, str2) -> { return func.apply(str1, str2).length() > 10; };' is correct implementation of BiPredicate<String, String>. Also note, lambda expression for BiPredicate uses BiFunction. This predicate returns true if combined length of passed strings is greater than 10.

For-each loop simply iterates over the String array elements and prints the string after pre-pending it with "pre" in case the combined length of result string is greater than 10. "prehistoric" has 11 characters and "presentation" has 12 characters and hence these are displayed in the output.

4.1.34 Answer: D

Reason:

Stream.of() returns blank stream. As Type of stream is specified, stream is of 'Stream<StringBuilder>', each element of the stream is considered to be of 'StringBuilder' type.

map method in this case accepts 'Function<? super StringBuilder, ? extends StringBuilder>'.

In Lambda expression 's -> s.reverse()', s is of StringBuilder type and hence no compilation error.

As stream is blank, hence map and forEach methods are not executed even once. Program executes fine but nothing is printed on to the console.

4.1.35 Answer: B

Reason:
Stream.of("red", "green", "blue", "yellow") => ["red", "green", "blue", "yellow"].

sorted() => ["blue", "green", "red", "yellow"].

findFirst() => ["blue"]. findFirst returns Optional<String> object.

4.1.36 Answer: B

Reason:
stream => ["and", "Or", "not", "Equals", "unary", "binary"].

Test::isFirstCharVowel is the predicate, to invoke negate() method, it needs to be type-casted to 'Predicate<String>'.

stream.filter(((Predicate<String>)Test::isFirstCharVowel).negate()) => ["not", "binary"].

findFirst() => Optional<String> object containing "not".

optional.get() => "not".

4.1.37 Answer: D

Reason:
It is very simple as you don't have to worry about return type of the code snippet. stream is of IntStream type. Even method filter returns instance of IntStream type. findFirst() returns an OptionalInt as it is called on IntStream.

Of all the given options, OptionalInt has 'ifPresent' method only. Hence correct answer is: 'ifPresent(System.out::println)'.

4.1.38 Answer: C

Reason:

There are 3 summary statistics methods available in JDK 8: IntSummaryStatistics, LongSummaryStatistics & DoubleSummaryStatistics.

summaryStatistics() method in IntStream class returns an instance of IntSummaryStatistics.
summaryStatistics() method in LongStream class returns an instance of LongSummaryStatistics.
summaryStatistics() method in DoubleStream class returns an instance of DoubleSummaryStatistics.

The 3 summary statistics classes override toString() method to print the data about count, sum, min, average and max.

All the 3 summary statistics classes have methods to extract specific stat as well: getCount(), getSum(), getMin(), getMax() and getAverage().

Summary Statistics are really useful if you want multiple stats, say for example you want to find both min and max. As min and max are terminal operation for finite stream so after using one operation stream gets closed and not possible to use the same stream for other terminal operations.

4.1.39 Answer: A,B

Reason:
'stream.reduce(0.0, (d1, d2) -> d1 + d2)' and 'stream.reduce(0.0, Double::sum)' are exactly same and adds all the stream contents.

stream.sum() causes compilation error as sum() method is declared only in primitive streams (IntStream, LongStream and DoubleStream) but not in generic stream, Stream<T>.

reduce method parameters are (Double, BinaryOperator).
0 (int literal) cannot be converted to Double and hence compilation error for 'stream.reduce(0, (d1, d2) -> d1 + d2)' and 'stream.reduce(0, Double::sum)'.

You can easily verify this by writing below code:
```
public class Test {
   public static void main(String[] args) {
      print(0); //Compilation error as int can't be converted to Double
   }

   private static void print(Double d) {
      System.out.println(d);
   }
}
```

4.1.40 Answer: B

Reason:
Current code displays below output:
d
a
mm
bb
zzz
www

if string's length is same, then insertion order is preserved.

Requirement is to sort the stream in ascending order of length of the string and if length is same, then sort on natural order.

lengthComp is for sorting the string on the basis of length, thenComparing default method of Comparator interface allows to pass 2nd level of Comparator.

Hence replacing 'stream.sorted()' with
'stream.sorted(lengthComp.thenComparing(String::compareTo))' will do the trick.

stream.sorted(lengthComp.reversed()) will simply reversed the order, which means longest string will be printed first, but this is not expected.

4.1.41 Answer: C

Reason:
stream.collect(Collectors.toList()) returns an instance of ArrayList and hence output will always be in ascending order as stream was sorted using sorted() method before converting to list.

4.1.42 Answer: D

Reason:
Variable id has package scope and as class Test is in the same package hence p.id doesn't cause any compilation error.
'Collectors.toMap(p -> p.id, Function.identity())' and 'Collectors.toMap(p -> p.id, p -> p)' are exactly same, as 'Function.identity()' is same as lambda expression 'p -> p'.
Collectors.toCollection(TreeMap::new) causes compilation error as TreeMap doesn't extend from Collection interface.

4.1.43 Answer: A

Reason:
findFirst() will never return empty Optional if stream is not empty. So no exception for get() method.

Also list and stream are not connected, which means operations done on stream doesn't affect the source, in this case list.
list.get(2) will print 'X' on to the console.

4.1.44 Answer: C

Reason:
Constructor of Boolean class accepts String argument.
If passed argument is null, then Boolean object for 'false' is created.
If passed argument is non-null and equals to "true" in case-insensitive manner, then Boolean object for 'true' is created otherwise Boolean object for 'false' is created.
So list contains 4 elements and all are Boolean objects for false.

As, BinaryOperator<T> extends BiFunction<T,T,T> so in this case signature of apply method will be: Boolean apply(Boolean, Boolean). Given lambda expression correctly implements the apply method.

To understand, 'stream.reduce(false, operator)' can be written as:

```
Boolean result = false;
for (Boolean element : stream) {
    result = operator.apply(result, element);
}
return result;
```

Above code is just for understanding purpose, you can't iterate a stream using given loop.

As 1st argument of reduce method (also known as identity) is set to false and all the 4 stream elements are also false, hence list.stream().reduce(false, operator) will return false.
So, in this case false will be printed on to the console.

If you change identity to true, then statement
'System.out.println(list.stream().reduce(true, operator));' will print true.

4.1.45 **Answer: A**

Reason:
Even though method m1() declares to throw IOException but at runtime an instance of FileNotFoundException is thrown.

A catch handler for FileNotFoundException is available and hence X is printed on to the console.

After that finally block is executed, which prints Z to the console.

4.1.46 **Answer: C**

Reason:
Even though an instance of FileNotFoundException is thrown by method m1() at runtime, but method m1() declares to throw IOException.

Reference variable s is of Super type and hence for compiler call to s.m1(); is to method m1() of Super, which throws IOException.

And as IOException is checked exception hence calling code should handle it.

As calling code doesn't handle IOException or its super type, so s.m1(); causes compilation error.

4.1.47 Answer: C

Reason:
NullPointerException extends RuntimeException and in multi-catch syntax we can't specify multiple Exceptions related to each other in multilevel inheritance.

4.1.48 Answer: B

Reason:
NullPointerException extends RuntimeException, but there are no overriding rules related to unchecked exceptions.
So, method m1() in Derived class correctly overrides Base class method.
Rest is simple polymorphism. obj refers to an instance of Derived class and hence obj.m1(); invokes method m1() of Derived class, which prints "Derived: m1()" to the console.

4.1.49 Answer: C

Reason:
Resources used in try-with-resources statement are implicitly final, which means they can't be reassigned.

scan = null; will fail to compile as we are trying to assign null to variable scan.

4.1.50 Answer: A

Reason:
Variable 'e' used in multi-catch block is implicitly final and can't be re-initialized.
e = null; causes compilation failure.

4.1.51 Answer: C

Reason:
close() method in AutoCloseable interface has below declaration:
void close() throws Exception;

MyResource class correctly overrides close() method.

try-with-resources statement internally invokes resource.close() method after executing resource.execute().

Output is:
Executing
Closing

4.1.52 Answer: C

Reason:
Variable r is implicitly final and hence can't be re-initialized.

'r = new Resource();' causes compilation error.

4.1.53 Answer: A

Reason:
'java -ea:com.udayan...' enables the assertion in com.udayan package and its sub packages. Test class is defined under 'com.udayan.ocp' package, hence assertion is enabled for Test class.

'assert flag = true : flag = false;' => On the left side 'flag = true' is a valid boolean expression, so no issues and on right side 'flag = false' assigns false to flag and false is returned as well, which is not void. Hence no issues with right side as well.

On execution, flag is true, hence AssertionError is not thrown.

Nothing is printed on to the console and program terminates successfully.

4.1.54 Answer: E

Reason:
Line n3 throws an instance of RuntimeException. As catch(RuntimeException e) is available, hence control starts executing catch-block inside check() method.
1 is printed on to the console.
At Line n4, instance of super-class (RuntimeException) is type-casted to sub-class (ArithmeticException), hence Line n4 throws an instance of ClassCastException.
ClassCastException is a sub-class of RuntimeException, so catch-block of main method is executed and Line n1 prints the fully qualified name of ClassCastException.
java.lang.ClassCastException is printed on to the console.

4.1.55 Answer: D

Reason:
LocalDate ofYearDay(int year, int dayOfYear): Valid values for dayOfYear for non-leap year is 1 to 365 and for leap year is 1 to 366.
For other values, java.time.DateTimeException is thrown.

4.1.56 Answer: C

Reason:
LocalTime.parse(text); => text must represent a valid time and it is parsed using DateTimeFormatter.ISO_LOCAL_TIME.

ISO_LOCAL_TIME represents time in following format:
HH:mm (if second-of-minute is not available),
HH:mm:ss (if second-of-minute is available),
HH:mm:ss.SSS (if nano-of-second is 3 digit or less),
HH:mm:ss.SSSSSS (if nano-of-second is 4 to 6 digits),
HH:mm:ss.SSSSSSSSS (if nano-of-second is 7 to 9 digits).

Valid values for hour-of-day (HH) is: 0 to 23.
Valid values for minute-of-hour (mm) is: 0 to 59.
Valid values for second-of-minute (ss) is: 0 to 59.
Valid values for nano-of-second is: 0 to 999999999.

In the given expression, 'LocalTime.parse("14:14:59.1111");' all the values are within range and as nano-of-second is of 4 digit, hence toString() method appends 2 zeros to it.

Output is: '14:14:59.111100'.

4.1.57 Answer: C

Reason:
dt.toLocalDate() returns an instance of LocalDate and dt.toLocalTime() returns an instance of LocalTime.

But '+' operator is not overloaded for LocalDate and LocalTime objects OR 2 LocalDate objects OR 2 LocalTime objects OR in general for 2 Java Objects.

It would work if one of the operand is of String type.

Hence 'dt.toLocalDate() + " " + dt.toLocalTime()' doesn't cause any compilation error as '+' operator is Left to Right associative.

dt.toLocalDate() + " " + dt.toLocalTime()
= (dt.toLocalDate() + " ") + dt.toLocalTime()
= "2018-03-16 " + dt.toLocalTime()
= "2018-03-16 10:15:30.220"

4.1.58 Answer: D

Reason:
For Period.ofWeeks(int), the resulting period will be day-based, with the amount of days equal to the number of weeks multiplied by 7.

Period is represented in terms of Year, Month and Day only and toString() method uses upper case characters.

NOTE: Other 'of' methods of Period class are:
Period.of(int years, int months, int days) => Returns a Period instance with specified number of years, months and days.
Period.ofDays(int days) => Returns a Period instance with specified number of days.
Period.ofMonths(int months) => Returns a Period instance with specified number of months.
Period.ofYears(int years) => Returns a Period instance with specified number of years.

4.1.59 Answer: A

Reason:
Signature of between method defined in Duration class is: 'Duration between(Temporal startInclusive, Temporal endExclusive)'.

As both LocalTime and LocalDateTime implement 'Temporal' interface, hence there is no compilation error.

If the Temporal objects are of different types as in this case, calculation is based on 1st argument and 2nd argument is converted to the type of 1st argument. It is easy to convert LocalDateTime to LocalTime.

Program executes successfully and terminates successfully after displaying the Duration object on to the console.

4.1.60 Answer: B

Reason:

M -> Represents actual digit for the month (1 to 12).
MM -> Represents 2 digits for the month (01 to 12).
MMM -> Represents short name for the month, with first character in upper case, such as Jun, Sep
MMMM -> Represents full name for the month, with first character in upper case, such as June, September

DateTimeFormatter.ofPattern(String) method uses the default Locale and in this case default Locale is set to en_US, hence English month names will be printed.
"2018-09-10" will be formatted to "10-Sep-2018".

4.1.61 Answer: B

Reason:

new PrintStream("F:\\err.log") => This will create a new file 'err.log' under F: and will create a PrintStream instance.

System.setOut(new PrintStream("F:\\err.log")); => Sets the out PrintStream to passed object.

System.out.println("ONE"); => Writes 'ONE' to 'err.log' file.

System.out.println(1 / 0); => Throws ArithmeticException, which is caught by the catch handler.

System.err.println("TWO"); => Prints 'TWO' on to the console, default err Stream. err PrintStream was not changed using System.setErr(PrintStream) method.

So, 'err.log' file contains 'ONE' only.

4.1.62 Answer: C

Reason:

In format string, format specifier are just replaced.
2$ means 2nd argument, which is 20 and 1$ means 1st argument, which is 10.
Hence 'System.out.printf("%2$d + %1$d", 10, 20);' prints '20 + 10' on to the console.

NOTE: System.out.printf(...) is same as System.out.format(...).

4.1.63 Answer: D

Reason:

Student class implements Serializable, hence objects of Student class can be serialized using ObjectOutputStream.

State of transient and static fields are not persisted.

While de-serializing, transient fields are initialized to default values (null for reference type and respective Zeros for primitive types) and static fields refer to current value.

In this case, name is transient, so it is not persisted. On de-serializing, null is printed for name and 20 is printed for age.

4.1.64 Answer: E

Reason:

Given File methods return boolean and don't throw any checked exception at runtime.

dirs -> referring to File object for abstract path: F:\A\B\C.
Initially F: is blank.

System.out.println(dirs.mkdirs()); => Creates all the directories A, B, C as per abstract path and returns true.

dir -> referring to File object for abstract path: F:\A

System.out.println(dir.mkdir()); => returns false as F:\A directory exists.

System.out.println(dir.delete()); => returns false as F:\A is not empty directory, it contains directory 'B'.

4.1.65 Answer: B, D

Reason:

This code compiles successfully.

Code inside main method doesn't throw IOException or its subtype but main method is free to declare any exception in its throws clause.

Even though program is executed from command line but System.console() may return null, in case no console available for the underlying OS.
In that case, console.readLine(...) will cause NullPointerException at runtime.

readLine method is a blocking method, it waits for the user action. It waits until user presses Enter key or terminates the program.

4.1.66 Answer: C

Reason:
toRealPath() returns the path of an existing file. It returns the path after normalizing.

Let's first normalize the path.

"F:\\A\\.\\B\\C\\D\\..\\Book.java"
can be normalized to "F:\\A\\B\\C\\D\\..\\Book.java" [Single dot is for current directory, hence it is redundant].
can be further normalized to "F:\\A\\B\\C\\Book.java" [Double dot is for going to parent directory, hence dir 'D' is removed].

'F:\A\B\C\Book.java' exists on the file system, hence no exception.

4.1.67 Answer: C

Reason:
file1.resolve(file2) resolves file2 against file1. file1 is an absolute path and file2 is a relative path, hence resolve method returns Path object referring to 'F:\A\B\C\Book.java'.

file1.resolveSibling(file2) resolves file2 against parent path of file1. Parent path of file1 is: 'F:\A\B\', hence resolveSibling method returns Path object referring to 'F:\A\B\Book.java'.

4.1.68 Answer: D

Reason:
'Files.copy(src, tgt);' copies 'F:\A\B\C\Book.java' to 'F:\A\B\Book.java' and returns the Path of copied element.

src refers to 'F:\A\B\C\Book.java'.
tgt refers to 'F:\A\B\Book.java'.
copy refers to 'F:\A\B\Book.java'.

Files.isSameFile(Path path1, Path path2) returns true if both the paths locate the same physical file.

src and copy refer to different physical files, hence 'Files.isSameFile(src, copy)' returns false.
tgt and copy refer to same physical file, hence 'Files.isSameFile(tgt, copy)' returns true.

4.1.69 Answer: A

Reason:

Root folder or drive is not considered in count and indexing. In the given path A is at 0th index, B is at 1st index, C is at 2nd index and Book.java is at 3rd index.

In 'subpath(int beginIndex, int endIndex)' method beginIndex in inclusive and endIndex is exclusive. So, in the given question, starting index is 1 and end index is 4. In the given path there is no element at the 4th index, hence an exception is thrown at runtime.

In fact, subpath(int beginIndex, int endIndex) throws IllegalArgumentException if 'beginIndex >= No. of path elements', 'endIndex > No. of path elements' and 'endIndex <= beginIndex'.

4.1.70 Answer: A

Reason:

path refers to 'F:\A', path.getRoot() refers to 'F:\' and path.getParent() refers to 'F:\'. Hence result is 'true'.

4.1.71 Answer: B

Reason:
path1 --> [F:\Other\Logs].
path2 --> [..\..\Shortcut\Child.lnk\Message.txt].

path1.resolve(path2) --> [F:\Other\Logs\..\..\Shortcut\Child.lnk\Message.txt].
path3 --> [F:\Shortcut\Child.lnk\Message.txt].

path1.resolveSibling(path2) --> [F:\Other\..\..\Shortcut\Child.lnk\Message.txt].
path4 --> [F:\Shortcut\Child.lnk\Message.txt].

This is interesting, if you are at the root directory, and give the command cd .., then nothing happens, you stay at the root only.
System.out.println(Paths.get("F:\\..\\..\\..\\..").normalize()); would print F:\.

This is the reason, why path4 is referring to [F:\Shortcut\Child.lnk\Message.txt] and no exception is thrown at runtime.

As path3 and path4 refer to same location, hence path3.equals(path4) returns true.

4.1.72 Answer: B

Reason:
As SELECT statement returns one record, code inside while loop is executed.

'rs.getInt("IDD")' throws SQLException as column name 'IDD' will not be found at runtime. Exception handler for SQLException is available, which prints 'An Error Occurred!' on to the console.

4.1.73 Answer: B

Reason:
Given sql query returns below records:
101 John Smith   12000
102 SeanSmith   15000
103 Regina   Williams 15500
104 Natasha George   14600

'resultSetType' can accept 3 constants: TYPE_FORWARD_ONLY, TYPE_SCROLL_INSENSITIVE & TYPE_SCROLL_SENSITIVE.
'resultSetConcurrency' can accept 2 constants: CONCUR_READ_ONLY & CONCUR_UPDATABLE.

'rs.absolute(-2);' moves the cursor to 3rd record (2nd from last).
'rs.relative(-1);' moves the cursor to 2nd record (1 up from the current cursor position).

'rs.getInt(1)' returns 102.

NOTE: Column index starts with 1 and not 0.

4.1.74 Answer: B

Reason:
database url has the form: protocol:subprotocol:subname.

protocol is always 'jdbc'.

subprotocol is database specific, for MySQL it is 'mysql'.

subname contains database details, such as '//localhost:3306/ocp'.

Complete database url form MySQL db is: 'jdbc:mysql://localhost:3306/ocp'. So it always starts with 'jdbc:'.

4.1.75   Answer: D

Reason:
rs.getMetaData().getColumnCount(); definitely returns 2 as there are 2 columns in the table.

But ResultSet cursor is initially before the first record, hence 'rs.getString(i)' throws SQLException at runtime.

To print both the column values correctly, either use rs.absolute(1) OR rs.relative(1) OR rs.next() just before the for loop.

4.1.76   Answer: B

Reason:
There are 3 ResultSet types: TYPE_FORWARD_ONLY, TYPE_SCROLL_INSENSITIVE and TYPE_SCROLL_SENSITIVE.

4.1.77   Answer: C

Reason:
Given query returns below records:
101 John   Smith   12000
102 Sean   Smith   15000
103 Regina Williams   15500
104 Natasha George 14600

'rs.moveToInsertRow();' It moves the cursor to the insert row.
Please note, If the cursor is at insert row and refreshRow() or updateRow() or deleteRow() method is called, then SQLException is thrown.
Hence, in this case an exception is raised by Line n1.

4.1.78   Answer: A,E

Reason:
Locale.US; => Locale.US represents a Locale instance for en_US.
new Locale(Locale.US); => There is no Locale constructor which accepts a Locale object.
Locale.getInstance("us"); => There is no getInstance method, which accepts single String argument. Famous getInstance method has signature: 'getInstance(String language, String country, String variant)'.

Locale.getDefault(); => It will not always return Locale for en_US, it depends on the default locale of JVM.
new Locale("en", "US"); => This definitely creates a Locale instance for en_US.

4.1.79 Answer: C

Reason:
The search order for matching resource bundle is:
com.udayan.ocp.MyResourceBundle_en_US [1st: Complete, en_US].
com.udayan.ocp.MyResourceBundle_en [2nd: Only language, en].
com.udayan.ocp.MyResourceBundle_fr_IT [3rd: Complete Default Locale, fr_IT].
com.udayan.ocp.MyResourceBundle_fr [4th: Language of Default Locale, fr].
com.udayan.ocp.MyResourceBundle [5th: ResourceBundle's name without language or country].

If search reaches the 5th step and no matching resource bundle is found, then MissingResourceException is thrown at runtime.

In 4th step, matching resource bundle is found and hence '1001' is printed on to the console.

4.1.80 Answer: D

Reason:
There are no setCountry(...) and setLanguage(...) methods defined in Locale class.

4.1.81 Answer: C

Reason:
Locale.US represents a Locale instance for en_US. As locale is en_US, hence given files will be searched in below order:
ResourceBundle_en_US.properties (Not available)
ResourceBundle_en.properties (Available and works even in the file name "EN" is in upper-case, but convention is to use lowercase of language code)
ResourceBundle.properties (Available)
Note that 'ResourceBundle_US.properties' will not be considered.

Hence bundle.getKeys(); returns an Enumeration<String> instance containing (k3,k4) from 'ResourceBundle_EN.properties' file and (k1,k2) from 'ResouceBundle.properties' file.

You can iterate over Enumeration using hasMoreElements() and nextElement() methods.

Iteration logic prints key-value pair in the order of Enumeration elements (k3, k4, k1, k2).
Hence the output will be:
k3=EN3
k4=EN4
k1=1
k2=2

4.1.82   Answer: C

Reason:

Callable is of Void type and call() method returns null.

'es.submit(new Caller("Call"));' creates a Caller object and invokes the call method. This method prints 'CALL' on to the console and returns null.

'System.out.println(future.get());' prints 'null' on to the console.

As 'es.shutdown();' is not invoked, hence program doesn't terminate.

4.1.83   Answer: A

Reason:

ExecutorService interface extends Executor interface and it has 'void execute(Runnable command);'. Runnable is a Functional interface which has single abstract method 'public abstract void run();'.

Given lambda expression, '() -> "HELLO"' returns a String and it doesn't match with the implementation of run() method whose return type is void. Hence it causes compilation error.

Return type of execute method is void, hence another reason for compilation error is that result of ex.execute(...) cannot be assigned to Future<String>.

4.1.84   Answer: A

Reason:

All streams in Java implements BaseStream interface and this interface has parallel() and sequential() methods. Hence all streams can either be parallel or sequential.

4.1.85 Answer: B

Reason:
Method reference 'Test::print' is for the run() method implementation of Runnable and 'Test::get' is for the call() method implementation of Callable.

Future<?> is valid return type for both the method calls. get() method throws 2 checked exceptions: InterruptedException and ExecutionException, hence given code compiles fine.

get() method waits for task completion, hence 'PRINT' will be printed first.

future1.get() returns null and future2.get() returns 10.

4.1.86 Answer: A

Reason:
RecursiveAction class has an abstract method 'void compute()' and Adder class correctly overrides it.

new Adder(1, 20); instantiate an Adder object with from = 1, to = 20 and total = 0.

20 - 1 is not less than or equal to 4 hence else block will create multiple Adder objects, and compute() method will be invoked on these objects. More Adder objects will be created further.

Statement 'total+=sum;' will update the total filed of these objects but not the adder object created at Line 34. So when 'System.out.println(adder.total);' is executed, it prints 0 on to the console.

To get the expected output (which is sum of numbers from 1 to 20), add below code as the last statement in the else block so that total field of Adder object created at Line 34 is updated successfully:
total = first.total + second.total;

4.1.87   Answer: A,B,C

Reason:
ForkJoinPool class declares the invoke() method as: public <T> T invoke(ForkJoinTask<T> task) {...}

Instance of ForkJoinTask class can be easily passed to the invoke method.

As RecursiveAction and RecursiveTask extend from ForkJoinTask, hence their instances can also be passed to the invoke method.

4.1.88   Answer: B

Reason:
Parallel streams internally use fork/join framework only, so there is always an overhead of splitting the tasks and joining the results.

Parallel streams improves performance for streams with large number of elements, easily splittable into independent operations and computations are complex.

4.1.89   Answer: B

Reason:
list.parallelStream() returns a parallel stream.

Method reference 'RES::append' is same as lambda expression 's -> RES.append(s)'.
NOTE: In the lambda expression as static variable RES is used hence given code suffers from race condition.

Output cannot be predicted in this case.

4.1.90 Answer: A

Reason:
stream --> {1, 2, 3, 4, 5}.
stream.parallel() returns a parallel stream.

To understand, 'reduce((x, y) -> x + y)' is equivalent to:

```
boolean foundAny = false;
int result = null;
for (int element : this stream) {
 if (!foundAny) {
    foundAny = true;
    result = element;
 }
 else
    result = accumulator.applyAsInt(result, element);
}
return foundAny ? OptionalInt.of(result) : OptionalInt.empty();
```

result will be initialized to 1st element of the stream and output will be the result of '1 + 2 + 3 + 4 + 5', which is 15.

The whole computation may run in parallel, but parallelism doesn't impact final result. In this case as there are only 5 numbers, hence it is an overhead to use parallelism.

reduce((x, y) -> x + y) returns OptionalInt and it has getAsInt() method.

5   Practice Test-5

5.1   90 Questions covering all topics.

5.1.1   Consider the code of Test.java file:

```java
package com.udayan.ocp;

class Player {
    String name;
    int age;

    void Player() {
        this.name = "Virat";
        this.age = 29;
    }

    public String toString() {
        return "Name: " + this.name + ", Age: " + this.age;
    }
}

public class Test {
    public static void main(String[] args) {
        System.out.println(new Player());
    }
}
```

What will be the result of compiling and executing Test class?

A. Compilation error

B. Name: null, Age: 0

C. Name: Virat, Age: 29

D. An exception is thrown at runtime

5.1.2   Consider below code:

```
//Test.java
package com.udayan.ocp;

abstract class Animal {
    abstract void eat();
}

class Dog extends Animal {
    public void eat() {
        System.out.println("Dog eats biscuit.");
    }
}

class Cat extends Animal {
    public void eat() {
        System.out.println("Cat eats fish.");
    }
}

public class Test {
    public static void main(String[] args) {
        Animal [] animals = new Dog[2];
        animals[0] = new Dog();
        animals[1] = new Cat();

        animals[0].eat();
        animals[1].eat();
    }
}
```

What will be the result of compiling and executing Test class?

A.	Compilation error	B.	Runtime exception
C.	Dog eats biscuit. Cat eats fish.	D.	None of the other options.

5.1.3   Consider the code of Test.java file:

```
package com.udayan.ocp;

class Calculator {
    public static void add(int x, int y) {
        System.out.println("The sum is: " + x + y);
    }
}

public class Test {
    public static void main(String[] args) {
        Calculator.add(15, 25);
    }
}
```

What will be the result of compiling and executing Test class?

A. The sum is: 40

B. The sum is: 1525

C. Compilation error

5.1.4   What will be the result of compiling and executing Test class?

```
package com.udayan.ocp;
interface Operation {
    int operate(int x, int y);
}
public class Test {
    public static void main(String[] args) {
        int x = 10;
        int y = 20;
        Operation o1 = (x, y) -> x * y;
        System.out.println(o1.operate(5, 10));
    }
}
```

A. 50

B. 200

C. Compilation error

D. Exception is thrown at runtime

461

5.1.5   Consider the code of Test.java file:

```
package com.udayan.ocp;

enum Flags {
    TRUE;

    Flags() {
        System.out.println("HELLO");
    }
}

public class Test {
    public static void main(String[] args) {
        Flags f1 = Flags.TRUE;
        Flags f2 = Flags.TRUE;
        Flags f3 = Flags.TRUE;
    }
}
```

What will be the result of compiling and executing Test class?

A. HELLO is printed once.

B. HELLO is printed twice.

C. HELLO is printed thrice.

D. HELLO Is not printed on to the console.

5.1.6   Below is the code of Test.java file:

```java
public class Test {
    enum TrafficLight {
        RED, YELLOW, GREEN;
    }

    public static void main(String[] args) {
        TrafficLight tl = TrafficLight.valueOf(args[0]);
        switch(tl) {
            case RED:
                System.out.println("STOP");
                break;
            case YELLOW:
                System.out.println("SLOW");
                break;
            case GREEN:
                System.out.println("GO");
                break;
        }
    }
}
```

What will be the output if Test class is executed by the commands:
```
javac Test.java
java Test GREEN AMBER
```

A. GO

B. IllegalArgumentException is thrown at runtime

C. NullPointerException is thrown at runtime

D. Compilation error

5.1.7   What will be the result of compiling and executing Test class?

```
package com.udayan.ocp;

class A {
    A() {
        System.out.print(1);
    }
    class B {
        B() {
            System.out.print(2);
        }
    }
}

public class Test {
    public static void main(String [] args) {
        B obj = new A().new B();
    }
}
```

A. 12

B. 21

C. 2

D. Compilation error

5.1.8 Given code:

```
package com.udayan.ocp;

class Outer {
    Outer() {
        System.out.print(2);
    }
    /*INSERT 1*/

    class Inner {
        Inner() {
            System.out.print(4);
        }
        /*INSERT 2*/
    }
}

public class Test {
    public static void main(String[] args) {
        new Outer().new Inner();
    }
}
```

Currently on executing Test class, 24 is printed in the output.

Which of the following pairs will correctly replace /*INSERT 1*/ and /*INSERT 2*/ so that on executing Test class, 1234 is printed in the output?

A.	Replace /*INSERT 1*/ with {System.out.print(1);} Replace /*INSERT 2*/ with {System.out.print(3);}
B.	Replace /*INSERT 1*/ with static {System.out.print(1);} Replace /*INSERT 2*/ with {System.out.print(3);}
C.	Replace /*INSERT 1*/ with {System.out.print(1);} Replace /*INSERT 2*/ with static {System.out.print(3);}
D.	Replace /*INSERT 1*/ with static {System.out.print(1);} Replace /*INSERT 2*/ with static {System.out.print(3);}

5.1.9   Given Code:

```
package com.udayan.ocp;

class Outer {
    private String msg = "A";
    public void print() {
        final String msg = "B";
        class Inner {
            public void print() {
                System.out.println(this.msg);
            }
        }
        Inner obj = new Inner();
        obj.print();
    }
}

public class Test {
    public static void main(String[] args) {
        new Outer().print();
    }
}
```

What will be the result of compiling and executing Test class?

A. Compilation error

B. A

C. B

D. Exception is thrown at runtime

5.1.10 Given code:

```
package com.udayan.ocp;

class Message {
    public void printMessage() {
        System.out.println("Hello!");
    }
}

public class Test {
    public static void main(String[] args) {
        Message msg = new Message() {
            public void PrintMessage() {
                System.out.println("HELLO!");
            }
        };
        msg.printMessage();
    }
}
```

What will be the result of compiling and executing Test class?

A. Compilation error

B. Runtime error

C. Hello!

D. HELLO!

5.1.11 Below is the code of Test.java file:

```
package com.udayan.ocp;

class A {
    static class B {

    }
}

public class Test {
    /*INSERT*/
}
```

Which of the following options can replace /*INSERT*/ such that there are no compilation errors?

A.   B obj = new B();

B.   B obj = new A.B();

C.   A.B obj = new A.B();

D.   A.B obj = new A().new B();

5.1.12 Will below code compile successfully?

```
package com.udayan.ocp;

class Outer {
    interface I1 {
        void m1();
    }
}
```

A. Yes

B. No

5.1.13 For the given code:

```
package com.udayan.ocp;

interface Printable {
    void print(String msg);
}

public class Test {
    public static void main(String[] args) {
        Printable obj = new Printable() {
            public void print(String msg) {
                System.out.println(msg);
            }
        };
        obj.print("Welcome!");
    }
}
```

Which of the following options successfully replace anonymous inner class code with lambda expression code?
Select ALL that apply.

A.	`Printable obj = (String msg) -> {System.out.println(msg);};`
B.	`Printable obj = (msg) -> {System.out.println(msg);};`
C.	`Printable obj = (msg) -> System.out.println(msg);`
D.	`Printable obj = msg -> System.out.println(msg);`
E.	`Printable obj = x -> System.out.println(x);`
F.	`Printable obj = y - > System.out.println(y);`

5.1.14 **What will be the result of compiling and executing Test class?**

```java
package com.udayan.ocp;

@FunctionalInterface
interface I4 {
    void print();
    boolean equals(Object obj);
}

public class Test {
    public static void main(String[] args) {
        I4 obj = () ->
                    System.out.println("Lambda expression");
        obj.print();
    }
}
```

A. Compilation error

B. Lambda expression

C. No output

D. Runtime error

5.1.15 **What will be the result of compiling and executing Test class?**

```java
package com.udayan.ocp;

@FunctionalInterface
interface I7 {
    void print();
}

public class Test {
    String var = "Lambda";
    class Inner {
        int var = 1000;
        I7 obj = () -> System.out.println(this.var);
    }

    public static void main(String[] args) {
        Inner inner = new Test().new Inner();
        inner.obj.print();
    }
}
```

A. Lambda

B. 1000

C. Compilation Error

D. None of the other options

5.1.16 Does below code compile successfully?

```
class A{}
interface M{}
interface N{}

class B extends A {}
class C extends A implements M {}
class D extends A implements M, N {}

class Generic<T extends M & N & A> {}
```

A. Yes

B. No

5.1.17 Given code of Test.java file:

```
package com.udayan.ocp;

public class Test {
    public static <T> T get(T t) {
        return t;
    }

    public static void main(String[] args) {
        String str = get("HELLO");
        System.out.println(str);
    }
}
```

What will be the result of compiling and executing Test class?

A. HELLO

B. Compilation error in 'get' method

C. Compilation error in 'main' method

D. Runtime Exception

5.1.18   Given code of Test.java file:

```
package com.udayan.ocp;

public class Test {
    private static <T extends Number> void print(T t) {
        System.out.println(t.intValue());
    }

    public static void main(String[] args) {
        /*INSERT*/
    }
}
```

Which of the following statements, if used to replace /*INSERT*/, will not cause any compilation error?

A. `print(new Integer(1));`

B. `print(new Number(0));`

C. `print(new Object());`

D. `print(new Character('a'));`

E. `print(new Double(5.5));`

5.1.19 **What will be the result of compiling and executing Test class?**

```
package com.udayan.ocp;

interface Operator<T> {
    public abstract T operation(T t1, T t2);
}

public class Test {
    public static void main(String[] args) {
        Operator<String> opr1 = (s1, s2) -> s1 + s2;
        Operator<Integer> opr2 = (i1, i2) -> i1 + i2;
        opr1.operation("Hello", "World");
        opr2.operation(10, 40);
    }
}
```

A.	Compilation error	B.	HelloWorld 50
C.	Program compiles and executes successfully but nothing is printed on to the console	D.	HelloWorld 1040

5.1.20 Given code of Test.java file:

```java
package com.udayan.ocp;

import java.util.*;

class Student {
    private String name;
    private int age;

    Student(String name, int age) {
        this.name = name;
        this.age = age;
    }

    public String toString() {
        return "Student[" + name + ", " + age + "]";
    }

    public boolean equals(Object obj) {
        if(obj instanceof Student) {
            Student stud = (Student)obj;
            return this.name.equals(stud.name)
                          && this.age == stud.age;
        }
        return false;
    }
}

public class Test {
    public static void main(String[] args) {
        Set<Student> students = new HashSet<>();
        students.add(new Student("James", 20));
        students.add(new Student("James", 20));
        students.add(new Student("James", 22));

        System.out.println(students.size());
    }
}
```

What will be the result of compiling and executing Test class?

A. 3

B. 2

C. Runtime Exception

5.1.21 Given code of Test.java file:

```
package com.udayan.ocp;

import java.util.*;

public class Test {
    public static void main(String[] args) {
        NavigableMap<Integer, String> map
                              = new TreeMap<>();
        map.put(25, "Pune");
        map.put(32, "Mumbai");
        map.put(11, "Sri Nagar");
        map.put(39, "Chennai");

        System.out.println(map.headMap(25));
        System.out.println(map.tailMap(25));
    }
}
```

What will be the result of compiling and executing Test class?

A.	`{11=Sri Nagar, 25=Pune}` `{25=Pune, 32=Mumbai, 39=Chennai}`
B.	`{11=Sri Nagar}` `{32=Mumbai, 39=Chennai}`
C.	`{11=Sri Nagar}` `{25=Pune, 32=Mumbai, 39=Chennai}`
D.	`{11=Sri Nagar, 25=Pune}` `{32=Mumbai, 39=Chennai}`

5.1.22 Given code of Test.java file:

```
package com.udayan.ocp;

import java.util.ArrayDeque;
import java.util.Deque;

public class Test {
    public static void main(String[] args) {
        Deque<Character> chars = new ArrayDeque<>();
        chars.add('A');
        chars.add('B');
        chars.remove();
        chars.add('C');
        chars.remove();

        System.out.println(chars);
    }
}
```

What will be the result of compiling and executing Test class?

A. [A]

B. [B]

C. [C]

5.1.23 **What will be the result of compiling and executing TestPoint class?**

```java
package com.udayan.ocp;

import java.util.ArrayList;
import java.util.Collections;
import java.util.Comparator;
import java.util.List;

class Point {
    private int x;
    private int y;

    public Point(int x, int y) {
        this.x = x;
        this.y = y;
    }

    @Override
    public String toString() {
        return "Point(" + x + ", " + y + ")";
    }
}

public class TestPoint {
    public static void main(String [] args) {
        List<Point> points = new ArrayList<>();
        points.add(new Point(4, 5));
        points.add(new Point(6, 7));
        points.add(new Point(2, 2));

        Collections.sort(points, new Comparator<Point>() {
            @Override
            public int compare(Point o1, Point o2) {
                return o1.x - o2.x;
            }
        });
    }
}
```

A. [Point(2, 2), Point(4, 5), Point(6, 7)]

B. [Point(6, 7), Point(4, 5), Point(2, 2)]

C. [Point(4, 5), Point(6, 7), Point(2, 2)]

D. Compilation error

5.1.24 A bank's swift code is generally of 11 characters and used in international money transfers:

```
An example: ICICINBBRT4
ICIC: First 4 letters for bank code
IN: Next 2 letters for Country code
BB: Next 2 letters for Location code
RT4: Next 3 letters for Branch code
```

Given code of SortSwiftCode.java file:

```java
package com.udayan.ocp;

import java.util.Arrays;
import java.util.Collections;
import java.util.Comparator;
import java.util.List;

public class SortSwiftCode {
    public static void main(String[] args) {
        List<String> swiftCodes = Arrays.asList(
            "ICICINDD016", "ICICINBBRT4", "BOTKINDD075",
            "BARBINBB011", "SBBJINDD062", "ABNATHBK865",
            "BKCHTHBK012");

        Comparator<String> countryLocationBank =
            Comparator.comparing(SortSwiftCode::extractCountry)
                .thenComparing(SortSwiftCode::extractLocation)
                .thenComparing(SortSwiftCode::extractBank);

        Collections.sort(swiftCodes, countryLocationBank);
        printCodes(swiftCodes);

    }

    private static String extractCountry(String swiftCode) {
        return swiftCode.substring(4, 6);
    }

    private static String extractLocation(String swiftCode) {
        return swiftCode.substring(6, 8);
    }
```

478

```
    private static String extractBank(String swiftCode) {
        return swiftCode.substring(0, 4);
    }

    private static void printCodes(List<String> list) {
        for (String str : list) {
            System.out.println(str);
        }
    }
}
```

What will be the result of compiling and executing SortSwiftCode class?

A.	ABNATHBK865 BKCHTHBK012 BARBINBB011 ICICINBBRT4 BOTKINDD075 ICICINDD016 SBBJINDD062	B.	BARBINBB011 ICICINBBRT4 BOTKINDD075 ICICINDD016 SBBJINDD062 ABNATHBK865 BKCHTHBK012
C.	BARBINBB011 BOTKINDD075 ICICINBBRT4 ICICINDD016 SBBJINDD062 ABNATHBK865 BKCHTHBK012	D.	None of the other options

5.1.25 Given code of Test.java file:

```
package com.udayan.ocp;

import java.util.Arrays;
import java.util.List;

public class Test {
    public static void main(String[] args) {
        List<String> list = Arrays.asList("A", "A", "b",
                                "B", "c", "c");
        list.stream().distinct().forEach(System.out::print);
    }
}
```

What will be the result of compiling and executing Test class?

A. AAbBcc

B. AbBc

C. ABbc

D. Abc

E. ABc

5.1.26   Given code of Test.java file:

```java
package com.udayan.ocp;

import java.util.*;

class Employee {
    private String name;
    private double salary;

    public Employee(String name, double salary) {
        this.name = name;
        this.salary = salary;
    }

    public String getName() {
        return name;
    }

    public double getSalary() {
        return salary;
    }

    public void setSalary(double salary) {
        this.salary = salary;
    }

    public String toString() {
        return "{" + name + ", " + salary + "}";
    }
}
```

```
public class Test {
  public static void main(String[] args) {
      List<Employee> employees = Arrays.asList(
          new Employee("Jack", 10000),
          new Employee("Lucy", 12000));
      employees.stream().filter(x -> x.getSalary() > 10000)
        .map(e -> e.getName()).forEach(System.out::println);
  }
}
```

What will be the result of compiling and executing Test class?

A.	Jack	B.	Lucy
C.	Jack Lucy	D.	Lucy Jack

5.1.27 Given code of Test.java file:

```
package com.udayan.ocp;

import java.util.stream.IntStream;

public class Test {
    public static void main(String[] args) {
        IntStream.iterate(1, i -> i + 1)
            .limit(11).filter(i -> i % 2 != 0)
            .forEach(System.out::print);
    }
}
```

What will be the result of compiling and executing Test class?

A. 13579

B. 1357911

C. 246810

D. 24681012

5.1.28 Given code of Test.java file:

```
package com.udayan.ocp;

import java.util.stream.IntStream;

public class Test {
    public static void main(String[] args) {
        System.out.println(
            IntStream.range(-10, -10).count());
        System.out.println(
            IntStream.rangeClosed(-10, -10).count());
    }
}
```

What will be the result of compiling and executing Test class?

A.	0 0	B.	0 1
C.	1 1	D.	1 0

5.1.29 Which of the following pairs correctly represent the Functional interface and its single abstract method?

A.	Consumer : apply Function : accept Supplier : test Predicate : get	B.	Consumer : apply Function : accept Supplier : get Predicate : test
C.	Consumer : accept Function : apply Supplier : get Predicate : test	D.	Consumer : accept Function : apply Supplier : test Predicate : get

5.1.30 **What will be the result of compiling and executing Test class?**

```
package com.udayan.ocp;

import java.util.function.Function;

public class Test {
    public static void main(String[] args) {
        Function<char [], String> obj = String::new; //Line 5
        String s = obj.apply(
            new char[] {'j', 'a', 'v', 'a'}); //Line 6
        System.out.println(s);
    }
}
```

What will be the result of compiling and executing Test class?

A. java

B. Compilation error at Line 5

C. Compilation error at Line 6

D. Exception is thrown at runtime

5.1.31 **Given code of Test.java file:**

```
package com.udayan.ocp;

import java.util.function.Function;

public class Test {
    public static void main(String[] args) {
        Function<String, Integer> f1 = Integer::new;
        Function<String, String> f2 = s ->
            new StringBuilder(s).reverse().toString();
        System.out.println(f1.compose(f2).apply("12345"));
    }
}
```

What will be the result of compiling and executing Test class?

A. 12345

B. 54321

C. Compilation error

D. NumberFormatException is thrown at runtime

5.1.32 Given code of Test.java file:

```java
package com.udayan.ocp;

import java.util.function.Predicate;

public class Test {
    public static void main(String[] args) {
        String [] arr = {"*", "**", "***", "****",
                                    "*****", "******"};
        Predicate<String> pr1 = s -> s.length() > 3;
        print(arr, pr1.negate());
    }

    private static void print(String [] arr,
                        Predicate<String> predicate) {
        for(String str : arr) {
            if(predicate.test(str)) {
                System.out.println(str);
            }
        }
    }
}
```

What will be the result of compiling and executing Test class?

A.	``` * * * * * * * * * * * * * * * ```	B.	``` * * * * * * ```
C.	``` * * * ```	D.	``` * * * * * * * * * * * * * * * * * * * * * ```

5.1.33 Given code of Test.java file:

```
package com.udayan.ocp;

import java.util.function.BiFunction;

public class Test {
    public static void main(String[] args) {
        BiFunction<String, String, String> func
                = (s1, s2) -> s2.concat(s1).trim();
        System.out.println(func.apply(" CD", " AB"));
    }
}
```

What will be the result of compiling and executing Test class?

A. AB CD

B. ABCD

C. CD AB

D. CDAB

5.1.34 Given code of Test.java file:

```
package com.udayan.ocp;

import java.util.function.DoubleFunction;
import java.util.function.DoubleUnaryOperator;

public class Test {
    public static void main(String[] args) {
        DoubleFunction<DoubleUnaryOperator> func =
                        m -> n -> m + n; //Line n1
        System.out.println(func.apply(11)
                    .applyAsDouble(24)); //Line n2
    }
}
```

What will be the result of compiling and executing Test class?

A. 22.0

B. 48.0

C. 35.0

D. Line n1 causes compilation error

E. Line n2 causes compilation error

5.1.35 Given code of Test.java file:

```
package com.udayan.ocp;

import java.util.function.UnaryOperator;

public class Test {
    public static void main(String[] args) {
        UnaryOperator<String> opr =
            s -> s.toString().toUpperCase(); //Line n1
        System.out.println(opr.apply(
            new StringBuilder("Hello"))); //Line n2
    }
}
```

What will be the result of compiling and executing Test class?

A. Compilation error at Line n1

B. Compilation error at Line n2

C. Hello

D. HELLO

5.1.36 Given code of Test.java file:

```java
package com.udayan.ocp;

import java.util.stream.Stream;

public class Test {
    public static void main(String[] args) {
        Stream.of().map(s ->
            s.reverse()).forEach(System.out::println);
    }
}
```

What will be the result of compiling and executing Test class?

A. Compilation error

B. NullPointerException is thrown at runtime

C. ClassCastException is thrown at runtime

D. Program executes successfully but nothing is printed on to the console

5.1.37 Given code of Test.java file:

```java
package com.udayan.ocp;

import java.util.stream.Stream;

public class Test {
    public static void main(String[] args) {
        Stream.of(true, false, true).map(b -> b.toString()
          .toUpperCase()).peek(System.out::println).count();
    }
}
```

What will be the result of compiling and executing Test class?

A.	TRUE FALSE TRUE 3	B.	TRUE FALSE TRUE
C.	true false true 3	D.	true false true

5.1.38 Given code of Test.java file:

```
package com.udayan.ocp;

import java.util.Optional;
import java.util.stream.Stream;

public class Test {
    public static void main(String[] args) {
        Optional<Integer> optional
                = Stream.of(10).findFirst();
        System.out.println(optional);
    }
}
```

What will be the result of compiling and executing Test class?

A. 10

B. Optional[10]

C. Text containing @ symbol

5.1.39 Given code of Test.java file:

```
package com.udayan.ocp;

import java.time.LocalDate;
import java.util.Optional;
import java.util.stream.Stream;

public class Test {
    public static void main(String[] args) {
        Stream<LocalDate> stream = Stream.of(
            LocalDate.of(2018, 1, 1),
            LocalDate.of(2018, 1, 1));
        Optional<LocalDate> optional = stream
                            .distinct().findAny();

        System.out.println(optional.isPresent()
                            + " : " + optional.get());
    }
}
```

What will be the result of compiling and executing Test class?

A. true : 2018-1-1

B. true : 2018-01-01

C. false : 2018-1-1

D. false : 2018-01-01

5.1.40 Given code of Test.java file:

```
package com.udayan.ocp;

import java.util.Random;
import java.util.stream.IntStream;

public class Test {
    public static void main(String[] args) {
        IntStream stream = new Random().ints(1, 7).limit(2);
        System.out.println(stream.max().getAsInt());
    }
}
```

Above code compiles and executes successfully and generates random integers.

Which of the following is not the possible output of above code?

A. 4

B. 5

C. 6

D. 7

5.1.41 Given code of Test.java file:

```
package com.udayan.ocp;

import java.util.Arrays;
import java.util.IntSummaryStatistics;
import java.util.stream.Stream;

public class Test {
    public static void main(String[] args) {
        String text =
            "I am going to pass OCP exam in first attempt";
        Stream<String> stream
                        = Arrays.stream(text.split(" "));
        IntSummaryStatistics stat = stream.map(s ->
                        s.length()).summaryStatistics();
        System.out.println(stat.getMax());
    }
}
```

Which of the following needs to be done, so that output is 7?

A. No need to make any changes, on execution given code prints 7 on to the console.

B. Replace 'text.split(" ")' with 'text.split(",")'

C. Replace 'stream.map(s -> s.length())' with 'stream.mapToInt(s -> s.length())'

D. Replace 'stat.getMax()' with 'stat.getCount()'

5.1.42 Given code of Test.java file:

```
package com.udayan.ocp;

import java.util.Comparator;
import java.util.stream.Stream;

public class Test {
    public static void main(String[] args) {
        Comparator<Integer> comp = (i1, i2) ->
                                    i2.compareTo(i1);
        Stream<Integer> stream = Stream
                            .of(55, 23, -9, 8, 42);
        stream.sorted(comp.reversed())
            .forEach(i -> System.out.print(i + " "));
    }
}
```

What will be the result of compiling and executing Test class?

A. 55 42 23 8 -9

B. -9 8 23 42 55

C. 55 23 -9 8 42

D. 42 8 -9 23 55

5.1.43 Given code of Test.java file:

```java
package com.udayan.ocp;

import java.util.List;
import java.util.Map;
import java.util.stream.Collectors;
import java.util.stream.Stream;

class Certification {
    String studId;
    String test;
    int marks;

    Certification(String studId, String test, int marks) {
        this.studId = studId;
        this.test = test;
        this.marks = marks;
    }

    public String toString() {
        return "{" + studId + ", " + test + ", "
                                    + marks + "}";
    }

    public String getStudId() {
        return studId;
    }

    public String getTest() {
        return test;
    }

    public int getMarks() {
        return marks;
    }
}

public class Test {
    public static void main(String[] args) {
        Certification c1 = new Certification("S001", "OCA", 87);
        Certification c2 = new Certification("S002", "OCA", 82);
        Certification c3 = new Certification("S001", "OCP", 79);
        Certification c4 = new Certification("S002", "OCP", 89);
        Certification c5 = new Certification("S003", "OCA", 60);
        Certification c6 = new Certification("S004", "OCA", 88);
```

```
    Stream<Certification> stream =
                Stream.of(c1, c2, c3, c4, c5, c6);
    Map<String, List<Certification>> map = stream.collect(
            Collectors.groupingBy(Certification::getTest));
    System.out.println(map.get("OCP"));
    }
}
```

What will be the result of compiling and executing Test class?

A. [{S001, OCA, 87}, {S002, OCA, 82}, {S003, OCA, 60}, {S004, OCA, 88}]

B. []

C. [{S001, OCA, 87}, {S002, OCA, 82}, {S001, OCP, 79}, {S002, OCP, 89}, {S003, OCA, 60}, {S004, OCA, 88}]

D. [{S001, OCP, 79}, {S002, OCP, 89}]

5.1.44 Given code of Test.java file:

```
package com.udayan.ocp;

import java.util.stream.Stream;

public class Test {
    public static void main(String[] args) {
        Stream<Double> stream = Stream.of(9.8, 2.3, -3.0);
        System.out.println(stream.min());
    }
}
```

What will be the result of compiling and executing Test class?

A. Compilation error

B. Runtime Exception

C. -3.0

D. 2.3

5.1.45 Given code of Test.java file:

```
package com.udayan.ocp;

import java.util.stream.Stream;

public class Test {
    public static void main(String[] args) {
        Stream<Double> stream = Stream.generate(() ->
                            new Double("1.0")).limit(10);
        System.out.println(stream.filter(d -> d > 2)
                            .allMatch(d -> d == 2));
    }
}
```

What will be the result of compiling and executing Test class?

A. false

B. true

5.1.46 Given code of Test.java file:

```
package com.udayan.ocp;

import java.util.function.LongFunction;
import java.util.function.LongUnaryOperator;
import java.util.stream.Stream;

public class Test {
    public static void main(String[] args) {
        long seed = 10;
        Stream<Long> stream = Stream.iterate(
                seed, i -> i + 2).limit(2); //Line n1
        LongFunction<LongUnaryOperator> func =
                            m -> n -> n / m; //Line n2
        stream.mapToLong(i -> i).map(func.apply(2))
                .forEach(System.out::println); //Line n3
    }
}
```

What will be the result of compiling and executing Test class?

A.	10 12	B.	0 0
C.	1 1	D.	5 6
E.	Compilation error		

5.1.47 Given code of Test.java file:

```
package com.udayan.ocp;

public class Test {
    private static void m1() {
        System.out.println(1/0);
    }

    public static void main(String[] args) {
        try {
            m1();
        } finally {
            System.out.println("A");
        }
    }
}
```

What will be the result of compiling and executing Test class?

A. A is printed to the console and program ends normally

B. A is printed to the console, stack trace is printed and then program ends normally

C. A is printed to the console, stack trace is printed and then program ends abruptly

D. Compilation error

5.1.48 Which of the following keywords is used to manually throw an exception?

A. throw

B. throws

C. thrown

D. catch

5.1.49 Given code of Test.java file:

```
package com.udayan.ocp;

import java.io.FileNotFoundException;

public class Test {
    public static void main(String[] args) {
        try {
            System.out.println(1);
        } catch (NullPointerException ex) {
            System.out.println("ONE");
        } catch (FileNotFoundException ex) {
            System.out.println("TWO");
        }
        System.out.println("THREE");
    }
}
```

What will be the result of compiling and executing Test class?

A.	ONE THREE	B.	TWO THREE
C.	THREE	D.	None of the System.out.println statement is executed
E.	Compilation error		

5.1.50 Given code of Test.java file:

```java
package com.udayan.ocp;

import java.sql.SQLException;

public class Test {
    private static void m() throws SQLException {
        try {
            throw new SQLException();
        } catch (Exception e) {
            e = null; //Line 10
            throw e; //Line 11
        }
    }

    public static void main(String[] args) {
        try {
            m(); //Line 17
        } catch(SQLException e) {
            System.out.println("Caught Successfully.");
        }
    }
}
```

What will be the result of compiling and executing Test class?

A. Caught Successfully.

B. Program ends abruptly.

C. Line 10 causes compilation failure.

D. Line 11 causes compilation failure.

E. Line 17 causes compilation failure.

5.1.51 Given code of Test.java file:

```java
package com.udayan.ocp;

import java.util.Scanner;

public class Test {
    public static void main(String[] args) {
        System.out.print("Enter some text: ");
```

```
try(Scanner scan = new Scanner(System.in)) {
    String s = scan.nextLine();
    System.out.println(s);
    scan.close();
    scan.nextLine();
}
    }
}
```

What will be the result of compiling and executing Test class?
User input is: HELLO

A. Compilation error

B. Runtime Exception

C. On execution program terminates successfully after printing 'HELLO' on to the console

5.1.52 Given code of Test.java file:

```
package com.udayan.ocp;

import java.io.PrintWriter;

public class Test {
    public static void main(String[] args) {
        try(PrintWriter writer;) {
            writer = new PrintWriter(System.out);
            writer.println("HELLO");
        }
    }
}
```

What will be the result of compiling and executing Test class?

A. HELLO

B. Compilation error

C. Runtime exception

5.1.53 Given code of Test.java file:

```java
package com.udayan.ocp;

class MyException1 extends RuntimeException {}

class MyException2 extends RuntimeException {}

public class Test {
    private static void m() {
        try {
            throw new RuntimeException();
        } catch(RuntimeException ex) {
            throw new MyException1();
        } finally {
            throw new MyException2();
        }
    }

    public static void main(String[] args) {
        try {
            m();
        } catch(MyException1 e) {
            System.out.println("MyException1");
        } catch(MyException2 e) {
            System.out.println("MyException2");
        } catch (RuntimeException e) {
            System.out.println("RuntimeException");
        }
    }
}
```

What will be the result of compiling and executing Test class?

A. MyException1

B. MyException2

C. RuntimeException

5.1.54 Given code of Test.java file:

```java
package com.udayan.ocp;

class MyResource implements AutoCloseable {
    public void execute() {
        System.out.println("Executing");
    }

    @Override
    public void close() throws Exception {
        System.out.println("Closing");
    }
}

public class Test {
    public static void main(String[] args) {
        try(MyResource resource = new MyResource()) {
            resource.execute();
        }
    }
}
```

What will be the result of compiling and executing Test class?

A.	Compilation Error	B.	Executing
C.	Executing Closing	D.	Runtime Exception

5.1.55 Given code of Test.java file:

```
package com.udayan.ocp;

public class Test {
    private static void checkStatus() {
        /*INSERT*/
    }

    private static String get() {
        return "TEST";
    }

    public static void main(String[] args) {
        try {
            checkStatus();
        } catch (AssertionError ae) {
            System.out.println(ae.getCause());
        }
    }
}
```

Which of the following options can replace /*INSERT*/ such that there are no compilation error?

A. `assert 1 == 2 : () -> "a";`

B. `assert 1 == 2 : 1;`

C. `assert 1 == 2 : return 1;`

D. `assert 1 == 2 : Test::get;`

5.1.56 Given code of Test.java file:

```
package com.udayan.ocp;

import java.time.LocalDate;

public class Test {
    public static void main(String [] args) {
        LocalDate date = LocalDate.ofYearDay(2018, 32);
        System.out.println(date);
    }
}
```

What will be the result of compiling and executing Test class?

A. Runtime exception

B. 2018-02-01

C. 2018-02-02

D. 2018-2-1

E. 2018-2-2

5.1.57 Given code of Test.java file:

```
package com.udayan.ocp;

import java.time.LocalDateTime;

public class Test {
    public static void main(String [] args) {
        LocalDateTime dt =
            LocalDateTime.parse("2018-03-16t10:15:30.22");
        System.out.println(dt.toLocalDate() + " "
                                    + dt.toLocalTime());
    }
}
```

What will be the result of compiling and executing Test class?

A. 2018-03-16 10:15:30.22

B. 2018-03-16 10:15:30.220

C. Compilation error

D. Runtime exception

5.1.58 Given code of Test.java file:

```java
package com.udayan.ocp;

import java.time.LocalDate;
import java.time.Month;
import java.time.Period;

public class Test {
    public static void main(String [] args) {
        LocalDate startDate
            = LocalDate.of(2018, Month.MARCH, 1);
        LocalDate endDate
            = LocalDate.of(2018, Month.MARCH, 11);

        System.out.println(
            Period.between(endDate, startDate));
    }
}
```

What will be the result of compiling and executing Test class?

A. P10D

B. P11D

C. P-10D

D. P-11D

5.1.59   Given code of Test.java file:

```
package com.udayan.ocp;

import java.time.*;

public class Test {
    public static void main(String [] args) {
        LocalDate date1 = LocalDate.of(2019, 1, 1);
        Duration d = Duration.ofDays(1);
        System.out.println(date1.plus(d));
    }
}
```

What will be the result of compiling and executing Test class?

A. 2019-01-02

B. 2019-01-01

C. Runtime exception

D. Compilation error

5.1.60   Given code of Test.java file:

```
package com.udayan.ocp;

import java.time.*;
import java.time.format.DateTimeFormatter;

public class Test {
    public static void main(String [] args) {
        LocalDate date = LocalDate.of(2018, 2, 1);
        DateTimeFormatter formatter = DateTimeFormatter
            .ofPattern("DD'nd day of' uuuu");
        System.out.println(formatter.format(date));
    }
}
```

What will be the result of compiling and executing Test class?

A. Runtime Exception

B. 01nd day of 2018

C. 02nd day of 2018

D. 32nd day of 2018

5.1.61   Below represents ZonedDateTime data:

```
2018-02-01T10:30+05:30[Asia/Kolkata]
2018-01-31T21:00-08:00[America/Los_Angeles]
```

Do above times represent same instance of time?

A. Yes

B. No

5.1.62   Given code of Test.java file:

```
package com.udayan.ocp;

import java.io.*;

public class Test {
    public static void main(String[] args) {
        Console console = System.console();
        if(console != null) {
            console.format("%d %<x", 10);
        }
    }
}
```

What will be the output of compiling and executing Test class from command prompt?

javac Test.java

java Test

A. 10 10

B. 10 12

C. 10 a

D. 10

E. Runtime Exception

5.1.63 F: is accessible for reading/writing and currently doesn't contain any directories.

Which of the code snippet allows to create below directory structure under F:?

```
F:.
  └──A
      └──B
          └──C
```

A.	```File file = new File("F:\\A\\B\\C");``` ```file.mkdir();```
B.	```File file = new File("F:\\A\\B\\C");``` ```file.mkdirs();```
C.	```File file = new File("F:\\A\\B\\C");``` ```file.createNewDirectory();```
D.	```File file = new File("F:\\A\\B\\C");``` ```file.createNewDirectories();```

5.1.64 Given code of Test.java file:

```
package com.udayan.ocp;

import java.io.*;

public class Test {
    public static void main(String[] args) {
        File dir = new File("F:" + System.getProperty(
                                "path.separator") + "A");
        dir.mkdir();
    }
}
```

F: is accessible for reading/writing and currently doesn't contain any files/directories.

Will above code create directory 'A' inside F:?

A. Yes

B. No

5.1.65 Given code of Test.java file:

```
package com.udayan.ocp;

import java.io.*;

public class Test {
    public static void main(String[] args)
                                throws IOException {
        File f1 = new File("F:\\f1.txt");
        FileWriter fw = new FileWriter("F:\\f2.txt");
        PrintWriter pw = new PrintWriter("F:\\f3.txt");
    }
}
```

F: is accessible for reading/writing and currently doesn't contain any files/directories.

On executing Test class, how many physical files will be created on the disc?

A. 0

B. 1

C. 2

D. 3

5.1.66 Given code of Test.java file:

```java
package com.udayan.ocp;

import java.io.*;

class Person {
    private String name;
    private int age;

    public Person(String name, int age) {
        this.name = name;
        this.age = age;
    }

    public String getName() {
        return name;
    }

    public int getAge() {
        return age;
    }
}

class Student extends Person implements Serializable {
    private String course;

    public Student(String name, int age, String course) {
        super(name, age);
        this.course = course;
    }

    public String getCourse() {
        return course;
```

```
        }
    }

public class Test {
    public static void main(String[] args)
            throws IOException, ClassNotFoundException {
        Student stud = new Student("John", 20,
                                    "Computer Science");
        try (ObjectOutputStream oos = new ObjectOutputStream(
                new FileOutputStream(("F:\\stud.ser")));
            ObjectInputStream ois = new ObjectInputStream(
                new FileInputStream("F:\\stud.ser")))
        {
            oos.writeObject(stud);

            Student s = (Student) ois.readObject();
            System.out.printf("%s, %d, %s",
                    s.getName(), s.getAge(), s.getCourse());
        }
    }
}
```

F: is accessible for reading/writing and currently doesn't contain any files/directories.

What will be the result of compiling and executing Test class?

A. John, 20, Computer Science

B. null, 0, Computer Science

C. null, 0, null

D. Runtime Exception

5.1.67   F: is accessible for reading and below is the directory structure for F:

```
F:.
 └──A
     └──B
         └──C
                Book.java
```

'Book.java' file is available under 'C' directory.

Given code of Test.java file:

```java
package com.udayan.ocp;

import java.nio.file.Path;
import java.nio.file.Paths;

public class Test {
    public static void main(String[] args) {
        Path file = Paths.get(
            "F:\\A\\.\\B\\C\\D\\..\\Book.java");
        System.out.println(file.toRealPath());
    }
}
```

What will be the result of compiling and executing Test class?

A.   Compilation Error

B.   NoSuchFileException is thrown at runtime.

C.   F:\A\B\C\Book.java

D.   F:\A\.\B\C\D\..\Book.java

E.   Book.java

5.1.68 Given code of Test.java file:

```
package com.udayan.ocp;

import java.nio.file.*;
import java.util.*;

public class Test {
    public static void main(String[] args) {
        Path path = Paths.get("F:\\A\\B\\C\\Book.java");
        /*INSERT*/
    }
}
```

Which of the following statements, if used to replace /*INSERT*/, will print below output on to the console?

```
A
B
C
Book.java
```

Select ALL that apply.

A.	`for(Path p : path) {`
	`    System.out.println(p);`
	`}`

B.	`for(int i = 0; i < path.getNameCount(); i++) {`
	`    System.out.println(path.getName(i));`
	`}`

C.	`Iterator<Path> iterator = path.iterator();`
	`while(iterator.hasNext()) {`
	`    System.out.println(iterator.next());`
	`}`

D.	`path.forEach(System.out::println);`

5.1.69 **F: is accessible for reading/writing and below is the directory structure for F:**

```
F:.
 └──A
     └──B
             Book.java
```

Given code of Test.java file:

```java
package com.udayan.ocp;

import java.io.File;
import java.io.IOException;
import java.nio.file.*;

public class Test {
    public static void main(String[] args)
                                    throws IOException{
        Path path = Paths.get("F:\\A\\B\\Book.java");
        long size1 = Files.size(path);

        File file = new File("F:\\A\\B\\Book.java");
        long size2 = file.length();

        System.out.println(size1 == size2);
    }
}
```

What will be the result of compiling and executing Test class?

A. true

B. false

C. Compilation error

5.1.70 **F: is accessible for reading/writing and below is the directory structure for F:**

```
F:.
 └──A
     └──B
                Book.java
```

Book.java is a text file.

Given code of Test.java file:

```java
package com.udayan.ocp;

import java.io.BufferedReader;
import java.io.IOException;
import java.nio.file.*;

public class Test {
    public static void main(String[] args)
                                    throws IOException{
        Path src = Paths.get("F:\\A\\B\\Book.java");
        try(BufferedReader reader =
                    Files.newBufferedReader(src))
        {
            String str = null;
            while((str = reader.readLine()) != null) {
                System.out.println(str);
            }
        }
    }
}
```

What will be the result of compiling and executing Test class?

A. Compilation error

B. Contents of Book.java are printed on to the console.

C. An exception is thrown at runtime.

5.1.71 **F: is accessible for reading/writing and below is the directory structure for F:**

```
F:.
└──Parent
    │   a.txt
    │   b.txt
    │
    └──Child
            c.txt
            d.txt
```

Given code of Test.java file:

```java
package com.udayan.ocp;

import java.io.IOException;
import java.nio.file.Files;
import java.nio.file.Path;
import java.nio.file.Paths;
import java.nio.file.attribute.BasicFileAttributes;
import java.util.function.BiPredicate;
import java.util.stream.Stream;

public class Test {
    public static void main(String[] args)
                                    throws IOException {
        Path root = Paths.get("F:");
        BiPredicate<Path, BasicFileAttributes> predicate
                        = (p,a) -> p.endsWith("txt");
        try(Stream<Path> paths
                    = Files.find(root, 2, predicate))
        {
            paths.forEach(System.out::println);
        }
    }
}
```

What will be the result of compiling and executing Test class?

A.	Above program executes successfully and prints nothing on to the console.
B.	Above program executes successfully and prints below lines on to the console: F:Parent\a.txt F:Parent\b.txt
C.	Above program executes successfully and prints below lines on to the console: F:Parent\Child\c.txt F:Parent\Child\d.txt F:Parent\a.txt F:Parent\b.txt

5.1.72 **F: is accessible for reading/writing and below is the directory structure for F:**

```
F:.
└──Parent
    │    a.txt
    │    b.txt
    │
    └──Child
            c.txt
            d.txt
```

Given code of Test.java file:

```java
package com.udayan.ocp;

import java.io.IOException;
import java.nio.file.Files;
import java.nio.file.Path;
import java.nio.file.Paths;
import java.nio.file.attribute.BasicFileAttributes;
import java.util.function.BiPredicate;
import java.util.stream.Stream;
```

```
public class Test {
    public static void main(String[] args)
                                throws IOException {
        Path root = Paths.get("F:");
        BiPredicate<Path, BasicFileAttributes> predicate
                    = (p,a) -> p.endsWith(null);
        try(Stream<Path> paths
                    = Files.find(root, 2, predicate))
        {
            paths.forEach(System.out::println);
        }
    }
}
```

What will be the result of compiling and executing Test class?

A.	Above program executes successfully and prints nothing on to the console.
B.	Above program executes successfully and prints below lines on to the console: F:Parent\a.txt F:Parent\b.txt
C.	Above program executes successfully and prints below lines on to the console: F:Parent\Child\c.txt F:Parent\Child\d.txt F:Parent\a.txt F:Parent\b.txt
D.	Compilation error

5.1.73 Given structure of EMPLOYEE table:

```
EMPLOYEE (ID integer, FIRSTNAME varchar(100), LASTNAME
varchar(100), SALARY real, PRIMARY KEY (ID))
```

Given code of Test.java file:

```java
package com.udayan.ocp;

import java.sql.*;

public class Test {
    public static void main(String[] args) {
        try {
            Connection con = DriverManager.getConnection(
                "jdbc:mysql://localhost:3306/ocp",
                "root", "password");
            String query = "Select * FROM EMPLOYEE";
            Statement stmt = con.createStatement();
            ResultSet rs = stmt.executeQuery(query);
            while (rs.next()) {
                System.out.println("ID: "
                        + rs.getInt("IDD"));
                System.out.println("First Name: "
                        + rs.getString("FIRSTNAME"));
                System.out.println("Last Name: "
                        + rs.getString("LASTNAME"));
                System.out.println("Salary: "
                        + rs.getDouble("SALARY"));
            }
            rs.close();
            stmt.close();
            con.close();
        } catch (SQLException ex) {
            System.out.println("An Error Occurred!");
        }
    }
}
```

Also assume:

URL, username and password are correct.

SQL query is correct and valid.

The JDBC 4.2 driver jar is configured in the classpath.

EMPLOYEE table doesn't have any records.

What will be the result of compiling and executing Test class?

A. Compilation Error

B. 'An Error Occurred!' is printed on to the console.

C. Code executes fine and doesn't print anything on to the console.

D. NullPointerException is thrown at runtime.

5.1.74 Given structure of EMPLOYEE table:

```
EMPLOYEE (ID integer, FIRSTNAME varchar(100), LASTNAME
varchar(100), SALARY real, PRIMARY KEY (ID))
```

EMPLOYEE table contains below records:

```
101 John    Smith  12000
102 Sean    Smith  15000
103 Regina Williams  15500
104 Natasha    George 14600
```

Given code of Test.java file:

```
package com.udayan.ocp;

import java.sql.*;

public class Test {
    public static void main(String[] args)
                                throws SQLException {
        String url = "jdbc:mysql://localhost:3306/ocp";
        String user = "root";
        String password = "password";
        String query = "Select ID, FIRSTNAME, LASTNAME, " +
            "SALARY FROM EMPLOYEE ORDER BY ID";

        try (Connection con =
            DriverManager.getConnection(url, user, password);
            Statement stmt = con.createStatement();
            ResultSet rs = stmt.executeQuery(query);)
        {
                rs.absolute(3);
                rs.relative(-1);
                rs.deleteRow();
        }
    }
}
```

Also assume:

URL, username and password are correct.

SQL query is correct and valid.

The JDBC 4.2 driver jar is configured in the classpath.

What will be the result of compiling and executing Test class?

A. An exception is thrown at runtime.

B. Record corresponding to ID 101 is deleted successfully.

C. Record corresponding to ID 102 is deleted successfully.

D. Record corresponding to ID 103 is deleted successfully.

E. Record corresponding to ID 104 is deleted successfully.

5.1.75 Given structure of LOG table:

```
LOG (ID integer, MESSAGE varchar(1000), PRIMARY KEY (ID))
```

Given code of Test.java file:

```java
package com.udayan.ocp;

import java.sql.*;
import java.util.Properties;

public class Test {
    public static void main(String[] args)
                                    throws Exception {
        String url = "jdbc:mysql://localhost:3306/ocp";
        Properties prop = new Properties();
        prop.put("user", "root");
        prop.put("password", "password");
        String query = "Select count(*) FROM LOG";
        try (Connection con =
                DriverManager.getConnection(url, prop);
            Statement stmt = con.createStatement();
            ResultSet rs = stmt.executeQuery(query);)
        {
            System.out.println(rs.getInt(1));
        }
    }
}
```

Also assume:
URL is correct and db credentials are: root/password.
SQL query is correct and valid.
The JDBC 4.2 driver jar is configured in the classpath.
LOG table doesn't have any records.

What will be the result of compiling and executing Test class?

A. An exception is thrown at runtime.

B. 0

C. 1

5.1.76 Which of the following is a valid ResultSet concur type?

    A. CONCUR_WRITE_ONLY

    B. CONCUR_READ_WRITE

    C. CONCUR_READ_ONLY

    D. CONCUR_BOTH

5.1.77 Given structure of MESSAGES table:

```
MESSAGES (msg1 varchar(100), msg2 varchar(100))
```

MESSAGES table contains below records:

```
'Happy New Year!', 'Happy Holidays!'
```

Given code of Test.java file:

```java
package com.udayan.ocp;
import java.sql.*;
import java.util.Properties;

public class Test {
    public static void main(String[] args)
                                        throws Exception {
        String url = "jdbc:mysql://localhost:3306/ocp";
        Properties prop = new Properties();
        prop.put("user", "root");
        prop.put("password", "password");
        String query = "Select count(*) FROM MESSAGES";
        try (Connection con =
                DriverManager.getConnection(url, prop);
            Statement stmt = con.createStatement(
                ResultSet.TYPE_SCROLL_INSENSITIVE,
                ResultSet.CONCUR_READ_ONLY);
            ResultSet rs = stmt.executeQuery(query);)
        {
            rs.absolute(0);
            System.out.println(rs.getInt(1));
        }
    }
}
```

Also assume:

URL is correct and db credentials are: root/password.

SQL query is correct and valid.

The JDBC 4.2 driver jar is configured in the classpath.

What will be the result of compiling and executing Test class?

A. 0

B. 1

C. 2

D. An exception is thrown at runtime

5.1.78   Given structure of EMPLOYEE table:

```
EMPLOYEE (ID integer, FIRSTNAME varchar(100), LASTNAME
varchar(100), SALARY real, PRIMARY KEY (ID))
```

EMPLOYEE table contains below records:

```
101 John     Smith     12000
102 Sean     Smith     15000
103 Regina   Williams    15500
104 Natasha George   14600
```

Given code of Test.java file:

```
package com.udayan.ocp;

import java.sql.*;

public class Test {
    public static void main(String[] args) throws Exception
    {
        String url = "jdbc:mysql://localhost:3306/ocp";
        String user = "root";
        String password = "password";
```

```
String query = "Select ID, FIRSTNAME, LASTNAME,
                    SALARY FROM EMPLOYEE ORDER BY ID";
try (Connection con =
    DriverManager.getConnection(
                        url, user, password);
    Statement stmt =
    con.createStatement(
            ResultSet.TYPE_FORWARD_ONLY,
                    ResultSet.CONCUR_UPDATABLE);
) {
    ResultSet rs = stmt.executeQuery(query);
    rs.absolute(1);
    rs.moveToInsertRow();
    rs.updateInt(1, 105);
    rs.updateString(2, "Chris");
    rs.updateString(3, "Morris");
    rs.updateDouble(4, 25000);
    rs.deleteRow();
    rs.refreshRow();
    System.out.println(rs.getInt(1));
    }
    }
}
```

Also assume:

URL is correct and db credentials are: root/password.

SQL query is correct and valid.

The JDBC 4.2 driver jar is configured in the classpath.

What will be the result of compiling and executing Test class?

A. 102

B. 104

C. 105

D. An exception is raised by rs.deleteRow();

E. An exception is raised by rs.refreshRow();

5.1.79 Given code of Test.java file:

```
package com.udayan.ocp;

import java.util.Locale;

public class Test {
    public static void main(String[] args) {
        Locale l1 = new Locale.Builder()
            .setLanguage("en").setRegion("US").build();
        Locale l2 = Locale.US;
        Locale l3 = new Locale("en");

        System.out.println(l1.equals(l2));
        System.out.println(l2.equals(l3));
    }
}
```

What will be the result of compiling and executing Test class?

A.	true true	B.	true false
C.	false true	D.	false false

5.1.80 Given code of 3 Java files:

```
//1. MyResourceBundle.java
package com.udayan.ocp;
import java.util.ListResourceBundle;

public class MyResourceBundle
            extends ListResourceBundle {
    @Override
    protected Object[][] getContents() {
        Object [][] arr = {{"surprise", "SURPRISE!"}};
        return arr;
```

```
        }
}

//2. MyResourceBundle_en_CA.java
package com.udayan.ocp;
import java.util.ListResourceBundle;

public class MyResourceBundle_en_CA
                extends ListResourceBundle {
    @Override
    protected Object[][] getContents() {
        Object [][] arr = {{"surprise", 12.64}};
        return arr;
    }
}

//3. Test.java
package com.udayan.ocp;
import java.util.Locale;
import java.util.ResourceBundle;

public class Test {
    public static void main(String[] args) {
        Locale.setDefault(new Locale("fr", "IT"));
        Locale loc = new Locale("en", "US");
        ResourceBundle rb = ResourceBundle.getBundle(
                "com.udayan.ocp.MyResourceBundle", loc);
        System.out.println(rb.getObject("surprise"));
    }
}
```

What will be the result of compiling and executing Test class?

A. SURPRISE!

B. 12.64

C. 1001

D. MissingResourceException is thrown at runtime

5.1.81 Which of the following correctly specifies the entries in resource bundle properties file?

A.	country=Sri Lanka continent=Asia
B.	country="Sri Lanka" continent="Asia"
C.	country=Sri Lanka;continent=Asia
D.	country=Sri Lanka:continent=Asia

5.1.82 Given code of Test.java file:

```
package com.udayan.ocp;

import java.text.NumberFormat;
import java.util.Locale;

public class Test {
    public static void main(String[] args) {
        Locale loc = new Locale("en", "US");
        NumberFormat nf =
            NumberFormat.getCurrencyInstance(loc);
        System.out.printf("Amount %s is in %s" ,
                    nf.format(10), nf.getCurrency());
    }
}
```

What will be the result of compiling and executing above program?

A. Amount $10.00 is in USD

B. Amount $10.00 is in US Dollar

C. Amount 10.00 is in US Dollar

D. Amount 10.00 is in USD

5.1.83 Given code of Test.java file:

```java
package com.udayan.ocp;

import java.util.concurrent.*;

class MyCallable implements Callable<Integer> {
    private Integer i;

    public MyCallable(Integer i) {
        this.i = i;
    }

    public Integer call() throws Exception {
        return --i;
    }
}

class MyThread extends Thread {
    private int i;

    MyThread(int i) {
        this.i = i;
    }

    public void run() {
        i++;
    }
}

public class Test {
    public static void main(String[] args)
            throws ExecutionException, InterruptedException{
        ExecutorService es =
                Executors.newSingleThreadExecutor();
        MyCallable callable = new MyCallable(10);
        MyThread thread = new MyThread(10);
        System.out.println(es.submit(callable).get());
        System.out.println(es.submit(thread).get());
        es.shutdown();
    }
}
```

What will be the result of compiling and executing Test class?

A.	9 10	B.	9 11
C.	9 0	D.	9 null

5.1.84 Given code of Test.java file:

```java
package com.udayan.ocp;

import java.util.concurrent.ExecutionException;
import java.util.concurrent.atomic.AtomicInteger;

public class Test {
    public static void main(String [] args)
            throws InterruptedException, ExecutionException{
        AtomicInteger ai = new AtomicInteger(10);
        /*INSERT*/

    }
}
```

Which of the following statements, if used to replace /*INSERT*/, will print '11:11' on to the console? Select ALL that apply.

A. `System.out.println(ai.addAndGet(1) + ":" + ai);`

B. `System.out.println(ai.getAndAdd(1) + ":" + ai.get());`

C. `System.out.println(ai.getAndIncrement() + ":" + ai.get());`

D. `System.out.println(ai.incrementAndGet() + ":" + ai.get());`

E. `System.out.println(ai.incrementAndGet(1) + ":" + ai.get());`

5.1.85 Given code of Adder.java file:

```java
package com.udayan.ocp;

import java.util.concurrent.ForkJoinPool;
import java.util.concurrent.RecursiveTask;

public class Adder {
    private static long LIMIT = 1000000000;
    private static final int THREADS = 100;

    static class AdderTask extends RecursiveTask<Long> {
        long from, to;

        public AdderTask(long from, long to) {
            this.from = from;
            this.to = to;
        }

        @Override
        protected Long compute() {
            if ((to - from) <= LIMIT/THREADS) {
                long localSum = 0;
                for(long i = from; i <= to; i++) {
                    localSum += i;
                }
                return localSum;
            }
            else {
                long mid = (from + to) / 2;
                AdderTask first = new AdderTask(from, mid);
                AdderTask second
                                = new AdderTask(mid + 1, to);
                first.fork();
                /*INSERT*/
            }
        }
    }

    public static void main(String[] args) {
        ForkJoinPool pool = new ForkJoinPool(THREADS);
        long sum = pool.invoke(new AdderTask(1, LIMIT));
        System.out.printf(
            "sum of the number from %d to %d is %d %n",
                                1, LIMIT, sum);
    }
}
```

Which of the following statement, if used to replace /*INSERT*/, will EFFICIENTLY add the numbers from 1 to 1000000000?

A. `return first.join() + second.compute();`

B. `return second.compute() + first.join();`

C. `return first.join();`

D. `return second.compute();`

5.1.86 Which of the following problems can be efficiently solved using Fork/Join framework?

A. Problems that can be divided into sub tasks, where each sub-task can be computed independently in asynchronous manner.

B. Problems that can be divided into sub tasks, where each sub-task can be computed independently in synchronous manner.

C. Problems that has lots of File Input/Output activities.

5.1.87 Given code of Test.java file:

```java
package com.udayan.ocp;

import java.util.Arrays;
import java.util.List;

public class Test {
    public static void main(String[] args) {
        List<String> list =
            Arrays.asList("A", "E", "I", "O", "U");
        System.out.println(
            list._____.isParallel());
    }
}
```

Which of the options correctly fills the blank, such that output is true?
Select ALL that apply.

A. `stream().parallel()`

B. `stream()`

C. `parallel()`

D. `parallelStream()`

5.1.88 Given code of Test.java file:

```java
package com.udayan.ocp;

import java.util.ArrayList;
import java.util.Collections;
import java.util.List;
import java.util.stream.IntStream;

public class Test {
    public static void main(String[] args) {
        List<Integer> list =
            Collections.synchronizedList(new ArrayList<>());
        IntStream stream = IntStream.rangeClosed(1, 7);
        stream.parallel().map(x -> {
            list.add(x); //Line 13
            return x;
        }).forEach(System.out::print); //Line 15
        System.out.println();
        list.forEach(System.out::print); //Line 17
    }
}
```

Which of the following statement is true about above code?

A. Line 15 and Line 17 will print exact same output on to the console.

B. Line 15 and Line 17 will not print exact same output on to the console.

C. Output cannot be predicted.

5.1.89 Given code of Test.java file:

```java
package com.udayan.ocp;

import java.util.Arrays;

public class Test {
    public static void main(String[] args) {
        String s1 = Arrays.asList("A", "E", "I", "O", "U")
            .stream().reduce("_", String::concat);
        String s2 = Arrays.asList("A", "E", "I", "O", "U")
            .parallelStream().reduce("_", String::concat);
        System.out.println(s1.equals(s2));
    }
}
```

What will be the result of compiling and executing Test class?

A. It will always print true.

B. It will always print false.

C. Output cannot be predicted.

5.1.90 Given code of Test.java file:

```
package com.udayan.ocp;

import java.util.stream.Stream;

public class Test {
    public static void main(String[] args) {
        String str1 = Stream.iterate(1, i -> i + 1)
            .limit(10).reduce("", (i, s) -> i + s,
                                (s1, s2) -> s1 + s2);
        String str2 = Stream.iterate(1, i -> i + 1)
            .limit(10).parallel().reduce("",
                (i, s) -> i + s, (s1, s2) -> s1 + s2);
        System.out.println(str1.equals(str2));
    }
}
```

What will be the result of compiling and executing Test class?

A. It will always print true.

B. It will always print false.

C. Output cannot be predicted.

5.2   Answers of Practice Test - 5 with Explanation

5.1.1   Answer: B

Reason:
Methods can have same name as the class. Player() is method and not constructor of the class, note the void return type of this method.

As no constructors are provided in the Player class, java compiler adds default no-argument constructor. That is why "new Player()" doesn't cause any compilation error.

Default values are assigned to instance variables, hence null is assigned to name and 0 is assigned to age.

In the output, Name: null, Age: 0 is displayed.

5.1.2   Answer: B

Reason:
Dog and Cat are siblings as both extend from Animal class.
animals refer to an instance of Dog [] type. Each element of Dog [] can store Dog instances and not Cat instances. But as we are using reference variable of Animal [] type hence compiler allows to add both Cat and Dog instances. So, animals[0] = new Dog(); and animals[1] = new Cat(); don't cause any compilation error.

But at runtime, while executing the statement: "animals[1] = new Cat();", a Cat instance is assigned to Dog array's element hence java.lang.ArrayStoreException is thrown.

5.1.3   Answer: B

Reason:
Operator + is left to right associative, so given expression can be grouped as:

"The sum is: " + x + y
= ("The sum is: " + x) + y
= (("The sum is: " + x) + y)
= (("The sum is: " + 15) + 25)
= ("The sum is: 15" + 25)
= "The sum is: 1525"

5.1.4   Answer: C

Reason:
Lambda expression's variables x and y cannot redeclare another local variables defined in the enclosing scope.

5.1.5   Answer: A

Reason:
Enum constructor is invoked once for every constant. There is only one constant, hence constructor is invoked only once.

For first 'Flags.TRUE', enum constructor is invoked but for later statements enum constructor is not invoked.

5.1.6   Answer: A

Reason:
args[0] refers to "GREEN" and args[1] refers to "AMBER".

TrafficLight.valueOf(args[0]); -> TrafficLight.valueOf("GREEN");

GREEN is a valid enum constant, hence case label for GREEN is executed and "GO" is printed to the console.

5.1.7   Answer: D

Reason:
To refer to inner class name from outside the top level class, use the syntax: outer_class.inner_class.
In this case, correct syntax to refer B from Test class is: A.B and not B.

5.1.8   Answer: A, B

Reason:
Regular inner class cannot define anything static, except static final variables. So static {System.out.print(3);} will cause compilation error.

If a class contains, constructor, instance initialization block and static initialization block and constructor is invoked, then the execution order is:

static initialization block, instance initialization block and then constructor.

5.1.9 Answer: A

Reason:
Keyword "this" inside method-local inner class refers to the instance of inner class.

In this case this.msg refers to msg variable defined inside Inner class but there is no msg variable inside Inner class. Hence, this.msg causes compilation error.

System.out.println(msg); would print B (msg shadows Outer class variable) and System.out.println(Outer.this.msg); would print A.

5.1.10 Answer: C

Reason:
It is a valid anonymous inner class syntax. But anonymous inner class code doesn't override printMessage() method of Message class rather it defines a new method PrintMessage (P in upper case).

Anonymous inner class allows to define methods not available in its super class, in this case PrintMessage() method.

But msg.printMessage(); statement invokes the printMessage method of super class, Message and thus "Hello!" gets printed in the output.

5.1.11 Answer: C

Reason:
In this case, you have to write code outside class A. B is a static nested class and outside class A it is referred by A.B.

Instance of class B can be created by 'new A.B();'.

5.1.12 Answer: A

Reason:
interface can be nested inside a class. Class Outer is top-level class and interface I1 is implicitly static.
Static nested interface can use all 4 access modifiers(public, protected, default and private).

5.1.13 Answer: A,B,C,D,E

Reason:
print(String) method accepts parameter of String type, so left side of lambda expression should specify one parameter, then arrow operator and right side of lambda expression should specify the body.

(String msg) -> {System.out.println(msg);}; => Correct.

(msg) -> {System.out.println(msg);}; => Correct, type of variable can be removed from left side. Java compiler handles it using type inference.

(msg) -> System.out.println(msg); => Correct, if there is only one statement in the right side then semicolon inside the body, curly brackets and return statement(if available) can be removed.

msg -> System.out.println(msg); => Correct, if there is only one parameter in left part, then round brackets can be removed.

x -> System.out.println(x); => Correct, any valid java identifier can be used in lambda expression.

y - > System.out.println(y); => Compilation error as there should not be any space between - and > of arrow operator.

5.1.14 Answer: B

Reason:
Functional interface must have only one non-overriding abstract method but Functional interface can have constant variables, static methods, default methods and overriding abstract methods [equals(Object) method, toString() method etc. from Object class]. I4 is a Functional Interface.

5.1.15 Answer: B

Reason:
Lambda expression is written inside Inner class, so this keyword in lambda expression refers to the instance of Inner class.
Hence, System.out.println(this.var); prints 1000.

5.1.16 Answer: B

Reason:
If multiple bounds are available and one of the bounds is a class, then it must be specified first.

class Generic<T extends M & N & A> {} => A is specified at last and hence compilation error.

5.1.17 Answer: A

Reason:
Return type of generic method 'get' is T, which is correctly defined before the return type of the method.
get("HELLO"); passed String so return value should be String only. String result is stored in str variable and same is printed using System.out.println statement.

5.1.18 Answer: A,E

Reason:
Number is an abstract class, so 'new Number(0)' cannot be used.
Character class doesn't extend Number.
Object class doesn't extend Number.

5.1.19 Answer: C

Reason:
Operator is a generic interface, hence it can work with any java class. There are absolutely no issues with lambda expressions but we are not capturing or printing the return value of operation method, hence nothing is printed on to the console.

System.out.println(opr1.operation("Hello", "World")); => Prints HelloWorld.

System.out.println(opr2.operation(10, 40)); => Prints 50. Over here int literals 10 and 40 are converted to Integer instances by auto-boxing.

5.1.20 Answer: A

Reason:
HashSet makes use of hashCode to find out the correct bucket, it then makes use of equals(Object) method to find out duplicate objects.

Student class correctly overrides equals(Object) method but it doesn't override hashCode() method. This means you get different hashCode for different objects. HashSet in this case cannot find out duplicate Student objects and 3 Student objects are added to the Set.

System.out.println(students.size()); => Prints 3 on to the console.

To avoid duplicate in the given Set, override hashCode() method in Student class:
```
public int hashCode() {
   return name.hashCode() + age;
}
```

5.1.21 Answer: C

Reason:
If you don't use 2nd parameter for headMap() and tailMap() methods to indicate whether keys are inclusive or exclusive,
then by default 'toKey' used in headMap() method is exclusive and 'fromKey' used in tailMap() method is inclusive.

You can confirm this by checking the definition of headMap() and tailMap() methods in TreeMap class.

Methods defined in TreeMap class:
```
public SortedMap<K,V> headMap(K toKey) {
   return headMap(toKey, false);
}

public SortedMap<K,V> tailMap(K fromKey) {
   return tailMap(fromKey, true);
}
```

5.1.22 Answer: C

Reason:
Deque's add() method invokes addLast(E) method and remove() method invokes removeFirst() method.

chars.add('A'); => [*A], {* represents HEAD element}
chars.add('B'); => [*A,B],
chars.remove(); => [*B],
chars.add('C'); => [*B,C],
chars.remove(); => [*C],
System.out.println(chars); => Prints [C] on to the console.

5.1.23 Answer: D

Reason:
x and y are private variables and are accessible within the boundary of Point class. TestPoint class is outside the boundary of Point class and hence o1.x and o2.x cause compilation error.

Make sure to check the accessibility before working with the logic.

5.1.24 Answer: B

Reason:
Default thenComparing method helps to chain the Comparators. First the list is sorted on the basis of country code, if matching country code is found then sorted on the basis of location code and if location code matches then list is sorted on bank code.

5.1.25 Answer: B

Reason:
Uppercase characters are different from Lowercase characters.
distinct() method of Stream returns a stream consisting of the distinct elements (according to Object.equals(Object)) of this stream.

"A" and "A" are same, "b" and "B" are different & "c" and "c" are same.

Arrays.asList(...) method returns sequential List object, so order of elements remain same.

Output is: AbBc

5.1.26 Answer: B

Reason:
employees.stream() => Gets the stream for employees list.

filter(x -> x.getSalary() > 10000) => Returns a stream consisting of elements of the stream that match the given Predicate. In this case {"Lucy", 12000} is returned.

map(e -> e.getName()) => Returns a stream consisting of the results of applying the given function to the elements of this stream. In this case {"Lucy"} is returned.

forEach(System.out::println) => Prints 'Lucy' on to the console.

5.1.27 Answer: B

Reason:
IntStream.iterate(1, i -> i + 1) => [1,2,3,4,5,6,7,...]. This is an infinite stream.

limit(11) => [1,2,3,4,5,...,11]. Eleven elements from the above stream.

filter(i -> i % 2 != 0) => [1,3,5,7,9,11]. Returns a stream consisting of all odd numbers.

forEach(System.out::print); => Prints '1357911' on to the console.

5.1.28 Answer: B

Reason:
IntStream.range(int start, int end) => start is inclusive and end is exclusive. If start >= end, then empty stream is returned.
IntStream.range(-10, -10) => returns empty stream.

IntStream.rangeClosed(int start, int end) => Both start and end are inclusive. If start > end, then empty stream is returned.
IntStream.rangeClosed(-10, -10) => returns a stream containing just 1 element, which is -10.

5.1.29 Answer: C

Reason:
It is always handy to remember the names and methods of four important built-in functional interfaces:
Supplier<T> : T get();
Function<T, R> : R apply(T t);
Consumer<T> : void accept(T t);
Predicate<T> : boolean test(T t);
Rest of the built-in functional interfaces are either similar to or dependent upon these four interfaces.

5.1.30 Answer: A

Reason:
String::new is the constructor reference for String(char []) constructor and obj.apply(new char[] {'j', 'a', 'v', 'a'}); would call the constructor at runtime, converting char [] to String. Variable s refers "java".

If you have issues in understanding method reference syntax, then try to write the corresponding lambda expression first.

For example, in Line 5, I have to write a lambda expression which accepts char [] and returns String object. It can be written as:
Function<char [], String> obj2 = arr -> new String(arr); It is bit easier to understand this syntax.

5.1.31 Answer: B

Reason:
f1.compose(f2) means first apply f2 and then f1.
f2.apply("12345") returns "54321" and then f1.apply("54321") returns 54321

5.1.32 Answer: B

Reason:
Lambda expression for Predicate is: s -> s.length() > 3. This means return true if passed string's length is > 3.
pr1.negate() means return true if passed string's length is <= 3. So first three array elements are printed.

5.1.33 Answer: A

Reason:
BiFunction<String, String, String> interface's apply method signature will be: String apply(String str1, String str2).

NOTE: Lambda expression's body is: 's2.concat(s1)' and not 's1.concat(s2)'. trim() method trims leading and trailing white spaces and not the white spaces in between.

func.apply(" CD", " AB") = " AB".concat(" CD").trim(); = " AB CD".trim(); = "AB CD"

5.1.34 Answer: C

Reason:
Though the lambda expression with 2 arrows seems confusing but it is correct syntax. To understand, Line n1 can be re-written as:
```
DoubleFunction<DoubleUnaryOperator> func = (m) -> {
  return (n) -> {
    return m + n;
  };
};
```

And corresponding anonymous class syntax is:
```
DoubleFunction<DoubleUnaryOperator> func = new
DoubleFunction<DoubleUnaryOperator>() {
  @Override
  public DoubleUnaryOperator apply(double m) {
    DoubleUnaryOperator duo = new DoubleUnaryOperator() {
      @Override
      public double applyAsDouble(double n) {
        return m + n;
      }
    };
    return duo;
  }
};
```

So, there is no issue with Line n1. Let's check Line n2.
'func.apply(11)' returns an instance of DoubleUnaryOperator, in which applyAsDouble(double) method has below implementation:

545

```
DoubleUnaryOperator duo = new DoubleUnaryOperator() {
    @Override
    public double applyAsDouble(double n) {
        return 11 + n;
    }
};
```

And hence, when applyAsDouble(24) is invoked on above instance of DoubleUnaryOperator, then it returns the result of 11 + 24, which is 35 and as return type is double, so 35.0 is returned.

5.1.35 Answer: B

Reason:
interface UnaryOperator<T> extends Function<T, T>, so its apply function has the signature: T apply(T).
In this case, UnaryOperator<String> is used and hence apply method will have the signature: String apply(String).
Lambda expression 's -> s.toString().toUpperCase()' is the correct implementation of 'String apply(String)' method and hence there is no issue with Line n1.
But at Line n2, argument passed to apply method is of StringBuilder type and not String type and hence Line n2 causes compilation error.

5.1.36 Answer: A

Reason:
Stream.of() returns blank stream. As Type of stream is not specified, stream is of 'Stream<Object>', each element of the stream is considered to be of 'Object' type.

map method in this case accepts 'Function<? super Object, ? extends R>'.

There is no 'reverse()' method in Object class and hence lambda expression causes compilation failure.

5.1.37 Answer: B

Reason:
count() is a terminal method for finite stream, hence peek(System.out::println) is executed for all the 3 elements of the stream.

count() method returns long value but it is not used.

5.1.38 Answer: B

Reason:
Optional<T> is a final class and overrides toString() method:

```
public String toString() {
    return value != null
        ? String.format("Optional[%s]", value)
        : "Optional.empty";
}
```

In the question, Optional is of Integer type and Integer class overrides toString() method, so output is: Optional[10]

5.1.39 Answer: B

Reason:
stream => [{2018-1-1}, {2018-1-1}].
stream.distinct() => [{2018-1-1}].
findAny() => Optional[{2018-1-1}].

optional.isPresent() => true. isPresent method returns true if optional is not empty otherwise false.
optional.get() => Returns LocalDate object {2018-1-1}, toString() method of LocalDate class pads 0 to single digit month and day.

'true : 2018-01-01' is printed on to the console.

NOTE: In real world projects, it is advisable to to check using isPresent() method before using the get() method.
```
if(optional.isPresent()) {
    System.out.println(optional.get());
}
```

5.1.40 Answer: D

Reason:
new Random().ints(start, end) => start is inclusive and end is exclusive. So this code generates random integers between 1 and 6. All the 6 integers from 1 to 6 are possible.

Above code will never generate 7.

Oracle Certified Professional: Java SE 8 Programmer II

5.1.41 Answer: C

Reason:
text.split(" ") => {"I", "am", "going", "to", "pass", "OCP", "exam", "in", "first", "attempt"}.
Arrays.stream(text.split(" ")); => ["I", "am", "going", "to", "pass", "OCP", "exam", "in", "first", "attempt"]. Stream<String> instance is returned.
stream.map(s -> s.length()) => [1, 2, 5, 2, 4, 3, 4, 2, 5, 7]. Stream<Integer> is returned.

summaryStatistics() method is declared in IntStream, LongStream and DoubleStream interfaces but not declared in Stream<Integer> interface and hence 'stream.map(s -> s.length()).summaryStatistics();' causes compilation failure.

Out of the given options, replacing 'stream.map(s -> s.length())' with 'stream.mapToInt(s -> s.length())' will correctly return an instance of IntStream and hence summaryStatistics() method can easily be invoked.

As you had to select only one option, so you can stop here. No need to validate other options. I am explaining other options just for knowledge purpose.

stat.getCount() will return 10 so not a correct option.

text.split(" ") delimits the text on the basis of single space. text.split(",") will delimit it on the basis of comma but as no comma is present in the given text, hence whole text will be returned and stat.getMax() will print 44.

5.1.42 Answer: B

Reason:
'(i1, i2) -> i2.compareTo(i1)' helps to sort in descending order. Code is: 'i2.compareTo(i1)' and not 'i1.compareTo(i2)'.

comp.reversed() returns a Comparator for sorting in ascending order. Hence, the output is: '-9 8 23 42 55 '.

5.1.43 Answer: D

Reason:
Collectors.groupingBy(Certification::getTest) => groups on the basis of test which is String type. Hence return type is: Map<String, List<Certification>>.

There are 4 records for OCA exam and 2 records for OCP exam, hence map.get("OCP") returns the list containing OCP records.

5.1.44 Answer: A

Reason:

stream is of Stream<Double> type, which is a generic stream and not primitive stream. There is no min() method available in generic stream interface, Stream<T> and hence, 'stream.min()' causes compilation error.

Generic Stream<T> interface has following methods:
Optional<T> min(Comparator<? super T> comparator);
Optional<T> max(Comparator<? super T> comparator);

To calculate min for generic Stream, pass the Comparator as argument:
stream.min(Double::compareTo), but note it will return an instance of Optional<Double> type.

5.1.45 Answer: B

Reason:
Method signatures:
boolean anyMatch(Predicate<? super T>) : Returns true if any of the stream element matches the given Predicate. If stream is empty, it returns false and predicate is not evaluated.

boolean allMatch(Predicate<? super T>) : Returns true if all the stream elements match the given Predicate. If stream is empty, it returns true and predicate is not evaluated.

boolean noneMatch(Predicate<? super T>) : Returns true if none of the stream element matches the given Predicate. If stream is empty, it returns true and predicate is not evaluated.

In the given code,
Stream.generate(() -> new Double("1.0")).limit(10); => returns a Stream<Double> containing 10 elements and each element is 1.0.

stream.filter(d -> d > 2) => returns an empty stream as given predicate is not true for even 1 element.

allMatch method, when invoked on empty stream, returns true.

5.1.46   Answer: D

Reason:

As variable seed is of long type, Hence Stream.iterate(seed, i -> i + 2) returns an infinite stream of Stream<Long> type. limit(2) returns the Stream<Long> object containing 2 elements 10 and 12. There is no issue with line n1.

Though the lambda expression with 2 arrows seems confusing but it is correct syntax. To understand, Line n2 can be re-written as:

```
LongFunction<LongUnaryOperator> func = (m) -> {
  return (n) -> {
    return n / m;
  };
};
```

And corresponding anonymous class syntax is:

```
LongFunction<LongUnaryOperator> func = new LongFunction<LongUnaryOperator>() {
  @Override
  public LongUnaryOperator apply(long m) {
    LongUnaryOperator operator = new LongUnaryOperator() {
      @Override
      public long applyAsLong(long n) {
        return n / m;
      }
    };
    return operator;
  }
};
```

So, there is no issue with Line n2. Let's check Line n3.
stream.mapToLong(i -> i) returns an instance of LongStream and LongStream has map(LongUnaryOperator) method.
'func.apply(2)' returns an instance of LongUnaryOperator, in which applyAsLong(long) method has below implementation:

```
LongUnaryOperator operator = new LongUnaryOperator() {
  @Override
  public long applyAsLong(long n) {
    return n / 2;
  }
};
```

As stream has elements 10 and 12, so map(func.apply(2)) returns an instance of LongStream after dividing each element by 2, so resultant stream contains elements 5 and 6.

forEach(System.out::println) prints 5 and 6 on to the console.

5.1.47 Answer: C

Reason:
Method m1() throws an instance of ArithmeticException and method m1() doesn't handle it, so it forwards the exception to calling method main.

Method main doesn't handle ArithmeticException so it forwards it to JVM, but just before that finally block is executed. This prints A on to the console.

After that JVM prints the stack trace and terminates the program abruptly.

5.1.48 Answer: A

Reason:
catch is for catching the exception and not throwing it.
thrown is not a java keyword.
throws is used to declare the exceptions a method can throw.
To manually throw an exception, throw keyword is used. e.g., throw new Exception();

5.1.49 Answer: E

Reason:
Java doesn't allow to catch specific checked exceptions if these are not thrown by the statements inside try block. catch(FileNotFoundException ex) {} causes compilation error in this case as System.out.println(1); will never throw FileNotFoundException.

NOTE: Java allows to catch Exception type. catch(Exception ex) {} will never cause compilation error.

5.1.50 Answer: D

Reason:
Exception is a java class, so e = null; is a valid statement and compiles successfully.

If you comment Line 10, and simply throw e, then code would compile successfully as compiler is certain that e would refer to an instance of SQLException only.

But the moment compiler finds 'e = null;', 'throw e;' (Line 11) causes compilation error as at runtime e may refer to any Exception type.

NOTE: No issues with Line 17 as method m() declares to throw SQLException and main method code correctly handles it.

5.1.51 Answer: B

Reason:
Even though Scanner is created in try-with-resources block, calling close() method explicitly doesn't cause any problem.
Scanner class allows to invoke close() method multiple times.

But once Scanner object is closed, other search operations should not be invoked. If invoked on closed scanner, IllegalStateException is thrown.

5.1.52 Answer: B

Reason:
Resources used in try-with-resources statement must be initialized.

'try(PrintWriter writer;)' causes compilation error as writer is not initialized in this statement.

5.1.53 Answer: B

Reason:
If finally block throws exception, then exception thrown by try or catch block is ignored.

In this case, method m() throws an instance of MyException2 class.

5.1.54 Answer: A

Reason:
close() method in AutoCloseable interface has below declaration:
void close() throws Exception;

MyResource class correctly overrides close() method.

try-with-resources statement internally invokes resource.close() method after executing resource.execute().

Overriding close method declares to throw Exception (checked exception) and hence handle or declare rule must be followed.

As main method neither declares to throw Exception nor provides catch block for Exception type, hence try-with-resources statement causes compilation error.

5.1.55 Answer: B

Reason:
assert 1 == 2 : () -> "a"; => Right expression can't specify any lambda expression.
assert 1 == 2 : return 1; => Right expression can't use return keyword, it should just specify the value.
assert 1 == 2 : Test::get; => Right expression can't specify any method reference syntax.
assert 1 == 2 : 1; => Legal. Left expression '1 == 2' returns boolean and right expression '1' is a non-void value.

5.1.56 Answer: B

Reason:
LocalDate ofYearDay(int year, int dayOfYear) returns an instance of LocalDate from a year and day-of-year.
January has 31 days, so 32nd day of the year means 1st Feb of the given year.

Output is: '2018-02-01' as toString() method of LocalDate class prints the LocalDate object in ISO-8601 format: "uuuu-MM-dd".

5.1.57 Answer: B

Reason:
LocalDateTime.parse(text); => text is parsed using DateTimeFormatter.ISO_LOCAL_DATE_TIME.

ISO_LOCAL_DATE_TIME is a combination of ISO_LOCAL_DATE and ISO_LOCAL_TIME, and it parses the date-time in following format:
[ISO_LOCAL_DATE][T][ISO_LOCAL_TIME]: T is case-insensitive.

ISO_LOCAL_DATE represents date in following format:
uuuu-MM-dd

Valid values for year (uuuu) is: 0000 to 9999.
Valid values for month-of-year (MM) is: 01 to 12.
Valid values for day-of-month (dd) is: 01 to 31 (At runtime this value is validated against month/year).

ISO_LOCAL_TIME represents time in following format:

HH:mm (if second-of-minute is not available),
HH:mm:ss (if second-of-minute is available),
HH:mm:ss.SSS (if nano-of-second is 3 digit or less),
HH:mm:ss.SSSSSS (if nano-of-second is 4 to 6 digits),
HH:mm:ss.SSSSSSSSS (if nano-of-second is 7 to 9 digits).

Valid values for hour-of-day (HH) is: 00 to 23.
Valid values for minute-of-hour (mm) is: 00 to 59.
Valid values for second-of-minute (ss) is: 00 to 59.
Valid values for nano-of-second is: 0 to 999999999.

dt.toLocalDate() returns an instance of LocalDate, whose toString() method prints date part: '2018-03-16'.

dt.toLocalTime() returns an instance of LocalTime, whose toString() method prints time part: '10:15:30.220'. As nano-of-second is of 2 digit, hence single zero is appended to its value.

5.1.58   Answer: C

Reason:
Signature of Period.between method is: Period between(LocalDate startDateInclusive, LocalDate endDateExclusive) {...}

Difference between 1st March 2018 and 11th March 2018 is 10 days and the result of this method is negative period as 1st argument is later date.

5.1.59   Answer: C

Reason:
Duration works with time component and not Date component.

plus(TemporalAmount) method of LocalDate class accepts TemporalAmount type and Duration implement TemporalAmount, so no compilation error. But at runtime date1.plus(d) causes exception.

Don't get confused with 'Duration.ofDays(1);', it is a convenient method to work with large time.

5.1.60   Answer: D

Reason:
In the parse string, anything between opening and closing quote is displayed as it is.

DD -> 2 digit representation for the day-of-year.
'nd day of' -> nd day of is displayed.
uuuu -> 4 digit representation for the year.

Output is: 32nd day of 2018.

NOTE: To display single quote, escape it with one more single quote. For example, 'DateTimeFormatter.ofPattern("'It''s' DD'nd day of' uuuu");' this will help to print: [It's 32nd day of 2018] whereas 'DateTimeFormatter.ofPattern("'It's' DD'nd day of' uuuu");' causes runtime exception.

5.1.61 Answer: A

Reason:
To know whether 2 instances represent same time or not, convert the time to GMT time by subtracting the offset.

2018-02-01T10:30 -(+05:30) = 2018-02-01T05:00 GMT.
and
2018-01-31T21:00 -(-08:00) = 2018-02-01T05:00 GMT.

So both represents same instance of time.

5.1.62 Answer: C

Reason:
'<' within format string is used to reuse the argument matched by the previous format specifier.

d is for Integer and x is for hexadecimal. Hexadecimal value for 10 is a.

So, 'console.format("%d %<x", 10);' prints '10 a' on to the console.

NOTE: console.format(...) and console.printf(...) methods are same. In fact, printf(...) method invokes format(...) method.

5.1.63 Answer: B

Reason:
createNewDirectory() and createNewDirectories() are not available in java.io.File class.

createNewFile() is for creating new file but not directory.

mkdir() is for creating just 1 directory, in this case abstract path is: 'F:\A\B\C', for mkdir() to create directory, 'F:\A\B\' path must exist.

As per question F: doesn't contain any directories, hence mkdir() doesn't create any directory and returns false.

mkdirs() creates all the directories (if not available), specified in the given abstract path and returns true.

5.1.64 Answer: B

Reason:
System.getProperty("path.separator") returns the path-separator, semicolon(;) on Windows system and colon(:) on Linux system.

So, above code will definitely not create directory named, 'A'. On windows system, it created directory with name ';A'.

You can get file separator by using below code:
System.getProperty("file.separator") OR File.separator.

5.1.65 Answer: C

Reason:
Initially F:\ is blank.

new File("F:\\f1.txt"); => It just creates a Java object containing abstract path 'F:\f1.txt'. NO physical file is created on the disc.

new FileWriter("F:\\f2.txt"); => It creates 'f2.txt' under F:.

new PrintWriter("F:\\f3.txt"); => It creates 'f3.txt' under F:.

NOTE: Constructors of FileWriter and PrintWriter can create a new file but not directory.

5.1.66 Answer: D

Reason:
Class Student implements Serializable but it's super class Person is not Serializable.

While de-serializing of Serializable class, constructor of that class is not invoked. But if Parent class is not Serializable, then to construct the Parent class object, a no-argument constructor in Parent class is needed. This no-argument constructor initializes the properties to their default values.

As Person class doesn't have no-argument constructor, hence 'ois.readObject();' throws runtime exception.

5.1.67   Answer: A

Reason:
toRealPath() returns the path of an existing file. It returns the path after normalizing.

As toRealPath() works with existing file, there is a possibility of I/O error hence toRealPath() method declares to throw IOException, which is a checked exception.

Given code doesn't handle or declare IOException and that is why 'file.toRealPath()' causes compilation error.

5.1.68   Answer: A,B,C,D

Reason:
All 4 are the correct way to iterate through path elements.

Root folder or drive is not considered in count and indexing. In the given path A is at 0th index, B is at 1st index, C is at 2nd index and Book.java is at 3rd index.

path.getNameCount() returns 4.

5.1.69   Answer: A

Reason:
static method Files.size(path) method is equivalent to instance method length() defined in java.io.File class.

Both returns length of the file, in bytes.

5.1.70   Answer: B

Reason:
Files class has methods such as newInputStream(...), newOutputStream(...), newBufferedReader(...) and newBufferedWriter(...) for files reading and writing. Given code doesn't cause any compilation error.

As Book.java is a text file and accessible, hence its contents are printed on to the console.

5.1.71 Answer: A

Reason:

endsWith method is overloaded in Path interface:
boolean endsWith(Path other);
boolean endsWith(String other);

Even though endsWith(String) accepts String but it should evaluate to pathname, such as "Child" OR "a.txt" but not just a part of pathname, such as "txt".

p.endsWith("txt") will return false for all the available paths and hence nothing will get printed on to the console.

NOTE: If you want to find the files ending with "txt" then use 'p.toString().endsWith("txt")' in the lambda expression.

5.1.72 Answer: D

Reason:

endsWith method is overloaded in Path interface:
boolean endsWith(Path other);
boolean endsWith(String other);

'p.endsWith(null)' causes compilation error as it is an ambiguous method call.

5.1.73 Answer: C

Reason:

Even if there are no records in EMPLOYEE table, ResultSet object returned by 'stmt.executeQuery(query);' will never be null.

rs.next() returns false and control doesn't enter while loop.

'rs.getInt("IDD")' statement has wrong column name but as this statement is not executed, hence SQLException is not thrown at runtime.

Code executes fine and doesn't print anything on to the console.

5.1.74 Answer: A

Reason:
By default ResultSet is not updatable.

'rs.deleteRow();' throws an exception at runtime.

To update the ResultSet in any manner (insert, update or delete), the ResultSet must come from a Statement that was created with a ResultSet type of ResultSet.CONCUR_UPDATABLE.

NOTE: If you want to successfully delete the row, then replace 'con.createStatement();' with 'con.createStatement(ResultSet.TYPE_SCROLL_SENSITIVE, ResultSet.CONCUR_UPDATABLE);' OR 'con.createStatement(ResultSet.TYPE_SCROLL_INSENSITIVE, ResultSet.CONCUR_UPDATABLE);'

5.1.75 Answer: A

Reason:
As credentials are passed as java.util.Properties so user name should be passed as "user" property and password should be passed as "password" property.

In the given code, correct property names 'user' and 'password' are used. As URL and DB credentials are correct, hence no issues in connecting the database.

Given query returns just one column containing no. of records, 0 in this case.

But ResultSet cursor is initially before the first record, hence 'rs.getInt(1)' throws SQLException at runtime.

5.1.76 Answer: C

Reason:
There are 2 ResultSet concur types: CONCUR_READ_ONLY and CONCUR_UPDATABLE.

5.1.77 Answer: D

Reason:

Initially cursor is just before the first record. 'rs.absolute(0);' also moves the cursor to just before the first record.

As ResultSet cursor is initially before the first record, hence 'rs.getInt(1)' throws SQLException at runtime.

5.1.78 Answer: D

Reason:
Given query returns below records:
101 John   Smith   12000
102 Sean   Smith   15000
103 Regina Williams   15500
104 Natasha George 14600

'rs.absolute(1);' It moves the cursor to 1st record
'rs.moveToInsertRow();' It moves the cursor to the insert row.
Please note, If the cursor is at insert row and refreshRow() or updateRow() or deleteRow() method is called, then SQLException is thrown.
Hence, in this case an exception is raised by rs.deleteRow();

5.1.79 Answer: B

Reason:
Builder is a static nested class added in Locale class in JDK 7.

NOTE: Builder's region is same as Locale's country.

l1 refers to Locale object for 'en_US'. l2 also refers to Locale object for 'en_US' but l3 doesn't refer to Locale object for 'en_US'. It just refers to Locale object for 'en'.

In fact, l3.getCountry() and l3.getDisplayCountry() return blank string.

l1 and l2 are same but l3 is different.

5.1.80 Answer: A

Reason:
The search order for matching resource bundle is:
com.udayan.ocp.MyResourceBundle_en_US [1st: Complete, en_US].
com.udayan.ocp.MyResourceBundle_en [2nd: Only language, en].
com.udayan.ocp.MyResourceBundle_fr_IT [3rd: Complete Default Locale, fr_IT].
com.udayan.ocp.MyResourceBundle_fr [4th: Language of Default Locale, fr].
com.udayan.ocp.MyResourceBundle [5th: ResourceBundle's name without language or country].

If search reaches the 5th step and no matching resource bundle is found, then MissingResourceException is thrown at runtime.

In 5th step, matching resource bundle is found and hence 'SURPRISE!' is printed on to the console.

5.1.81 Answer: A

Reason:
Format of resource bundle properties file is:
key1=value1
key2=value2

There must be a newline between 2 pairs of key and value. Colon(:) and Semicolon(;) are not used as separators.

Even if value has space in between, double quotes are not used.

NOTE: Generally as a good convention spaces in keys are not OK but if you have to have the space, then escape it properly.
country name=Sri Lanka => NOT OK.
country\ name=Sri Lanka => OK.

5.1.82 Answer: A

Reason:
As Locale instance is for en_US, hence 'NumberFormat.getCurrencyInstance(loc);' returns NumberFormat instance for US.
Currency code for US is USD and it is represented as $.
nf.getCurrency() returns the Currency object with currency Code "USD" and nf.format(10) returns $10.00

5.1.83 Answer: D

Reason:

Method submit is overloaded to accept both Callable and Runnable: <T> Future<T> submit(Callable<T> task); and Future<?> submit(Runnable task);

Both returns a Future object. call() method of MyCallable returns 9 and get() method returns this value.

run() method of MyThread doesn't return anything, hence get() method of Future object returns null.

5.1.84 Answer: A, D

Reason:

AtomicInteger overrides toString() method hence when ai is passed to println method, its value is printed.

'ai.addAndGet(1)' first adds 1 (10+1) and returns 11. 'ai' also prints 11.
'ai.getAndAdd(1)' first returns 10 and then adds 1.
'ai.getAndIncrement()' first returns 10 and then adds 1.
'ai.incrementAndGet()' increments the value by 1 (10+1) and returns 11.
'ai.incrementAndGet(1)' causes compilation failure.
'ai.get()' returns the current value of ai.

5.1.85 Answer: B

Reason:

After invoking fork() on 1st subtask, it is necessary to invoke join() on 1st subtask and compute() on 2nd subtask. Hence 'return first.join();' and 'return second.compute();' are not valid options.

The order of execution of calling join() and compute() on divided subtasks is important in a fork/join framework.

For the statement 'return first.join() + second.compute();' as join() is called so each task waits for its completion before starting execution of a new thread. Even though you will get the correct output but it is not utilizing the fork/join framework efficiently.

If you are interested in finding out the time difference then I will suggest to modify main(String[]) method as below and run the program for both the statements separately.

public static void main(String[] args) {

```
LocalTime start = LocalTime.now();
ForkJoinPool pool = new ForkJoinPool(THREADS);
long sum = pool.invoke(new AdderTask(1, LIMIT));
System.out.printf("sum of the number from %d to %d is %d %n", 1, LIMIT, sum);
LocalTime end = LocalTime.now();
System.out.println(ChronoUnit.NANOS.between(start, end));
}
```

5.1.86 Answer: A

Reason:
Fork/Join framework is for the problems that can be divided into sub tasks and result of computation can be combined later. Each sub-task should be computed independently without depending upon other tasks and result can be combined later.

Input/Output operations may block and hence this framework is not suitable for any type of I/O operations.

Synchronization defeats the purpose of fork/join framework to compute the tasks in parallel.

5.1.87 Answer: A,D

Reason:
Collection interface has a default method stream() to return a sequential() stream for the currently executing Collection.
Collection interface has a default method parallelStream() to return a parallel stream for the currently executing Collection.

Stream class has parallel() method to convert to parallel stream and sequential() method to convert to sequential stream.
isParallel() method of Stream class returns true for parallel Stream.

list is a Collection. So,

list.stream() returns a sequential stream and list.stream().parallel() returns a parallel stream. list.stream().parallel().isParallel() returns true.
stream() returns a sequential stream and list.stream().isParallel() returns false.
list.parallel() causes compilation error.
list.parallelStream() returns a parallel stream. list.parallelStream().isParallel() returns true.

5.1.88 Answer: C

Reason:
Line 13 is changing the state of list object and hence it should be avoided in parallel stream. You can never predict the order in which elements will be added to the stream.

Line 13 and Line 15 doesn't run in synchronized manner, hence as the result, output of Line 17 may be different from that of Line 15.

On my machine below is the output of various executions:
Execution 1:
5427163
5412736

Execution 2:
5476231
5476123

Execution 3:
5476231
5476231

5.1.89 Answer: C

Reason:
reduce method in Stream class is declared as: T reduce(T identity, BinaryOperator<T> accumulator)
By checking the reduce method, 'reduce("", String::concat)', we can say that:
Identity is String type, accumulator is BinaryOperator<String> type.

Though you may always get false but result cannot be predicted as identity value ("_") used in reduce method is not following an important rule.

For each element 't' of the stream, accumulator.apply(identity, t) is equal to t.

'String::concat' is equivalent to lambda expression '(s1, s2) -> s1.concat(s2);'.

For 1st element of the stream, "A" accumulator.apply("_", "A") results in "_A", which is not equal to "A" and hence rule is not followed.

s1 will always refer to "_AEIOU" but s2 may refer to various possible string objects depending upon how parallel stream is processed.

s2 may refer to "_A_E_I_O_U" or "_AE_I_OU" or "_AEIOU". So output cannot be predicted.

5.1.90 Answer: A

Reason:

reduce method in Stream class is declared as: <U> U reduce(U identity, BiFunction<U,? super T,U> accumulator, BinaryOperator<U> combiner)
By checking the reduce method 'reduce("", (i, s) -> i + s, (s1, s2) -> s1 + s2)', we can say that:
Identity is String type, accumulator is BiFunction<String, ? super Integer, String> type, combiner is BinaryOperator<String> type.

To get consistent output, there are requirements for reduce method arguments:
1. The identity value must be an identity for the combiner function. This means that for all u, combiner(identity, u) is equal to u.
   As u is of String type, let's say u = "X", combiner("", "X") = "X". Hence, u is equal to combiner("", "X"). First rule is obeyed.

2. The combiner function must be compatible with the accumulator function; for all u and t, the following must hold:
   combiner.apply(u, accumulator.apply(identity, t)) == accumulator.apply(u, t).
   Let's consider, u = "Y", t is element of Stream, say t = 1, identity = "".
   combiner.apply(u, accumulator.apply(identity, t))
   = combiner.apply("Y", accumulator.apply("", 1))
   = combiner.apply("Y", "1")
   = "Y1"

   and

   accumulator.apply(u, t)
   = accumulator.apply("Y", 1)
   = "Y1"

 Hence, combiner.apply(u, accumulator.apply(identity, t)) == accumulator.apply(u, t).
2nd rule is also followed.

3. The accumulator operator must be associative and stateless. Operator + is associative and lambda expression is stateless. 3rd rule is followed.

4. The combiner operator must be associative and stateless. Operator + is associative and lambda expression is stateless. 4th rule is followed.

As all the rules are followed in this case, hence str1 refers to "12345678910" and str2 refers to "12345678910"

6   Practice Test-6

6.1   90 Questions covering all topics.

6.1.1   Consider below code:

```java
//Test.java
package com.udayan.ocp;

class Animal {
    void eat() {
        System.out.println("Animal is eating.");
    }
}

class Dog extends Animal {
    public void eat() {
        System.out.println("Dog is eating biscuit.");
    }
}

public class Test {
    public static void main(String[] args) {
        Animal [] animals = new Dog[2];
        animals[0] = new Animal();
        animals[1] = new Dog();

        animals[0].eat();
        animals[1].eat();
    }
}
```

What will be the result of compiling and executing Test class?

A.	Compilation error	B.	Runtime exception
C.	Animal is eating. Dog is eating biscuit.	D.	Animal is eating. Animal is eating.

6.1.2   Consider the code of Test.java file:

```
package com.udayan.ocp;

class Player {
    String name;
    int age;

    Player() {
        this.name = "Yuvraj";
        this.age = 36;
    }

    protected String toString() {
        return name + ", " + age;
    }
}

public class Test {
    public static void main(String[] args) {
        System.out.println(new Player());
    }
}
```

What will be the result of compiling and executing Test class?

A. Compilation error

B. null, 0

C. Yuvraj, 36

D. Text containing @ symbol

6.1.3 Consider the code of Test.java file:

```
package com.udayan.ocp;

abstract class Animal {
    public static void vaccinate() {
        System.out.println("Vaccinating...");
    }

    private abstract void treating();
}

public class Test {
    public static void main(String[] args) {
        Animal.vaccinate();
    }
}
```

What will be the result of compiling and executing Test class?

A. Compilation error in Test class

B. Compilation error in Animal class

C. Vaccinating...

6.1.4 Which of the following are Functional Interface in JDK 8?

A. java.util.Comparator

B. java.lang.Runnable

C. java.awt.event.ActionListener

D. java.io.Serializable

E. java.lang.Cloneable

6.1.5   **What will be the result of compiling and executing Test class?**

```
package com.udayan.ocp;

interface Formatter {
    public abstract String format(String s1, String s2);
}

public class Test {
    public static void main(String[] args) {
        Formatter f1 = (str1, str2) ->
            str1 + "_" + str2.toUpperCase();
        System.out.println(f1.format("Udayan", "Khattry"));
    }
}
```

A. Udayan_Khattry

B. UDAYAN_Khattry

C. Udayan_KHATTRY

D. UDAYAN_KHATTRY

6.1.6 Consider the code of Test.java file:

```
package com.udayan.ocp;

public class Test {
    enum Directions {
        NORTH("N"), SOUTH("S"), EAST("E"), WEST("W")

        private String notation;

        Directions(String notation) {
            this.notation = notation;
        }

        public String getNotation() {
            return notation;
        }
    }

    public static void main(String[] args) {
        System.out.println(
            Test.Directions.NORTH.getNotation());
    }
}
```

What will be the result of compiling and executing Test class?

A. N

B. NORTH

C. Compilation error

D. Exception is thrown at runtime

6.1.7 What will be the result of compiling and executing Test class?

```
package com.udayan.ocp;

enum Status {
    PASS, FAIL, PASS;
}

public class Test {
    public static void main(String[] args) {
        System.out.println(Status.FAIL);
    }
}
```

A. FAIL

B. fail

C. Fail

D. None of the other options

6.1.8 Given code:

```
package com.udayan.ocp;

class Foo {
    public static void m1() {
        System.out.println("Foo : m1()");
    }
    class Bar {
        public static void m1() {
            System.out.println("Bar : m1()");
        }
    }
}

public class Test {
    public static void main(String [] args) {
        Foo foo = new Foo();
        Foo.Bar bar = foo.new Bar();
        bar.m1();
    }
}
```

A. Foo : m1()

B. Bar : m1()

C. Compilation error

D. Runtime exception

6.1.9   Given Code:

```java
package com.udayan.ocp;

class Message {
    public void printMessage() {
        System.out.println("Hello!");
    }
}

public class Test {
    public static void main(String[] args) {
        Message msg = new Message() {}; //Line 9
        msg.printMessage(); //Line 10
    }
}
```

What will be the result of compiling and executing Test class?

A. Compilation error at Line 9

B. NullPointerException is thrown by Line 10

C. Hello!

D. HELLO!

6.1.10 Given code:

```
package com.udayan.ocp;

interface I1 {
    void m1();
}

public class Test {
    public static void main(String[] args) {
        I1 i1 = new I1() {
            @Override
            public void m1() {
                System.out.println(1234);
            }
        };
        i1.m1();
    }
}
```

What will be the result of compiling and executing Test class?

A. 1234

B. No output

C. Compilation error

D. Runtime exception

6.1.11 Below the code of A.java file:

```
package com.udayan.ocp;

public class A {
    private static class B {
        private void log() {
            System.out.println("static nested class");
        }
    }

    public static void main(String[] args) {
        /*INSERT*/
    }
}
```

Which of the following options can replace /*INSERT*/ such that there on executing class A, output is: static nested class?

A.	`B obj1 = new B();` `obj1.log();`
B.	`B obj3 = new A().new B();` `obj3.log();`
C.	`A.B obj2 = new A.B();` `obj2.log();`
D.	`A.B obj4 = new A().new B();` `obj4.log();`

6.1.12 Which of the following operator is used in lambda expressions?

A. =>

B. = >

C. ->

D. - >

6.1.13 Does below code compile successfully?

```
package com.udayan.ocp;

@FunctionalInterface
interface I1 {
    void print();
    boolean equals();
}
```

A. Yes

B. No

6.1.14 What will be the result of compiling and executing Test class?

```
package com.udayan.ocp;

interface I1 {
    void print();
}

public class Test {
    public static void main(String[] args) {
        I1 obj = () -> System.out.println("Hello");
    }
}
```

A. Compilation error

B. Hello

C. Program compiles and executes successfully but nothing is printed on to the console

D. Runtime error

6.1.15 What will be the result of compiling and executing Test class?

```java
package com.udayan.ocp;

interface I6 {
    void m6();
}

public class Test {
    public static void main(String[] args) {
        I6 obj = () ->  {
            int i = 10;
            i++;
            System.out.println(i);
        };
        obj.m6();
    }
}
```

A. Compilation error

B. 10

C. 11

D. Exception is thrown at runtime

6.1.16 Given code of Test.java file:

```java
package com.udayan.ocp;

class Printer<T extends String> {}

public class Test {
    public static void main(String[] args) {
        Printer<String> printer = new Printer<>();
        System.out.println(printer);
    }
}
```

What will be the result of compiling and executing Test class?

A. Some text containing @ symbol

B. Compilation error for Printer class

C. Compilation error for Test class

6.1.17 Given code of Test.java file:

```
package com.udayan.ocp;

public class Test {
    private static final <X extends Integer,
        Y extends Integer> void add(X x, Y y) {
            System.out.println(x + y);
    }

    public static void main(String[] args) {
        add(10, 20);
    }
}
```

What will be the result of compiling and executing Test class?

A. Compilation error

B. Runtime Exception

C. 30

D. 1020

6.1.18 Given code of Test.java file:

```
package com.udayan.ocp;

public class Test<T> {
    T [] obj;

    public Test() {
        obj = new T[100];
    }

    public T [] get() {
        return obj;
    }

    public static void main(String[] args) {
        Test<String> test = new Test<>();
        String [] arr = test.get();
        System.out.println(arr.length);
    }
}
```

What will be the result of compiling and executing Test class?

A. 100

B. Compilation error

C. Runtime exception

6.1.19 Given code of Test.java file:

```
package com.udayan.ocp;

import java.util.ArrayList;
import java.util.List;

abstract class Animal {}
class Dog extends Animal{}

public class Test {
    public static void main(String [] args) {
        List<Animal> list = new ArrayList<Dog>();
        list.add(0, new Dog());
        System.out.println(list.size() > 0);
    }
}
```

What will be the result of compiling and executing Test class?

A. true

B. false

C. Compilation error

D. Runtime exception

6.1.20 Given code of Test.java file:

```java
package com.udayan.ocp;

import java.util.*;

class Student {
    private String name;
    private int age;

    Student(String name, int age) {
        this.name = name;
        this.age = age;
    }

    public int hashCode() {
        return name.hashCode() + age;
    }

    public String toString() {
        return "Student[" + name + ", " + age + "]";
    }

    public boolean equals(Object obj) {
        if(obj instanceof Student) {
            Student stud = (Student)obj;
            return this.name.equals(stud.name)
                            && this.age == stud.age;
        }
        return false;
    }
}

public class Test {
    public static void main(String[] args) {
        Set<Student> students = new TreeSet<>();
        students.add(new Student("James", 20));
        students.add(new Student("James", 20));
        students.add(new Student("James", 22));

        System.out.println(students.size());
    }
}
```

What will be the result of compiling and executing Test class?

A. 2

B. 3

C. Runtime Exception

6.1.21 Given code of Test.java file:

```
package com.udayan.ocp;

import java.util.*;

public class Test {
    public static void main(String[] args) {
        Deque<Integer> deque = new ArrayDeque<>();
        deque.add(100);
        deque.add(200);
        deque.addFirst(300);
        deque.addLast(400);
        deque.remove(200);

        System.out.println(deque.getFirst());
    }
}
```

What will be the result of compiling and executing Test class?

A. 100

B. 200

C. 300

D. 400

6.1.22 Given code of Test.java file:

```java
package com.udayan.ocp;

import java.util.*;

public class Test {
    public static void main(String[] args) {
        Set<String> set = new HashSet<>(
                    Arrays.asList(null, null, null));
        long count = set.stream().count();
        System.out.println(count);
    }
}
```

What will be the result of compiling and executing Test class?

A. 0

B. 1

C. 3

D. Runtime Exception

6.1.23 Given code of Test.java file:

```
package com.udayan.ocp;

import java.util.ArrayList;
import java.util.List;

public class Test {
    public static void main(String[] args) {
        List list = new ArrayList<Integer>();
        list.add(1);
        list.add(2);
        list.add("3"); //Line 11
        list.removeIf(i -> i % 2 == 1); //Line 12
        System.out.println(list);
    }
}
```

What will be the result of compiling and executing Test class?

A. Compilation error at Line 11

B. Compilation error at Line 12

C. Runtime Exception

D. [2]

6.1.24 **What will be the result of compiling and executing Test class?**

```java
package com.udayan.ocp;

import java.util.ArrayList;
import java.util.Collections;
import java.util.Comparator;
import java.util.List;

class Point {
    private int x;
    private int y;
    public Point(int x, int y) {
        this.x = x;
        this.y = y;
    }
    public int getX() {
        return x;
    }
    public int getY() {
        return y;
    }
    @Override
    public String toString() {
        return "Point(" + x + ", " + y + ")";
    }
}

public class Test {
    public static void main(String [] args) {
        List<Point> points = new ArrayList<>();
        points.add(new Point(4, 5));
        points.add(new Point(6, 7));
        points.add(new Point(2, 2));

        Collections.sort(points, new Comparator<Point>() {
            public int compareTo(Point o1, Point o2) {
                return o1.getX() - o2.getX();
            }
        });

        System.out.println(points);
    }
}
```

A. [Point(2, 2), Point(4, 5), Point(6, 7)]

B. [Point(6, 7), Point(4, 5), Point(2, 2)]

C. [Point(4, 5), Point(6, 7), Point(2, 2)]

D. Compilation error

6.1.25 Given code of Test.java file:

```java
package com.udayan.ocp;
import java.util.Arrays;
import java.util.Collections;
import java.util.Comparator;
import java.util.List;

public class Test {
    public static void main(String[] args) {
        List<String> list = Arrays.asList(
                "#####", "#", "##", "####", "###");
        Comparator<String> comp =
                    Comparator.comparing(s -> s);
        Collections.sort(list, comp.reversed());
        printCodes(list);
    }

    private static void printCodes(List<String> list) {
        for (String str : list) {
            System.out.println(str);
        }
    }
}
```

What will be the result of compiling and executing Test class?

A.	B.
##### # ## #### ###	### #### ## # #####
C.	D.
##### #### ### ## #	# ## ### #### #####

6.1.26 **Given code of Test.java file:**

```java
package com.udayan.ocp;

import java.util.*;

class Employee {
    private String name;
    private double salary;

    public Employee(String name, double salary) {
        this.name = name;
        this.salary = salary;
    }

    public String getName() {
        return name;
    }

    public double getSalary() {
        return salary;
    }

    public void setSalary(double salary) {
        this.salary = salary;
    }

    public String toString() {
        return "{" + name + ", " + salary + "}";
    }
}

public class Test {
    public static void main(String[] args) {
        List<Employee> employees = Arrays.asList(
            new Employee("Jack", 10000),
            new Employee("Lucy", 12000));
        employees.forEach(e -> e.setSalary(
            e.getSalary() + (e.getSalary() * .2)));
        employees.forEach(System.out::println);
    }
}
```

What will be the result of compiling and executing Test class?

A.	{Jack, 12000.0} {Lucy, 14400.0}	B.	{Jack, 12000} {Lucy, 14400}
C.	{Jack, 10000.0} {Lucy, 12000.0}	D.	{Jack, 10000} {Lucy, 12000}

6.1.27 Given code of Test.java file:

```
package com.udayan.ocp;

import java.util.*;
import java.util.stream.IntStream;

public class Test {
    public static void main(String[] args) {
        IntStream.range(1, 10).forEach(System.out::print);
    }
}
```

What will be the result of compiling and executing Test class?

A. 123456789

B. 12345678910

C. 13579

D. 246810

6.1.28 Given code of Test.java file:

```
package com.udayan.ocp;

import java.util.stream.LongStream;

public class Test {
    public static void main(String[] args) {
        LongStream.iterate(0, i -> i + 2).limit(4)
                            .forEach(System.out::print);
    }
}
```

What will be the result of compiling and executing Test class?

A. 02

B. 024

C. 0246

D. 02468

6.1.29 Given code of Test.java file:

```
package com.udayan.ocp;

import java.util.ArrayList;
import java.util.List;

public class Test {
    public static void main(String[] args) {
        List<StringBuilder> list = new ArrayList<>();
        list.add(new StringBuilder("abc"));
        list.add(new StringBuilder("xyz"));
        list.stream().map(x -> x.reverse());
        System.out.println(list);
    }
}
```

What will be the result of compiling and executing Test class?

A. [cba, zyx]

B. [abc, xyz]

C. Compilation error

D. Runtime Exception

6.1.30 Given code of Test.java file:

```
package com.udayan.ocp;

import java.util.function.Predicate;

public class Test {
    public static void main(String[] args) {
        printNumbers(i -> i % 2 != 0);
    }

    private static void printNumbers(
                    Predicate<Integer> predicate) {
        for(int i = 1; i <= 10; i++) {
            if(predicate.test(i)) {
                System.out.print(i);
            }
        }
    }
}
```

What will be the result of compiling and executing Test class?

A. 12345678910

B. 1234567891011

C. 246810

D. 13579

E. 1357911

6.1.31 Given code of Test.java file:

```
package com.udayan.ocp;

import java.util.function.Predicate;

public class Test {
    public static void main(String[] args) {
        String [] arr = {"A", "ab", "bab", "Aa", "bb",
                                    "baba", "aba", "Abab"};

        processStringArray(arr, /*INSERT*/);
    }

    private static void processStringArray(String [] arr,
                            Predicate<String> predicate) {
        for(String str : arr) {
            if(predicate.test(str)) {
                System.out.println(str);
            }
        }
    }
}
```

Which of the following options can replace /*INSERT*/ such that on executing Test class all the array elements are displayed in the output?
Select ALL that apply.

A. `p -> true`

B. `p -> !false`

C. `p -> p.length() >= 1`

D. `p -> p.length() < 10`

6.1.32 Which of the import statements correctly imports the functional interface Comparator?

A. import java.util.function.Comparator;

B. import java.util.Comparator;

C. import java.function.Comparator;

D. import java.lang.Comparator;

6.1.33 Given code of Test.java file:

```
package com.udayan.ocp;

import java.util.function.IntConsumer;
import java.util.stream.IntStream;

public class Test {
    public static void main(String[] args) {
        IntConsumer consumer = i -> i * i * i;
        int result = IntStream.range(1, 5).sum();
        System.out.println(result);
    }
}
```

What will be the result of compiling and executing Test class?

A. 100

B. 225

C. Runtime Exception

D. Compilation error

6.1.34 Given code of Test.java file:

```
package com.udayan.ocp;

import java.util.function.BiFunction;

public class Test {
    public static void main(String[] args) {
        BiFunction<Double, Double, Integer> compFunc
                                = Double::compareTo;
        System.out.println(compFunc.apply(10.01, 11.99));
    }
}
```

What will be the result of compiling and executing Test class?

A. Compilation error

B. 0

C. 1

D. -1

E. 2

F. -2

6.1.35 Given code of Test.java file:

```
package com.udayan.ocp;

import java.util.function.LongFunction;
import java.util.function.LongUnaryOperator;

public class Test {
    public static void main(String[] args) {
        LongFunction<LongUnaryOperator> func =
                        a -> b -> b - a; //Line n1
        System.out.println(calc(
                        func.apply(100), 50)); //Line n2
    }

    private static long calc(LongUnaryOperator op,
                                        long val) {
        return op.applyAsLong(val);
    }
}
```

What will be the result of compiling and executing Test class?

A. 100

B. -100

C. 50

D. -50

E. Line n1 causes compilation error

F. Line n2 causes compilation error

6.1.36 Given code of Test.java file:

```
package com.udayan.ocp;

import java.util.function.UnaryOperator;

public class Test {
    public static void main(String[] args) {
        final String password = "Oracle";
        UnaryOperator<String> opr1 =
                    s -> s.replace('a', '@'); //Line n1
        UnaryOperator<String> opr2 =
                    s -> password.concat(s); //Line n2
        System.out.println("Password: " +
                opr1.apply(opr2.apply("!"))); //Line n3
    }
}
```

What will be the result of compiling and executing Test class?

A. Compilation error at Line n1

B. Compilation error at Line n2

C. Compilation error at Line n3

D. Password: Or@cle!

E. Password: Oracle!

6.1.37 Given code of Test.java file:

```
package com.udayan.ocp;

import java.util.stream.Stream;

public class Test {
    public static void main(String[] args) {
        Stream.of(true, false, true).map(b -> b.toString()
            .toUpperCase()).peek(System.out::println);
    }
}
```

What will be the result of compiling and executing Test class?

A.	Compilation error	B.	TRUE FALSE TRUE
C.	true false true	D.	Program executes successfully but nothing is printed on to the console

6.1.38 Given code of Test.java file:

```
package com.udayan.ocp;
import java.util.Optional;

public class Test {
    public static void main(String[] args) {
        Optional<Integer> optional = Optional.of(null);
        System.out.println(optional);
    }
}
```

What will be the result of compiling and executing Test class?

A. Optional.empty

B. Optional[null]

C. Optional[0]

D. NullPointerException is thrown at runtime

6.1.39 Given code of Test.java file:

```
package com.udayan.ocp;
import java.util.OptionalLong;

public class Test {
    public static void main(String[] args) {
        OptionalLong optional = OptionalLong.empty();
        System.out.println(optional.isPresent()
                    + " : " + optional.getAsLong());
    }
}
```
What will be the result of compiling and executing Test class?

A. true : 0

B. false : 0

C. false : null

D. true : null

E. Runtime Exception

6.1.40 Given code of Test.java file:

```java
package com.udayan.ocp;

import java.util.stream.Stream;

class Employee {
    private String name;
    private double salary;

    public Employee(String name, double salary) {
        this.name = name;
        this.salary = salary;
    }

    public String getName() {
        return name;
    }

    public double getSalary() {
        return salary;
    }

    public String toString() {
        return "{" + name + ", " + salary + "}";
    }

    public static int salaryCompare(double d1, double d2) {
        return new Double(d2).compareTo(d1);
    }
}

public class Test {
    public static void main(String[] args) {
        Stream<Employee> employees = Stream.of(
            new Employee("Jack", 10000),
            new Employee("Lucy", 12000),
            new Employee("Tom", 7000));

        highestSalary(employees);
    }

    private static void highestSalary(Stream<Employee> emp){
        System.out.println(emp.map(e -> e.getSalary())
                        .max(Employee::salaryCompare));
    }
}
```

What will be the result of compiling and executing Test class?

A. Optional[10000.0]

B. Optional[12000.0]

C. Optional[7000.0]

D. Optional.empty

6.1.41 Given code of Test.java file:

```
package com.udayan.ocp;

import java.util.Arrays;
import java.util.stream.Stream;

public class Test {
    public static void main(String[] args) {
        Stream<Double> stream =
            Arrays.asList(1.8, 2.2, 3.5).stream();
        System.out.println(
            stream.reduce((d1, d2) -> d1 + d2)); //Line 9
    }
}
```

What will be the result of compiling and executing Test class?

A. Optional[7.5]

B. 7.5

C. Line 9 causes Compilation error

6.1.42   Given code of Test.java file:

```
package com.udayan.ocp;

import java.util.Arrays;

public class Test {
    public static void main(String[] args) {
        String [] names = {"Peter", "bonita", "John"};
        Arrays.stream(names).sorted(
            (s1, s2) -> s1.compareToIgnoreCase(s2))
            .forEach(System.out::println);
    }
}
```

What will be the result of compiling and executing Test class?

A.	Peter bonita John	B.	John bonita Peter
C.	bonita John Peter	D.	John Peter bonita

6.1.43 Given code of Test.java file:

```
package com.udayan.ocp;

import java.util.Arrays;
import java.util.stream.Stream;

public class Test {
    public static void main(String[] args) {
        String [] arr1
            = {"Virat", "Rohit", "Shikhar", "Dhoni"};
        String [] arr2 = {"Bumrah", "Pandya", "Sami"};
        String [] arr3 = {};

        Stream<String[]> stream
                        = Stream.of(arr1, arr2, arr3);
        stream.flatMap(s -> Arrays.stream(s)).sorted()
            .forEach(s -> System.out.print(s + " "));
    }
}
```

What will be the result of compiling and executing Test class?

A. Virat Rohit Shikhar Dhoni Bumrah Pandya Sami

B. Virat Rohit Shikhar Dhoni Bumrah Pandya Sami null

C. null Bumrah Dhoni Pandya Rohit Sami Shikhar Virat

D. Bumrah Dhoni Pandya Rohit Sami Shikhar Virat

E. Bumrah Dhoni Pandya Rohit Sami Shikhar Virat null

6.1.44 Given code of Test.java file:

```
package com.udayan.ocp;

import java.util.stream.LongStream;

public class Test {
    public static void main(String[] args) {
        LongStream stream = LongStream.empty();
        System.out.println(stream.average());
    }
}
```

What will be the result of compiling and executing Test class?

A. null

B. 0.0

C. OptionalDouble.empty

D. Runtime exception

6.1.45 Given code of Test.java file:

```
package com.udayan.ocp;

import java.util.stream.Stream;

public class Test {
    public static void main(String[] args) {
        Stream<Double> stream =
            Stream.generate(() -> new Double("1.0"));
        System.out.println(stream.sorted().findFirst());
    }
}
```

What will be the result of compiling and executing Test class?

A. Optional[1.0] is printed and program terminates successfully.

B. Optional[1.0] is printed and program runs infinitely.

C. Nothing is printed and program runs infinitely.

D. Compilation error.

6.1.46 Given code of Test.java file:

```
package com.udayan.ocp;

import java.util.Optional;
import java.util.stream.Stream;

public class Test {
    public static void main(String[] args) {
        Stream<String> stream = Stream.of("a",
                                "as", "an", "and");
        Optional<String> first = stream.findFirst();
        if(first.ifPresent()) {
            System.out.println(first.get());
        }
    }
}
```

What will be the result of compiling and executing Test class?

A. a

B. Any element from the stream is printed

C. Compilation error

D. Runtime Exception

6.1.47 Given:

```
package com.udayan.ocp;

import java.util.Arrays;
import java.util.List;
import java.util.function.UnaryOperator;

public class Test {
    public static void main(String[] args) {
        /* INSERT */
        List<Character> vowels =
                Arrays.asList('A', 'E', 'I', 'O', 'U');
        vowels.stream().map(x -> operator.apply(x))
                .forEach(System.out::print); //Line n1
    }
}
```

Line n1 is causing compilation error as variable 'operator' is not found. Which of the following two options can replace /* INSERT */ such that output is: BFJPV?

A. `UnaryOperator<Integer> operator = c -> c + 1;`

B. `UnaryOperator<Character> operator = c -> c + 1;`

C. `UnaryOperator<Character> operator =`
`                        c -> c.charValue() + 1;`

D. `UnaryOperator<Character> operator =`
`                        c -> (char)(c.charValue() + 1);`

E. `Function<Character, Character> operator =`
`                        x -> (char)(x + 1);`

F. `Function<Character, Integer> operator = x -> x + 1;`

6.1.48 Given code of Test.java file:

```java
package com.udayan.ocp;

import java.io.FileNotFoundException;
import java.io.IOException;

abstract class Super {
    public abstract void m1() throws IOException;
}

class Sub extends Super {
    @Override
    public void m1() throws IOException {
        throw new FileNotFoundException();
    }
}

public class Test {
    public static void main(String[] args) {
        Super s = new Sub();
        try {
            s.m1();
        } catch (IOException e) {
            System.out.print("A");
        } catch (FileNotFoundException e) {
            System.out.print("B");
        } finally {
            System.out.print("C");
        }
    }
}
```

What will be the result of compiling and executing Test class?

A. AC

B. BC

C. class Sub causes compilation error

D. class Test causes compilation error

6.1.49 Given code of Test.java file:

```java
package com.udayan.ocp;

public class Test {
    private static void div(int i, int j) {
        try {
            System.out.println(i / j);
        } catch (ArithmeticException e) {
            Exception ex = new Exception(e);
            throw ex;
        }
    }
    public static void main(String[] args) {
        try {
            div(5, 0);
        } catch (Exception e) {
            System.out.println("END");
        }
    }
}
```

What will be the result of compiling and executing Test class?

A. Compilation error

B. END is printed and program terminates successfully

C. END is printed and program terminates abruptly

D. END is not printed and program terminates abruptly

6.1.50   Given code of Test.java file:

```java
package com.udayan.ocp;

import java.sql.SQLException;

public class Test {
    private static void m() throws SQLException {
        throw null; //Line 7
    }

    public static void main(String[] args) {
        try {
            m(); //Line 12
        } catch(SQLException e) {
            System.out.println("Caught Successfully.");
        }
    }
}
```

What will be the result of compiling and executing Test class?

A.   Caught Successfully.

B.   Program ends abruptly.

C.   Line 7 causes compilation failure.

D.   Line 12 causes compilation failure.

6.1.51 Given code of Test.java file:

```
package com.udayan.ocp;

class TestException extends Exception {
    public TestException() {
        super();
    }

    public TestException(String s) {
        super(s);
    }
}

public class Test {
    public void m1() throws _____ {
        throw new TestException();
    }
}
```

For the above code, fill in the blank with one option.

A. Exception

B. Object

C. RuntimeException

D. Error

6.1.52 Given code of Test.java file:

```
package com.udayan.ocp;

import java.io.IOException;
import java.sql.SQLException;

class MyResource implements AutoCloseable {
    @Override
    public void close() throws IOException{

    }

    public void execute() throws SQLException {
        throw new SQLException("SQLException");
    }
}

public class Test {
    public static void main(String[] args) {
        try(MyResource resource = new MyResource()) {
            resource.execute();
        } catch(Exception e) {
            System.out.println(e.getSuppressed().length);
        }
    }
}
```

What will be the result of compiling and executing Test class?

A. 1

B. 0

C. NullPointerException is thrown

6.1.53 Given code of Test.java file:

```
package com.udayan.ocp;

class Resource implements AutoCloseable {
    public void close() {
        System.out.println("CLOSE");
    }
}

public class Test {
    public static void main(String[] args) {
        try(Resource r = null) {
            System.out.println("HELLO");
        }
    }
}
```

What will be the result of compiling and executing Test class?

A.	HELLO	B.	HELLO CLOSE
C.	Compilation error	D.	NullPointerException is thrown at runtime

6.1.54 Given code of Test.java file:

```
package com.udayan.ocp;

public class Test {
    private static void checkStatus(boolean flag) {
        assert flag : flag = true;
    }

    public static void main(String[] args) {
        checkStatus(false);
    }
}
```

What will be the result of executing Test class with below command?
java -ea:com.udayan... com.udayan.ocp.Test

A. No output and program terminates successfully

B. AssertionError is thrown and program terminates abruptly

C. Compilation error

6.1.55   Given code of Test.java file:

```java
package com.udayan.ocp;

public class Test {
    private static void checkStatus() {
        assert 1 == 2 : 2 == 2;
    }

    public static void main(String[] args) {
        try {
            checkStatus();
        } catch (AssertionError ae) {
            System.out.println(ae.getMessage());
        }
    }
}
```

What will be the result of executing Test class with below command?
java -ea com.udayan.ocp.Test

A. true

B. false

C. null

D. Compilation error

6.1.56 Given code of Test.java file:

```
package com.udayan.ocp;

import java.time.LocalDate;

public class Test {
    public static void main(String [] args) {
        LocalDate ocpCouponPurchaseDate
                    = LocalDate.of(2018, 3, 1);
        System.out.println("Coupon expiry date: "
            + ocpCouponPurchaseDate.plusDays(10));
    }
}
```

What will be the result of compiling and executing Test class?

A. Coupon expiry date: 2018-3-11

B. Coupon expiry date: 2018-03-11

C. Compilation error

D. Runtime exception

6.1.57 Given code of Test.java file:

```
package com.udayan.ocp;

import java.time.LocalDateTime;

public class Test {
    public static void main(String [] args) {
        LocalDateTime dt =
            LocalDateTime.parse("2018-03-16t10:15:30.22");
        System.out.println(dt);
    }
}
```

What will be the result of compiling and executing Test class?

A. 2018-03-16t10:15:30.22

B. 2018-03-16T10:15:30.22

C. 2018-03-16t10:15:30.220

D. 2018-03-16T10:15:30.220

6.1.58 Given code of Test.java file:

```
package com.udayan.ocp;

import java.time.*;

public class Test {
    public static void main(String [] args) {
        System.out.println(LocalDate.of(2018, 6, 6)
            .plus(Period.parse("P9M")));
    }
}
```

What will be the result of compiling and executing Test class?

A. 2018-3-6

B. 2018-03-06

C. 2019-3-6

D. 2019-03-06

6.1.59 Given code of Test.java file:

```
package com.udayan.ocp;

import java.time.*;
import java.time.format.DateTimeFormatter;

public class Test {
    public static void main(String [] args) {
        LocalDate valDay = LocalDate.of(2018, 2, 14);
        DateTimeFormatter formatter
            = DateTimeFormatter.ofPattern("DD-MM-uuuu");
        System.out.println(valDay.format(formatter));
    }
}
```

What will be the result of compiling and executing Test class?

A. Compilation Error

B. Runtime Exception

C. 14-02-2018

D. 45-02-2018

6.1.60 Which of the following classes support time zone?

A. LocalDate

B. LocalTime

C. LocalDateTime

D. ZonedDateTime

6.1.61 Given code of Test.java file:

```java
package com.udayan.ocp;

import java.time.*;
import java.time.format.DateTimeFormatter;

public class Test {
    public static void main(String [] args) {
        LocalDate date = LocalDate.of(2018, 11, 4);
        DateTimeFormatter formatter
            = DateTimeFormatter.ofPattern("DD-MM-uuuu");
        System.out.println(formatter.format(date));
    }
}
```

What will be the result of compiling and executing Test class?

A. Compilation Error

B. Runtime Exception

C. 04-11-2018

6.1.62 Given code of Test.java file:

```java
import java.io.*;

public class Test {
    public static void main(String[] args) {
        Console console = System.console();
        if(console != null) {
            console.format("%d %x", 10);
        }
    }
}
```

What will be the output of compiling and executing Test class from command prompt?
javac Test.java
java Test

A. 10 10

B. 10 12

C. 10 a

D. 10

E. Runtime Exception

6.1.63 Given code of Test.java file:

```
package com.udayan.ocp;

public class Test {
    public static void main(String[] args) {
        System.out.printf("%2$d + %1$d", 10, 20, 30);
    }
}
```

What will be the result of compiling and executing Test class?

A. 30

B. 10 + 20

C. 20 + 10

D. None of the other options

6.1.64   Given code of Test.java file:

```java
package com.udayan.ocp;

import java.io.*;

class Student implements Serializable {
    private String name;
    private int age;

    Student(String name, int age) {
        this.name = name;
        this.age = age;
    }

    public String getName() {
        return name;
    }

    public int getAge() {
        return age;
    }

    public void setName(String name) {
        this.name = name;
    }

    public void setAge(int age) {
        this.age = age;
    }
}

public class Test {
    public static void main(String[] args)
        throws IOException, ClassNotFoundException {
        Student stud = new Student("John", 20);

        try(ObjectOutputStream oos = new ObjectOutputStream(
            new FileOutputStream("C:\\Student.dat")) ){
            oos.writeObject(stud);
        }

        stud.setName("James");
        stud.setAge(21);

        try( ObjectInputStream ois = new ObjectInputStream(
```

```
        new FileInputStream("C:\\Student.dat")) ){
        stud = (Student)ois.readObject();
        System.out.printf("%s : %d", stud.getName(),
                                     stud.getAge());
    }
  }
}
```

There is full permission to list/create/delete files and directories in C:.
What will be the result of compiling and executing Test class?

A. Runtime Exception

B. John : 20

C. James : 21

6.1.65 Which of the following methods a class must implement/override to implement
        java.io.Serializable interface? Select ALL that apply.

A. `public void writeObject(Object);`

B. `public Object readObject();`

C. `public void serialize(Object);`

D. `public Object deserialize();`

E. `None of the other options`

6.1.66 Given code of Test.java file:

```
package com.udayan.ocp;

import java.io.*;

class Person {
    private String name;
    private int age;

    public Person(){}

    public Person(String name, int age) {
        this.name = name;
        this.age = age;
    }

    public String getName() {
        return name;
    }

    public int getAge() {
        return age;
    }
}

class Student extends Person implements Serializable {
    private String course;

    public Student(String name, int age, String course) {
        super(name, age);
        this.course = course;
    }

    public String getCourse() {
        return course;
    }
}

public class Test {
    public static void main(String[] args)
            throws IOException, ClassNotFoundException {
        Student stud = new Student("John", 20,
                                    "Computer Science");
        try (ObjectOutputStream oos = new ObjectOutputStream(
                new FileOutputStream(("F:\\stud.ser")));
```

```
        ObjectInputStream ois = new ObjectInputStream(
            new FileInputStream("F:\\stud.ser")))
    {

        oos.writeObject(stud);

        Student s = (Student) ois.readObject();
        System.out.printf("%s, %d, %s", s.getName(),
                        s.getAge(), s.getCourse());
    }
  }
}
```

F: is accessible for reading/writing and currently doesn't contain any files/directories.

What will be the result of compiling and executing Test class?

A. John, 20, Computer Science

B. null, 0, Computer Science

C. null, 0, null

D. Runtime Exception

6.1.67 **F: is accessible for reading and below is the directory structure for F:**

```
F:.
└──A
    └──B
        └──C
                Book.java
```

'Book.java' file is available under 'C' directory.

Given code of Test.java file:

```java
package com.udayan.ocp;

import java.nio.file.Path;
import java.nio.file.Paths;

public class Test {
    public static void main(String[] args) {
        Path file = Paths.get(
                "F:\\A\\.\\B\\C\\D\\..\\Book.java");
        System.out.println(file.toAbsolutePath());
    }
}
```

What will be the result of compiling and executing Test class?

A. Compilation Error

B. NoSuchFileException is thrown at runtime

C. F:\A\B\C\Book.java

D. F:\A\.\B\C\D\..\Book.java

E. Book.java

6.1.68 Given code of Test.java file:

```
package com.udayan.ocp;

import java.nio.file.Path;
import java.nio.file.Paths;

public class Test {
    public static void main(String[] args) {
        Path file1 = Paths.get("F:\\A\\B");
        Path file2 = Paths.get("F:\\A\\B\\C\\Book.java");
        System.out.println(file1.resolve(file2)
                    .equals(file1.resolveSibling(file2)));
    }
}
```

What will be the result of compiling and executing Test class?

A. true

B. false

6.1.69 **F: is accessible for reading and below is the directory structure for F:**

```
F:.
 └───A
      └───B
           └───C
                     Book.java
```

Given code of Test.java file:

```java
package com.udayan.ocp;

import java.io.IOException;
import java.nio.file.Files;
import java.nio.file.Path;
import java.nio.file.Paths;
import java.nio.file.attribute.BasicFileAttributes;

public class Test {
    public static void main(String[] args)
                                    throws IOException{
        Path path = Paths.get("F:\\A\\B\\C\\Book.java");
        /*INSERT*/
    }
}
```

Which of the following statements, if used to replace /*INSERT*/, will successfully print creation time of 'Book.java' on to the console?
Select 3 options.

A.	`System.out.println(Files.getAttribute(path, "creationTime"));`
B.	`System.out.println(Files.readAttributes(path, "*").get("creationTime"));`
C.	`System.out.println(Files.readAttributes(path, "*").creationTime());`
D.	`System.out.println(Files.readAttributes(path, BasicFileAttributes.class).get("creationTime"));`
E.	`System.out.println(Files.readAttributes(path, BasicFileAttributes.class).creationTime());`

6.1.70 **F: is accessible for reading/writing and below is the directory structure for F:**

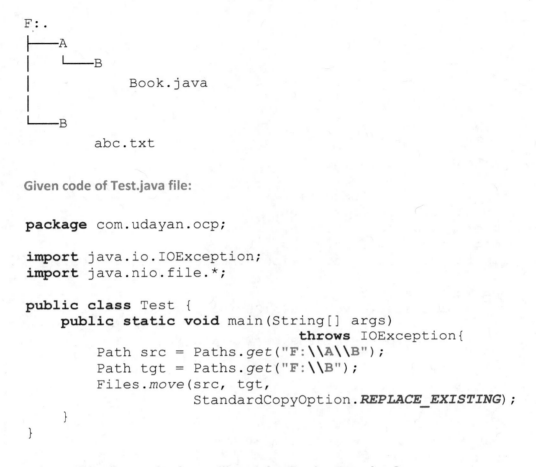

```
F:.
├──A
│   └──B
│
│           Book.java
│
│
└──B
        abc.txt
```

Given code of Test.java file:

```java
package com.udayan.ocp;

import java.io.IOException;
import java.nio.file.*;

public class Test {
    public static void main(String[] args)
                            throws IOException{
        Path src = Paths.get("F:\\A\\B");
        Path tgt = Paths.get("F:\\B");
        Files.move(src, tgt,
                StandardCopyOption.REPLACE_EXISTING);
    }
}
```

What will be the result of compiling and executing Test class?

A. Directory B with its contents will move successfully from 'F:\A\B' to 'F:\B'

B. An exception is thrown at runtime

C. Compilation error

6.1.71 Given code of Test.java file:

```
package com.udayan.ocp;

import java.nio.file.Path;
import java.nio.file.Paths;

public class Test {
    public static void main(String[] args) {
        Path path = Paths.get(
            "F:\\A\\.\\B\\C\\D\\..\\Book.java");
        path.normalize();
        System.out.println(path);
    }
}
```

What will be the result of compiling and executing Test class?

A. F:\A\B\C\Book.java

B. F:\A\B\C\D\Book.java

C. F:\A\.\B\C\D\..\Book.java

D. None of the other options

6.1.72 F: is currently blank and accessible for Reading/Writing.

Given code of Test.java file:
```
package com.udayan.ocp;

import java.io.IOException;
import java.nio.file.Files;
import java.nio.file.Path;
import java.nio.file.Paths;

public class Test {
    public static void main(String[] args)
                            throws IOException {
        Path path = Paths.get("F:", "A", "B", "File.txt");

        /*INSERT*/
    }
}
```

Test.class file is under 'C:\classes\com\udayan\ocp'.

Which of the following statements, if used to replace /*INSERT*/, will successfully create the file "File.txt" under F:\A\B directory?

A.	`Files.createFile(path);`
B.	`Files.createDirectories(path);` `Files.createFile(path);`
C.	`Files.createDirectories(path.getParent());` `Files.createFile(path.getFileName());`
D.	`Files.createDirectories(path.getParent());` `Files.createFile(path);`

6.1.73 Given structure of EMPLOYEE table:

```
EMPLOYEE (ID integer, FIRSTNAME varchar(100), LASTNAME
varchar(100), SALARY real, PRIMARY KEY (ID))
```

EMPLOYEE table contains below records:
```
101 John    Smith   12000
102 Sean    Smith   15000
103 Regina Williams  15500
104 Natasha    George 14600
```

Given code of Test.java file:

```java
package com.udayan.ocp;

import java.sql.*;

public class Test {
    public static void main(String[] args) {
        String url = "jdbc:mysql://localhost:3306/ocp";
        String user = "root";
        String password = "password";
        String query = "Select ID, FIRSTNAME, LASTNAME, " +
            "SALARY FROM EMPLOYEE WHERE " +
            "SALARY > 14900 ORDER BY ID";

        try (Connection con = DriverManager
                    .getConnection(url, user, password);
            Statement stmt = con.createStatement(
                ResultSet.TYPE_SCROLL_SENSITIVE,
                ResultSet.CONCUR_UPDATABLE);
            ResultSet rs = stmt.executeQuery(query);) {
            rs.absolute(-1);
            rs.updateDouble("SALARY", 20000);
            rs.updateRow();
        } catch (SQLException ex) {
            System.out.println("Error");
        }
    }
}
```

Also assume:

URL, username and password are correct.

SQL query is correct and valid.

The JDBC 4.2 driver jar is configured in the classpath.

What will be the result of compiling and executing Test class?

A. 'Error' is printed on to the console.

B. Program executes successfully but no record is updated in the database.

C. Program executes successfully and salary of Sean Smith is updated to 20000.

D. Program executes successfully and salary of Regina Williams is updated to 20000.

6.1.74 Given structure of EMPLOYEE table:

```
EMPLOYEE (ID integer, FIRSTNAME varchar(100), LASTNAME
varchar(100), SALARY real, PRIMARY KEY (ID))
```

EMPLOYEE table contains below records:

```
101 John    Smith  12000
102 Sean    Smith  15000
103 Regina Williams  15500
104 Natasha    George 14600
```

Given code of Test.java file:

```
package com.udayan.ocp;

import java.sql.*;

public class Test {
    public static void main(String[] args)
                                    throws SQLException {
        String url = "jdbc:mysql://localhost:3306/ocp";
        String user = "root";
        String password = "password";
        String query = "Select ID, FIRSTNAME, LASTNAME, " +
            "SALARY FROM EMPLOYEE ORDER BY ID";

        try (Connection con = DriverManager
                        .getConnection(url, user, password);
            Statement stmt = con.createStatement();
            ResultSet rs = stmt.executeQuery(query);) {
            rs.moveToInsertRow();
            rs.updateInt(1, 105);
            rs.updateString(2, "Smita");
            rs.updateString(3, "Jain");
            rs.updateDouble(4, 16000);
            rs.insertRow();
        }
    }
}
```

Also assume:
URL, username and password are correct.
SQL query is correct and valid.
The JDBC 4.2 driver jar is configured in the classpath.

What will be the result of compiling and executing Test class?

A. An exception is thrown at runtime.

B. Program executes successfully but no new record is inserted in the database.

C. Program executes successfully and a new record is inserted in the database.

6.1.75 Given structure of EMPLOYEE table:

```
EMPLOYEE (ID integer, FIRSTNAME varchar(100), LASTNAME
varchar(100), SALARY real, PRIMARY KEY (ID))
```

EMPLOYEE table contains below records:
```
101 John    Smith  12000
102 Sean    Smith  15000
103 Regina Williams  15500
104 Natasha    George 14600
```

Given code of Test.java file:

```java
package com.udayan.ocp;

import java.sql.*;
import java.util.Properties;

public class Test {
    public static void main(String[] args)
                                    throws Exception {
        String url = "jdbc:mysql://localhost:3306/ocp";
        Properties prop = new Properties();
        prop.put("user", "root");
        prop.put("password", "password");
        String query = "Select ID, FIRSTNAME, LASTNAME, " +
            "SALARY FROM EMPLOYEE ORDER BY ID";
        Class.forName(url);

        try (Connection con = DriverManager
                            .getConnection(url, prop);
            Statement stmt = con.createStatement(
                ResultSet.TYPE_SCROLL_INSENSITIVE,
                ResultSet.CONCUR_READ_ONLY);
            ResultSet rs = stmt.executeQuery(query);) {
            rs.relative(1);
            System.out.println(rs.getString(2));
        }
    }
}
```

Also assume:
URL is correct and db credentials are: root/password.
SQL query is correct and valid.

The JDBC 4.2 driver jar is configured in the classpath.

What will be the result of compiling and executing Test class?

A. John

B. Sean

C. Smith

D. An exception is thrown at runtime.

6.1.76 Given structure of MESSAGES table:

```
MESSAGES (msg1 varchar(100), msg2 varchar(100))
```

MESSAGES table contains below records:
```
'Happy New Year!', 'Happy Holidays!'
```

Given code of Test.java file:

```java
package com.udayan.ocp;

import java.sql.*;

public class Test {
    public static void main(String[] args)
                                    throws SQLException {
        String url = "jdbc:mysql://localhost:3306/ocp";
        String user = "root";
        String password = "password";
        String query = "DELETE FROM MESSAGES";
        try (Connection con = new Connection(
                                url, user, password);
            Statement stmt = con.createStatement())
        {
            System.out.println(stmt.executeUpdate(query));
        }
    }
}
```

Also assume:
URL is correct and db credentials are: root/password.
SQL query is correct and valid.

The JDBC 4.2 driver jar is configured in the classpath.

What will be the result of compiling and executing Test class?

A. 0

B. 1

C. Compilation error

D. An exception is thrown at runtime

6.1.77 By default a Connection object is in auto-commit mode.

A. true

B. false

6.1.78 Consider below statement:

Any _____ drivers that are found in your class path are automatically loaded.
Which of the following options correctly fills the blank space?

A. JDBC 4 and later

B. JDBC 3 and later

C. JDBC 2 and later

D. JDBC 1 and later

6.1.79 Assume that proper import statements are available, which of the following statements will compile successfully?

Select ALL that apply.

A. `List<Locale> list = Locale.getAvailableLocales();`

B. `Object [][] arr = Locale.getAvailableLocales();`

C. `Locale [] loc = Locale.getAvailableLocales();`

D. `Map<String, String> map = Locale.getAvailableLocales();`

E. `Object [] locale = Locale.getAvailableLocales();`

6.1.80 Following resource bundle files are defined for the project:

```
ResourceBundle_CA.properties
ResourceBundle_hi.properties
ResourceBundle_IN.properties
ResourceBundle.properties
```

The default locale of the system is 'fr_CA'

Which of the resource bundle will be loaded for Locale en_IN?

A. `ResourceBundle_CA.properties`

B. `ResourceBundle_hi.properties`

C. `ResourceBundle_IN.properties`

D. `ResourceBundle.properties`

6.1.81 Given code of Test.java file:

```java
package com.udayan.ocp;

import java.util.Locale;

public class Test {
    public static void main(String[] args) {
        Locale loc = Locale.ENGLISH;
        System.out.println(loc.getDisplayCountry());
    }
}
```

What will be the result of compiling and executing Test class?

A. United States

B. US

C. English

D. en

E. No text is displayed in the output

6.1.82 Which of the following method a concrete class must override if it extends from ListResourceBundle?

A. abstract protected String[][] getContents();

B. abstract protected String[] getContents();

C. abstract protected Object[][] getContents();

D. abstract protected Object[] getContents();

6.1.83 Consider below code:

```
package com.udayan.ocp;

import java.text.NumberFormat;

public class Test {
    public static void main(String[] args) {
        System.out.println(
                NumberFormat._____.format(5));
    }
}
```

The default locale of the system is 'en_US'. Which of the options correctly fills the blank, such that output is $5.00?

A. getCurrencyInstance()

B. getCurrencyInstance(java.util.Locale.US)

C. getInstance()

D. getInstance(java.util.Locale.US)

6.1.84   Given code of Test.java file:

```
package com.udayan.ocp;

import java.util.concurrent.*;

public class Test {
    public static void main(String[] args) {
        ExecutorService es =
            Executors.newSingleThreadExecutor();
        es.execute(() -> System.out.println("HELLO"));
        es.shutdown();
    }
}
```

What will be the result of compiling and executing Test class?

A. Compilation error

B. null

C. HELLO

D. An exception is thrown at runtime

6.1.85   To efficiently use fork/join framework, after invoking fork() on first subtask, the order of invoking join() and compute() is as follows:

A. Invoke compute() on 2nd subtask and then join() on 1st subtask.

B. Invoke join() on 1st subtask and then compute() on 2nd subtask.

C. Invoke compute() on 1st subtask and then join() on 2nd subtask.

D. Invoke join() on 2nd subtask and then compute() on 1st subtask.

6.1.86 Which of the below classes help you to define recursive task? Select ALL that apply.

    A. Recursion

    B. RecursionAction

    C. RecursionTask

    D. RecursiveAction

    E. RecursiveTask

6.1.87 Given code of Test.java file:

```java
package com.udayan.ocp;

import java.util.ArrayList;
import java.util.Collections;
import java.util.List;
import java.util.stream.IntStream;

public class Test {
    public static void main(String[] args) {
        List<Integer> list = Collections
                    .synchronizedList(new ArrayList<>());
        IntStream stream = IntStream.rangeClosed(1, 7);
        stream.parallel().map(x -> {
            list.add(x); //Line 13
            return x;
        }).forEachOrdered(System.out::print); //Line 15
        System.out.println();
        list.forEach(System.out::print); //Line 17
    }
}
```

Which of the following statement is true about above code?

    A. Line 15 and Line 17 will print exact same output on to the console.

    B. Line 15 and Line 17 will not print exact same output on to the console.

    C. Output of Line 15 can be predicted.

    D. Output of Line 17 can be predicted.

    E. Output of both Line 15 and Line 17 can be predicted.

6.1.88 Given code of Test.java file:

```
package com.udayan.ocp;

import java.util.Arrays;

public class Test {
    public static void main(String[] args) {
        String s1 =
            Arrays.asList("A", "E", "I", "O", "U")
                .stream().reduce("", String::concat);
        String s2 =
            Arrays.asList("A", "E", "I", "O", "U")
                .parallelStream().reduce("", String::concat);
        System.out.println(s1.equals(s2));
    }
}
```

What will be the result of compiling and executing Test class?

A. It will always print true.

B. It will always print false.

C. Output cannot be predicted.

6.1.89 Given code of Test.java file:

```
package com.udayan.ocp;

import java.util.stream.Stream;

public class Test {
    public static void main(String[] args) {
        Stream<String> stream =
            Stream.of("J", "A", "V", "A");
        String text = stream.parallel()
                        .reduce(String::concat).get();
        System.out.println(text);
    }
}
```

What will be the result of compiling and executing Test class?

A. It will always print JAVA on to the console.

B. Output cannot be predicted.

C. None of the other options.

6.1.90 Given code of Test.java file:

```
package com.udayan.ocp;

import java.util.ArrayList;
import java.util.List;

class Book {
    String isbn;
    double price;

    Book(String isbn, double price) {
        this.isbn = isbn;
        this.price = price;
    }

    public String toString() {
        return "Book[" + isbn + ":" + price + "]";
    }
}

public class Test {
    public static void main(String[] args) {
        List<Book> books = new ArrayList<>();
        books.add(new Book("9781976704031", 9.99));
        books.add(new Book("9781976704032", 15.99));

        Book b = books.stream().reduce(
            new Book("9781976704033", 0.0), (b1, b2) -> {
            b1.price = b1.price + b2.price;
            return new Book(b1.isbn, b1.price);
        });

        books.add(b);
        books.parallelStream().reduce((x, y) ->
            x.price > y.price ? x : y)
            .ifPresent(System.out::println);
    }
}
```

What will be the result of compiling and executing Test class?

A. Book[9781976704033:25.98]

B. Book[9781976704031:9.99]

C. Book[9781976704032:15.99]

D. Book[9781976704033:9.99]

E. Book[9781976704033:15.99]

6.2   Answers of Practice Test - 6 with Explanation

6.1.1   Answer: B

Reason:

animals refer to an instance of Dog [] type. Each element of Dog [] can store Dog instances but not Animal instances(sub type can't refer to super type). But as we are using reference variable of Animal [] type hence compiler allows to add both Animal and Dog instances. So, animals[0] = new Animal(); and animals[1] = new Dog(); don't cause any compilation error.

But at runtime, while executing the statement: "animals[0] = new Animal();", an Animal instance is assigned to Dog array's element hence java.lang.ArrayStoreException is thrown.

6.1.2   Answer: A

Reason:
The toString() method in Object class has below definition:
public String toString() {
    return getClass().getName() + "@" + Integer.toHexString(hashCode());
}

toString() method cannot be overridden using protected modifier.

6.1.3   Answer: B

Reason:
'abstract' and 'private' cannot be used together.

6.1.4   Answer: A,B,C

Reason:
Comparator has only one non-overriding abstract method, compare. Runnable has only one non-overriding abstract method, run.

ActionListener has only one non-overriding abstract method, actionPerformed. Serializable and Cloneable are marker interfaces.

6.1.5   Answer: C

Reason:

Dot (.) operator has higher precedence than concatenation operator, hence toUpperCase() is invoked on str2 and not on the result of (str1 + "_" + str2)

6.1.6   Answer: C

Reason:

As enum Directions contains more code after constant declarations, hence last constant declaration must be followed by a semicolon.

Correct constant declaration is:
NORTH("N"), SOUTH("S"), EAST("E"), WEST("W");

6.1.7   Answer: D

Reason:

enum Status will cause compilation error as constant name should be unique, but PASS is declared twice.

6.1.8   Answer: C

Reason:

Regular inner class Bar cannot define any static methods. Method m1() is static and hence compilation error.

NOTE: Regular inner class cannot define anything static, except static final variables.

6.1.9   Answer: C

Reason:

Message msg = new Message() {}; means msg doesn't refer to an instance of Message class but to an instance of un-named sub class of Message class, which means to an instance of anonymous inner class.

In this case, anonymous inner class code doesn't override printMessage() method of super class, Message.

So at runtime, msg.printMessage() method invokes the printMessage() method defined in super class (Message) and Hello! is printed to the console.

6.1.10 Answer: C

Reason:
Semicolon is missing just before the statement i1.m1(); Wrong syntax of anonymous inner class.

6.1.11 Answer: A, C

Reason:
static nested class can use all 4 access modifiers (public, protected, default and private) and 2 non-access modifiers (final and abstract).
static nested class can contain all type of members, static as well as non-static. This behavior is different from other inner classes as other inner classes don't allow to define anything static, except static final variables. This is the reason static nested class is not considered as inner class.

There are 2 parts in accessing static nested class: 1st one to access the static nested class's name and 2nd one to instantiate the static nested class.
Within the top-level class, a static nested class can be referred by 2 ways: TOP-LEVEL-CLASS.STATIC-NESTED-CLASS and STATIC-NESTED-CLASS.

In this case, either use A.B or simply use B. Now for instantiating the static nested class, an instance of enclosing class cannot be used, which means in this case, I can't write new A().new B(). Correct way to instance static nested class is: new A.B(); but as main method is inside class A, hence I can even write new B(); as well.

Top-level class can easily access private members of inner or static nested class, so no issues in invoking log() method from within the definition of class A.

6.1.12 Answer: C

Reason:
Arrow operator (->) was added in JDK 8 for lambda expressions.
NOTE: there should not be any space between - and >.

6.1.13 Answer: B

Reason:
@FunctionalInterface annotation cannot be used here as interface I1 specifies two non-overriding abstract methods. This code causes compilation error.

6.1.14 Answer: C

Reason:
Lambda expression is defined correctly but print() method is not invoked on obj reference. So, no output.

6.1.15 Answer: C

Reason:
No issues with lambda syntax: curly brackets and semicolon are available.
Variable i is declared within the body of lambda expression so don't confuse it with local variable of main method.
i is declared and initialized to 10, i is incremented by 1 (i becomes 11) and finally value of i is printed.

6.1.16 Answer: A

Reason:
Even though String is a final class but T extends String is a valid syntax. As no class extends from java.lang.String class so parameterized type will always be Printer<String>.

Generic class Printer doesn't override toString() method, hence Object version is invoked.

6.1.17 Answer: C

Reason:
If a generic method is defined in a non-generic class then type parameters must appear before the return type of the method.

Integer is also a final class so parameters X and Y can only be of Integer type.

add(10, 20); => Auto-boxing converts int literals to Integer objects. 30 is printed on to the console.

6.1.18 Answer: B

Reason:
Instantiation of a type parameter 'new T()' or an array of type parameter 'new T[5]' are not allowed.

'obj = new T[100];' causes compilation failure.

6.1.19 Answer: C

Reason:

List is super type and ArrayList is sub type, hence List l = new ArrayList(); is valid syntax.
Animal is super type and Dog is sub type, hence Animal a = new Dog(); is valid syntax.
Both depicts Polymorphism.

But in generics syntax, Parameterized types are not polymorphic, this means
ArrayList<Animal> is not super type of ArrayList<Dog>. Remember this point. So below
syntaxes are not allowed:
ArrayList<Animal> list = new ArrayList<Dog>(); OR List<Animal> list = new
ArrayList<Dog>();

6.1.20 Answer: C

Reason:

TreeSet requires you to provide either Comparable or Comparator. If you don't provide
Comparator explicitly, then for natural ordering your class should implement
Comparable interface.

Student class doesn't use Comparable, hence ClassCastException is thrown at runtime.

6.1.21 Answer: C

Reason:
deque.add(100); => {*100}. * represents HEAD of the deque.
deque.add(200); => {*100, 200}. add(E e) invokes addLast(e) method.
deque.addFirst(300); => {*300, 100, 200}.
deque.addLast(400); => {*300, 100, 200, 400}.
deque.remove(200); => {*300, 100, 400}. Deque interface doesn't have remove(int
index) method.

System.out.println(deque.getFirst()); => Prints 300 on to the console.

You should be aware of other methods from Deque interface as well, such as:
removeFirst(); => Removes the first element from the Deque.
removeLast(); => Removes the last element from the Deque.

6.1.22 Answer: B

Reason:
HashSet cares about uniqueness and allows 1 null value.

6.1.23 Answer: B

Reason:

list is of List (raw) type. So, it can accept any object. Line 11 doesn't cause any compilation error.

As list is raw list, which means it is of Object type, hence in Predicate's lambda expression, i is of Object type. Modulus operator (%) cannot be applied to Object type. So, Line 12 causes compilation error.

NOTE: This questions checks whether you can find out the issues when raw and generic types are mixed.

6.1.24 Answer: D

Reason:

Comparator interface has compare(...) method and not compareTo(...) method. Anonymous inner class's syntax doesn't implement compare(...) method and thus compilation error.

Make sure to check the accessibility and interface method details before working with the logic.

6.1.25 Answer: C

Reason:

Comparator.comparing(s -> s); compares the passed Strings only. As all the characters in the String are '#', this means strings are sorted on the basis of their lengths. Comparator referred by comp sorts on the basis of strings' lengths. Default reversed() method just reverses the ordering of the Comparator referred by comp, which means sorts the strings in descending order of their lengths.

6.1.26 Answer: A

Reason:

Iterator<T> interface has forEach(Consumer) method. As Consumer is a Functional Interface and it has 'void accept(T t)' method, hence a lambda expression for 1 parameter can be passed as argument to forEach(...) method.
'e -> e.setSalary(e.getSalary() + (e.getSalary() * .2))' => increments the salary of all the employees by 20%.
'System.out::println' => prints employee object on to the console.

As salary is of double type, so decimal point (.) is shown in the output.

6.1.27 Answer: A

Reason:

IntStream.range(int start, int end) => start is inclusive and end is exclusive and incremental step is 1. So, stream consists of value from 1 to 9 and these values are printed by forEach method.

NOTE: For IntStream.rangeClosed(int start, int end), both start and end are inclusive.

6.1.28 Answer: C

Reason:

LongStream.iterate(long seed, LongUnaryOperator f) => 'seed' is the initial element and 'f' is a function to be applied to the previous element to produce a new element.

LongUnaryOperator is a functional interface and has method 'long applyAsLong(long operand);'. This means lambda expression should accept long parameter and return long value.
'i -> i + 2' is the correct lambda expression.

LongStream.iterate(0, i -> i + 2) => This results in an infinite stream consisting of elements [0,2,4,6,8,10,12,...]

limit(4) => Returns a stream consisting of 4 elements [0,2,4,6] from the given stream.

Hence, the output is: 0246

6.1.29 Answer: B

Reason:

Streams are lazily evaluated, which means if terminal operations such as: forEach, count, toArray, reduce, collect, findFirst, findAny, anyMatch, allMatch, sum, min, max, average etc. are not present, the given stream pipeline is not evaluated and hence map() method doesn't reverse the stream elements.

'[abc, xyz]' is printed on to the console.

If you replace 'list.stream().map(x -> x.reverse());' with 'list.stream().map(x -> x.reverse()).count();' then output will be: '[cba, zyx]'.

6.1.30 Answer: D

Reason:
In the boolean expression (predicate.test(i)): i is of primitive int type but auto-boxing feature converts it to Integer wrapper type.
for loops works for the numbers from 1 to 10. test(Integer) method of Predicate returns true if passed number is an odd number, so given loop prints only odd numbers.

6.1.31 Answer: A,B,C,D

Reason:
p -> true means test method returns true for the passed String.
p -> !false means test method returns true for the passed String.
p -> p.length() >= 1 means test method returns true if passed String's length is greater than or equal to 1 and this is true for all the array elements.
p -> p.length() < 10 means test method returns true if passed String's length is less than 10 and this is true for all the array elements.

6.1.32 Answer: B

Reason:
java.util.Comparator interface is available with Java since JDK 1.2. So, even though it is a functional interface but Java guys didn't move it to java.util.function package.

Had Comparator interface moved to java.util.function package, then millions of lines of existing Java codes would have broken. That's why package of all the existing functional interface was not changed.

6.1.33 Answer: D

Reason:
IntConsumer has single abstract method, 'void accept(int value);'. accept(int) method doesn't return anything.

Lambda expression 'i -> i * i * i' returns an int value and hence given lambda expression causes compilation failure.

6.1.34 Answer: D

Reason:
BiFunction<T, U, R> : R apply(T t, U u);

BiFunction interface accepts 3 type parameters, first 2 parameters (T,U) are passed to apply method and 3rd type parameter is the return type of apply method.

In this case, 'BiFunction<Double, Double, Integer>' means apply method will have declaration: 'Integer apply(Double d1, Double d2)'.

Lambda expression should accept 2 Double type parameters and must return Integer object. Lambda expression is:

(d1, d2) -> d1.compareTo(d2); and corresponding method reference syntax is: 'Double::compareTo'.

This is an example of "Reference to an Instance Method of an Arbitrary Object of a Particular Type" and not "method reference to static method".

If d1 < d2, then -1 is returned and if d1 > d2, then 1 is returned.

6.1.35 Answer: D

Reason:
Though the lambda expression with 2 arrows seems confusing but it is correct syntax. To understand, Line n1 can be re-written as:

```
LongFunction<LongUnaryOperator> func = (a) -> {
   return (b) -> {
     return b - a;
   };
};
```

And corresponding anonymous class syntax is:

```
LongFunction<LongUnaryOperator> func = new LongFunction<LongUnaryOperator>() {
   @Override
   public LongUnaryOperator apply(long a) {
     LongUnaryOperator operator = new LongUnaryOperator() {
       @Override
       public long applyAsLong(long b) {
         return b - a;
       }
     };
```

```
      return operator;
   }
};
```

So, there is no issue with Line n1. Let's check Line n2.

'func.apply(100)' returns an instance of LongUnaryOperator, in which applyAsLong(long) method has below implementation:
```
LongUnaryOperator operator = new LongUnaryOperator() {
   @Override
   public long applyAsLong(long b) {
      return b - 100;
   }
};
```

When calc(LongUnaryOperator op, long val) is invoked using calc(func.apply(100), 50), op refers to above LongUnaryOperator instance and val is 50.
op.applyAsLong(50); returns 50 - 100, which is -50.

6.1.36 Answer: D

Reason:
interface UnaryOperator<T> extends Function<T, T>, so its apply function has the signature: T apply(T).
In this case, UnaryOperator<String> is used and hence apply method will have the signature: String apply(String).
Lambda expression 's -> s.replace('a', '@')' is the correct implementation of 'String apply(String)' method and hence there is no issue with Line n1.
Lambda expression 's -> str.concat(s)' is also the correct implementation of 'String apply(String)' method. Don't get confused with final modifier being used for 'str' reference, it is safe to invoke methods on final reference variable but yes you can't assign another String object to final reference variable. By invoking str.concat(s) a new String object is returned. So, no there is no issue with Line n2 as well.
Let's solve Line n3:
System.out.println("Password: " + opr1.apply(opr2.apply("!")));
System.out.println("Password: " + opr1.apply("Oracle!")); //opr2.apply("!") returns "Oracle!"
System.out.println("Password: " + "Or@cle!"); //opr1.apply("Oracle!") returns "Or@cle!"
Hence, output is: Password: Or@cle!

6.1.37   Answer: D

Reason:

Streams are lazily evaluated, which means for finite streams, if terminal operations such as: forEach, count, toArray, reduce, collect, findFirst, findAny, anyMatch, allMatch, sum, min, max, average etc. are not present, the given stream pipeline is not evaluated and hence peek() method doesn't print anything on to the console.

6.1.38   Answer: D

Reason:

If null argument is passed to of method, then NullPointerException is thrown at runtime.

6.1.39   Answer: E

Reason:

In this case, value variable inside Optional instance is null.

optional.isPresent() => false. isPresent method returns true if optional is not empty otherwise false.

If value variable inside Optional instance is null (empty optional), then NoSuchElementException is thrown at runtime.

In real world projects, it is advisable to to check using isPresent() method before using the get() method.
```
if(optional.isPresent()) {
    System.out.println(optional.getAsLong());
}
```

NOTE: There are 3 primitive equivalents of Optional<T> interface available. Remember their similarity with Optional<T> class.

```
Optional<T>:
Optional<T> empty(),
T get(),
boolean isPresent(),
Optional<T> of(T),
void ifPresent(Consumer<? super T>),
T orElse(T),
T orElseGet(Supplier<? extends T>),
T orElseThrow(Supplier<? extends X>),
Optional<T> filter(Predicate<? super T>),
```

Optional<U> map(Function<? super T, ? extends U>),
Optional<U> flatMap(Function<? super T, Optional<U>>).

OptionalInt:
OptionalInt empty(),
int getAsInt(),
boolean isPresent(),
OptionalInt of(int),
void ifPresent(IntConsumer),
int orElse(int),
orElseGet(IntSupplier),
int orElseThrow(Supplier<X>).
[filter, map and faltMap methods are not available in primitive type].

OptionalLong:
OptionalLong empty(),
long getAsLong(),
boolean isPresent(),
OptionalLong of(long),
void ifPresent(LongConsumer),
long orElse(long),
long orElseGet(LongSupplier),
long orElseThrow(Supplier<X>).
[filter, map and faltMap methods are not available in primitive type].

OptionalDouble:
OptionalDouble empty(),
double getAsDouble(),
boolean isPresent(),
OptionalDouble of(double),
void ifPresent(DoubleConsumer),
double orElse(double),
double orElseGet(DoubleSupplier),
double orElseThrow(Supplier<X>).
[filter, map and faltMap methods are not available in primitive type].

6.1.40 Answer: C

Reason:
In real exam, don't predict the output by just looking at the method name.

It is expected that highestSalary(...) method will print 'Optional[12000.0]' on to the console but if you closely check the definition of Employee.salaryCompare(...) method you will note that it helps to sort the salary in descending order and not ascending order.

Rest of the logic is pretty simple.

emp => [{"Jack", 10000.0}, {"Lucy", 12000.0}, {"Tom", 7000.0}].

emp.map(e -> e.getSalary()) => [10000.0, 12000.0, 7000.0].

max(Employee::salaryCompare) => Optional[7000].

NOTE: There are 3 methods in Stream interface, which returns Optional<T> type:
1. Optional<T> max(Comparator<? super T> comparator);
2. Optional<T> min(Comparator<? super T> comparator);
3. Optional<T> reduce(BinaryOperator<T> accumulator);

6.1.41 Answer: A

Reason:
'stream.reduce((d1, d2) -> d1 + d2)' returns 'Optional<Double>' type whereas 'stream.reduce(0.0, (d1, d2) -> d1 + d2)' returns 'Double'.

6.1.42 Answer: C

Reason:
In this example, Stream<String> is used. sorted method accepts Comparator<? super String> type.

compareToIgnoreCase is defined in String class and it compares the text by in case-insensitive manner. Even though 'b' is in lower case it is printed first, followed by 'J' and 'P'.

6.1.43 Answer: D

Reason:
stream is not of Stream<String> type rather it is of Stream<String[]> type.
flatMap method combines all the non-empty streams and returns an instance of Stream<String> containing the individual elements from non-empty stream.

stream => [{"Virat", "Rohit", "Shikhar", "Dhoni"}, {"Bumrah", "Pandya", "Sami"}, {}].
stream.flatMap(s -> Arrays.stream(s)) => ["Virat", "Rohit", "Shikhar", "Dhoni", "Bumrah", "Pandya", "Sami"].
sorted() => ["Bumrah", "Dhoni", "Pandya", "Rohit", "Sami", "Shikhar", "Virat"].

6.1.44 Answer: C

Reason:

average() method in IntStream, LongStream and DoubleStream returns OptionalDouble.

As stream is an empty stream, hence 'stream.average()' returns an empty optional.

OptionalDouble.empty is printed on to the console for empty Optional.

6.1.45 Answer: C

Reason:

Stream.generate(() -> new Double("1.0")); generates an infinite stream of Double, whose elements are 1.0.

stream.sorted() is an intermediate operation and needs all the elements to be available for sorting. As all the elements of infinite stream are never available, hence sorted() method never completes. So among all the available option, correct option is: 'Nothing is printed and program runs infinitely.'

6.1.46 Answer: C

Reason:

Method isPresent() returns boolean whereas method ifPresent accepts a Consumer parameter. 'first.ifPresent()' causes compilation failure.

6.1.47 Answer: D, E

Reason:

As 'vowels' refers to List<Character>, hence vowels.stream() returns Stream<Character> type. So, map method of Stream<Character> type has signature: <R> Stream<R> map(Function<? super Character, ? extends R> mapper);

Since forEach(System.out::print) is printing BFJPV, hence result of map(x -> operator.apply(x)) should be Stream<Character> and not Stream<Integer>.

This means correct reference type of 'operator' variable is Function<Character, Character>. Now as UnaryOperator<T> extends Function<T, T>, so UnaryOpeartor<Character> is also correct reference type of 'operator' variable.

Out of 6, we are left with 4 options. Let's check the options one by one:

'UnaryOperator<Character> operator = c -> c + 1;': 'c + 1' results in int and int can be converted to Integer but not Character, so this causes compilation failure.
'UnaryOperator<Character> operator = c -> c.charValue() + 1;': 'c.charValue() + 1' results in int and int can be converted to Integer but not Character, so this causes compilation failure.
'UnaryOperator<Character> operator = c -> (char)(c.charValue() + 1);': This expression adds 1 to the current char value (primitive char is compatible with primitive int) and resultant int value is type-casted to char, which is converted to Character by auto-boxing. Hence, this is correct option.
'Function<Character, Character> operator = x -> (char)(x + 1);': This is also correct option. x + 1 results in int, which is type-casted to char and finally converted to to Character by auto-boxing.

6.1.48   Answer: D

Reason:

FileNotFoundException extends IOException and hence catch block of FileNotFoundException should appear before the catch block of IOException.
Hence, class Test causes compilation error.

6.1.49   Answer: A

Reason:

throw ex; causes compilation error as div method doesn't declare to throw Exception (checked) type.

6.1.50   Answer: B

Reason:

Classes in Exception framework are normal java classes, hence null can be used wherever instances of Exception classes are used, so Line 7 compiles successfully.
No issues with Line 12 as method m() declares to throw SQLException and main method code correctly handles it.

Program compiles successfully but on execution, NullPointerException is thrown, stack trace is printed on to the console and program ends abruptly.

If you debug the code, you would find that internal routine for throwing null exception causes NullPointerException.

6.1.51 Answer: A

Reason:
Method m1() throws an instance of TestException, which is a checked exception as it extends Exception class.
So in throws clause we must provide:
1. Checked exception.
2. Exception of TestException type or it's super types (Exception, Throwable), Object cannot be used in throws clause.

6.1.52 Answer: B

Reason:
execute() method throws an instance of SQLException.

Just before finding the matching handler, Java runtime executes close() method. This method executes successfully.

An instance of SQLException is thrown. No exceptions was suppressed so 'e.getSuppressed()' returns Throwable [] of size 0.

'e.getSuppressed().length' prints 0 on to the console.

6.1.53 Answer: A

Reason:
For null resources, close() method is not called and hence NullPointerException is not thrown at runtime.

HELLO is printed on to the console.

6.1.54 Answer: B

Reason:
'java -ea:com.udayan...' enables the assertion in com.udayan package and its sub packages. Test class is defined under 'com.udayan.ocp' package, hence assertion is enabled for Test class.

assert flag : flag = true; => flag is a boolean variable, so 'assert flag' has no issues and right expression must not be void. 'flag = true' assigns true to flag and true is returned as well. Hence no issues with right side as well.

On execution, flag is false, hence AssertionError is thrown and program terminates abruptly.

6.1.55 Answer: A

Reason:
assert 1 == 2 : 2 == 2; => throws AssertionError and as 2 == 2 is true, hence message is set as true.

main method catches AssertionError (though you are not supposed to handle Error and its subtype) and 'ae.getMessage()' returns true.

6.1.56 Answer: B

Reason:
In LocalDate.of(int, int, int) method, 1st parameter is year, 2nd is month and 3rd is day of the month.

ocpCouponPurchaseDate --> {2018-03-01} and ocpCouponPurchaseDate.plusDays(10) --> {2018-03-11}.

toString() method of LocalDate class prints the LocalDate object in ISO-8601 format: "uuuu-MM-dd".

6.1.57 Answer: D

Reason:
LocalDateTime.parse(text); => text is parsed using DateTimeFormatter.ISO_LOCAL_DATE_TIME.

ISO_LOCAL_DATE_TIME is a combination of ISO_LOCAL_DATE and ISO_LOCAL_TIME, and it parses the date-time in following format:
[ISO_LOCAL_DATE][T][ISO_LOCAL_TIME]: T is case-insensitive.

ISO_LOCAL_DATE represents date in following format:
uuuu-MM-dd

Valid values for year (uuuu) is: 0000 to 9999.
Valid values for month-of-year (MM) is: 01 to 12.
Valid values for day-of-month (dd) is: 01 to 31 (At runtime this value is validated against month/year).

ISO_LOCAL_TIME represents time in following format:
HH:mm (if second-of-minute is not available),
HH:mm:ss (if second-of-minute is available),
HH:mm:ss.SSS (if nano-of-second is 3 digit or less),
HH:mm:ss.SSSSSS (if nano-of-second is 4 to 6 digits),
HH:mm:ss.SSSSSSSSS (if nano-of-second is 7 to 9 digits).

Valid values for hour-of-day (HH) is: 00 to 23.
Valid values for minute-of-hour (mm) is: 00 to 59.
Valid values for second-of-minute (ss) is: 00 to 59.
Valid values for nano-of-second is: 0 to 999999999.

toString() method of LocalDateTime class has following definition: return date.toString()
+ 'T' + time.toString();

NOTE: 'T' is in upper case and as nano-of-second is of 2 digit, hence single zero is
appended to its value.

6.1.58   Answer: D

Reason:
Period.parse(CharSequence) method accepts the String parameter in "PnYnMnD"
format, over here P,Y,M and D can be in any case. "P9M" represents period of 9 months.

Signature of plus method of LocalDate is: 'LocalDate plus(TemporalAmount)', Period
implements ChronoPeriod and ChnonoPeriod extends TemporalAmount. Hence Period
type can be passed as an argument of plus method. Adding 9 months to 6th June 2018
returns 6th March 2019.

6.1.59   Answer: D

Reason:
New Date/Time API has format method in DateTimeFormatter as well as LocalDate,
LocalTime, LocalDateTime, ZonedDateTime classes, so valDay.format(formatter) doesn't
cause compilation error.

D represents day-of-year and DD is for printing 2 digits. If you calculate, day of the year
for 14th Feb 2018, then it is 45th day of the year (as January has 31 days).
45 is a 2-digit number and hence can be easily parsed by 'DD'.

Output in this case is: 45-02-2018.

6.1.60 Answer: D

Reason:
LocalDate, LocalTime and LocalDateTime don't have concepts of time zones. ZonedDateTime class is used for time zones.

6.1.61 Answer: B

Reason:
D represents day-of-year and DD is for printing 2 digits. If you calculate, day of the year for 4th Nov 2018, it will be of 3 digit value as year has 365 days and date is in November month.

Pattern DD (for 2 digits) will cause Runtime Exception in this case.

If you get confused with pattern letters in lower case and upper case, then easy way to remember is that Bigger(Upper case) letters represent something bigger. M represents month & m represents minute, D represents day of the year & d represents day of the month.

6.1.62 Answer: E

Reason:
console.format("%d %x", 10); => There are 2 format specifiers (%d and %x) in the format string but only one argument (10) is passed.
MissingFormatArgumentException is thrown at runtime.

NOTE: console.format(...) and console.printf(...) methods are same. In fact, printf(...) method invokes format(...) method.

6.1.63 Answer: C

Reason:
In format string, format specifier are just replaced.
2$ means 2nd argument, which is 20 and 1$ means 1st argument, which is 10.
Hence 'System.out.printf("%2$d + %1$d", 10, 20);' prints '20 + 10' on to the console.

Having more arguments than the format specifiers is OK, extra arguments are ignored but having less number of arguments than format specifiers throws MissingFormatArgumentException at runtime.

NOTE: System.out.printf(...) is same as System.out.format(...).

6.1.64 Answer: B

Reason:

Student class implements Serializable, hence objects of Student class can be serialized using ObjectOutputStream.

setName() and setAge() are called after executing 'oos.writeObject(stud);' hence these are not reflected in the serialized data.

On de-serializing, persisted Student data is printed on to the console.

6.1.65 Answer: E

Reason:

java.io.Serializable is a marker interface and hence classes which implement this interface are not required to implement any methods for serialization to work.

6.1.66 Answer: B

Reason:

Class Student implements Serializable but it's super class Person is not Serializable.

While de-serializing of Serializable class, constructor of that class is not invoked. But if Parent class is not Serializable, then to construct the Parent class object, a no-argument constructor in Parent class is needed. This no-argument constructor initializes the properties to their default values.

Person class has no-argument constructor. So while de-serialization name and age are initialized to their default values: null and 0 respectively. course refers to "Computer Science" as it belongs to Serializable class, Student.

In the output, you get 'null, 0, Computer Science'.

6.1.67 Answer: D

Reason:

toAbsolutePath() method doesn't care if given path elements are physically available or not and hence it doesn't declare to throw IOException. It just returns the absolute path without any normalization.

'F:\A\.\B\C\D\..\Book.java' is displayed on to the console.

6.1.68 Answer: A

Reason:

As file2 refers to an absolute path and not relative path, hence both 'file1.resolve(file2)' and 'file1.resolveSibling(file2)' returns Path object referring to 'F:\A\B\C\Book.java'. equals method returns true in this case.

6.1.69 Answer: A, B, E

Reason:

Files.getAttribute(Path path, String attribute, LinkOption... options) returns the value corresponding to passed attribute. IllegalArgumentException is thrown if attribute is not spelled correctly.
Files.getAttribute(path, "creationTime") returns an object containing value for 'creationTime' attribute.

Files.readAttributes is overloaded method:
public static Map<String,Object> readAttributes(Path path, String attributes, LinkOption... options) throws IOException {...}
public static <A extends BasicFileAttributes> A readAttributes(Path path, Class<A> type, LinkOption... options) throws IOException {...}

If 2nd parameter is of String type, readAttributes method returns Map<String, Object> and if 2nd parameter is of Class<A> type, it returns A. And A should pass IS-A test for BasicFileAttributes type.

To retrieve value from Map object, use get(key) method.

Files.readAttributes(path, "*").get("creationTime") returns an object containing value for 'creationTime' attribute.

Files.readAttributes(path, "*").creationTime() causes compilation error as creationTime() method is not defined in Map interface.

Files.readAttributes(path, BasicFileAttributes.class) returns an instance of BasicFileAttributes class and it has creationTime() method to return the creation time.

But BaseFileAttributes class doesn't have get(String) method, so 'Files.readAttributes(path, BasicFileAttributes.class).get("creationTime")' causes compilation error.

NOTE: There are other important methods in BaseFileAttributes class which you should know for the OCP exam: size(), isDirectory(), isRegularFile(), isSymbolicLink(), creationTime(), lastAccessedTime() and lastModifiedTime().

6.1.70 Answer: B

Reason:

Files.move(Path source, Path target, CopyOption... options) method throws following exceptions-
[Copied from the Javadoc]
1. UnsupportedOperationException - if the array contains a copy option that is not supported
2. FileAlreadyExistsException - if the target file exists but cannot be replaced because the REPLACE_EXISTING option is not specified (optional specific exception)
3. DirectoryNotEmptyException - the REPLACE_EXISTING option is specified but the file cannot be replaced because it is a non-empty directory (optional specific exception)
4. AtomicMoveNotSupportedException - if the options array contains the ATOMIC_MOVE option but the file cannot be moved as an atomic file system operation.
5. IOException - if an I/O error occurs
6. SecurityException - In the case of the default provider, and a security manager is installed, the checkWrite method is invoked to check write access to both the source and target file.

As target directory is not empty and StandardCopyOption.REPLACE_EXISTING is used hence DirectoryNotEmptyException is thrown at runtime.

6.1.71 Answer: C

Reason:
Implementations of Path interface are immutable, hence path.normalize() method doesn't make any changes to the Path object referred by reference variable 'path'.

System.out.println(path); prints the original path, 'F:\A\.\B\C\D\..\Book.java' on to the console.

If you replace 'path.normalize();' with 'path = path.normalize();', then 'F:\A\B\C\Book.java' would be printed on to the console.

6.1.72 Answer: D

Reason:
Files.createFile(path); => throws IOException as parent directories don't exist.

Files.createDirectories(path); => Creates the directories 'A', 'B' and 'File.txt'. Path after creation is: 'F:\A\B\File.txt\'.
Files.createFile(path); => FileAlreadyExistsException as directory with the same name already exists.

path.getParent() returns 'F:\A\B', which is an absolute path and path.getFileName() returns 'File.txt', which is a relative path.
Files.createDirectories(path.getParent()); => Creates the directories 'A' and 'B'. Path after creation is: 'F:\A\B\'.
Files.createFile(path.getFileName()); => Creates the file under current directory, Path after creation is: 'C:\classes\com\udayan\ocp\File.txt'.

Files.createDirectories(path.getParent()); => Creates the directories 'A' and 'B'. Path after creation is: 'F:\A\B\'.
Files.createFile(path); => Creates the file, 'File.txt' under 'F:\A\B\'. Path after creation is: 'F:\A\B\File.txt'.

6.1.73 Answer: D

Reason:
Given sql statement returns below records:
102   SeanSmith   15000
103   Regina   Williams 15500

'rs.absolute(-1);' moves the cursor pointer to 2nd record (1st record from the bottom).

'rs.updateDouble("SALARY", 20000);' updates the salary of 2nd record to 20000.

'rs.updateRow();' statement updates the record in the database.

Hence, Program executes successfully and salary of Regina Williams is updated to 20000.

Please note: there is no need to invoke con.commit(); method as by default Connection object is in auto-commit mode.

6.1.74 Answer: A

Reason:
By default ResultSet is not updatable.

'rs.moveToInsertRow();' throws an exception at runtime.

To update the ResultSet in any manner (insert, update or delete), the ResultSet must come from a Statement that was created with a ResultSet type of ResultSet.CONCUR_UPDATABLE.

NOTE: If you want to successfully insert a new record, then replace 'con.createStatement();' with 'con.createStatement(ResultSet.TYPE_SCROLL_SENSITIVE, ResultSet.CONCUR_UPDATABLE);' OR 'con.createStatement(ResultSet.TYPE_SCROLL_INSENSITIVE, ResultSet.CONCUR_UPDATABLE);'.

6.1.75 Answer: D

Reason:
It is assumed that JDBC 4.2 driver is configured in the classpath, hence Class.forName(String) is not required. But no harm in using Class.forName(String).

Class.forName(String) expects fully qualified name of the class but in this case url refers to database url and not fully qualified name of the class, hence ClassNotFoundException is thrown at runtime.

6.1.76 Answer: C

Reason:
Connection is an interface, hence 'new Connection(url, user, password);' causes compilation error.

Correct way to create Connection object in this case will be: 'DriverManager.getConnection(url, user, password);'

6.1.77 Answer: A

Reason:
According to javadoc of java.sql.Connection, "By default a Connection object is in auto-commit mode, which means that it automatically commits changes after executing each

statement. If auto-commit mode has been disabled, the method commit must be called explicitly in order to commit changes; otherwise, database changes will not be saved".

6.1.78 Answer: A

Reason:
Starting with JDBC 4, there is no need to manually load the driver class. For JDBC 3 drivers, java.lang.Class.forName method is used to load the driver class.

6.1.79 Answer: C,E

Reason:
'public static Locale[] getAvailableLocales() {...}' returns the Locale [] containing all the available locales supported by the JVM. Hence, 'Locale [] loc = Locale.getAvailableLocales();' will compile successfully.

As Object is the ultimate base class, hence 'Object [] locale = Locale.getAvailableLocales();' also works.

NOTE: Object [] is not the parent of Locale [] but array allows above syntax because it has ArrayStoreException.

6.1.80 Answer: D

Reason:
Default Locale is: fr_CA and passed Locale to getBundle method is: en_IN

The search order for matching resource bundle is:
ResourceBundle_en_IN.properties [1st: Complete en_IN].
ResourceBundle_en.properties [2nd: Only language en].
ResourceBundle_fr_CA.properties [3rd: Complete default Locale fr_CA].
ResourceBundle_fr.properties [4th: Language of default Locale fr].
ResourceBundle.properties [5th: ResourceBundle's name without language or country].

Out of the given resource bundles, 'ResourceBundle.properties' matches.

6.1.81 Answer: E

Reason:
Locale.ENGLISH is equivalent to new Locale("en", "");
So, language is 'en' and country is blank.

loc.getDisplayCountry() returns blank string, hence no text is displayed in the output.

6.1.82 Answer: C

Reason:
ListResourceBundle has one abstract method: 'abstract protected Object[][] getContents();'. All the concrete sub classes of ListResourceBundle must override this method.

6.1.83 Answer: A, B

Reason:
As expected output is: $5.00, which means formatter must be for the currency and not the number.
NumberFormat.getInstance() and NumberFormat.getInstance(Locale) return the formatter for the number and hence will display 5 on to the console.
NumberFormat.getCurrencyInstance() returns the currency formatter for default Locale which is en_US, hence format(5) will display $5.00 on to the console.
NumberFormat.getCurrencyInstance(java.util.Locale.US) returns the currency formatter for the specified Locale, which is again en_US, hence format(5) will display $5.00 on to the console.

6.1.84 Answer: C

Reason:
ExecutorService interface extends Executor interface and it has 'void execute(Runnable command);'. Runnable is a Functional interface which has single abstract method 'public abstract void run();'.

Given lambda expression, '() -> System.out.println("HELLO")' accepts no parameter and doesn't return anything, hence it matches with the implementation of run() method.

'HELLO' is printed on to the console.

6.1.85 Answer: A

Reason:
After invoking fork() on 1st subtask, it is necessary to invoke join() on 1st subtask and compute() on 2nd subtask.

The order of execution of calling join() and compute() on divided subtasks is important in a fork/join framework. First invoke compute() on 2nd subtask and then join() on 1st subtask.

6.1.86 Answer: D, E

Reason:

There are no classes in concurrent package with the names 'Recursion', 'RecursionAction' and 'RecursionTask'.

Both RecursiveAction and RecursiveTask can be used to define a recursive task.

RecursiveTask is used to define tasks which returns a value whereas RecursiveAction is used to define tasks that don't return a value.

6.1.87 Answer: C

Reason:

Line 13 is changing the state of list object and hence it should be avoided in parallel stream. You can never predict the order in which elements will be added to the stream.

Line 13 and Line 15 doesn't run in synchronized manner, hence as the result, output of Line 17 may be different from that of Line 15.

forEachOrdered() will processes the elements of the stream in the order specified by its source, regardless of whether the stream is sequential or parallel.

As forEachOrdered() method is used at Line 15, hence Line 15 will always print '1234567' on to the console.

On my machine below is the output of various executions:
Execution 1:
1234567
1352764

Execution 2:
1234567
6514327

Execution 3:
1234567
1732645

6.1.88 Answer: A

Reason:
reduce method in Stream class is declared as: T reduce(T identity, BinaryOperator<T> accumulator)
By checking the reduce method, 'reduce("", String::concat)', we can say that:
Identity is String type, accumulator is BinaryOperator<String> type.

'String::concat' is equivalent to lambda expression '(s1, s2) -> s1.concat(s2);'.

To get consistent output, there are requirements for reduce method arguments:
1. For each element 't' of the stream, accumulator.apply(identity, t) is equal to t.
   For 1st element of the stream, "A" accumulator.apply("", "A") results in "A", which is equal to "A" and hence 1st rule is followed.

2. The accumulator operator (concat) in this case must be associative and stateless.
   concat is associative as (s1.concat(s2)).concat(s3) equals to s1.concat(s2.concat(s3)).
Given method reference syntax is stateless as well.

As both the rules are followed, hence reduce will give the same result for both sequential and parallel stream.

6.1.89   Answer: A

Reason:
reduce method in Stream class is declared as: 'Optional<T> reduce(BinaryOperator<T> accumulator);'

'String::concat' is equivalent to lambda expression '(s1, s2) -> s1.concat(s2);'.
By checking the reduce method, 'reduce(String::concat)' we can say that:
accumulator is BinaryOperator<String> type.

To get consistent output, accumulator must be associative and stateless. concat is associative as (s1.concat(s2)).concat(s3) equals to s1.concat(s2.concat(s3)). Given method reference syntax is stateless as well.

Hence, reduce will give the same result for both sequential and parallel stream.

As per Javadoc, given reduce method is equivalent to:

```
boolean foundAny = false;
T result = null;
for (T element : this stream) {
 if (!foundAny) {
    foundAny = true;
    result = element;
 }
 else
    result = accumulator.apply(result, element);
}
return foundAny ? Optional.of(result) : Optional.empty();
```

This means, output will be JAVA.

6.1.90 Answer: A

Reason:
books --> [Book[9781976704031:9.99], Book[9781976704032:15.99]].
books.stream() --> {Book[9781976704031:9.99], Book[9781976704032:15.99]}. It is sequential stream.

To understand, first reduce() method can be somewhat written as:

```
Book book = new Book("9781976704033", 0.0);
for(Book element : stream) {
    book = accumulator.apply(book, element);
}
return book;
```

Above code is just for understanding purpose, you can't iterate a stream using given loop.

apply(book, element) invokes the code of lambda expression:
```
(b1, b2) -> {
    b1.price = b1.price + b2.price;
    return new Book(b1.isbn, b1.price);
}
```

This means, price of Book object referred by book will be the addition of 9.99 and 15.99, which is 25.98 and its isbn will remain 9781976704033.

b --> Book[9781976704033:25.98].

Above book is added to the books list.
books --> [Book[9781976704031:9.99], Book[9781976704032:15.99], Book[9781976704033:25.98]].

books.parallelStream().reduce((x, y) -> x.price > y.price ? x : y) returns Optional<Book>, the Book object inside Optional has highest price.

Hence, output is: Book[9781976704033:25.98].

Udemy Courses By The Author

Courses for Java 17 Certification:

Topic-Wise Tests:-

Java Certification (1Z0-829) Topic-wise Tests Part-1 [2023]
Assess your preparation of Java SE 17 Developer exam (includes 602 questions)

https://www.udemy.com/course/ocp_java-se-17_1z0-829_p1/?referralCode=7C3BC4B0A074FC5BFCD1

Java Certification (1Z0-829) Topic-wise Tests Part-2 [2023]
Assess your preparation of Java SE 17 Developer exam (includes 610 questions)

https://www.udemy.com/course/ocp_java-se-17_1z0-829_p2/?referralCode=380CD98469BA5D4843DC

Exam Simulation Tests:-

Java Certification (1Z0-829) Exam Simulation Part-1 [2023]
Assess your preparation of Java SE 17 Developer exam (includes 303 questions)

https://www.udemy.com/course/java-11_1z0-829_p1/?referralCode=B84DE9AF0FCC009B726B

Java Certification (1Z0-829) Exam Simulation Part-2 [2023]
Assess your preparation of Java SE 17 Developer exam (includes 303 questions)

https://www.udemy.com/course/java-11_1z0-829_p2/?referralCode=704CEFBDE75B17CB2C2C

Java Certification (1Z0-829) Exam Simulation Part-3 [2023]
Assess your preparation of Java SE 17 Developer exam (includes 303 questions)

https://www.udemy.com/course/java-11_1z0-829_p3/?referralCode=1FDBB124B2F5F8A7EBD6

Java Certification (1Z0-829) Exam Simulation Part-4 [2023]

Assess your preparation of Java SE 17 Developer exam (includes 303 questions)

https://www.udemy.com/course/java-11_1z0-829_p4/?referralCode=0E9648DAD625420184CB

Courses for Java 11 Certification:

Topic-Wise Tests:-

Java Certification (1Z0-819) Topic-wise Tests Part-1 [2023]

Assess your preparation of Java SE 11 Developer exam (includes 535 questions)

https://www.udemy.com/course/ocp_java-se-11_1z0-819_p1/?referralCode=94723C1A0CB233CD799E

Java Certification (1Z0-819) Topic-wise Tests Part-2 [2023]

Assess your preparation of Java SE 11 Developer exam (includes 567 questions)

https://www.udemy.com/course/ocp_java-se-11_1z0-819_p2/?referralCode=0E765C48B618E866CB79

Exam Simulation Tests:-

Java Certification (1Z0-819) Exam Simulation Part-1 [2023]

Assess your preparation of Java SE 11 Developer exam (includes 300 questions)

https://www.udemy.com/course/java-11_1z0-819_p1/?referralCode=360ED8841D658B856247

Java Certification (1Z0-819) Exam Simulation Part-2 [2023]

Assess your preparation of Java SE 11 Developer exam (includes 300 questions)

https://www.udemy.com/course/java-11_1z0-819_p2/?referralCode=9A6070157511183345C8

Java Certification (1Z0-819) Exam Simulation Part-3 [2023]

Assess your preparation of Java SE 11 Developer exam (includes 251 questions)

https://www.udemy.com/course/java-11_1z0-819_p3/?referralCode=019E14731CC414A03B1D

Java Certification (1Z0-819) Exam Simulation Part-4 [2023]

Assess your preparation of Java SE 11 Developer exam (includes 251 questions)

https://www.udemy.com/course/java-11_1z0-819_p4/?referralCode=0876CB0955C2942C81CF

Courses for Java 8 Certification:

1Z0-808:-

[New Pattern] OCA Topic Wise (1Z0-808) [2023]

New questions to prepare for Java SE 8 Programmer I EXAM

https://www.udemy.com/course/java-se-8_1z0-808/?referralCode=76BC955CCA9433B7B81B

[New Pattern] OCA Exam Sim (1Z0-808) [2023]

New questions to practice for Java SE 8 Programmer I EXAM

https://www.udemy.com/course/java-8_1z0-808/?referralCode=DD0A5563E81820B89DC8

Java Certification - OCA (1Z0-808) Topic-wise Tests [2023]

Multiple choice questions covering all the exam objectives of Oracle Certified Associate, Java SE 8 Programmer I

https://www.udemy.com/course/java-ocajp/?referralCode=AAD655BA1CE88EEE7DDC

Java Certification : OCA (1Z0-808) Exam Simulation [2023]

Master the essentials to pass the Oracle Certified Associate(OCA): Java SE 8 Programmer I EXAM

https://www.udemy.com/course/java-oca/?referralCode=2337F77572B062EB41D6

1Z0-809:-

Java Certification - OCP (1Z0-809) Topic-wise Tests [2023]

Multiple choice questions covering all the exam objectives of Oracle Certified Professional, Java SE 8 Programmer II

https://www.udemy.com/course/java-ocpjp/?referralCode=22BEEDC2D666C97BA703

Java Certification : OCP (1Z0-809) Exam Simulation [2023]

Pass the Oracle Certified Professional(OCP): Java SE 8 Programmer II EXAM

https://www.udemy.com/course/java-ocp/?referralCode=13982FCB1E0CAA5B94FB

Other Courses:

Java For Beginners - 1st step towards becoming a Java Guru!

Become a Core Java Expert easily and in step-by-step manner

https://www.udemy.com/course/corejava/?referralCode=831CD22E895230578AF2

Test your Core Java skills

139 multiple choice questions to test your Core Java skills

https://www.udemy.com/course/testcorejava/?referralCode=B8C939C8E3AEDA4EC4FD

Test Java Functional Programming (Lambda & Stream) skills

180+ questions on Inner classes, Lambda expressions, Method References, Functional Interfaces & Stream API

https://www.udemy.com/course/test-functional-programming/?referralCode=6A6A598EDD16CF40AA8E

Java Certification (1Z0-815) Topic-wise Tests [2023]

492 Multiple choice questions arranged in topic-wise manner covering all the exam objectives of 1Z0-815 exam

https://www.udemy.com/course/java-11_1z0-815/?referralCode=B0A027B28ACC27976961

Java Certification (1Z0-815) Exam Simulation [2023]

492 Multiple choice questions covering all the exam objectives of 1Z0-815 exam

https://www.udemy.com/course/java-se-11_1z0-815/?referralCode=F409C96F9DD47698A3AE

Python Quiz - Test your Python knowledge in 1 Day!

11th hour preparation for Python interviews, exams and tests with multiple choice questions

https://www.udemy.com/course/python-test/?referralCode=F070ABFC34905F36FF71

NOTE: Access above links to avail maximum discount on the courses.

OR

You may also send an email to udayan.khattry@outlook.com to request for **MAXIMUM Discount coupon code** for above courses.

www.ingramcontent.com/pod-product-compliance
Lightning Source LLC
LaVergne TN
LVHW080109070326
832902LV00015B/2483